The New Media Handbook

D0209992

The New Media Handbook deals with the essential diversity of new media by combining critical commentary and descriptive and historical accounts with a series of edited interviews with new media practitioners, including young web developers, programmers, artists, writers and producers.

The New Media Handbook provides an understanding of the historical and theoretical development of new media, emphasising the complex continuities in the technological developments associated with particular cultural uses of media, rather than understanding new media as replacing or breaking what has gone before.

The New Media Handbook focuses upon the key concerns of practitioners and how they create their work and develop their projects – from artists to industry professionals, web designers to computer programmers. It includes a discussion of key concepts such as digital code, information, convergence, interactivity and interface and, finally, identifies key debates and locates the place of new media practice within contemporary culture.

The New Media Handbook includes:

- interviews with new media practitioners
- case studies, examples and illustrations
- a glossary of technical acronyms and key terms
- a bibliography and list of web resources.

Andrew Dewdney is Professor of Media Education and Head of the Department of Arts, Media and English at London South Bank University. He is the Chair of the Digital Arts Development Agency (DA2) and the Director of the New Media Gallery at London South Bank University.

Peter Ride is Senior Research Fellow at the University of Westminster and Director of the Centre for Arts Research, Technology and Education (CARTE). As a curator and new media producer he has worked with leading international artists and is artistic Director of the Digital Arts Development Agency (DA2).

Media Practice

Edited by James Curran, Goldsmiths College, University of London

The *Media Practice* handbooks are comprehensive resource books for students of media and journalism, and for anyone planning a career as a media professional. Each handbook combines a clear introduction to understanding how the media work with practical information about the structure, processes and skills involved in working in today's media industries, providing not only a guide on 'how to do it' but also a critical reflection on contemporary media practice.

The New Media Handbook

Andrew Dewdney
and Peter Ride

Routledge
Taylor & Francis Group

LONDON AND NEW YORK

First published 2006
by Routledge
2 Park Square, Milton Park, Abingdon, Oxon OX14 4RN

Simultaneously published in the USA and Canada
by Routledge
270 Madison Ave, New York, NY 10016

*Routledge is an imprint of the Taylor & Francis Group,
an informa business*

© 2006 Andrew Dewdney and Peter Ride

Typeset in Times by
Florence Production Ltd, Stoodleigh, Devon
Printed and bound in Great Britain by
The Cromwell Press, Trowbridge, Wiltshire

British Library Cataloguing in Publication Data
A catalogue record for this book is available from the British Library

Library of Congress Cataloging in Publication Data
A catalog record for this book has been requested

ISBN10: 0–415–30711–2 (hbk)
ISBN10: 0–415–30712–0 (pbk)
ISBN10: 0–203–64578–2 (ebk)

ISBN13: 978–0–415–30711–6 (hbk)
ISBN13: 978–0–415–30712–3 (pbk)
ISBN13: 978–0–203–64578–9 (ebk)

Contents

31 A framework for considering new media in contemporary culture **285**

Illustrations

Notes on interviewees

Justin Bennett, artist (Netherlands/Spain); work includes 'Site' (2000) and 'Berlaymont Dreaming' (2004)

David Bickerstaff, Australian, based in London, is the Creative Director of Newangle Multimedia (UK) and a practising new media artist

Susan Collins, artist (UK) and head of the Slade Centre for Electronic Media, University College London; projects include 'In Conversation' (1997) and 'Fenlandia' (2004)

Ana Kronschnabl, independent producer and artist (UK); Director of Plugincinema.com

Joe Lister, web designer (UK)

Matt Locke, Head of New Media Innovation, BBC, and new media writer and critic (UK)

Rafael Lozano-Hemmer, artist (Canada/Spain); projects include 'Vectorial Elevation' (2000) and 'Body Movies' (2001)

Anne Nigten, Manager (Netherlands), V2_labs at V2_Institute for the Unstable Media, Rotterdam

Tim Olden, artist and Network Manager of Interaction Design, Royal College of Art (UK)

Nina Pope, artist (UK); work includes 'A Hypertext Journal' (1996) and 'Bataville' (2004)

Jane Prophet, artist (UK); work includes 'TechnoSphere' (1996) and 'Decoy' (2000)

David Rokeby, artist (Canada); work includes 'Very Nervous System' (1988) and 'n-Cha(n)t' (2001)

Rob Saunders, freelance programmer (Australia/UK)

Vivienne Stone, independent producer (New Zealand); formerly with Saatchi & Saatchi, New Zealand

Maria Stukoff, independent producer (UK); formerly Director of Media Training North West

Benjamin Weil, independent curator (USA); founder of äda'web and Curator of New Media at San Francisco Museum of Modern Art

Tim Wright, writer and producer (UK); projects include 'Online Caroline' (2000) and 'In Search of Oldton' (2004)

Sites relating to case studies

www.adaweb.com (Benjamin Weil)
www.janeprophet.com (Jane Prophet)
www.somewhere.org.uk (Nina Pope)
www.onlinecaroline.com (Tim Wright)
www.robsaunders.net (Rob Saunders)
www.newangle.co.uk (David Bickerstaff)
www.plugincinema.com (Ana Kronschnabl)
www.saatchinzonline.com (Viv Stone)
www.breastlink.com (Viv Stone)
www.v2.nl (Anne Nigten)
www.lozano-hemmer.com (Rafael Lozano-Hemmer)
homepage.mac.com/davidrokeby/home.html (David Rokeby)
www.inconversation.com/ (Susan Collins)
www.ucl.ac.uk/slade/sac (Susan Collins)
www.bmbcon.demon.nl/justin (Justin Bennett)
www.mtnw.co.uk (Maria Stukoff: Media Training North West)
www.idea.org.uk/maria (Maria Stukoff)
www.test.org.uk (Matt Locke)

Acknowledgements

....

We would like to acknowledge the help and support of the following people, without whom this project would not have been possible.

Peter

....

I would like to thank the interviewees for their significant participation, Helen Idle, for editorial assistance with Chapter 29, 'Case Study: Innovation and media institutions – Matt Locke', Newangle for contributing a website design for the cover, Rachel Drummond-Hay for help in transcribing interviews, Jane Prophet, Professor Sandra Kemp, the Trustees of the Quintin Hogge Trust and Professor Margaret Blunden. I would also like to thank Professor David Ride for his guidance and Ian Iqbal Rashid for endless support.

Andrew

....

I would like to thank my Arts Management students who have engaged so positively and with healthy scepticism with my course on New Media and Digital Arts over the past three years. To my colleagues at London South Bank who gave constant encouragement and support while I sat in my office wrestling with the text. To Catherine for her total support, and to Alice and Max who stiffened my resolve at many crucial points.

Part I

New media frameworks

1 Introduction

What kind of book is this?

This is one of a number of books in a series of handbooks produced by Routledge for students of the arts, media and cultural studies and social sciences. Existing titles include the mainstream media of newspapers, radio, advertising, television, photography, magazines and public relations. *The Cyberspace Handbook* in this series is a useful companion to this book. The style and approach of each book is different; there is no house style, but they have in common the aim to articulate what is involved in the professional practice of contemporary media. To paraphrase the series editor, James Curran, the aim of the series is to provide comprehensive resource books that are something between a 'how-to-do-it' manual and a critical reflection of contemporary media. In the case of new media this is no easy task because, as the reader will soon discover, new media is, by its very nature, a hybrid practice involving a wide range of practical skills and intellectual resources as well as numerous competing critical commentaries. We have chosen to grapple with the essential diversity of our subject by combining critical commentary, descriptive and historical accounts with a series of edited interviews with new media practitioners. In doing this we hope that we provide a sufficiently broad selection of material to construct a kind of 'map' of some of the established and emergent 'territories' of new media practice.

Metaphors abound in new media, and critical commentary and reflection are, in our view, essential components of practice. 'New territory', 'emergent fields', 'uncharted space', 'new frontiers', a series of spatial metaphors, whose roots lie in an historical time-frame and discourse of physical geography, science and colonialism, which is itself the subject of other critical reflections. In uncovering the roots and sources for the spatialisation of human–computer interaction, the book draws upon a number of academic disciplines, most notably cultural and media studies.

Handbooks and guides have to be useful. The comparison with travel guides again springs to mind. Imagine that you are on a journey in a place unknown to you and you need to orientate yourself to the people, place and culture. In this place you need to get your bearings and find somewhere to stay. There are many ways in which you could set about doing these things, but a guide book is a good starting point. It is a feature of the moment we are in, and one we examine throughout this book, that more and more people are 'travelling' in cyberspace and using the Internet rather than guide books to plan travel in the real world. The exponential expansion of the use of the Internet is not, however, making the printed book redundant, only changing the way we use books. This book is designed to help you find your way around an emergent subject and a set of complex, multimedia practices. It will, we hope, show the main contours of the new subject, locate the main centres of interest and even chart many of the routes and connections between them. But, like all guides and maps, it is important to recognise that this book constructs an order upon our landscape, which is inescapably partial and selective. The guide comes with built-in perspective. It inevitably has its omissions and, in relationship to the emerging field, its uncharted territories. This is only to be expected in a fast developing field such as new media. The mapping task is like trying to represent something that is in a state of flux, possibly like attempting to map the surface of the sea. The map provided in this book contains conceptual definitions, accounts of technologies and a selection of cultural practices based upon new media. The book is, thankfully, not the first attempt to do this, since new media is already being studied from a variety of different viewpoints and disciplines. We start the book by identifying some of the different ways in which new media is being approached by media professionals and academics.

Any book with the word 'new' in its title willingly draws attention to the period in which it was written. In the globalised world everything labelled 'new' quickly becomes the 'established' and, in a shorter and shorter space of time, is passed over as the old or obsolete. The reason for this is that in everyday use the term 'new' has become bonded to consumer products, from fashions, to films to food, and, as a label, means simply the latest. We can put this another way and say that the meaning of the word 'new' is currently defined by a consumer world in which novelty and the disposability of objects and things is now a norm. In such a world, 'new' has come to denote a kind of superficiality, the very opposite of things that have significance or depth. The term 'new', understood simply as novelty, is not the way this book uses it. In many ways our working definition of new media is neither about the current moment in time, nor about media as the latest technologies. In this book the term 'new', as we apply it to media, will refer to what people do with technologies and is, therefore, about the possibilities for, and realisation of, human thinking, feeling and communication in a new medium. The significance of the new for us, here, lies in identifying ideas, feelings and experiences that are, and can be, grasped and understood through a new medium in different and challenging ways. In this process some kind of individual or social communication occurs such that new insights and discoveries about ourselves and the world take place. This is a definition of the new that emphasises the social and cultural significance of change, a process that can also be defined as a paradigm shift in the mode of thinking.

One of the guiding principles of this book is that we resist any reductive notion of new media as novelty or fashion, in favour of the idea of new media as representing significant cultural and social change. In adopting this view we have found that we also need to provide an understanding of the historical and theoretical development of new media that emphasises the complex continuities in the technological developments associated with particular cultural uses of media, rather than understand new media as replacing what has gone before. The book is organised around the practices of new media as a direct consequence of attempting to understand new media as embedded in concrete cultural developments.

The invention and spread of the printing press in Europe from the 1450s led to the development of print culture. The spread of print media was the basis of new forms of reading and writing and the general diffusion of knowledge in a continuous process over the next 500 years. In the twenty-first century, long after print media could be considered as new, it continues to be a major means for communication of ideas, feelings and experience. While this book was produced with the use of computers, written with word processing software and edited, designed and laid-out on screen, its form and material existence is still words printed in black ink on bleached paper on pages in a fixed order and bound together with glue. Academic publishers still make their living from selling books, although they are interested in the possibilities presented by online publishing. At the same time readers in general do not want to sit and read text from a screen, nor download chapters or whole books for printing. Academics and teachers know that today's busy, cash-strapped students do not want to have to buy large quantities of books or spend long uninterrupted periods of time reading. Given an 'A level' or undergraduate assessment essay on the topic of new media, the majority of students will increasingly use online sources for their writing. The old medium of books continues in a world in which more and more knowledge or data are stored, transferred and accessed electronically. Culturally, reading and writing cross and re-cross the old and new forms. This crossing of boundaries and convergence of forms is the territory we explore.

Our approach

Within the broad theoretical approach outlined above, we can identify three things that mark this book out from the growing literature on the subject of new media. First, it looks at new media from the point of view of the practitioner. By this we mean that the book is organised around new media artefacts, their producers and production. It aims to stay close to the many issues that beset the new media producer, half of which are about making machines do what you want them to do and the other half about wondering why you are trying to do it in the first place. New media practitioners worry away, alternately, about technical detail and the personal and social implications of technology. This is why so many new media projects have technology as their apparent subject. Second, the book looks at the practitioner as primarily a creative, rather than technical person. We are not writing a computer or software manual and this is not a how-to-do-it, but more a how-to-think-it guide. The book's interest in hardware and software is from the point of view of how they are used creatively. This means looking at what people are doing with technologies as well as how they understand what they are doing. In this respect the case studies and examples always privilege the position of the creative producer working in specific cultural and institutional contexts. Most of the case studies and examples are drawn from people working outside of the corporate mainstream of new media commerce. We focus upon a range of independent producers because they illustrate many of the wider understandings and problems we discuss about what is characteristic about new media practice. The fact that we have chosen people working in contemporary cultural contexts, rather than in science or commerce, is again because we consider that their projects illustrate the links between ideas, forms and audiences. Many of our case studies point up the collaborative nature of the practice of new media and, interestingly, point to the fact that people collaborate across different specialisations.

Education and training

Because of this social approach to new media practice the book includes a chapter discussing the meaning of that much used and abused term 'creativity' and its relationship to craft skills. Traditionally, training arts practitioners was carried out 'on the job', so to speak, which involved a lot of watching and copying what other trained people did. This watching and copying was the way in which knowledge, skills and techniques necessary to production were acquired, in the process of doing, rather than being formally taught. At the height of analogue broadcast and print media, up until the end of the 1970s, media training was organised under a system of apprenticeships. Apprenticeships had a much longer history as a system of craft and industrial training in which the necessary knowledge and skills of a practice were passed on. Such training was done as an inseparable part of the process of production. Today, the widespread formal apprenticeship system has gone and has been replaced by training programmes that take place at a distance from the production process, mostly in colleges. The apprentice, working alongside the 'craftsman', or skilled operator in the production process, learnt by copying and doing. The apprentice would know that something had been done the right way and was of a high standard, as the artefact was produced and approved by those who were already trained. On-the-job training still takes place, but in more casual and, importantly, more short-term ways. Changes in the social organisation of industrial and commercial training reflect the global restructuring of industrial production. Today, products are no longer produced all in one place (the vertical factory system), they require much shorter turn-around time in consumer markets and involve ever greater levels of automation brought about by the introduction of new technologies.

When considering the training and education of a new media practitioner, we still have to take into account a differentiation of knowledge and skills in the production process itself. One of the biggest distinctions in conventional media production is that between so-called creatives and technicians. The production of media is still organised under a system in which labour is divided into separate specialist tasks. The system of media training reflects this division of labour in different ways. There is, first and foremost, a primary distinction between those who develop and define the content of programming and those who put programmes together. The first group (content providers) which includes writers, producers and directors, are deemed to be the creatives, and the second group, the film and studio crews who operate the equipment of production and post-production, are deemed to be technicians. Within each of these groups production is refined into further specialisations that reflect the degree of either technical or creative complexity – the differences between front-end and back-end programming, for instance, reflected in the interview with Joe Lister.

In contrast to the divisions of labour that operate in the industrial and commercial production of media, the production of art is conceived of as a holistic process under the direction and control of the artist. Novels, poetry, plays, music and works of visual art are still largely the products of individual creators, even if groups are then needed to technically produce or perform them. In most of these artforms it is assumed that the artist both conceives of the work and has the personal skills to produce the artefact itself. Even when an artform requires technical assistance, for example the large-scale public sculpture that needs industrial production techniques and is factory produced, the resulting work is valued and understood as that of the artist, rather than the result of a team of people.

How these different traditions and divisions of production relate to new media is a question this book continually considers, partly because new media practice is continuous with existing art and media practices and partly because at points it has a new and challenging organisation. What is clear is that new media represents a convergence of previously distinct communication forms in which skills and practices overlap and boundaries between previously distinct operations of production blur.

Creativity

The other issue arising from our discussion of creativity relates to the conceptual and imaginative dimension of the production process. 'Where do creative ideas come from?' would be a practical question here. For the new student of new media to be told something they have done is, or is not, a creative solution, can be a complete mystery. What is considered creative in practice at any one time can follow fashion as much as it can a more enduring set of rules. Creativity can also be as much about breaking rules as it can be about following them. The approach we explore in this book is to think of creativity not as an inherent property of either an object/artefact, nor an exclusive quality of the producer/artist. Instead, we define creativity as a given set of common values in a process of communication, which involves not only the artist and their product, but also those who listen, see, read and appreciate what has been made. We go on to say that it is important to consider what creativity in new media entails and where the prevailing models of creativity and imaginative practice come from.

Third, the book looks at new media in context. The book adopts the view that the artefacts of new media are not simply the outcomes of the creative use of new machines, but are also shaped by the cultural, institutional and financial conditions in which the people who make new media artefacts work. In fact, in many instances of new media projects, there is no artefact as such, not in the obvious cultural sense of permanent works, but rather a record of a temporary process of communication. By keeping the creative practitioner and their projects at the centre of the book we hope to provide a closer, more textual definition of the relationship between technology, media practices and our contemporary culture, bearing in mind that these are changing relationships.

Theory and practice

The book is written from a producer or practitioner point of view, while at the same time continually 'signposting' the relevance of theory to practice. Theory is another one of those thorny terms we need to be clear about, since it has different meanings for different groups and in different contexts. Theory can mean either the direct explanation of how things work, what we might called applied theory, or an explanation about why and how a thing exists at all, which we might call abstract theory. Certainly all theory is an abstraction from concrete objects in the world and the difference between applied and abstract theory is a matter of degree, rather than a matter of kind. However, in British culture, the distinction between abstract and applied theory is perceived and lived as marking a hard-walled separation between the speculation about, and the application of, knowledge in 'the real world'. The real world here is that of business and production where there is literally little or no time for speculation or reflection upon practice. Speculation on causes, purposes and meanings can, and often does, appear as an idle or unprofitable waste of time measured against the urgent process of getting the job done. The more theory questions the meanings and purposes of a practice the more likely it will be perceived as not belonging to 'the real world'. Operational knowledge, on the other hand, is experienced as contingent and necessary and unquestioningly belonging to the real world. The problem with this distinction is that operational knowledge (what we might call know-how as opposed to know-why) always has, embedded within it, assumptions and precepts derived, at some point, from abstract theory (know-why). This is what we mean by saying the two are not distinct but continuous. But in the real world theory and practice are separated and organised so that some people are involved as theorists in the institution of the academy, while practitioners belong to the world of commerce and industry. This is fine as far as it goes, in fact it is the way our society organises and naturalises the separation. Operational knowledge is a kind of theoretical shorthand, since it is not necessary to rehearse first causes and principles in order to get on with the job. The primary difficulty with theory for practitioners is that, while applied theory appears immediately relevant to understanding how something 'works', abstract theory appears to overly question or even negate the value of practice. Of course reaching a point where theory replaces the practice rather than illuminates it is an extreme, but it has been said many times in our experience, as teachers and producers, that too much theory, or the wrong theory, or theory badly explained, 'does your head-in'. The counter to theoretical overload is not to reject all theory and theory teaching, but to require theory to be made clear, accessible and relevant to the pressing issues of practice. While much of mainstream media practice is conducted every day at a distance from conceptual-based theorising, innovative or progressive work is often much closer to ideas, debates and issues that are also being analysed at the theoretical level. The book deals with the theory–practice relationship in a number of ways: first, in the body text where accounts of key concepts and ideas are explained; second, in the course of the edited interviews; and third, in the summaries that accompany the case studies.

What is new media?

As we discuss throughout this book, the question of what is and is not new media remains open and ongoing. Some definitions of new media focus exclusively upon computer technologies while others stress the cultural forms and contexts in which technologies are used, for example, art, film, commerce, science and, above all, the Internet. For us there is a third term in the new media equation, technologies and cultural forms, that of cultural concepts. Cultural concept refers to an active and shaping set of ideas, and the underlying theories or wider discourses to which they belong, that informs what the practitioner does. The active 'ideas' which are worked upon in practice arise from the technology, the cultural context and the cultural concepts and, as our case studies and examples show, carry over cultural concepts from one context into another. We also argue throughout this book that our understandings of technology are themselves a product of a given set of received ideas, which means that we can't easily separate our general ideas of technology, as socially good, bad or indifferent, from machines designed for particular uses. The motor car is a good example of a conflictual relationship with technology because we like the convenience and reliability of motor travel, but not its environmental impact. As with all of our attempts in this book at defining new media, they remain necessarily fluid by virtue of its developing and evolving character; however, our underlying formula of technology plus concepts plus contexts will serve as a guide.

Who are the new media practitioners?

One of the recurring observations to be made about people working in new media is how varied their backgrounds are. No two people, it would appear, share the same set of skills, aptitudes and knowledge. In part this is to be expected of a relatively new discipline with relatively new formal training routes and where, instead, people seem to have an existing practice from which they develop an evolving interest in the possibilities presented by email, websites, digital animation or interactivity. The case studies are all demonstrations of this principle that practitioners, in general, migrate from one set of practices into another, often retaining elements of previous practices. This is an example of the hybrid nature of new media in which the skills of, say, the writer or film-maker are configured and developed in a different technological and organisational context. The hybrid and fluid nature of 'practice migration' makes it difficult, but not impossible, to describe at a general level what skills and training are needed to work in new media. In fact, there is no one set of skills or established body of knowledge that will fit a person to work in the area. Thinking in terms of fixed skills or progression routes goes against the grain of the fast moving, fluid and still evolving nature of new media practice. Also, we have demonstrated that new media practices are largely made up from the established media practices of, for example, scriptwriting, image making, graphics, editing, composing and so on. Each of the case studies explores a different configuration of established and emerging skills. They show how a combination of grounded knowledge of a media discipline together with an operational familiarity with computer systems and software is in evidence in practice. But how this combinatory set of knowledge and skills is achieved varies widely, depending upon the context in which someone is working and the models of practice adopted.

Models of practice inform how media is produced and how individual roles are understood. Models of practice become established over time and serve to set out the rules and procedures of how things get done and who does what. The production of novels, paintings or films each contain work for many more people than an author, artist or director. Art and media products entail a pre-production stage involving, in different ways, the initial expression of an idea, its development within a particular form and the commissioning and financing of a work. There is, of course, great variation in the control over pre-production, which takes us back to different models of practice. Work produced for an established client and market will conform tightly to the boundaries of what is agreed financially and contractually. In contrast, work produced speculatively, by an individual working on their own, will operate in a context specified only by the implicit discipline of the practitioner. This is not to say, however, that the model of practice of the individual working for themselves is any more or less unencumbered or 'free' than that of a practitioner working in a group or for a client. The model of practice that privileges the unconstrained context of individuals, operating within exclusively self-regulating boundaries set by themselves, belongs, of course, to the European Romantic tradition (see the discussion on creativity). Models of practice remain largely implicit to the contexts of practice, rather like trade secrets, and are understood through acquired practice, that is, on the job. The purpose of reflecting upon models of practice in new media is to demonstrate the range of practice strategies in operation and to identify what a number of them have in common.

The organisation of the case studies

At the beginning of each case study there is a short overview of an individual's practice and their operational role. The case studies have been carefully edited and synthesised from much larger interviews and email correspondence in order to make them relevant to the issues discussed in each section of the book. In this way it is hoped that the reader will be able to move between the direct reflections of practice to the wider discussion of concepts and ideas. There is a common a set of 'generic skills' that we have identified across the practitioner accounts. The skill set we are identifying encompasses technical skills, conceptual skills and social skills and can be defined around the following terms: visioning, development, research, networking, collaboration and production.

Generic skill sets

Visioning is essentially the process of having ideas, or, more properly, beginning to articulate your ideas in various forms of personal notation and informal discussion. Ideas that are more than ideas have to become proposals and proposals are a first articulation of how an idea might be realised. Development is the process of beginning to turn abstract possibilities, the vision and idea, into concrete realities and is a process of engaging others through the proposal in ideas. Development is an open process in which a proposal will go through changes as it is engaged and related to the resources and support needed to realise the idea. Ideas can, and most often do, change in subtle or drastic ways during the developmental stages as they are tested out in the context of possible realisation. Research is a generic skill which happens at all stages of pre-production and post-production. At very early stages of visioning and development, research is focused upon the content and intellectual coherence of ideas, whereas at later stages research might focus upon resources and responses. Networking has become a contemporary generic skill in many occupations and in media has always been a strong aspect of how opportunities are seized and work commissioned. Networking, as distinct from nepotism, is not only about who you know, but also about good communication and awareness of the field of opportunities at any one time. Networking is about establishing connections between people and their roles in order to maximise the possibilities of realisation. Collaboration is again a common skill in media and extends naturally to new media, since by nature new media is a group and collaborative activity. Collaboration can of course take many forms from jointly authoring and producing work, working with people from different disciplines, or working within an agreed division of labour within a set production. Production will take many forms depending on the particular expertise of the practitioner. It will encompass organisational, managerial and communication roles, through specific skills in the cultural forms of writing, programming and design, through to marketing and promotion. Any and all of the aspects of realising a new media work for a given or new audience is included in the production process.

While it might be said that such skills or qualities relate to a wide spectrum of human activities, we argue that it is the combination of all of these activities which mark out new media at this point in time. All of these attributes are given their specific meaning in definite contexts, which will mark out their significance to a particular activity. In new media contexts each of these 'roles', as we are calling them, take on specific characteristics.

The actual roles of the practitioners in our case studies are of course more known and conventional. The case studies encompass the role of the writer, film-maker, sculptor, curator, software designer and company director working with, in, and on new media. The creative identity of individuals highlighted in the case studies indicates that, at present, it is the established rather than the emergent cultural role that is retained. The role of the artist is a case in point since it provides an obvious identity and role in relationship to certain kinds of production. But the case studies reveal people who combine distinct knowledge and skills from different practices in the hybrid mixture that is new media.

The case studies – contexts of practice

Our discussion of the generic roles of the new media practitioner is to be understood in relationship to the contexts of new media practice. Context can and does mean many things, from your place of work right through to the accumulation of your life experiences. Context is therefore practical, social and intellectual and it should be borne in mind that at its widest all of these dimensions of our context set and shape a given set of possibilities. This is not to say that we have no control over what immediate context we choose to work in, or that we are incapable of changing our context and ourselves in the process. However, the recognition of, and reflection upon, the dimensions of our full context, our historical, social, cultural and economic formation, does allow us to understand the conditions in which we operate. The value of this point is to focus attention on the need for, and process of, gaining insight into our context as one measure of gaining control over how we approach our own productions within any given set of circumstances. Context remains a crucial aspect of how practices are organised and institutionalised in the production process. Context is also central to the ways in which the products of practice are received. The context of the reception of work will, in large part, determine how work is interpreted, appreciated and valued. The context of reception will also determine who gets to value and use work because it establishes the audience and their expectations. For a practitioner of new media, understanding both the production and reception contexts of work is important precisely because the designation of cultural value is not yet established or settled. What, after all, is the context of 'net art', which, unlike its object counterpart in an art gallery, has no institutional context to confirm an artefact status and provenance? The work in the gallery carries with it the approval of the institution, whereas a website, which claims to be a work of art, remains undifferentiated within the horizontal plane of TCP addresses. The web is a differentiated but non-hierarchical organisation of cultural material in which the good jostles with the bad, or worse. As a context it has been embraced by a generation of artists and new media practitioners who value precisely what they take to be its democratic and accessible characteristic over that of what is perceived as the hierarchical and exclusive character of national and international cultural organisations. Whatever the merits of the argument in this particular case, it is a demonstration that the context in which work is produced or in which it is received is significant and shapes the limits and possibilities of practitioner roles.

Generic institutional contexts of new media

What then, in more detail, are the contexts for the production of new media? From our case studies we get a generic picture of the institutional contexts of production and consumption of new media. There is the obvious context of business and commerce built around the dot.com industry which emerged in the 1990s, which is increasingly based around creative and advertising agencies as well as the new media end of established media production. Then there is the context of cultural institutions, mostly in the public sector, but including private charities and trusts, operating at international, national and regional levels. These could include museums, galleries, dance companies, orchestras, arts centres, arts projects and arts organisations. In the UK, for example, there are a small number of Arts Council-supported new media organisations. Mainstream media institutions in film and animation production, television production and broadcasting, graphic and architectural design studios, print journalism and music companies all have some relationship to new media either because they have new media offshoots, mostly related websites, or because aspects of their production processes are based in digital technologies. Finally, we should consider that educational institutions provide a serious context for new media development and practice in the form of teaching, research and training. Schools, colleges and universities have all had considerable government investment in information technologies, which are used by teachers, pupils, lecturers and students alike. Universities are also able to invest in up-to-date hardware for research purposes in a variety of subject disciplines from the obvious context of computer science and engineering, through to media production, art and design to the social sciences and health. In all of these educational contexts the possibility of using digital technologies for cross-disciplinary and collaborative projects is present.

Commercial, media, cultural and educational, these are the four broad operating contexts of new media. In each case they provide the resources and funding, the plant and hardware for work to be undertaken; they provide employment and fees for work to be produced. We recognise that not all new media practice can be neatly fitted into this scheme, but we consider that the great majority will have some relationship to this pattern. One exception to our scheme, where work is produced outside of these major institutional and productive work contexts, is that of freelance artist/producer. With the miniaturisation of computer memory and the lowering of costs of originating digital capture, many more practitioners can work independently, often using the physical space of home or a small studio. For the freelance producer, this amounts to a form of 'cottage industry' where it is unnecessary to attend a 'factory' or the modern office, because the productive workstations are personally owned and access to the network can be from anywhere. But the fact that many freelance new media practitioners can work from home is not the same as saying that their production has no relationship to the main institutional contexts that we have indicated. In fact, 'outsourcing' and 'subcontracting' have been familiar modes of the organisation of media labour for the last two decades and, in some cases, photography for instance, are the dominant historical model.

The significance of the major institutional contexts here is that they play a large part in defining the parameters of what is produced. The commercial world of dot.com, for instance, has, over the past decade, settled into relatively stable patterns of production with a much more formal division of markets and labour, the three most obvious areas being advertising, online services and entertainment. Markets and divisions of labour are much less differentiated in new media practice in the cultural sector of museums and galleries because this sector is not 'driven' primarily by the commercial imperatives of profit and loss. A consequence of its 'not for profit' financial standing is that 'start-up' capital is wholly dependent upon public funding or private donation and the whole economy of the public cultural sector, in the UK and Europe in particular, is a tiny fraction in comparison to the major economies of dot.com or online entertainment.

This is also true of the education sector, although in comparison to the cultural sector there has, over the last decade, been a marked increase in funding for research and teaching in new media areas. The paradigm case for research development of new media in an educational context remains that of the Massachusetts Institute of Technology (MIT). In Europe and the UK, such levels of government funding are more specifically targeted at the hard, scientific, rather than soft, cultural end of technological research and the corporate investment in UK universities for new media research is on a much smaller scale.

Generic intellectual contexts of new media

The institutional and industrial organisation define the practical context of new media production, but what of the more nebulous cultural and intellectual contexts; how are we to define a scheme here? This is the realm of biographical experience and the formation of ideas, obsessions and interests which, many would say, is particular to the individual. There is no doubt that each one of us does carry and embody a unique set of experiences and understanding. At the same time, that unique body of experience has been acquired in a given historical, social, psychological and cultural context. Common accounts, versions and understandings of human experience are carried and recounted, in part, by the same practical institutions and organisations of education and media that we have already identified. Any one such institution, let alone the total, contains a richness and diversity of intellectual and cultural knowledge and experience which, as individuals, we actively engage with. We might say that each individual has a unique pathway through a common and available cultural stock. Further than this, in any one historical context or period, there exist common preoccupations and focuses of attention – what we, elsewhere, have also referred to as discourses or narratives. Such discourses are another dimension of context, which set the parameters or frameworks of our ideas and questions. In our case studies the reader will see some of these at work. In the case of Ana Kronschnabl, for instance, avant-garde film is an important informing intellectual context, just as for Tim Wright the historical context of authorship is a central concern.

There are a number of related discourses in new media, which are currently being worked through, in the different institutional contexts of commerce, culture, education and training. We characterise three main inter-related discourses as: (a) the human–machine relationship, (b) access and control of networked communication, and (c) representational–non-representational systems. These discourses, or debates, form the wider theoretical context within which more particular practical interests, in non-linearity, authorship, montage, immersion or emergence, for example, fit. The intellectual frameworks, or discourses, are also historically traceable in the formation of new media from the intellectual disciplines of European philosophy, science and literature.

Fluidity

Tim Wright created an online interactive novel, Susan Collins created a link between public exchange between the urban street and an online audience and Justin Bennett created a sound sculpture in an art gallery. Tim Wright used HTML in developing his website, Susan Collins exploited the possibilities of the development of the software

'Realplayer' and Justin Bennett used the software of Max/MSP, to programme sound by the movement of people in a defined space. The locations of each of their works varies: the urban street, the Internet and an art gallery. The cultural context for their work is that of the contemporary arts. They are all working with computers and available software. Although the specific historical context of their work is that of arts, the use of live weblinks, online exchange and spatial interfaces have come to have a much wider set of cultural and commercial contexts in clubs, events and advertising. These particular case studies illustrate a number of our broader points about the hybrid nature of new media and how we can understand the media practitioner as someone who crosses boundaries between media technologies, concepts and contexts. Conversely, the products of their work, the work itself, can readily be understood in different ways once the cultural context in which it is presented changes. This is most certainly true of the two pieces of work that had a web presence. Susan Collins points out that the audience for her website shot up after someone from the 'Realplayer' company included it in their software listing, 'Timecast'. It would not be at all clear how many of the viewers of 'In Conversation' received it as an artwork, and in many respects it doesn't matter. Equally, Tim Wright's 'Online Caroline' deliberately exploited the ambiguity of a personal rather than fictitious game or artsite. In these examples the loose and heterogeneous cultural context of the web meant that the viewer's context had to be deemed to be unknown.

Writers' context
....

Our own historical and intellectual context as writers also informs the approach of this book. Everyone has a context and our current one, the one that impinges upon this book, is foremost fashioned by working in higher education. Beyond this immediate context is a much longer shared history of working in the independent and community arts sector during the 1970s and 1980s, which has shaped our perspectives on new media. The paths of our working lives crossed at numerous points prior to coming together to write this book. Peter, for instance, was the Director of Photography at the Watershed Media Centre in Bristol in the late 1980s, eighteen months before Andrew took up the same post. Between 1993 and 1997, Andrew was associated with Artec, a London-based new media training agency funded by the Arts Council of Great Britain and the European Social Fund, working on the new media project 'Silver to Silicon'. Subsequently, Peter went to work at Artec after leaving Cambridge Darkroom. We came together again in 1999, with the establishment of the Digital Arts Development Agency, in which Peter was the Artistic Director and Andrew was the Chair of the Board of Directors. The Watershed Media Centre in Bristol was Britain's first dedicated Media Centre, largely funded by the British Film Institute, and later the Arts Council's Photography Panel. Cambridge Darkroom was, for a time, also supported by the Arts Council, as was Watershed, to be centres for the educational development of photography by providing darkroom production and exhibition facilities. They were just two of a network of regional centres in the UK which supported the exhibition of contemporary independent media projects. The importance of these shared points to the project of this book lies in the fact that this network was committed to the critical exploration of contemporary media and the development of greater opportunities for practitioners working outside of the mainstream of publishing, broadcasting and national museums and galleries. The aim of this media network was to provide a resource that was relevant to local and regional cultures of place and identity and to bring the means of media production to a wider and more diverse group of practitioners. Today, some of these same centres are at the forefront of the exploration of new media along with newer organisations, which have sprung up in less than a decade. The history of independent practice in film and photography in the UK, and the cultural politics of that tradition, connect in important ways with the project of this book both through the case studies, often examples of independent producers, and in the perspective on the importance of focusing upon practice itself.

Organisation of the book

The book is divided into four parts: the first provides an overview of the history and study of new media; the second focuses on producers and consumers; the third studies three key concepts – interface, interactivity and digitality; and the fourth looks at the wider issues of convergence, databases and digital aesthetics. Each section is organised to include a combination of three things: descriptions and definitions of key ideas, case studies of projects and key examples of practitioners' working methods and processes. The material is organised so that the case studies and examples are related to the general explanations of concepts and ideas. The case studies and key examples comprise over a third of the book and contain a wide variety of discussion on nearly all aspects of new media practice. They include how people became involved in new media, how they organised and funded projects and how they set up companies or worked in existing institutions. They also include the process of project development from ideas to real-isation, and how people collaborate and network. Finally, they include accounts of completed works and how they have been received and what happens to them after-wards. In the last section the interviews increasingly focus upon the wider discussion of issues affecting the practices of the future. The case studies were produced from research interviews and are edited to be relevant to the specific sections of the book and the ideas they discuss.

The material within each part is structured by a set of underlying questions that students, producers and users of new media might reasonably want to ask, such as, what is new media and how is it being used?; what are the key concepts and issues in new media and what are the emergent forms and skills of new media?

Part I – new media as a subject, language and history

Part I is essentially an attempt to look at the different ways in which new media is being defined in both theory and practice. It characterises the different ways in which new media is given definition within different practices and disciplines. It also considers the social language in which new media is practised and, again, recognises differences in approaches and ideas contained within technical or theoretical language. Building upon this it also considers the 'representational', or 'coded' language, nature of new media artefacts and communications. It considers the problems of defining the expressive, creative and organisational codes and conventions of computer-based communication. Part I sets the contemporary discussion of new media as a subject, practice and language in a historical context by looking at various ways in which new media is rapidly gaining a history and the ways in which different approaches are taken to what a history of new media might look like.

The case studies in Part I explore the way that many of the ideas in the preceding chapters are demonstrated through the work that practitioners do and in the ways that they think about new media. These case studies are intended to put flesh on the issues that have been discussed and to show how the different contexts in which people operate affect the way they present their work. In particular, they demonstrate how practitioners place themselves in a history of new media, a history that is sometimes personal and sometimes about external developments.

Four practitioners have been interviewed: Nina Pope, an artist who was involved in a series of early web projects; Jane Prophet, an artist and academic who reflects on the way that she became involved in working with new media; Tim Wright, who discusses the writing and producing of a work of online entertainment, 'Online Caroline', that was a commercial as well as artistic enterprise; and a curator, Benjamin Weil, who organised and developed projects with artists in a range of institutions and organisations for many years. They cover a breadth of work and expertise, and demonstrate different approaches. A recurrent interest that is being addressed in this book is the roles that people play in new media, and how they define themselves. In these studies the practitioners describe themselves and their activities in many ways, and also what they understand the roles of other people as being.

When describing a project it is easy to think of it in only one context, for example as a work of fine art, or a commercial project that applies a particular historical technological innovation. One of the things that case studies demonstrate is that people do not think of their work as operating in one context and that they often span many fields. Single projects can be presented in a particular way but the development of a number of projects across a career often shows a more varied sense of the way that new media operates.

Practitioners are often acutely aware of the contemporary and the historical context of the work that they do. They discuss not only the works that they have made but also their approach to them as being 'of a particular time'. But although works can be contextualised by particular technologies, this is not to suggest that they should be seen as being 'locked into' that period. However, this unravels a series of complexities: a work needs to be seen as being part of the culture that made it possible in terms of the current ideas and of the methods of production available, but when being discussed in retrospect it is problematic to think of it in terms of being limited to that period. Once technology has advanced, or approaches evolved, there is danger in thinking of a work as being simplistic or naive. One of the points that is made through these case studies is that the concerns of the practitioners in making their works often transcend the issues of the time in which it was produced. Although the technology changes and people take different approaches to talking about current concerns, underlying issues are often remarkably consistent.

Social understanding of new media is shown to be as crucial as a technological understanding in these case studies. All four practitioners discuss the way that the public, audiences and users understood what new media was capable of and how it fitted within their lives. They make it clear that the means of technology to deliver a project is no more important to the practitioner than the way that expectations of the public can be addressed, and that the work that they are making can fit within the capacity of the public to experience it, be that as a challenge or as a more easy fit.

There are additional contexts that need to be considered and these are addressed in these studies, such as the way that practitioners have approached ideas of hybridity and convergence of media forms in very practical terms that have ensured their works make sense to their audience. They discuss the various ways that they have worked with their audiences and defined or shaped their roles as users of or as participants in their work. Lastly, they reflect on the notion of innovation and how it has shaped their practices and their careers.

Part II – producers and consumers

Part II, 'New media practice', is largely given over to case studies that have been selected to reflect the different contexts of new media practice in commerce, technical application, workshop production and creative business. The introduction to Part II provides an overview of the contemporary context in which practice takes place and considers issues of access, software and health and safety.

The seven case studies in Part II focus on the ways in which practitioners think about themselves as creative people, or as functioning in a work context. It asks how they define their roles and how they evaluate what they do. These case studies are organised so that they give a sense of how and why people operate professionally, but from the ground up, focusing on individuals rather than on categories.

We see from these examples how there is a diversity of experience for new media practitioners and that people call upon a wide variety of skills to undertake their tasks. Some of these skills come from formal training but many of the skills they value are a combination of social and managerial skills learned over time that give them their unique way of working in the area of technology and in the context of a new media project.

This series of case studies starts by looking at the generic roles that producers take and how work is produced in different contexts. In the commercial sector, Vivienne Stone, a media producer in advertising, describes her role on projects for high profile clients, and David Bickerstaff develops interactive installations for museums and galleries. Working at a different level as new media technical specialists with commercial projects, Rob Saunders discusses the role of a freelance programmer and Joe Lister explains how a web developer operates within a company team. To examine how the development of artists' creative projects can be facilitated in a laboratory environment, Anne Nigten describes activity in a creative research lab and Tim Olden describes how learning is supported in an educational context. The role of creative entrepreneurs, and how they blend their work with their creative practice, is discussed by Ana Kronschnabl and David Bickerstaff.

In each of these interviews the practitioners describe the experience that they have gained in order to skill themselves to do their jobs and what they value in the approach that they take. The key points of interest are in how they have used these skills and how this determines the approach they take. As such, they identify the learning curve that they have undertaken. They also un-package how they have gone about specific jobs, describing in detail the stages involved in each one. Through this we can gain a sense of the complexity of their activity and how it draws on many of the concerns and areas discussed elsewhere in the book, demonstrating both practical and theoretical knowledge.

Part III – analogue to digital code, interface and interactivity

Part III focuses specifically upon three key concepts in new media: interface, interactivity and digital code. The digital is explained in relationship to a discussion of the differences between digital and analogue technologies and media as well as a discussion of the importance of understanding the concept of code. 'Human–computer interface' considers both the physical apparatus we use to communicate through and with a computer, as well as the conceptual, metaphorical and practical designs of graphical user interfaces. 'Interactivity' rehearses the arguments for and against interactivity being the defining feature of new media as a radically new cultural form. The four case studies in Part III look at the way that artists explore within their work a range of interests in new media practice that are not contained in single issues but are complex fusions of diverse concerns.

The practitioners interviewed here are: Justin Bennett, who works primarily with sound installation; Susan Collins, who describes a project that created a junction between a website and public space; Rafael Lozano-Hemmer, whose large-scale installations employ public spectacle, but also enable public participation; and David Rokeby, whose software underpins all the interactive projects he creates.

The case studies all talk about the works as having arisen out of a range of contexts, but all of them have in common that the practitioners are defining new areas of activity or innovative ways of working. Sometimes using low-end technology and sometimes using hugely complicated and expensive resources, each of them is pushing at the boundaries of what is possible. Similarly, they all try to explore what it means to operate in innovative ways, where their difficulties lie and how they try to deal with them. They give a sense of the various conditions that apply and that affect the ways that a work is developed and produced in the 'real-world' scenario of project management. They also illustrate how projects are born out of a sense of cultural and intellectual exploration needs as well as through innovations with technology and how sometimes the two can work together to their mutual advantage.

The interviews also make it clear that projects rarely develop in isolation and that artists and practitioners most often evolve work through building upon their understanding of how audiences have responded to previous work. The audience for a specific work need know nothing of this ongoing process of research, but it remains an important part of the practitioners' skill and experience.

The audience is fundamental to the practitioners in these case studies, and each of them demonstrates that they evolve a very complex understanding of the way to work with their audience over time and through the various approaches and disciplines from which their practices arise. So, for example, Rafael Lozano-Hemmer has a background in theatre, and Susan Collins began her practice in media installation. Each of the artists is finely attuned to the way that this sense of how their approach to key concepts, such as interactivity or interface, emerges from their specific discipline. Their discussions about the way they define key concepts give a very clear sense of the way that definitions are worked through in practice.

Part IV – convergence, information and digital aesthetic

Part IV discusses the importance to new media of two further key concepts, convergence and information, and relates them to the question of whether new media has a distinct digital aesthetic and what that might consist of and in. This section also considers whether new media can be thought of as a single new medium, a new paradigm with the database as its essential form, or whether we should think about new media as the umbrella term under which a range of continuing media practices and cross-disciplinary interests intersect. In discussing the character of new media we address the question of how new media is changing aesthetic responses to existing art practices and analogue media artefacts. Convergence is explained not only as a technical feature of digital systems and code, but also in terms of the social and economic convergence of communication systems. Possibly the most over-used yet least understood term in new media and digital technologies is that of 'information'. Most of us are familiar with the linguistic currency of living in an 'information age' or that there has been an 'information revolution', phrases that are most often used to signal the greater importance of computers in work practices and the phenomenal rise of networked computers. But what is information and how has the computer database come to be the repository of so much information? In our discussion we attempt to distinguish the different ways in which knowledge, experience and cultural texts are considered as information and data. The discussion of convergence, data and information is important for the ways in which we go on to discuss the question of a digital aesthetic, which we consider in three ways: new media as an extension of existing media, new media as a break with existing media and new media as a crisis in culture. In each of these terms we consider the rules of representation, breaking the rules, and the constitution of a new system, respectively. There are two case studies in the concluding section, which have been included because they provide a wide discussion of how new media relates to the direction of future training and production. Maria Stukoff, who was Director of Media Training North West, an agency established to develop new media skills in the North West of England and based at the BBC in Manchester, discusses how graduate profiles relate to the current and future training needs of new media industries. Matt Locke, who is Head of Innovation at the BBC, discusses the impact of digital technologies upon television broadcasting and upon the role of public service broadcasting in particular. The BBC plays a significant role in shaping perceptions of the social and cultural use of digital technologies in the UK and how the corporation conceptualises the possibilities of the digital will inform its policy and practice.

2 New media as a subject

....

Throughout writing this book we have been conscious of adding one more volume to the growing literature on the subject. 'New media' is becoming the preferred term for a range of media practices that employ digital technologies and the computer in some way or another. New media is also emerging as a key institutional term in education and culture. New media is the title of university departments and degrees and the title of a distinct canon of artistic practice. This makes new media an academic and intellectual subject as well as a practice. As such, a growing body of writing is emerging that constitutes the history and theory of the subject and its objects and practices in the wider world. As writers we are also readers of the work of others in this developing field and we have come to the view that part of our task is to provide something of a useful summary of the field.

New media or digital media?

....

There are a growing number of digital media titles on the bookshelves and in some important respects there is an overlap between work being described as new media and that defined as digital media. The main problem with the term 'digital media' is that it has a tendency to privilege technology itself as the defining aspect of a medium, as if all digital media practice will be first and foremost about, or will reflect, the character of digital technology. In contrast, the term 'new media' signals more about the contemporary cultural concepts and contexts of media practices than it does about simply a new set of technologies. It is important and absolutely central to this way of thinking that technologies and cultural and expressive practices are thought of as inseparable. The relationship between technologies and cultural and media practices needs to be understood as linked at every stage, from invention to development and use. While this book has adopted the term new media over that of digital media, it is important to add that new media builds in its own redundancy. It takes little mental effort to reflect that all media must have been new at some point in their history and the question is then quickly begged: when will new media stop being new and become old or just media? The general answer is, of course, that new media will become old media when something else comes along that is significantly different. Superficially, the term 'new media' suggests that at the core of its meaning it is its 'newness', or novelty, that interests and excites. But novelty is by nature ephemeral and the excitement of the new quickly wears thin. The new, by definition, has not stood the test of time, but historically we are aware that the new can also indicate a set of more radical and fundamental shifts and changes in the ways in which human affairs are conducted. Hindsight has taught us that the twentieth century contains a catalogue of 'the new' in many areas of everyday life as well as in extraordinary scientific and cultural achievement. Indeed, the twentieth century was established on the legacy of progress bequeathed by the industrial revolution. Ideas about the newness of new media and its technological base are deeply rooted in the historical notion of social and scientific progress.

New media and electronic media

Electronic media also has a bearing upon our use of the term 'new media'. Electronic media privileges the power source of a group of related technologies as its defining feature. Electronic media groups together all those media that are dependent upon and structured through the medium of the science and technology of electrical transmission. At this general level electronic media is also a historical term for grouping together a characteristic element of electronic communication, which developed from the late nineteenth century and includes the media of telegraphy, telephone, radio, television and computing. Electronic media can be considered as a transparent transmission system for the content of previous human communication media, the medium itself being considered a neutral carrying system for sound and image. Conversely, electronic media can also be considered to profoundly shape its content, so that, for example, radio represents the one-way transmission of a disembodied human voice, whereas speech could be considered as embodied in a two-way human interaction. Marshall McLuhan (1964) generalises this understanding to the idea that the content of any medium is always another medium, that is to say that the content of writing is speech and that speech is the content of telegraphy. The term 'electronic media' also connotes many things about the characteristic of the communications which are electronically based. McLuhan also articulates that since the content of any medium is always another medium then the medium is also, always, the message. From this thinking it is possible to say that the content of electronic media is electricity. An example here would be electronic music. We all know and accept, as a matter of course, that the majority of music we listen to is recorded and transmitted using electronic and, increasingly, digital technologies. We still demand a high degree of high-fidelity to an original source of sound in our music technology. At the same time we also accept that there is a category, or genre, of music that we distinguish by the overall organisation of sound as electronic. We also know that electronic music is something quite different from music produced by acoustic instruments that have been electrified and amplified. We long ago accepted that electronic amplification of instruments and the human voice changed – mediated – the sound we heard. But in listening to electronic music we expect to hear sounds that have been made by a specifically electronic instrument, namely that range of music technologies that come under the banner of synthesisers.

'Electronic media' is a useful term for categorising those cultural media forms that have emerged as a sub-set or genre within a larger practice: art or music on the one hand, printing on the other. The use of language to create new terms, by which we can mark out significant changes in our experience of cultural products, does tell us something about how we are thinking about those changes. For example, it is interesting that, while we are happy to think of electronic music, art or print journals, we don't think of electronic film or electronic photography. So, at one level, the term 'electronic media' distinguishes little other than telling us that electricity is the basis for the medium, in the literal sense of the materials and machines that drive a given cultural media; the daily newspaper, for instance, has an electronic version. Like digital media, electronic media foregrounds the technological means as the defining feature of our experience of a medium.

Cyberstudies

New media also has an overlap with cyberculture and its academic counterpart cyber-studies, which refer to those writings dedicated to the discussion and description of how people are using the Internet and the World Wide Web. There are several strands to the discourse of cyberspace. Technically cyberspace can be defined simply as a worldwide network of computer networks that use the TCP/IP protocols to facilitate data trans-mission and exchange. Culturally, and in terms of the popular imagination, William Gibson's fictional definition of cyberspace as 'a consensual hallucination experienced daily by billions of legitimate operators' (1986: 51) extends the idea of cyberspace to the social and psychological meanings of the operations and exchanges between users of the network of computers. In addition we would also have to include cybernetics, as a branch of learning that brings together theories and studies on communication and control as a part of cyberstudies. The term 'cybernetics' gained currency in its use by Norbert Wiener to define studies in the interaction of goals, predictions, actions, feed-back and response in human and machine systems. Cyberspace encompasses interests in human–machine interaction and in the human presence within computer data systems. Studies of the current cultural practices focus upon screen-based textual or graphic inter-action and communication in online multi-user communications, email or gaming. However, research, sponsored by governmental or commercial agencies for military or civic purposes, is interested in the development of human–machine interaction and human presence within computer data systems in more far reaching ways. Research in artificial intelligence (AI) and intelligent software agents (IA), together with advanced robotics, moves along the lines of the creation of cyborgs as various kinds of hybrids between humans and machines. Research into the human presence and interaction within computer data systems takes a number of current forms through the development of more complex simulators, which can create highly immersive virtual or simulated 'real' environments. In addition, current research is focusing upon the augmentation of reality (AR), through the use of computer data systems and wireless receiving systems to deliver new levels of spatially specific information. From the perspective of new media prac-tice, cyborgs, robots and virtual reality largely remain the province of advanced research, while the concepts and, indeed, the language, operate within the cultural currency of the techno-imaginary.

New media and cyberspace

Clearly, what happens in cyberspace is directly related to new media, which, as you will remember, is defined here more widely as the media and cultural practices of working with computers. We have included key case studies of art projects that are based upon the Internet and which, therefore, at one level can be considered projects in cyberspace. Cyber-theory and cybercultural studies have rapidly developed analyses and descriptions of online communication as a parallel virtual world. Bell (Bell and Kennedy 2000) offers a broad definition of cyberstudies as consisting of 'domains of digital communication and information technologies', which include 'the Internet, email, chat rooms, MUDs, digital imaging systems, virtual reality, new biomedical technologies, artificial life and interactive digital entertainment systems'. Such an inclusive definition unites around technological systems and our interaction with them. Bell is quick to point out that, in his terms, these are all 'technocultural constructions' in which the place of human imagination and presentation remain central. Bell's emphasis is squarely upon the cultural use and value of technological systems, and the inclusive definition of cyber-studies offered by him above places cyberstudies as an extension of the established academic arena of cultural studies. In a similar way, new media is to media studies what cyberstudies is to cultural studies. Put another way, the current need to understand the impact of new digital technologies upon established cultural and media practices and organisations is also changing cultural and media studies as a subject.

The difference between cultural and media studies approaches to new media

While media and cultural studies are closely related, they are also historically distinct in their focus of attention as well as in their methods. Traditionally media studies focused upon five key aspects of the production and consumption of broadcast and print media: the institutions, industries, media, texts and audiences. Within this framework media studies developed specific studies of radio, television, newspapers, magazines and cinema, although cinema has had another academic context in film studies. This division of media into production and consumption and into discrete stages and specific forms also produced two distinct types of analysis. The first type of analysis consisted of empirical studies, largely drawing upon the research methodologies of social science, which sought to find out (a) the effects of media upon individuals and groups, and (b) the ways in which ownership, regulatory legislation and industrial production shaped media products. The second type of analysis drew upon distinctly different traditions in linguistics, literature and philosophy, in order to analyse the media object itself. Such analysis separated out the media 'text' from its immediate context of production and consumption in order to look in detail at how meaning was constructed. We could simplify these traditions and say that media studies in Europe and North America has for the last twenty years primarily focused upon two things, the economic and social organisation of public media and media products as textual representations. The intro-duction of new technologies in mainstream media production, initially in the print industry, then in music production and, later, in broadcasting, required media studies to reconsider questions of technology. The rapid development of the Internet and the World Wide Web from the mid-1990s required media studies to consider a wholly new medium. It is not surprising that media studies initially approached the study of cyberspace primarily as a new, global form of communication based upon the network of networked computers. Media studies as an academic discipline is continuing to adapt to the conver-gence of media in digital forms as well as extensions of new media and, not unnaturally, it is building upon its existing frameworks of study, types of analysis, theories and concepts.[1]

Cultural studies and cyberspace

Cultural studies clearly overlaps with media studies, since media plays a large part in everyday life, which was the founding object of cultural studies. Cultural studies focuses specifically upon the experience of everyday life and of the shared traditions, occupations, pastimes and customs of specific groups. In the now famous definition, culture was defined as a whole way of life,[2] which enlarged the academic study of culture from a narrow concentration on a selective tradition of literature, science and arts, to include studies of popular and everyday culture. Cultural studies certainly shares with media studies the broad tradition of social science research methods of empirical study. It has also developed forms of textual analysis to account for specific cultural practices, dress and fashion and popular music for instance, as well as more theoretical models of culture and the role of culture in social reproduction. Unlike media studies, cultural studies has been more pronounced in focusing upon subordinate and marginal cultures and, through this, has focused more fully upon resistance and transgression in the face of dominant and official cultures of communication. While cultural studies reflects its sociological roots in examining the social organisation and reproduction of culture, it also allowed for the ethnographic exploration of the cultural experience of the individual within the group. This interest in the local and specific experiences of individuals and sub-groupings defines one of the ways in which cultural studies has sought to define cyberstudies. It is not surprising, therefore, to find debates about sexuality, the body and subjectivity in the forefront of interest in what is happening in cyberspace. Cyberculture has been defined as an alternative to actual social and spatial cultures and online identities have been described as offering the individual freedoms not otherwise available in real space (Turkle 1997). But from the perspective of new media practice, cyberstudies is, at its best, a necessary extended research project, drawing upon a number of empirically and theoretically based forms of analysis, attempting to understand and define what we are doing when we are online, or engaged in certain interactions with a computer programme and a screen.

New media and visual culture

Before leaving academic approaches to the study of new media, we need, briefly, to make reference to visual culture. Visual cultural studies have a claim to be an emergent field of study, if not a discipline (Mirzoeff 1999), which holds some explanatory power in relationship to new media. The basic argument of visual cultural studies is that human culture has become more and more reliant upon the visual dimension of human sense perception in communication. The development of large-scale media technologies throughout the twentieth century is pointed to as evidence of the growing emphasis and social reliance upon visual communication. Photography, film, television and photo-print create a visual environment, which has moved a culture dominated by the word to a culture dominated by the image. It follows, in this argument, that academic study needs to take on the full significance of this fact and to bring together what have previously been separate objects of attention with their own distinct modes of study. Visual cultural studies constructs a new genealogy in which the study of visual and plastic arts are the precursors of the study of photography, film and television. Visual cultural studies conceptualises the rise of the visual in communication in two ways. It does this, first, by arguing that vision is a cultural practice that has changed over time, rather than a biologically fixed function of the human eye and brain, and, second, by redefining the autographic and later mechanical modes of visual reproduction as visual technologies. The first argument leads visual cultural studies to place visuality at the centre of communication, requiring a renewed interest in the science of vision and perception and in how and what can be represented. In bringing autographic reproduction in painting and printing and mechanical reproduction in photography, film and later video together as visual technologies, a renewed emphasis is placed upon the role of the medium in defining the message. The study of visual culture, then, includes the production and consumption of vision, or the operations and modes of vision in a given cultural and historical context. Within the study of visual culture the increasing application of digital imaging technologies strengthens the argument for the centrality of visuality in contemporary cultural experience. The argument is supported by the convergence of the telephone, television and computer in new screen-based interactive systems which are increasingly centred on the potential realisation of full-screen, real-time video streaming as the most desired and popular form of interface. The characteristics of such future screen-based visual interfaces, their aesthetics and effects, have been considered to be either those of the highly immersive, which moves the argument from visuality to virtuality, or of the depthless surface of the hypermediated screen.

New media, electronic and digital art

New media also has increasing currency as a distinct category of twenty-first-century art. The current moment is one in which a range of new media practices is being (re)contextualised within historical and contemporary curatorial fields and institutions. This is taking place through art institutions commissioning installation or networked projects, creating archives and in constructing a canon of works and a historical narrative of their development. The main argument being advanced is that new media art practice is a new avant-garde, an art practice of the future, ahead of its time and, as yet, not fully capable of being recognised or accepted (Rush 1999). Defining new media practice as the latest avant-garde locates our thinking about it firmly within the European modernist tradition. In such a context new media practice takes on the mantle of the modernist/post-modernist goal of pushing the boundaries of the medium of art itself. Paul (2003: 9) distinguishes two categories of digital art, one that uses digital technologies as a tool for the creation of traditional art objects and the other 'that employs digital technologies as its very own medium, being produced stored and presented exclusively in the digital form and making use of its interactive or participatory features'. Paul acknowledges the difficulties of categorisation in a period in which new media practice is evolving and changing, nevertheless, her categories distinguish between 'tradition' and 'new media', and, like Rush (1999), she sees the medium-specific definition as forward looking.

New media studies reshaping the media studies agenda

Established media studies tends to divide the media field into a number of discrete areas of study, each of which is intended to denote sections of the overall process of media production and consumption. Media studies is still thought about and taught in terms of the categories of institutions, industries, audiences, forms and languages. Such categories had explanatory currency in a post-war period of relative stability within the major, nationally organised media organisations. But with the internationalisation of media ownership and deregulation of public broadcasting the idea of a unified 'mass media' became increasingly challenged. The expansion of satellite transmission and reception and the rise of the Internet have created a much more diversified pattern of media production and consumption. As media studies as a discipline begins to account for the introduction of new media technologies and practices in the established media landscape as well as accounting for the emergence of distinct new media forms, its explanatory paradigms will be tested and modified.

Returning to the mapping metaphor

Mapping is probably the strongest metaphor and ordering concept of the book. It is a mapping exercise. But unlike a map of the earth's surface, our subject is not already unified, it is not already one thing, but rather has a number of different layers and surfaces that are not simply visible or exposed. To extend the metaphor, we can't spatialise all the dimensions of the subject on one plane. New media is a complex and layered subject that includes technical, historical, practical and theoretical knowledge. New media is characterised by its hybridity, or by the convergence or overlap of previously distinct media operations, skills and techniques. It follows, therefore, that it will contain different orders of knowledge and understanding.

Academic books on new media

There are a growing number of excellent books that offer the student of new media a range of perspectives on the subject. It should be remembered that all accounts of new media will be partial and will be written from a certain perspective or position, whether such positions are made explicit or not. The best books will be able to critically reflect on their own position and may well engage in debate with other views and positions. Two recent books that we have found useful and important in giving an overview and history of the subject are Lister *et al.*, *New Media: A Critical Introduction* (2003) and Wardrip-Fruin and Montfort, *The New Media Reader* (2003). The first book was written by academic colleagues of ours working in a university department of Cultural and Media Studies, from a cultural studies perspective and agenda. Indeed, we think of our book as a practical companion to it. *New Media: A Critical Introduction* does the difficult job of locating and tracing the underlying strands of argument which, in one sense, make up the academic study of new media. The book has a cultural constructivist framework, which seeks explanations of technology in what people do with technology rather than in the technology itself. The book consistently takes to task technological determinism in all its forms, resisting an account of new media as so many (determined) effects of a technologically based medium. In an important section the book re-examines the debates generated by the very different work of Marshall McLuhan and Raymond Williams writing in the 1960s and 1970s in relationship to television. In effect, *New Media: A Critical Introduction* adopts the approach of showing how new media can be thought of as part of a continuously evolving pattern of media codes and conventions.

In contrast, *The New Media Reader* sets out to provide us with the seminal historical texts of the computer, not as an advanced calculator, but as a new 'poetic' medium. The book carries two positioning introductions by Janet H. Murray and Lev Manovich, both of which argue for a conception of computing as a new medium of expression, which has taken over sixty years to emerge in its own right. *The New Media Reader* selects and assembles published articles and papers from computer scientists, engineers, artists and philosophers over six decades (1941–1994). It does this in order to create a new canon, or intellectual context, for contemporary practice.

Two other important books which advance a general theoretical view of new media are Manovich, *The Language of New Media* (2001) and Bolter and Grusin, *Remediation* (2000). Manovich (2001) encompasses both continuity and radical rupture in his account of new media. His argument for continuity is that the cultural language of new media is derived from ways of seeing and communicating derived from the predominance of film and cinema in the twentieth century. He then argues that the digital basis of new media, rather than the analogue medium of film, requires us to develop a new language of computer code. Manovich essentially argues that numerical representation, modularity, variability and transcoding, radically change what can be done, expressed, thought and communicated with a medium, and that we need to develop a new software theory, rather than cultural theory, to account for new media objects.

Bolter and Grusin (1999) offer a further and distinct framework for understanding new media. They also provide a historical contextualisation of new media, which articulates two distinct, if not binary opposite, traditions within cultural media. These they define as hypermediacy, our human interest in multiple, mediating processes, and immediacy, our desire for the eradication of all traces of mediation and to have absolute transparency. These twin tendencies, previously separated in cultural representations as different from each other as medieval churches – hypermediated environments – and photography – the transparent window on the world – now battle it out on the computer screen. For Bolter and Grusin the presence of immediacy and hypermediacy in new media is the remediation of all previous media. They point to television as the current battleground between two cultural forms and technologies and conclude that the computer will remediate television.

All of the four books we have cited focus on a set of common issues and debates about how we should conceive of new media and its practices. All four books provide historical contexts which differ but overlap. At the core of all the debates is the struggle to understand the relationship between the cultural language of new media and the scientific and technical apparatuses and systems upon which it is based. The complex relationship between culture and technology lies at the heart of understanding and practising new media. The histories provided in these four works share a common framework in the development of computing. They differ in the degree to which they include histories of representational media as essentially part of the history of new media.

Many of the ideas and points raised in the above summaries are expanded upon in greater depth in Part II in the discussion of new media languages, and in Part III which looks at the key debates. There are, of course, many more valuable books that appear on book lists and bibliographies which the student of new media would need to read and refer to over sustained study. The four we have singled out are important because they are all recent attempts to provide a specific framework for new media, as opposed to discussion of new technologies within different disciplinary boundaries.

Key titles

Everett, A. and Caldwell, J.T. (2003) *New Media: Theories and Practices of Digitextuality*. London: Routledge.

Lister, M., Dovey, J., Giddings, S., Grant, I. and Kelly, K. (2003) *New Media: a critical introduction*. London: Routledge.

Lovejoy, M. (2004) *Digital Currents: art in the electronic age*. London: Routledge.

Manovich, L. (2001) *The Language of New Media*. Massachusetts: MIT Press.

Paul, C. (2003) *Digital Art*. London: Thames & Hudson.

Rush, M. (1999) *New Media in Late 20th-century Art*. London: Thames & Hudson.

CASE STUDY

Contextualising creative practice: Jane Prophet

....

Jane Prophet is internationally established as an artist and writer. Among the best known of her wide ranging works are the projects 'TechnoSphere', a virtual world inhabited by thousands of digital creatures, which ran as an Internet project from 1995 till 2003, and was arguably one of the first artist-led web projects in the UK, and 'Decoy' (2001), a series that looked at the cultivated English landscape in which trees 'grew', and the landscape took on new shapes.

In this interview, Jane talks about the beginning of her practice and her approach to working with new media as an artist. She also identifies what to her are some of the specific characteristics of making artwork with teams and collaborators.

Background and creative influences
....

How did you start working with new media? Can you discuss what were the early influences upon the direction you took?

I think that I need to reflect on the situations in which I first used new media. What underpins my whole approach to using whatever media I've worked with, including new media, is the experience that I had on my undergraduate degree course and foundation art course. I actually didn't use new media on either of those two courses, but I was lucky in that when I did my undergraduate course I worked with people who encouraged me to make sound works and installations and who were very much aware of the art language and conceptual art movements. I didn't realise till much later on how lucky I was to have tutors who were that broad-based, as opposed to focusing on life drawing which many other students experienced. Later I did a degree in Live Art and in effect what I did was create installations and perform in them, which used old media such as 16 mm film, light-reactive materials and light effects.

Now when I look back at the work that I made, like 'Heart of the Cyborg' [a CD-ROM piece that explored ideas about the virtual and technological body] or 'Techno-Sphere', which were the first digital media works I made, I see them as performative works. I could look at them and talk about the way that they operate as digital art, and that would not be unrepresentative, but I think it more accurate to see them in terms

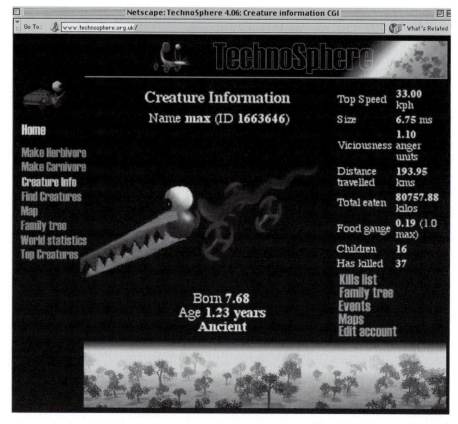

Figure 3.1   Jane Prophet and Gordon Selly, 'TechnoSphere' (1995)
'TechnoSphere' was a virtual world, populated by artificial life forms created by online users. The digital ecology of the 3-D world depended on the participation of the public and supported many tens of thousands of competing life forms: typically 20,000 creatures were alive at any one time. Detail from webpage showing information on artificial life creatures.

of my trajectory as an artist and to think of them as works about the body, about the audience becoming participants, and spatial awareness. I think the reason why I felt able to go into new media was that I never saw it as separate from my fine art practice. I saw it as another set of tools that I could use in my practice. Of course, as soon as I looked into it, I realised that this was a medium that was going to change my practice, it was about interacting with the world in a whole new way. Thinking about digital arte-facts and digital media as communication media has been really important to me.

Storyboarding with Hypercard and experiments with software

What led to your interest in digital technology? You have described it as providing 'another set of tools'. Did you start to work with new media as a way of solving prob-lems and to enable you to make more complex works than you could with other media?

I think if anything I was technophobic as an undergraduate. Some of my contemporaries made extraordinarily technologically advanced works. But to me technology was a means to an end – a way of getting my message across. When I went into my postgraduate course in 1988 I had never used a computer. It sounds mad now but I was at the only arts school in the country where you could use an Apple Mac. People came from all over because it was a place where they could make art with computers in a formal way. We began with Hypercard and the first thing that I realised was that if you planned out and storyboarded your Hypercard stack it was like a concept diagram.

That was how I had always planned out my art works, it was the way I represented my thoughts. I realised like lots of artists that the way I was essentially working was non-linear and I became interested in hyper-textual structure. That's what kept me going – because what you could do at the time in terms of images was so limited, and the graphical output was so uninspiring, but the underlying ideas about linking, about interactivity, that we take for granted were really radical at the time and resonated with me. Having said that, the first digital piece I made, 'TechnoSphere', didn't have a flashy graphical quality, but it is more about 'site', the way we represent information and about the nature of the Internet. Ultimately I would say that 'TechnoSphere' was a social project, a tool for thinking, and I would say that most of my projects have that sort of conceptual edge to them.

Figure 3.2   Jane Prophet and Gordon Selly, 'TechnoSphere' (1995)
Detailed rendering of an artificial life creature contributed by online participants to the artificial world of 'TechnoSphere'. Users created their own artificial life forms, building carnivores or herbivores from component parts (heads, bodies, eyes and wheels). Their digital DNA, or genetic specification, was linked to each component part, determining speed, visual perception, rate of digestion and so forth. Once a creature was built, users named their digital creature and it was tagged with their email address, so that messages could be sent 'from' the creature to its creator.

What sort of technologies or programmes did you find useful? What directions did this early work take you in?

I made video installations, then a series of Chromakey pieces which enabled me to experiment with layering. I was interested in having something layered but that was also coloured and moving, and at the time, technology with Hypercard didn't allow you to do that. The restriction with Hypercard was that it was very difficult even to work with basic black and white images, and we were limited to things that would fit on floppy disks. Looking back, it is like a sketchbook work, in which I was working out how to get non-linearity using what was a tape-based format. This is what we were all struggling with at the time. And in some ways that way of working has not completely disappeared. A lot of my work is about layering meaning and images, but I don't always do it within a frame, it is much more spatial. As a visual artist, I found digital media terribly limiting and frustrating as a means of making and disseminating work and at the same time it was also incredibly liberating conceptually. However, over the last ten years I have understood the technology more and the technology has advanced a huge amount. Now there is a real convergence, a synergy between what the technology has to offer conceptually and what it can actually deliver. This enables a huge conceptual shift for all of us.

The experience I went through was, in some ways, hugely frustrating, not just for me but also for everybody around me who was on the same learning curve. I don't think that this was due to the management of the education but it was symptomatic of something on the brink, of working on the edge of what a technology can do. When people don't understand a technology they don't understand its limitations and so they demand more and more from it. I think it is typical of artists that when they use a technology they aren't familiar with they have all sorts of aspirations that get built up and then get frustrated.

Now, when I look around at contemporary new media work one of the things that I find disappointing about is how unadventurous it is. Because now we know and understand the limitations of the technology, it is pushed forward incrementally, whereas I think in the 1990s people were preposterously expecting things from it which led to some appalling works but it did contribute to this vision. It did contribute to people thinking, 'If I can't get it to achieve X what can I get it to do that will give the same result?' – and as a result this meant that artists didn't specialise so much as work across different media.

Mathematics

Do you think that learning about digital technology, and acquiring particular skills, gave you a determination to specialise in that as your field? Or were there more general interests about technology and new media that resonated with you?

I really resist the label of 'digital artist' because I don't see myself as that. I've never seen myself as that because I think that if I was a digital artist I couldn't make works like the site-specific installation, 'Conductor', made using light and water [shown at Wapping Hydraulic Power Station, London 2001]. It's just that often digital processes can deliver and reflect my thinking perfectly as an artist so I want to use them. One other important thing that happened during my education was that I met mathematicians and listened to them for the first time. Through them I discovered that their relationship with new media technology was at the level of programming. What that meant for them was that they didn't look at the machine as a machine that manipulated pixels, they looked at the computer as a machine that they programmed and that those equations made images. That is a really different way of thinking about making images, because if you are shifting images around in Photoshop or in 3-D Studio Max it is very top-down, you are not thinking about what happens if you write an equation and what that means, you are thinking about a particular outcome you want. What brought that home to me was when a mathematician showed me a Mandelbrot Set and said to me, 'What do you see in this image?'. I could talk about patterns, colour, meaning and he said, 'This is what I see,' and on a whiteboard wrote out a mathematical equation. And I was mind-blown by that.

I later heard Benoit Mandelbrot talk, which was an extraordinary experience, and I suddenly saw that there was something about chaos theory and its manifestation and in the way it was represented visually through his Julia sets that was potentially life changing. Hypercard had had that effect on me, it was a conceptual framework or concept that changed the way I saw the world. A mathematician had once said to me that he thought that maths was beautiful, and that it was frustrating that artists might not be able to see maths that way, but the visual impact of a Julia set could not be denied though it meant such different things to such different people.

I think I am still dealing with those ideas when I make images that are easily accessible like my projects 'Landscape Room' or 'Decoy' where I use fractal mathematics and you don't see the code but you see these faux landscapes. But the underlying concept is that I am still thinking about the relationship between mathematics and natural forms. I think that enough people who know nothing about mathematics know that connection through looking at the work to think that somehow this is transmitted in the works. I believe that they do contemplate the question, 'what is natural?'

Dealing with broader cultural and political agendas

A question like 'what is natural?' is asked by artists in many contexts, and rightly so. Do you see in your work that this is primarily about technology or is it broader?

I suppose that this is something that runs through the work that I have done since I was an undergraduate. When I was an undergraduate the question 'what is natural?' was often asked within the context of feminist theory. And this was a difficult time in feminist theory between resisting biological determinism and celebrating what was feminine, and I don't think that I necessarily resolved it in my own work. Now we just accept that mutually exclusive dualisms, such as the male versus the female, the natural versus the artificial, are over – we just accept that. But in the 1980s I don't think it was so easily accepted, and it was very challenging, particularly in art school, particularly when there was a tradition of life drawing. The debate was loaded and informed my practice: where is the boundary between my body and the outside world? What is the difference between being the subject of a life drawing and looking at or making life drawings myself? We can ask now, what is there to replace these dualisms? The answer has to be that there are more endless questions. For example: what is the boundary between undesirable genetic modification in plants and the sort of genetic modification that has gone on for hundreds of years through selective agriculture? Where are the boundaries between my body and the machine? And with nano-technology this is a very real question, not just a rhetorical one.

Figure 3.3
Jane Prophet, 'Decoy' (2001)
Sequence of stills from an evolving
landscape, 'Blickling Hall', in which
an avenue of trees is digitally
'grown'. English oaks once formed
an avenue in the parkland at
Blickling Hall but most were
removed by landscape designers to
create a 'picturesque' landscape.
Using the existing trees as a guide
the avenue is reinstated.

I use new media in a variety of ways, and sometimes I am using it to comment upon itself, because some of the projects are based upon fractal mathematics that are reflecting their own source. In comparison, when I make something like 'The Heart of the Cyborg', it is a very different project. When it starts off I am concerned with the body and technology but in the final instance the technology is the work's delivery mechanism. The self-critique is not embedded in the work to the same degree.

Skills and expertise

In thinking about the trajectory you have taken as an artist, what kind of skills have been important to you and enabled your development?

In terms of skills I think that learning how to HTML edit was essential because it gave me access to the Internet in a way that otherwise would not have been available. I was working with the web pre-Dreamweaver and other editing programmes. HTML editing allowed me to subvert and use the technology in ways that it wasn't used much online. I've always been aware of the battle between making work and developing a high level of technical skills because I don't think that the two necessarily go together. If you are an artist like me – by which I mean I am not a net artist, I am not a video or an installation artist – I make work in areas that are appropriate at different times and I can't become an expert in all those skills and all those technologies. So I've always learned only what I need to learn. This is one of the reasons why I work with people who have particular skills in other areas. I am not prepared to sit back and observe someone else with the skills though. It is important to understand how the technology works in order to be able to work meaningfully with the medium, like having programming knowledge. Right now I am in a situation where I am excited about non-linear editing. I am an opportunist in that way: I will learn something and then drop it and move on.

Framing collaborations

A lot of people have talked about working with new media as often being collaborative. In your projects you have worked with teams and collaborators. How has this shaped your approach to your work?

The most important skills that I have developed have been interpersonal and people have commented to me that the most important thing about my work is the interaction with other people as it comes about. I may spend months and months on a project and seemingly be making no work but I am spending huge amounts of time with a programmer or a scientist in a lab and what I am doing on the one hand may be hanging out but I quickly develop themes and areas of questions and I pursue these over time. The duration of the collaboration is important. It takes time to build trust and to get under the skin of another person and understand what makes them tick, what it is about the expertise they have in their discipline that is unique.

That is also the way that I would describe my approach to site-specific work. Like 'Conductor' which was made in response to a particular building at a particular moment in time and the people in it. And the Internet works are also about asking the question, 'What is the Internet, how do we understand it?' And how do you answer that question? You can't answer it on your own, it's best if you ask a lot of people the same question, so the work is dialogic.

*Do you also find yourself working with teams where there is an emphasis on function-
ality and where different people have specific roles (such as an animator or an a-life
programmer) but in something like a traditional model of the artist and the technicians?
Or do you find that most situations involve more open and fluid collaborations and that
roles may shift?*

There are situations where working with other people is about project management. And
there can also be straightforward jobbing work that goes on where people have very
specific functions.

There is a model that is long established, for example the Michelangelo model of the
artists and the technicians, and I don't work on a project like marble statues that require
studio assistants to chip away at stone, but I have people that chip away at pixels or
code. They manifest my ideas, it is as simple as that. But I think there is a very different
model, which is what I would call a bottom-up 'true collaboration' which is where the
interaction with an assistant changes to the point where they are a key collaborator and
they are having an impact upon the idea.

But interestingly I can have a very conventional task-oriented relationship with a
programmer where I am asked by them to come up with the ideas and they will carry
them out, and yet with the same person in a different situation I can have a bottom-up
emergent process where we evolve the idea together.

The importance of team work

....

*Would you go so far as to say that an important skill that you have developed is to
enable people to work in that context?*

Yes, I think it is an important skill – and there are strategies as well. Sometimes collaboration also operates as an exchange culture, a gift economy. It can be that members
of a team work because it is in our mutual interests, and because we will both gain
different things from the project. I also know that a lot of inputs won't be recognised
without a fight when the work has been made.

*Are you saying that the kind of team work that you are involved in on your projects
doesn't fit into a typical model in the art world?*

I still think, no matter how far we think that we have moved on, the idea of collaboration is a very hard idea to sell to the art world, where there is a very deep rooted notion
of what is an artist and a narrow view of what is a legitimate creative process. I have
had experiences where galleries have not listed my collaborators as makers of the
artwork, and recognising collaboration between different disciplines is deeply problematic in the artworks and it is just as problematic in the new media art world as in any
other. And what the art world is having to learn with new media is that there is another
model and it is qualitatively different.

Jane Prophet's art projects and writing are at www.janeprophet.com

4 The language of new media

....

How we communicate using computers is an important question and, since human communication has always involved the development and use of language, we need to consider how computer-based forms of communication relate to language. There are two related senses in which a language of new media can be discussed. First, we can consider whether the distinctive features of computer communication, the digitisation and storage of data, programming and software use, operate in any way like a language. The central interface of end-user computer communication remains, for the time being at least, language based, however, the ways in which we engage in textual communication with a computer, as opposed to written or printed text, is potentially new or at least different. Looking at how new media operates using a variety of language elements builds upon established ways of accounting for how meaning is achieved in other media forms such as literature, graphics, film or photography. The communication of meaning in film, for example, is achieved through a combination of the technical apparatus for creating moving images and synchronised sound and the cultural forms, or the rules and conventions of actions, events and scenes within the filmic image. Currently, film and photographic theory are having to reconsider how the introduction of digital technology is changing the ways in which we have come to understand the production and use of certain kinds of images in media forms such as Hollywood movies and photojournalism.[1]

The second sense of a language of new media is more straightforward, and refers to the specialist and technical set of words and concepts in which new media is discussed. But even here there is no one simple and agreed way of talking about computer communication. We make an important distinction between a technical operational language, used by those who are involved in the chain of new media production, i.e. scientists, engineers, technicians, producers and designers, and an equally technical but abstract language used by artists, academics and cultural theorists, who reflect upon the meaning of new media.

Computer-mediated forms of communication
....

The 'language' of computer-mediated forms of communication can be thought of as consisting of two connected levels. At the user/receiver level we can conceive of a language of the human–computer interface (HCI), which consists of software programmes together with the data assets, the electronic encoding of written texts, images, graphics, sounds they make available. At the computer processing and programming level we can consider a language of code, the mathematical algorithms which structure the computer processing and operating system. Our two levels are similar to what Manovich (2001: 46), distinguishes as the 'cultural layer' and the 'computer layer' which, he says, influence each other, or are composited in practice. Where, exactly, these two levels meet, between the design of computers and software and the ways in which a user engages with them, is a complex but important point of understanding. The design and production of any machine or technology needs to be understood as already containing cultural values or meanings, which are part of the structure of the language of any new media product, but are not immediately obvious to the user. One way of revealing the cultural/linguistic meanings built into the design of computers is through analysis of interfaces and software use. Thinking about software as culture leads us to see that software code is based upon usability concepts, based upon a set of assumptions and precepts about the purposes the machine or programme has been designed to solve or facilitate. The personal computer (PC) arrives culturally conceptualised as a machine with user intentions and purposes already prefigured in its design. The problem with the distinction between the machine and its organisational function on the one hand, and the human uses to which we put the machine on the other, is that it can lead us to assume the neutrality of the machine as a tool.

The distinction between our two levels of language (machine and its uses, or the computer level and the cultural level) is not recognised in practice, because the user experiences a seamless flow, from the interface metaphor (the desktop), through the controls it offers, through to the data it makes available. The user interacts with the computer through programmed instructions embedded in software that conceals the programming layer, while simulating the cultural layer of image, sound and text. The end user doesn't 'see' the layer of code, or even necessarily need to use the programming language, and hence doesn't need to think about it either. The computer layer constitutes the invisible part of the grammar of new media until, that is, something goes wrong with the operational commands, which forces the user to become, negatively, aware of it.

Level 1 Command	**Interface**
Metaphorical interface	Windows, icons, desktop, toolbars
Physical interface	Screen: keyboard, mouse, input devices
Level 2 Processing and memory	**Function**
Operating system	Software code
Central processing unit	Algorithmic code, electrical impulses and switches

The recognition of 'visible' and 'invisible' levels of interface command, the latter based upon mathematics, and the former on the simulated representation of existing forms of cultural communication, make the notion of a unified or consistent language of new media untenable. The reasons for this are threefold. First, new media is, by definition, continually evolving and developing and could, therefore, be said to be at a current stage where it has no developed language of its own. This is a view adopted by a number of commentators (Manovich 2001; Rush 2001). Second, new media is characterised more than anything else by its hybridity. The graphical user interface (GUI) of the PC, the desktop and its current applications, is the nearest we come to defining a coherent usable set of common communication tools. But the graphical user interface is, itself, based upon the previous and distinct analogue media disciplines, i.e. typewriting and printing, 2-D graphics, animation, film and photography, as well as being founded upon computing (Bolter and Grusin 2000). Third, there is a widespread social, cultural and institutional application of new media, in the office, home, laboratory, school, college or workshop, that differentiates user requirements and access. Within such contexts of computer-mediated communication, localised purposes, rules, conventions and under-standings will be defined that will contribute to the ways in which communication takes place. While there are distinct technical stages in new media production and different cultural contexts and uses, it is their convergence in a common set of digital technolo-gies that forms the basis upon which we say that there is something like a language of new media. The current position of computer-mediated language can, therefore, be summarised in the following way:

1 The language of new media is at an early stage of development.

2 The language of new media is highly dependent upon historical media forms and their discourses, which digital code simulates and represents.

3 The language of new media is characterised by a high degree of hybridity, based upon convergence.

We can now look at each of these aspects in turn.

The languages of established media and communication

As we have noted, the language of new media can be understood by a comparison with those of highly developed media communications. The ways in which film, photography, television, print culture, musical forms, drama, theatre, dance and the visual arts communicate constitutes an historical archive upon which computer-mediated communi-cation is being established.

Media communication is not the same thing as a specific media language, as the large volume of academic writing on the subject makes plain. Most critics would agree that media forms operate like a language, rather than strictly obeying the rules of human spoken and written languages. This is evident when we consider visual language, for instance. Paintings are not composed out of regulated, systematised linguistic elements because colour, shape and texture do not operate like letters, words and sentences, yet culturally we are able to talk of 'reading' as much as viewing or contemplating a painting. Whether the discussion is of painting, photography, film or television as a language, strictly speaking, an analogy with speech and writing is being made. Language is a mode of communication based upon a code, i.e. letters, words and sentences governed by a set of grammatical rules. In practice, none of our list of developed cultural and media forms of expression and communication can be strictly called a language, because we are unable to break them down totally to a rule-based code. Nevertheless, the 'language-like' nature of modern media has been extremely important in understanding how complex meanings, much of which go beyond the obvious or literal message, are encoded and decoded. New media language borrows, adapts and transforms elements of existing and established encoding methods of communication. How it does this is the subject of this section.

Over the past two decades the academic discipline of media studies has consistently attempted to analyse media forms in terms of their language-like properties. Television, film and photography have all been treated to systematic theoretical and empirical analysis in attempts to discover their underlying, or structural, organisation. The common core of this endeavour has been to identify the constituent parts of a media message, whether that is a single photographic image, or a discrete television programme, or a sequence of edited film. In breaking down the media message into its smallest units of meaning, media forms are being treated as if they were a formal language in the same way that words and sentences obey a set of grammatical rules. Of course, the study of media forms as languages does not represent the whole of the discipline of media studies, which is also interested in the social, political and economic organisation and regulation of media, as well as its reception by audiences. Nor does the specific tradition of analysis that flows from studying media texts as linguistic structures represent the only position on the analysis of the media text. However, it does remain a powerful general way of thinking about media messages that has been shaped by structuralist and semiological theory. If there is a current consensus on how the communicative structures of photography, film and television work, it is one that recognises a multiplicity of ways in which they can be analysed and the attempt to develop a single scientific method for analysis has been largely abandoned. But, with the advent of new media, the question arises again about structure and language because the emergent digital media forms all have a common technical code, and they are re-purposing, or hybridising all existing and highly developed media forms of communication.

Hybridity and convergence

The revaluation of old media through the prism of new media, or the visioning of new media possibilities through the lens of old media, is a response to the phenomenon of convergence in technologies and media ownership. Convergence is also a way of thinking about the current state of new media languages. Practical developments in new media language, as well as the cultural conversation about new media, can, at best, be regarded as a patchwork of knowledge and understanding. We can look at what some of the key knowledge and skill transfer consists of in terms of what is specific to new media and what remains generic to cultural language. From such an exercise it is possible to articulate what the 'new' or 'emerging' practices of new media are. Convergence suggests three identifiable processes that we might expect to find in both film and new media:

- overlapping practices;
- dissolving of conceptual boundaries of potential meaning;
- emergence of new hybrid practices.

Film, language and new media

Film as a medium of expression and communication consists of both a particular set of related apparatuses (cameras, lighting systems, sound recording equipment and editing), as well as a body of shared cultural knowledge about how to construct images and sounds and put them together in ways that make sense in particular cultural contexts.

The knowledge about film apparatuses and how to use them to make meaning is repro-duced in a variety of contexts, through publishing, education and the production companies that train and pass on the know-how of film-making. Film has developed a range of distinct forms each with its own rules or conventions that vary from culture to culture. For example, contemporary Indian cinema, 'Bollywood', happily mixes Hollywood naturalistic continuity editing with anti-illusionist traditions of Hindu myth-ology. The question of whether film is an exact language, or whether it functions like a language, is the subject of film theory, which has, over the last fifty years, generated a number of distinct conceptual approaches to the analysis of different film forms. It is useful to briefly characterise the key approaches to film analysis since they have a bearing on one of the primary ways in which new media is being discussed in terms of the remediation or re-purposing of old media.

How film 'works' to create meaning has been generally understood and studied in relationship to the various stages of film production and consumption. Different theoretical and analytical traditions have established themselves to account for how films are made and how they are valued and interpreted. The emphasis upon film as a language is most associated with forms of analysis that treat the film as a 'closed text'. Such analysis 'brackets out', or suspends attention to all those factors of the social and economic production and consumption of film other than the specific com-bination of image and sound that make up a discrete and completed object. Analysing film as a text is based upon the assumption that, over time, film apparatuses and the cultural conventions that govern actions, objects and events within the film frame, have combined to create a structure in which there is something like a film grammar, syntax and vocabulary. Such film language involves the combination of the distinct tech-nical practices of cinematography, acting, scripting and editing, which have coalesced over time and in different cultural contexts to form the distinctive 'rules' of specific cinemas.

Film theory has striven to reveal the underlying rules, both cultural and technical, of film language and meaning. In this endeavour, film theory has produced a number of distinct analytical positions that highlight key different perspectives of the cultural experience of cinema. Film theory focuses upon four inter-related but distinct aspects of the development and use of film as a medium from the producer to the receiver. These four aspects can be defined as: the intentions and role of the film-maker (auteur theory); types and styles of film (realism, genre, textual and structuralist theory); the cultural context in which film is produced and received (intertextuality, post-colonialism, feminist and queer theory); and the ways in which an individual is socio-psychologically positioned to experience the film (spectator theory, psychoanalysis, post-structuralist, post-modernist theory). Of course, any one of these positions within film theory is attempting to account not simply for a part of the process, but also for the overall meaning of film in culture. It is always a case of stressing the centrality of one of the four dimensions in (over)determining the others. Most recently there has been a recognition within film studies (Stam 2000) that it is unlikely that we will ever produce one overarching or totalising account of how film generates meaning and that it is more fruitful to see various theoretical accounts forming a grid which when applied to concrete examples of film illuminates their different aspects.

It would be quite possible to apply any of the perspectives on, and principles of, film theory to new media artefacts and yet very little detailed analysis of new media arte-facts and their user modes of engagement has, so far, been undertaken or published. By their nature (interactive), new media artefacts present a different set of difficulties for the researcher or critic, since by nature they do not present or represent themselves, whether on- or offline, as unitary and finite texts. In addition, interactive media embraces, if not celebrates, the idea that it is the user, not the producer, who is the author of the 'work' by virtue of the user's choice and navigational path through a programmed data-set. No two users, it is argued, will have the same experience of what constituted the work. Of course, no two people will experience a film in the same way, yet the film as cultural object is the same object for both, while the interactive media artefact is different for each viewer. But the close scrutiny and analysis of interactive media artefacts has to start somewhere and, we would argue, it is possible to set about analysing or critiquing interactive media artefacts using a range of theoretical tools derived, in part, from the analysis of film.

The application of digital technologies in compositing and editing moving images means that part of the emerging language in which new media is being understood and framed now relates to new ways of understanding film and, hence, is included in film studies. This is part of the phenomenon of media convergence in which the application of digital technologies to analogue film is changing, first and foremost, the distribution forms of film. One of the noticeable effects of digital distribution is that cinema is less separated from other media platforms. The installation of digital television and the scaling up of the domestic screen will make the 'home cinema' an established cultural experience. Further technical developments in broadband signalling will shortly complete the convergence of the computer and television as a new platform for home entertainment in which subscription or pay-as-you-go-based film-on-demand services will be the norm. The projection of 35 mm or 70 mm film in cinemas is also challenged by digital technologies' increasing ability to simulate the resolution of the projected chemical film image. Cinemas will be able to receive high-quality digital film online for projection, which could, potentially, radically change the ways in which cinema organises screenings and programming.

If digital technology is destabilising the boundary between film and television at the level of distribution and reception of the product of film, is it also changing the nature of film in production? At the time of writing most major film productions are shot on film and the film industry remains technologically based around the film camera. Where production requires shooting on video/digital video, it is subsequently transferred to film for exhibition. Film in the camera remains, for the time being, the gold standard against which the quality of digital video is measured, but digital recording of the moving image will very soon reach the stage when it can simulate all of the technical and aesthetic qualities of film. At this stage, rather as we have already seen with digital photography, the industry will adopt digital recording equipment and formats as standard. At the present time the greatest impact of digital technology upon film as a product is in post-production. Film may still be shot in the camera, but it is almost universally edited digitally. Once the film sequences are transferred to a digital format then it can be edited in the virtual environment of the computer where every element of the image can be altered and cloned and sequences moved endlessly and seamlessly in a virtual edit. The other major and more visible effect of digital technology in film post-production is in special effects (SFX). Special effects consists of producing effects that happen either in front of the camera, or by treating the film after it has been shot in post-production through montage and animation of other filmed material. Digital technology provides for the seamless layering and compositing of live action and animation in ways that produce a new photo-realist hybrid. Directors can now render a unified and credible moving image of any imagined world conjured up by writers. Another way of putting this is to say that computer generated image software programmes (CGI) merge material generated from external sources with animated material produced by computer algorithms.

The use of CGI in post-production film-making has had effects on the product of mainstream Hollywood film, which has been noted in film studies as another way in which film is becoming less distinct from new media. New media's capacity to incorporate, or remediate, all previous media suggests that film will develop new and as yet unlooked for outcomes in online, interactive or immersive media. Computer and video games already constitute a form of interactive digital film for game players.

Computer modelling and rendering of objects and spaces that can be given photo-realistic behaviours and properties also changes/extends the established language of film-making that evolved from the codes and conventions of the movement of the film camera and its implied point-of-view. In the virtual space created by vectoral graphics space and objects can be 'seen' from any position, defying the laws of physics that apply to the movement of objects in the real world or the positions and movements of the human body. In film, science fiction and cartoons have previously exploited and deployed special effects that allow characters in film to defy gravity or travel across time. But CGI also brings forwards the possibility of endlessly changing the position of the audience in relationship to space, objects and actions within space, by putting them in an all-seeing point-of-view relative to the position of the virtual camera. It is a computer algorithm that determines the position and angle of view, rather than the lens and frame of a real camera located in real space. The same is true of virtual lighting in CGI. The filmic image is produced by reflected light from either the sun or artificial lights or both. Lighting is part of the language of film, producing particular effects of place and space related to the natural world and of mental states. Lighting objects in a computer-rendered world follows the logic of lighting codes derived from previous film convention if it wishes to reproduce a given aesthetic style or look, but it can also assign different light values to different objects within the same scenes as well as lighting a scene from virtual positions.

Photography, language and new media

Mitchell (1998) eloquently describes in detail the technical differences between the chemical photograph and the digital image. In doing this he underlines the point that, while culturally there has been continuity in thinking about the digital image as a digital photograph, at the medium-specific and technical level they have little in common. The technical differences between analogue photography and the digital image could have led to a definition of a digital image as something other than photography. The digital camera is, in fact, an electronic capture device, with more in common with a mobile phone or computer than a camera. A digital photograph is more accurately understood as a simulation of an analogue photograph. The algorithms that determine each tonal and colour value of individual pixels in a mathematical grid substitute for the continuous tones and hues of the chemical photograph. Photography is, therefore, a good example of how the (cultural) language of the digital image is continuous with that which arose out of a previous technology, while the actual technology (digital coding) is significantly different. Here, we have new media simulating the form and language of an older medium, but with a radically different structure. This is conceptually confusing, as a number of commentators have pointed out,[2] because it tends to lead to misunderstanding the digital image as simply the production of a photograph using a different technology or, conversely, that the digital image is an inferior, less truthful or accurate kind of photograph. The better way to understand the digital image is in terms of technological and cultural convergence. First, the digital image is the technical convergence of some aspects of the photomechanical process, the light forming image of the pinhole camera and the properties of lenses, together with an electronic technology that converts light patterns into electrical currents which are then coded by a set of binary numeral values. Second, digital photography is a hybrid that combines the conventions of photography and graphics in a digital programme. As Mitchell (1998: 60) puts it, 'the practices of digital imaging and photography intersect at the moment of image capture, but thereafter the disjunction become increasingly significant'. Digital capture imitates the process of the mechanical camera shutter release allowing a measured amount of light to fall onto the light-sensitive film plane. It does this by replacing the film plane with a charge-coupled device (CCD), which records a light intensity and additive primary colour value for selected areas within a CCD array. The result of this image capture is a digital file and it is important to recognise that there are other image-capture technologies. The drum and flatbed scanner converts existing photographic and graphic imagery into digital image files and the video frame-grabber can convert the continuous analogue signal of video into a series of 'framed' digital files. It is the digital file that parts company with the photographic negative or print at the technical level, while in many contexts remaining firmly embedded in the cultural arena of photography. Digital imaging represents a concrete example of the more general point that new media language can only be approached at this point in culture and history as a hybrid in which established media languages provide a metaphorical equivalent to a computer-based science and technology for which there is no developed and systematic practical cultural language. Photoshop, a software programme created by Adobe Systems, Inc. in 1989 for the manipulation of scanned or raster images for PostScript output, is a good example of the hybrid identity of new media language.

Photoshop

What follows is a descriptive analysis of the organisation and functions of Photoshop that leads into a more analytical account of how these functions presuppose a cultural pattern of use. Upon launching Photoshop, version 7 you are reminded that it is a licensed product that has a legal agreement attached to it, making it illegal to make any further copies of the software. The opening credits read like film credits, citing a voluminous number of developers and giving their acknowledgements and thanks to friends and family. The style of the credits is both grand and relaxed at the same time. They have even thought to include the user's name in the acknowledgements as a personal touch, a suggestion of the fraternity of new media practitioners. The Photoshop launch logo colonises the human eye as its icon. It is a blue eye with long lashes, which is presented in a mute montage that also includes a partial picture frame, a camera lens, the sky and a number of birds.

Photoshop's graphic screen interface sits on top of the Windows or Mac OS X desktop. It has a narrow horizontal menu bar at the top and a tool bar down the left side. Upon opening a new file a document control box is created within which a blank canvas of specified dimensions is located. The menu bar contains the familiar options, file, edit, image, layer, select, filter, view, window and help. Each of the words is an active link to a drop-down menu containing further option commands. The file menu includes import and export, while the edit menu has the options to cut and paste. Image, select and filter have the largest range of option commands. In the image menu, there are the options of mode, adjust, duplicate, size, rotate, layer. A third layer of options, under 'adjust' for example, contains colour balance and brightness/contrast. Many of these menu items, such as file, edit, view and help, are the standard commands of word-processing software applications which allow for elements within a file to be edited, cut, pasted, copied, saved and printed. Photoshop becomes more specific in its image and filter menus, which offer a range of pre-determined adjusts of the whole or parts of the image. In Photoshop 7 the filters are pre-programmed special effects that can be applied to an existing image or graphic object. They include a range of effects that relate to other media, for example under the sub-menu 'artistic' there are a range of effects derived from European painting; watercolour is an effect, for instance. 'Video' is another sub-menu, while 'blur' and 'sharpen' are more directly related to the photographic enlarger. As the manual puts it, 'Photoshop's filters are used to produce myriad effects, from the slightly sharpened to wild distortion' (Weinmann and Lourekas 2003). The Photoshop menu thus contains generic commands common to all digital files (cut, paste and copy could equally apply to sound, for example), as well as commands that are specific to the visual image and which have been derived from existing media.

Tools

The Photoshop tool bar follows this duality, with some highly generic tools such as: zoom, select and text; other tools generic to drawing software, such as brush, pen and erase; medium-specific tools, such as dodge, blur and crop, derived from the chemical darkroom of photography; and then tools for which there was no existing media equivalent, such as magic wand, which selects similarly coloured pixels, history brush, which restores pixels from a designated state, the clone stamp and the slightly mystical and most recent tool, the healing brush which corrects flaws. Again, the reason for such descriptive detail is to underline the point that even the names of the tools reflect the hybrid and even somewhat schizophrenic nature of the command options. The result is a graphic interface that has the icons and titles of the tools and conventions of drawing and painting, combined with the operations of chemical photography together with a set of new options based upon preset computer behaviours and pixel cloning and adjustment.

Layers and compositing

In addition to what are considered the basic operations of the menu and tools, Photoshop 7 contains more advanced operations that control colour management, compositing, selection, history and navigation, gradients, layers and masks. Compositing groups the operations of the cut and paste of elements and selections and the cloning, resizing and pattern stamping of selections which can be precisely positioned and aligned with seamless edges or divisions between elements. Colour management and gradient control tone and hue in different layers, masks and selections. The very early versions of Photoshop only allowed for any two moves in selection before the new configuration became fixed. It was not possible to go back and undo previous moves. The introduction of layers in Photoshop 3.0 represented a quantum leap in digital image manipulation. Layers can be compared to clear acetate sheets, which are opaque where there is imagery and transparent where there is not. Each layer can be assigned a different opacity and a mode to control how that layer blends with the layers below it. The layers can be stacked in any order and remain active, with the user being able to turn layers on and off and to work on one active layer at a time. Because Photoshop makes it possible to keep all changed states active until a final version is required, a way of charting the changes is necessary, otherwise the user would easily lose the order of actions they have made. Photoshop has a history palette that allows users to selectively undo up to 1,000 previous states and to navigate through the moves they have made.

Photoshop 7's array of tools, each of which encodes a computer behaviour, is by any account formidable. It should be remembered that analogue photo-mechanical reproduction was lengthy and more time consuming, requiring separated skills and different technical processes. It is the convergence of many of these separate processes and skills in Photoshop which, at one level, is considerably impressive if not awe inspiring. To recognise the power of digital convergence as represented in Photoshop, in comparison to its analogue predecessors, is also to recognise a period of historic change in the process of representation and reproduction. The 'radical' moment that digital convergence represents can be, and has been, compared to the earlier historical period when photo-mechanical reproduction replaced reproduction by hand, which was illuminated so clearly by Walter Benjamin (1939) in his seminal essay, 'The Work of Art in the Age of Mechanical Reproduction'. In the decade and a half since Photoshop's appearance, there has been continual reflection upon what the use of Photoshop and the related digital capture and output technologies have achieved and what effects they have had upon all forms of (photo)graphic representation and reproduction. Manovich (2001) links Photoshop with post-modernism, arguing that it was no accident that the appearance of Photoshop coincided with what Frederic Jameson called the condition of post-modernity, with its characteristic emphasis upon surface rather than depth.

5 CASE STUDY
Shifting concerns in artists' projects: Nina Pope

his case study looks at the way that an artist situates her practice in relation to a wider development of and interest in ideas about new media.

Nina Pope and her collaborator Karen Guthrie have been working with new media since the mid-1990s. Their first new media project in 1996, 'A Hypertext Journal', was one of the first Internet arts projects in the UK. For this project they undertook a trip around Scotland in the path of the famous journey taken by Boswell and Johnson in the

Figure 5.1 Nina Pope and Karen Guthrie, 'A Hypertext Journal' (1996)
Detail from the website showing a portrait of the artists during their tour of Scotland, undertaken as an 'interactive artwork' in which they uploaded daily diary pages of their journey. This project was one of the first publicly funded Internet art projects in the UK.

Figure 5.2   Nina Pope and Karen Guthrie, 'An Artist's Impression' (1999)
Gallery installation of the physical representation of a social online game, a MUSH, under evolving
construction at the Institute of Contemporary Arts, London. The installation was created as a physical representation of the online space and participants in the online community designed aspects
of the virtual world, which were then modelled in the real world by Pope and Guthrie as a way of
teasing out the differences between an online and offline space.

seventeenth century, which led to what is arguably one of the first published travel journals. When Pope and Guthrie travelled they uploaded texts in an early version of a web
diary or a blog, with embedded images and animations. The project explored how to use
hypertext as a part of the narrative and as a reference to historical publishing. Later, Pope
and Guthrie went on to create other projects such as 'An Artist's Impression' (1999)
that used aspects of Internet culture, such as the multi-user virtual environments of
MUSHes, that were otherwise considered to be very technical, but used them as a space
for collaborative artistic expression. 'Broadcast (29 pilgrims, 29 tales)' used webcasting
as a contemporary approach to community folktales by reworking Chaucer's *Canterbury
Tales*, which was presented as the Tate Gallery Annual Event 1999, in London.

In this interview, Nina Pope explores how major issues in new media practice were
being thought of at the time that she and her colleague were first working. She reflects
on the way that some of these have changed in importance and how, with hindsight,
some of them can be seen to have a significance that wasn't considered at the time. The
case study also demonstrates the way that themes and subjects have shifted within new
media as key areas of interest. Some of these themes have a consistency and can be
seen to persist no matter what technology is being used or what levels of innovation
are occurring. Others seem to be more 'of the moment' and they cease to be concerns,
as particular aspects of new media cease to have the immediate importance or cease to
raise problematic issues.

Nina Pope's practice as an artist is also a good demonstration of the way that someone
working with new media may be interested in exploring its possibilities, but it is much

more likely that they are interested in broader creative or cultural issues. When they articulate what their practice is about, technology is not the thing that determines or controls the path they take, but it is part of the approach they are taking. Nina demonstrates how the concerns that trigger Karen Guthrie and herself to embark on each individual project are consistent, and sometimes they are investigated through the means of new technology, but sometimes through quite different approaches.

The impact of working with technology

Nina, how would you describe the way that technology impacted upon your practice? Was the opportunity to work new media a significant point of interest from the beginning in your artistic partnership with Karen?

When we both started using new technology it was for practical reasons and to enhance our more regular art practice. We had trained in print making so we began scanning in images and using them digitally, and as we learnt about technology it provided a key for us into a completely new way of working from the way that we had been trained at art school. Our experience of technology has led us to our current practice and really enabled us to take a new approach to live events and interacting with people. It's not fixated on technology, but it draws on it. Technology was the bridge for us out of a more traditional art practice.

Later you started developing projects in which digital technology was a central component. What where the challenges of working with new forms of media that particularly interested you?

Figure 5.3   Nina Pope and Karen Guthrie, 'An Artist's Impression' (1999)
Detail from the gallery installation.

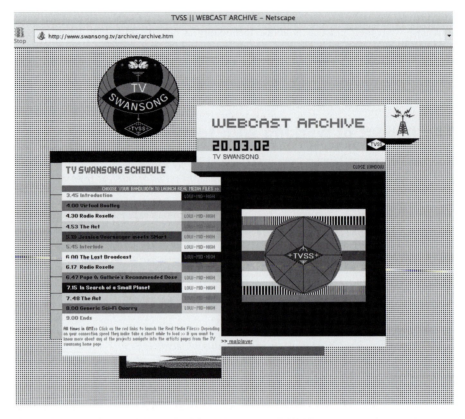

Figure 5.4   Nina Pope and Karen Guthrie, 'TV Swansong' (2002)
Detail from the 'TV Swansong' website linking to the archive of the webcast and to streaming media files. Eight artists were commissioned to produce media artworks for a day of live webcasting on 20 March 2002.

I suppose that one of the things that we found interesting was looking at technology at the point at which it was changing. When we did 'Hypertext Journal' it was at the point at which a fairly sizable number of people in the UK had access to the Internet for the first time and this was obviously something very new. Just the idea of this expanded the way that we could imagine how we might practise. Later, when we started to make work which used webcasting, such as 'Broadcast' and 'TV Swansong', that was the point when broadcasting was at a point of change. So, often, we would come to a project when there was a shift in technology and so the two interests would align. However, the technology has never been the sole focus of the work, it is much more content driven than that.

Consistent artistic concerns and influences

Your first projects were early approaches to artistic work on the web where the content tried to explore the technological possibilities. When you look back can you reflect on the key issues which, at that point, you thought were challenging for an artist to grapple with? With the benefit of hindsight do you think that those concerns have stood the test of time and remain interesting now?

With 'A Hypertext Journal' specifically the key thing that we were interested in was how you could interact with your audience live and that's certainly something that we have remained interested in. I think this idea has become more important, not just in visual arts but also broadcasting – a lot of the models we now see on TV were things that people were experimenting with in a more experimental way when the web started. Things that were once only part of artists' practice online have now become part of everyday online life. Blogs, for example, are now commonplace and in effect that is what 'A Hypertext Journal' was in 1996. It was written in HTML but basically it was a live online diary being regularly updated which people logged into. I guess it is significant that we were encouraging people to interact with us through that medium and that this is something that we certainly remain interested in. To a certain extent these things shifted the way that people thought about how artists could produce artwork.

Hypertext

At the time that you were developing 'A Hypertext Journal' the notion of exploiting the way the web used 'hyperlinks' as part of an arts project was actually quite experimental. In part, it challenged the more conventional way to approach an artwork as being a self-contained unit but it also emphasised that the artwork was dependent upon a networked experience and made reference to external material. At the time you described hypertext, as you used it in 'A Hypertext Journal', as a metaphor for the way that knowledge is reflected and expressed in publishing through footnotes. Shifts like this may seem slight but they were fundamental things that made the web unique and extraordinary as a media space for artists to play with. Do you think it is possible to contextualise projects in retrospect? Do the ideas that seemed remarkable and engaged so much attention seem less challenging in retrospect or can you assess their importance more critically?

You have to think back to that point where there was a different sense of experience of media. Now we hyperlink across all sorts of different media and expect to do this. You watch a TV programme then you go and look it up on the web to find out something that you missed in the programme, or replay a highlight, or tune into the live stream. In a way, that kind of cross-referencing between different media and content made by lots of different people is just part of the way that you expect to experience stuff now. That has remained significant and it reflects something that is social as well as about media. Something that has been consistent about some of this work, and very important to me, is that these sorts of 'linking' practices are about being embedded in communities of interest. People form links to you, and you form links to them, but this is not necessarily to do with where you are geographically. I see that with our work, each project will have a peculiar and particular group forming around it with a common interest, and the 'members' will be from all kinds of different places, generations, backgrounds. So I see hypertext as not just the linking of words but as a much bigger thing that can happen via the web.

Virtual spaces

In your project 'An Artist's Impression' you hosted an online community, a MUSH (which is often defined as a 'multi-user shared habitat' and is a text-based social medium in which multiple players are connected at the same time and share the experience of the virtual world). For this project, you 'created' a virtual island as a starting point, and invited people to join into the project by becoming members of the online community. Those participants then became the island's 'inhabitants' and through text descriptions they gave it shape and detail, defining what the different parts of the virtual space were like. Then, as part of the project, you also made a 'real' model of the island as a gallery installation, gradually adding to it as the members of the online community described it.

The project reflected a new wave of interest in virtual space. Do you think that it was able to make people think about the way that there is a strange juxtaposition between the way that we conceptualise data worlds and physical worlds?

We were never really interested in the kind of project that tries to create a simulation of reality or a VR environment. What we were interested in were the interactions that were happening in these spaces between people. The idea behind making the model was to make people engage with the human processes that take place, not to play into a sci-fi interest in virtual spaces. We hoped that by looking at this object they could imagine the dialogues and the kind of activities that might happen in this space – the way that people might play in online games. And actually it took the evolution of the project for many people to engage with the idea of there being virtual spaces that were made up of textual descriptions. So, again, it was driven by a shift in technology but it was very much focused on the content and what was happening within that. It seemed important to explore the idea of what that abstract space might be.

Recently I was looking at a student project set in an online game; it was the first time in ages I had looked at one. Technically gaming is much more advanced now, and everybody has a fairly realistic 3-D representation of themselves and the space they are moving around in and this would never have been possible in a shared online environment when we were making 'An Artist's Impression'. However, what was fascinating was that the things that were happening in the game were almost identical to what happened in our text-based space. So although we are not working in that sort of space directly at the moment I remain interested with it.

This underlines an observation that many new media artists appear to make, that the concerns that they explored in arts projects have a resonance that continues even if the technology they are using changes, or when the technology shifts from being experimental to more commercial and incorporated into everyday life.

Sometimes I think that some ideas are limited or do get easily exhausted, and it is definitely time to move on. But some things have infinite possibilities so, for example, there are always interesting ways of looking at a cross-over between a real and a virtual or data space, irrespective of whether it is expressed as a critiquing technology or as an investigation into social interactions.

New areas of experimentation with the Internet

When we look at the career of some artists we can see that they have a very clear relationship with technology in that it is one of the consistent things that they are always interested in working with, and as such it provides them with the subject matter for their work as well as the tools of production. However, as a result the work is often contextualised by the technology. Has being described as 'new media artists' been an issue for you? When you look back at some of your early work and that of your contemporaries, do you think that contextualising in this way might also have been a useful tactic in helping people to understand what new media might offer arts practice?

When we began making work there was a sense that there were lots of other people experimenting in the same area and so there was a particular critical mass and maybe the description 'new media' made sense. I don't know if that will happen again or if it is a necessary or useful term.

Also, the way that we could work with a context like the Internet was at that time technically very limited. So there were people like Heath Bunting or Jodi and us and we were all working with the Internet as we all understood it, and we were making very different pieces with it but we had a similar reference point. Now the Internet is a less meaningful term because what you can do with it, or how you approach it, is so broad. I don't think you are ever going to have that sense of cohesion again around lots of people working very closely together with a similar sort of focus but incredibly different ways of reaching that point.

Current approaches to new media

You have always had a professional career in education as well as being an artist so you are also involved in technology in a different context. What are the aspects of contemporary new media that you find are particularly significant in the context of education?

I teach in Interaction Design at the RCA so I am still very much embedded within the culture of new media. I like that because it keeps me in touch in a very easy way with what is happening in terms of innovation and currency of different concepts. I have got approximately thirty students who are all at the start of their careers and that is really stimulating.

Something that I now find less prevalent in students is the search for new breakthroughs in design or new 'killer applications' but they are much wiser about the ways that technology lets us think 'outside the corporate box'. So they are particularly interested in shareware and open source software, and the culture of that area is still a little like the culture we experienced when the web first started. It feels quite exciting in terms of the way people approach different things like peer-to-peer networks, and how these systems change the way people use technology in their everyday lives. So the creative challenges are in line with the new sorts of ways people consume and relate to media in very opportunistic ways. Take, for example, 'pod-casting' where users are likely to download very personalised daily news reports onto their I-pods and listen to them on the move. Just this activity alone presents all sorts of interesting design challenges not just to do with technology but also content production and people's behaviour patterns – Interaction Design now has to be about this complete system.

Can you describe some of the projects that you are working on at the moment and the themes that you are interested in?

At the moment we are doing a project, 'Almanac', which involves dynamic databases and digital time-lapse systems, which has given us access to a whole new system of digital projectors which are being rolled out to cinemas in the UK, and that has been fascinating. For this project, five static digital time-lapse cameras have been placed in diverse locations in East Anglia – all of which have been used for film and TV locations. These cameras will take images at regular intervals each day, throughout the year, and by the end of twelve months, the cameras will have recorded nearly one million frames, all to be fed into a bespoke database. Once installed, this database will configure and play a unique trailer for a randomly selected camera, specific to the day on which people are watching it at the cinema. Once again this is a project where something we are interested in in terms of content is coinciding with a shift in available technology, and we are making a project at that point to test out what this combination might look like.

Our other project at the moment is what you might commonly understand as a documentary. For several years we've been researching the UK historical re-enactment scene, where large numbers of people take on historical roles and personalities, dressing in historical costume. We've participated both as audience members and occasionally taking part in Tudor re-enactments ourselves. To date we've made a range of works which record our experiences, including pinhole photographs, video diaries and footage from tiny hidden cameras in our costumes. These are posted to a blog which documents this as an ongoing project.

Both these projects seem to illustrate something that appears consistently throughout your work, which is that new media is being used as a tool to enable or record a very distinct type of performance, sometimes in which you play an active role and sometimes in which you are absent. There is also a synergy between the way the web was used as the site of 'A Hypertext Journal' and the way the blog is used for the latter re-enactment project.

It is also remarkable how in the mid-1990s an online diary was classified as an experimental art work, and very 'off the wall'. Now, this is exactly what people think of as a standard way of posting information about one's daily activities, and the most obvious way of placing private observations and documents into a public sphere.

Nina Pope and Karen Guthrie's art projects can be seen at www.somewhere.org.uk

6 Talking new media

··

t is important to consider the actual spoken and written language in which the discussion of all of the stages in making a new media artefact, object or product and its reception and effect takes place. New media arts practices and their corresponding educational study are talked and written about in a particular way, which we could call a parlance or linguistic sub-set. We could also call it jargon or rhetoric, although that has the pejorative overtone of a use of language that is unnecessarily complex or exclusive. There is still a strong belief that if something is worth saying then it can be said simply. There is great merit in this tradition of plain speaking, but the communication of new thoughts and meanings is, itself, a hard task. In countering the emphasis in everyday life towards excessive simplicity, it should also be recognised that language is, itself, a means of discovering meaning, and that our ideas and experience change, i.e. we have new experiences that we struggle, through language, to communicate. It is in this later respect that we should see new media language as the attempt to grasp the significance of new media and to assess the possibilities of computer-mediated communications.

The typical ways in which new media products and systems are discussed among the community of producers and critical reviewers will include specialist technical terms and abstract concepts. This is what we will call the conversational language of new media and we discuss it in the following two sections. First, we deal with key concepts in new media and then discuss the ways in which they are entailed in discourses about technology.

For our purposes here we can define the two most prominent forms of new media language as the technical and the conceptual, both of which share buzz words, abbreviations and acronyms which, to the uninitiated, make little sense. Cookies, blogs and bluetooths, have the ring of an animated cartoon rather than the technical description of email protocols or wireless computer systems, while technical acronyms such as RAM and ROM, JAVA, HTML, HCI and GUI, to mention but a few, remain impenetrable. Conceptual terms, such as convergence, connectivity and conviviality, and immersive, immediacy and immanence, come from a language used to describe the human social exchange rather than a relationship to a machine. This combination of technical and conceptual terms creates a differentiated but shared cultural language of knowledge and interest as well as assumed aims and purposes. Take, for instance, the following piece, which is typical of new media journalism:

It's not that it's hard to use: the Symbian 7 user interface is not as friendly or straight-forward as the new Handspring/Palm Treo 600, but is very much better than the Widows CE-powered Orange SPV . . . The P900 offers a daunting number of features including Bluetooth, GPRS, SMS, MMS multimedia messaging.

(Jack Schofield *Guardian Online* 30.10.03)

Such technical writing and its language is, of course, typical and widespread in the mar-keting of high-tech consumer products. We are all familiar with the hobbyist, some might say 'nerdy', fascination with technical specifications, manuals and gizmos. There is nothing culturally new in this and it can, and should, be viewed as an extension of an existing popular fascination with machines. When thinking about the use of technologies in the production of new media we should note that the technical language of function-ality is also a language of purpose. When a technical review talks about a mobile being more or less friendly a strong value judgement is being made about what we want to do with wireless technology. Here, 'friendly' becomes synonymous with 'simple to use'. However, the more simple a powerful computer processor/and wireless receiver and trans-mitter (a mobile phone) becomes, the less we understand of its potential; the technology and its programming language become invisible in order that we can use it simply. There is, potentially, a large 'cost' in this trade-off between technology and simple use, which the other difficult, theoretical part of the language struggles to make visible.

Describing what a computer can do, the technical specifications of RAM and ROM, for instance, is not only descriptive of what a computer hard drive does, it also contains implicit cultural ideas about what we want a computer to be and how we want to relate to it. Why do we want/need faster and faster processors and greater and greater memory? The many answers to this question have to be sought in looking at the located purposes for which computers are used. The instances are many, from highly secretive military research contracts for intelligence gathering and weapons systems, through civil admin-istrative record keeping and surveillance, to the use of computers in health and education, and in many forms of media communications.

Technical language

The language of computer functionality is most obviously part of a technical language that has most agency in computing science and engineering and is evident in technical specifications and technical coding and hardware manuals. Software manuals are inter-esting in that they straddle the world of coded functionality and the end-user.

Software manuals

Software manuals are typically clearly written and contain copious diagrams alongside the text and are designed to be read in conjunction with using software programmes. Such manuals use the time-honoured training technique of, here is how you do it, now you try. The manuals are hierarchical and linear in structure, starting with simple instruc-tions and working up to more complex operations. Unproblematic and boring we might say. Boring because until you have memorised the commands and functions sufficiently, you have to keep referring to the manual for the next step, and unproblematic because they simply tell the user the functions of the programme so that they can use it in whatever way they like.

Software manuals are written as a language of instruction, rather like a knitting pattern, recipe, or the assembly instructions for model kits. This, for example, is taken from Macromedia's Flash Manual: 'Click the paint bucket's hot spot (the tip of the drip of paint) somewhere inside the outline shape or within the existing fill. The shape fills with the gradient currently selected in the Fill Focus color chip.'

Such an instruction would make perfect sense to those familiar with the PC or Mac operating environment and authoring interface. We know what 'click' means, without having to explain the function of the mouse and cursor; we know that the paint bucket is a graphic icon that operates as a functional command, and so on. As we acquire familiarity with the practice of using computers and their software, so we become familiar with uses of the language in which is it described. Equally, as competence in the use of software develops, including all the short-cuts and personalised uses of tools and commands, it becomes unnecessary to verbalise how we achieved a particular operation, it becomes what we have previously called know-how.

The technical language of software, like the technical language of hardware, also contains implicit linguistic pointers to assumed purposes as well as functions. Take, for instance, the following passage from the Macromedia Flash Manual:

> Flash 4. Sports an updated interface that brings Flash closer in look and feel to other Macromedia products. Some of the most exciting additions to Flash 4 are beyond the scope of this book but may spur you to learn the basics so that you can later soar with the full flexibility of Flash.

Paraphrasing somewhat we can see that an aspiration to be as flexible as possible is being marked out so that the user might achieve something like the experience of soaring, i.e. the imagined freedom of the human body in flight, the experience of speed, apparent weightlessness and uninterrupted vision. This is a conventional cultural metaphor for a certain kind of immediate bodily freedom and, in the case of Flash 4, it is being promised through the redesign of the 'look and feel of the interface'. In reality, of course, the user is physically confined by the keyboard and screen in the human–computer interface. This is just one small example of how wider purposes and aspirations become encoded in the technical language of computer hardware and software.

Conceptual language

The implicit and unproblematic references to the aims, aspirations and purposes of computer use in the technical vocabulary, i.e. the metaphorical allusions such as soaring or navigating, become the starting point for a conceptual language of new media developed within the context of education and academia (precisely the context of the production and consumption of this book). It is important to stress that the academic vocabulary of new media is not unitary or indeed homogeneous. We should say that there are a number of different conceptual vocabularies, reflecting different academic subjects, each containing its own historical direction and concerns, in short, its own 'take' on new media. While the conceptual lexicon reflects different disciplines, there are, nevertheless, a number of key conceptual terms that are now established as essential aspects of the practices and concerns of new media. Terms such as digital, digitality, digitextuality and cyberspace, and cyberbodies, now define essential characteristics and dimensions of the new computer environment. Interface, interactivity, hypermediacy, navigation and networks are key terms for discussing human–computer/machine exchange. Virtual worlds, identities and realities, characterised alternatively as rich, immersive or augmented, are key to the discussion of the qualitative and subjective experience of computer-based technologies that extend human sense perceptions. Smart architecture and conscious networks and distributed data systems are most often the conceptual signposts for the aspirations of artificial (machine) intelligence. These key terms, among others, provide the conceptual landscape in which current new media practices and future aspirations are grasped. On inspection, the conceptual vocabulary combines the cultural discussion of human purpose and intention with the technological discussion of applications. This distinction has been elaborated as the essential difference between the project of the engineers and that of the humanist scholars. The engineers have embraced a technological project in which instruments and machines (computers) organise not only our outer-world but also consciousness itself, while the humanist scholars recognise this world of technology as problematic and seek to focus on the manifest lack of clarity about our relationship to what we have brought into existence (Murray 1997: 4). While it is true that this distinction points us to two distinct discourses, in our terms, languages of new media, which primarily inform the technical on the one hand and the conceptual on the other, it is by no means a neat divide. As Murray points out, the engineers are not in a culturally and philosophically 'value free' technological world of instruments, and the humanist scholars are not without dreams of what machines can do. We would also add that these are two somewhat abstract groupings that do not translate neatly in the more messy social and cultural fabric of everyday and institutional life. Gaining an overview of new media and its development will involve a much more complex grasp of the material organisation and institutional systems (the apparatuses) in which all of the different, sectional interests in new media are maintained.

In setting out the terrain of technical and conceptual terms that define current electronic machines and how we are using them, we prefer to think in terms of discourses/historical narratives (tropes) through which technology, and its relationship to culture and society and communication and representation, is understood. While we discuss technological discourses in Part II, it is worth noting here that many of the 'buzz' words and phrases belong to these more extended accounts and narratives. New media studies, as much as old media studies, accepts that the communication and representation of human knowledge and experience necessarily involves language and technological systems: 500 years of print culture for instance; or 150 years of photography and 100 years of film. One of the crucial starting points for understanding the languages of new media is, therefore, to define how new media, as distinct from old media, requires us to rethink the intercession of media technologies in human experience.

This task of rethinking how media practices work in society and for individuals, how new media is changing existing patterns of communication and evolving new ones, is the larger task of the whole discipline of media studies. The question of the languages of new media becomes central to this task since there is an enormous continuity between, as well as transformation of, media practices. The production of newspapers and television has been technically transformed by the introduction of technologies which have, over two decades, transformed industrial working practices. Yet, at the same time, we continue to think of the newspaper and broadcast television as continuous with what has gone before, and in many ways discussed in the same ways using the same terms.

It must now be obvious from what we have said so far that in looking at the languages of new media it is necessary to have more than simple 'dictionary' definitions of the vocabulary of new media. Instead, we need a map that shows the various levels of connections and disconnections within and across the technical and conceptual terminologies.

CASE STUDY

Curating new media projects: Benjamin Weil

....

enjamin Weil is one of the leading international curators of new media art. He
was one of the founders of the network 'The Thing' in the early 1990s and in
New York set up the Internet arts organisation, äda 'web, which was one of the
first curated and organised web art projects in the world operating as a stand-alone
organisation and not associated with other institutions. It produced some of the most
important Internet art pieces in the 1990s, mostly through a series of commissioned
works with artists ranging from famous names with established careers in the art world
to unknown individuals experimenting with digital media. Subsequently, Benjamin
worked at the Institute of Contemporary Art (ICA) in London as the Director of the
New Media Centre and at the San Francisco Museum of Modern Art (SFMoMA) as the
Curator of New Media; in both positions he was responsible for bringing new media
arts projects into the confines of much more conventional arts institutions.

In this interview, he looks at the work that he did and places it in the context of other
arts initiatives and movements going on at the time. He explains how different organisations are able to work with different degrees of flexibility with new media and deal
with the problems and concerns that new areas of work create. This includes issues such
as setting up collaborations between artists and technologists, and archiving new media
work so that it could be maintained for future display in a museum. As a curator,
Benjamin has been highly instrumental in finding ways to work with digital technology
and to show how it plays an important part in our understanding of all media arts, not
just computer-based arts.

Background to new media work
....

*Benjamin, your career covers an extensive period of change. You started working in
what became called 'new media' at the point when digital technologies first came into
the reach of artists. Previously only people who had access to highly specialised
computer resources were able to make experimental work, but by the late 1980s and
early 1990s, artists were also able to access computers within the resources of the workplace or the studio. How did you first get involved in this as a distinct area of practice?
How did it relate to other creative practices that you were involved in at the time?*

In 1991 in New York the whole frenzy that predicated the mid-1980s' art world turned into complete depression – in other words everything collapsed. The economy was not doing well but also the art world, which had become a kind of refuge investment for people, stopped being so, and all of a sudden there was an amazing opportunity for a whole new generation of people to engage with art making in a way that was much more loose-ended. Exhibitions were being curated in abandoned offices – there was a little bit of that in London at some point too. And one thing that became very interesting at that time is that computers started emerging on the arts scene. They were still very complicated machines; for the most they were machines using Microsoft OS, but modems started appearing.

Technology was never really something that appealed to me as such, but technology as a means of communication was really what I found appealing. It served a purpose to help get away from the utterly commercial art scene. But context-specific work was interesting as well to me – the idea of making something that was related to where it was rather than being a finished product with portable value. Added to that was the layer of public space which was something that I was getting more and more interested in. Artists were starting to comprehend that the rules of communication are predicated by advertising. They were asking 'how do you radicalise a discourse that starts existing in a public space?'. It was also the time that artists' groups like Grand Fury were doing projects such as 'Kissing doesn't Kill' by mixing the realms of advertising and the realms of activism. Those things were all really important to me.

So when I discovered the web I realised, 'this is amazing!' It gave us the space to combine context-specific work and also address the structure of communication. At that point there was almost nobody else working in this area because the web was really much more of an academic concern at the beginning and barely making its way to become commercial.

From that I discovered all kinds of things that were happening. Early adopters of digital had previously been compelled to work in a very limited environment and had little to no involvement with the art world. But all of a sudden computing became so readily available that everyone started playing with it and because it was readily available, and becoming ubiquitous, it started to take a whole new meaning in people's lives. I think it's completely normal that artists were integrating more and more technology into their work because of all the technology around them. Gradually the boundary, the technology barrier, was getting erased. So to be able to include this work in a larger context of a critical discourse about what art can be became more relevant.

Developing Internet art projects

äda 'web was first set up in 1994 and ran until 1998 and was one of the first websites that was solely concerned with creating and presenting artworks online. It offered a sophisticated form of cultural communication. Over four years you worked with and commissioned a large number of artists' projects and you also collaborated with a range of arts institutions like the Museum of Modern Art New York. What were the kinds of things you were looking for in artists who you worked with? What were the kinds of things you were trying to do as a producer?

You have to remember that many people were interested in working in public space, and I was also interested in the idea of the experience of art not being delineated by the context in which it is being shown. I was also very interested in the idea of all kinds of forms that had been experimented with in the 1960s at the height of these conceptual fluxes – trying to get art out of its boundaries and creating networks. So the issue was how do you establish an interesting critical discourse and how do you at the same time help shape the language or structure, the vocabulary, the grammar, the communication of this system?

When I approached artists nobody knew what the web was to start with, but also nobody was an expert in web design. We didn't even know that to publish an image you had to downsize it so it wasn't too heavy to download, and make it in three colours and save it in a certain format. What I was really interested in was not so much people who were going to explore on the level of form as much as people really going to grasp a conceptual grounding of what could be done and then carry out an experiment with the collaboration of programmers and, eventually, web designers. That's why I chose to work primarily with artists who weren't coming from a technological background at all, artists like Jenny Holzer, Lawrence Weiner and Julia Scher, because I thought that these people had clearly spent time thinking about those issues.

Of course, the web was primarily text based at that time and it was primarily a lowband communication. The strategy was very different and, of course, the number of users was not even remotely close to what it is now, but I think it was interesting in a different way.

At that point did artists who were working online start to contact you?

Artists were interested in having their work contextualised within the scheme of what we were trying to develop because they had an understanding of what we were doing and they believed the conceptual grounds we were trying to establish made sense to them. Artists like Jodi did a project for äda 'web. That's how we expanded our horizons from being a digital foundry to being a digital foundry with a website that enabled people to actually post their work.

Understanding the context of technology

Many artists and curators at the time had talked about the need to come to grips with the formal qualities of new media so that it was being treated as something distinct with its own qualities and characteristics and didn't just reflect ways of working with other media. But also they were often interested in playing with the formal qualities as well, pushing the boundaries and experimenting with the way that things worked and the way that they appeared. Were you also concerned with these issues and trying to find ways to define a particular aesthetic, language or way of working that seemed the most appropriate way to approach the creative use of technology?

In retrospect, I was more interested in the idea of putting together two kinds of approaches to technology – in other words the very artistic approach and the very conceptual approach. This was the opposite approach to engineering. The emphasis was not on understanding the machine or the mechanism as much as understanding the context that it created. I chose to work with artists who had not even begun to understand what the web was but who had an incredibly sharp intuitive understanding of what a network was. For me the challenge was to bring in somebody who had good engineering skills and I would initiate a dialogue between them and a particular artist like Jenny Holzer

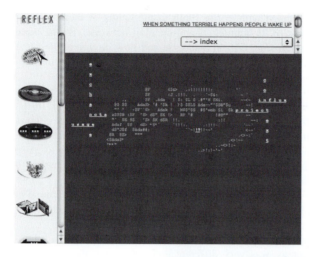

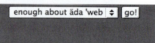

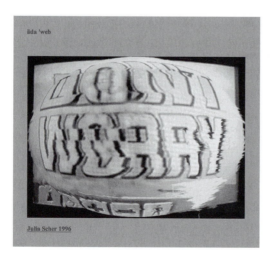

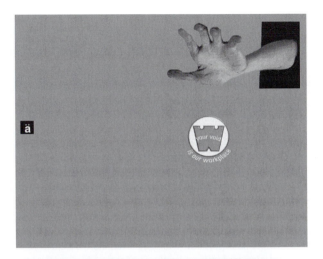

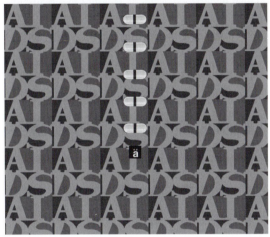

Figure 7.1   äda 'web (1997)

Selections of rotating front page designs from the äda 'web website including links to artists' projects including works by Jenny Hozer, Julia Scher and General Idea.

Established in 1995, äda 'web was one of the first cultural online projects to support and present experimental artists' projects on the World Wide Web. äda 'web aimed to offer artists the possibility of addressing the new medium without necessarily having any specific notion of computing and, through ongoing dialogue with artists and technologists, enabled a translation of concepts into the realm of the network.

or Lawrence Weiner, and from this would come a result. It was like being an artistic director in a situation where there is somebody who knows how to make things happen and somebody whose ideas are being carried out. This relationship worked pretty well with most of the artists and web producers I was working with. In that sense I was orchestrating things.

That approach is very different from one in which the artist is totally in charge of the technology or collaborating on the way the technology is being used, which is probably a more typical approach now. But managing a creative dialogue between different practitioners is an important part of the creative process.

It makes me think of the piece that we collaborated on with A. A. Bronson with ArtAIDS which was to make a screensaver for World AIDS Day in 1997. A. A. Bronson was from the artists' group General Idea and he clearly had no idea of how the Internet operated but he understood appropriation, understood multiples, understood things that have got a playful social awareness, understood things that are inherently in themselves disposable, understood that notion of art as a grenade which just has its own little fuse and operates in a particular way, and also understood aesthetic pleasure in a really low resolution, in a low-value way. You couldn't get anyone more appropriate who could work like that.

Developing projects within the context of arts institutions

After setting up äda 'web and curating its projects for several years you moved onto other projects, often working in high-profile international arts institutions. Did you face the same concerns working with artists in later years or do you think the main issues have been modified by time and by the way that technology has become available to the community of practitioners?

At the ICA (Institute of Contemporary Art) in London, I was the Director of New Media from 1998 to 1999. This was a very interesting definition because, on the one hand, it was a department that was coming from film and video but never really a production department, and yet it generated an extraordinary archive of recorded lectures. My predecessor evolved it into a new media department. When I was hired I started thinking I should take it from there. It had machines provided by Sun Microsystems but which were obviously machines that no artists, or few artists, could operate on their own, and I quickly realised that if I wanted it to be a production environment I would have to make this environment respond to the specific needs of artists. I began to realise that if we had engineering support those incredibly complicated and extraordinarily expensive machines would become an asset incredibly valued by the artistic community, or at least some of the artistic community.

So the context informed what I was trying to do. The same way I was wondering how I could involve the dot.com culture into all this because obviously there was the need to find money to finance our activities. The expectation was that industry people who were very intelligent and creative would love a place where they could come together and take part in intellectual debates, mingle with artists and exchange ideas. To an extent it worked, but not entirely, and there are all sorts of reasons why it was difficult, not least because of the economy, but it proved that you can bring together different worlds.

Models to enable collaboration

Obviously many people have said that a high level of hardware does not necessarily provide a fertile ground for creativity, and this applies not just in digital media but to technology and arts across the fields. However, at the same time, technological resources can both simulate and facilitate artists and projects at a high level that they could not otherwise reach. Many people found themselves in situations where it is expected that technology can lead to creative production. But are these problems resolvable? Did you find that you were able to develop a model for working with a high level of technology but one in which you could include the right human resources and technical support – and that out of this you were able to fuel creative projects in the way you needed to?

I have to say that whereas my model of äda 'web was very much the model of the open studio, the digital foundry, the place where people come to collaborate to create new things, my approach at the ICA was very much informed by the EAT programme (Experiments in Art and Technology, started by Billy Cluver and Robert Rauschenberg). My idea was to build on the relationship between Sun Microsystems and the ICA. I aimed to try to convince Sun that it was in their best interest to provide artists not only with machines but also with technical support and expertise that, in turn, could inform their own research and development. In other words, that this was something that should be regarded as an integral part of better engineering. That way we could have an interesting cultural product being produced and, at the same time, something that would become a real asset for Sun.

Bringing experimental work into the institution

In 2000 you became Curator of New Media at the San Francisco Museum of Modern Art. Was that a return to a more conventional form of curating?

When I went on to SFMoMA, having experimented outside of all this, my goal was to bring it back within the institution and to start thinking how a museum, which is really a collecting institution, can start addressing the issue of unstable media. I was contemplating what would be the best tools to try to address a cultural form that is yet to be determined, yet to have a critical frame applied to it, but at the same time could completely benefit from the continuum of history and be completely integrated within the activities of the museum. But also, how the museum needs to modify its understanding of what it was dealing with.

Documenting creative processes

When you were commissioning an artist as museum curator you had the intention that the work would be seen in the museum and it would be part of the museum's collection. What were the differences between working as a curator in a more informal context and working in the museum? Does working from within a museum mean that there were things you would expect of the artist that you wouldn't have expected in your previous curatorial contexts?

If I reflect upon the commissioning process, first and foremost my relationship with the artist is that I am engaging in a direct dialogue with them, asking them to produce something new. I am also asking them to be incredibly self-conscious about the way they do it. I don't think I have hindered at all the capacity of the artist to do their own work. But I have very carefully documented the stages that have helped construct the story that goes around the artwork. By doing so I am trying to script a scenario that enables us to understand where this work is coming from, how it locates itself within the larger scheme of the artist's work. It shows how the artist envisioned this work in relation to the rest of their production, how they started elaborating and determining the function of each of the elements of these projects. This also enables the museum to know when and what to replace and how to replace it.

Different models of commissioning

When you are working with artists have you found that there are some preferred ways of working with technology? Do you try to create a situation that is as flexible as possible when you commission an artist so that they can each work in their own way or do you prefer to plan more tightly with them what their approach will be?

Not many artists are really interested in the idea of being overly self-conscious so though we may work out a plan they may process it in their own time. So each of them comes up with different ways. For instance, when I commissioned Pipi Lotti to make a video installation at SFMoMA, 'Stir Heart Rinse Heart', she came to San Francisco with two crates of objects and numerous hard drives full of digital images and she literally crafted her piece in the gallery. For two weeks she worked non-stop in the gallery crafting her piece, checking the speed of one footage against the other, and then, when things started falling in place, creating the sound track that went with it.

On the other hand, when I commissioned the artist Christian Marclay he explained to me what he wanted to do, but that he didn't have the means to make it happen: the means being the fact that he didn't have a computer powerful enough to be able to edit of images on the fly. But he also didn't have access to the necessary infrastructure. When we established what his needs were in relation to engineering support he also realised that he needed technical support to understand the potential of the software he was using. He had an idea of what he wanted since he had done a lot of sound editing but he had never done image editing himself. So we set him up with a very good Macintosh with Final Cut Pro and then eventually he also used a version of Max. We documented all the equipment and all the software he used to produce the Quartet. Then when the piece was installed I asked him how we should go about understanding what it was we were looking at. Not just in terms of the meaning of the piece but also in terms of the whole technical background that informed the way the piece existed and what it looked like.

Anticipating future directions of work

When you have documented a work and it becomes part of the museum's collection do you expect that to be the end of the creative process or do you have to be flexible about the way that works can be presented in future?

Interestingly enough, with Christian Marclay's work, this issue started with something very simple – which was projectors. When the piece was installed at SFMoMA we used LCD projectors which had a certain specification and a fairly low contrast ratio. Later, the piece was installed in New York and they couldn't find projectors so eventually borrowed new projectors. All of a sudden the piece looked completely different. And then Christian said he preferred the quality of the installation in San Francisco. But the question was how we would go about inputting this information in order for people in the future to present the work. In addition, we knew that they might be able to pull out the four DVDs and import them all together as one file onto an MPEG player. Another consideration in future would be if it is important that the piece is projected or not, so whether the cinema idea is an integral part of the piece or whether it can appear on whatever surface or substance is going to be invented in the future. You can't predict what the future is going to be.

Looking back over the work that you have produced and commissioned across the years do you think that there are consistent concerns that you have as a curator that stand the test of time, regardless of the fashions or concerns of new media?

The important question is what are the conceptual roots of the project, what is important, how does it work, what are the mechanisms, what is the intellectual grounding, how does it relate to other aspects of culture that it inhabits? Basically this is very much what the art historian does with old work except it's being done on the fly as the art is produced so that you have a first understanding of what the work is.

For me, what's interesting is that I've realised that the museum has come to under-stand that, to a certain extent, it's no longer about the artwork and whatever surrounds the artwork. It's about the artwork becoming a constellation of elements that together form the experience of art. That for me is the most important element and distinction that has occurred by working closely with the artist and establishing this dialogue between the collecting institution and the artist so as to create this open slate.

Projects discussed in this case study are documented at www.adaweb.org and www.sfmoma.org

8 New media histories

....

Starting points

....

A history of new media will have to include a number of different strands of the historical development of art and media, their technologies, institutions and cultural forms. Initially such a history will involve something of the development of computing, electronics, robotics, optics, telecommunications, broadcasting, theatre, art, photography, film, literature, music and popular cultural pastimes. Such a list is daunting since it threatens to involve a history of every cultural means of expression and communication. The overriding reason why new media needs such a multi-layered history is because of the hybrid nature of both the technologies and cultural practices gathered under the umbrella title. There is not as yet a single technological apparatus that lines up with a developed cultural form; rather, the practices of new media currently use a combination of different media in both digital and analogue forms across a range of cultural forms. Equally there is no single, or unified, idea of what new media is, what knowledge and experience it deals with or the contexts in which it is applied. At present any history of new media will have to account for all of the diverse developments that are constituted as new media. A new media history is better understood as a provisional and relational process because, while a unified and linear history can provide compelling stories of technological advancement, it also reduces and narrows our conceptual understanding of the current possibilities and purposes of new mediums. Linear histories typically construct a chronological sequence of selectively significant events in order to argue that the present outcomes and configurations of technology and their uses are the logical and essential outcome of that history. An important cautionary point to remember is that any history, including this outline, is authored by individuals and groups working out of subjects, institutions, theories and perspectives, which will organise what is thought to be valuable to include, or stress. One should expect any new media history to be able to claim an authority that is based in, and reflective of, acknowledged and specific scholarship or practices. We have noted in the introduction how accounts of new media are cast and shaped within other disciplines and practices, which is only to be expected and should not be dismissed, since there is no absolute position of objectivity in operation here. Any new media history will, by definition, be an initial one, given the recent emergence of new media practice, but it will also have roots in other disciplines and developments. An understanding of calculating machines as the precursor of current

PCs, on the one hand, and the history of typographical layout, on the other, would be equally important to an understanding of websites, for example. New media history is, then, better thought of in the plural as historical strands.

There are three broad strands of a potential new media history, which are touched upon here: histories of material technologies; histories of telecommunication systems; and histories of cultural and media practices. Put more generally, a new media history requires an overview of the development of technological apparatuses, the ways in which they have been socially organised for communication purposes, and the cultural forms of communication they have been used for. In addition to historical accounts of machines, systems and products we also need to consider the social and cultural contexts in which such developments take place and the intellectual models within which histories are constructed. But how is such a history to be constructed? We can formulate the dimensions of new media histories as needing to take account of:

1 how reproductive and communication technologies have developed;

2 how the meanings of specific art and media artefacts relate to the technical possibilities of the medium and the cultural context in which they take place;

3 how media production embodies/reflects the larger economic organisation;

4 how the funding of scientific and technological research shapes the agendas and interests of its outcomes;

5 how prevailing theories of human perception and knowledge provide frameworks for thinking about the purposes and effects of media.

Problems of historical methodology

Having cautioned against attempts to provide reduced, linear versions of a history of new media, and stressing instead the need for more complex accounts, we are still faced with the need for historical selectivity. There are two main reasons for this. We cannot ignore the fact that there is something *new* about new media, which is not accountable for in terms of existing continuous histories of media. It is important, therefore, for us to ask how the newness of the current new media came about and to think about the distinct and different elements that have combined to produce such a powerful form of communication and reproduction. Second, understanding the newness of new media will not be achieved by treating the established history of media as an historical list of technological inventions. New media cannot be accounted for simply as the latest in a line of inventions, because, from the standpoint of how we use such inventions, new media is continuous with previous technologies as well as containing and reviving older media interests.

It is worth noting that the specific difficulty of the historical method we are discussing here has been encountered in existing accounts of new media. Let us go back to the idea, as Lister puts it, that there can be 'no single, linear history, which will account for all that that new media embraces' (2003: 45). Lister outlines three broad paradigms within which histories of new media have been constructed: the teleological, the genealogical and Modernist Aesthetics. These are useful categories with which to think about the problems of understanding the development of new media technologies and practices.

The logic of (technological) progress

Linear histories of new media, such as those of Howard Rheingold and Peter Weibel, cited in Lister (2003: 47), broadly fall into the category of historical accounts that create a narrative of (technological) progress. In such histories, progress is driven either by some grand design of history itself or, in a sub-set of the same argument, by human genius and invention. An account of new media in these terms would, therefore, argue that our current media technologies and practices are the culmination of the historical progress, sometimes involving false starts and dead-ends, of all previous media, which contained the 'seeds' of, or prefigured, the present. In this way of seeing history, the past is a preparation for the present and, by implication, the further unfolding of events into the future and towards some final goal. Such historical constructs are labelled by Lister as teleological. Teleology is a theoretical term in philosophy, which attempts to explain a series of events in terms of ends, goals or purposes. Aristotle argued that all nature reflects the purposes of an immanent final cause.

An example of a teleological history of media would be one in which each histori-cally ascending medium, television following radio for instance, emerged deliberately and inevitably in a process of continuous discovery and progress. A wider version of the same argument is one in which history is highly telescoped to suggest that the devel-opment of implements for hunting and cultivation contained the drive for space travel because tools, whether a stone axe or a rocket, are extensions of the human body in time and space. This is a powerful and persuasive view of human progress in which we come to see all of the subsequent historical refinements in tool-making as a preparation for our current ability to traverse outer space (this was alluded to in the opening sequence of Stanley Kubrick's film *2001*). Another example of the same argument applied retro-spectively from the vantage point of new media would be one which said that the 35,000-year-old cave paintings of flora and fauna in Southern Europe and Australia were made as immersive and virtual environments. In this example, the enclosure of the cave and the light from the fire illuminating the painted representations on the walls created a simulation of the external world. Our ancestors, looking at the flickering images of hunter and hunted, are likened to the game player in front of the computer screen. The painted image on the cave wall and the computer screen are assumed by us to be connected by the continuous human drive to augment reality. At a larger level the same argument can be advanced to say that the European history of art and representation, which links fresco painting, oil painting, lithography, engraving, photography, tele-graphy, film and television, are the inevitable intermediate steps between the cave and a totally immersive virtual reality.

Such grand historical narratives are, as Lister points out again, arguments rather than necessary or absolute histories. As such, they are of interest and attract attention precisely because of their selective view (what they leave out of account) and for their narrative content (the story they tell). In the case of digital technology, it is the larger drives towards convergence, miniaturisation and automation of information that linear pro-gressive histories have pointed up. These tendencies of technological development are, in the thinking of Baudrillard (1985) for instance, stages towards the visibility and, at the same time, the dematerialisation, of everything; in his terms, the 'satellitisation of the real'.

Modernism, art and the avant-garde

An emerging account of new media can be found in art historical and exhibition contexts. The basic premise for considering new media within a history of art is that over the twentieth century artists have used technological media (photography, video, electronics and computers) to make works of art, which have been exhibited and collected, bought and sold by museums and private collectors. As such, this collection of works can be thought of as a category of art, initially as electronic or digital art and, more recently, as new media art. As a category it can be included in the history and criticism of art. At the same time we can include 'new media art' as another strand of the wider category of a history of new media and consider how it is currently being framed. Rush (1999) advances an orthodox art historical view of new media in proposing that artists working with technologies represent a final avant-garde of the twentieth century. Following this argument through in outline is instructive because, while it shares the same argument as teleological histories of technologies, it also suggests that the artist is someone who can explore and subvert the received wisdom and potential of technological advances.

The orthodox European history of art encourages us to see the development of visual representation from the Stone Age to the Industrial Age as a history of continuous technical improvements in the artist's ability to render likenesses more accurately through the technical mastery of the medium. Such a history is usually said to culminate in the development of photography, which could render likenesses perfectly through a mechanical means. Benjamin (1939) pointed out that mechanical reproduction (the photograph) freed the hand of the most important artistic functions of pictorial reproduction. We will come back to consider Benjamin's fuller analysis of the impact of mechanical reproduction further on, since it has been highly influential in thinking about new media. In the conventional history of art the advent of photography is seen as loosening the artist's dependency on the need for hand-produced likenesses and hence hastening the end of the neo-classical academy, and ushering in modernism. During the period from the 1840s until the turn of the century, when Niepce, Fox Talbot and Daguerre were perfecting the photographic medium, painting and sculpture continued to be dominated by the Royal Academy of Arts. The annual Academy exhibitions exercised a form of control over what was considered to be the correct subjects for art and how they should be executed. Rush starts his account of new media in twentieth-century art by pointing out that twentieth-century art has had a persistent tendency to question painting as the privileged medium of representation. He points to the many renowned artists and art movements of the twentieth century whose work included everyday objects and used materials other than paint and canvas. The use of 'new' media with which to make art is characterised as being driven by the experimental nature of modernist art. It is not hard to see how this argument is developed to account for contemporary new media art. Picasso's and Braque's incorporation of everyday materials in their paintings is essentially the same 'experimental' approach to the medium as that of Jane Prophet, Susan Collins or David Rokeby whose work we discuss in this volume.

While a new media art history, constructed along the axis of the advancement of experimental media, is a meaningful narrative, it is also a reduction of the fuller meanings, contexts and relations of art, because, once again, it ties the motor of artistic development to technological progress. The history of the avant-garde as a self-absorbed preoccupation with the medium of art is simply another version of technological determinism. One of the significant meeting points for ideas about modernist art and contemporary technology lies in Marshall McLuhan's formulation that 'the medium is the message'.

In putting together an account of the development of digital art, Paul (2003) makes the distinction between art that uses digital technologies as a tool for the creation of traditional art objects, and art that employs technologies as its very own medium. While Paul is mindful that the distinction between technology as a tool and technology as a medium is a preliminary categorisation, it does become the organising principle of her material and reproduces the distinction between tradition and the new. Both Rush and Paul conclude that new technologies will become more pervasive in art and everyday life. Scientific research in the areas of artificial life and intelligent interfaces, in digital and biological engineering and nanotechnologies, is predicted to lead, inexorably, to some kind of final frontier of the human–machine interface in which brain-to-machine and brain-to-brain interactions are envisaged as an enfolding of the human body and the machine. In the visual arts, ideas such as these have been actively developed by individuals and groups of artists whose interests have focused upon cybernetic and electronic arts.

Future worlds

Many of the accounts of the relationship of art and technology we have come across are a specific version and reworking of the wider formulation of the relationship of society and technology. Hence, the general and common argument is that art is being propelled by technology into a future role, function and form that is unlike anything that has gone before. The argument runs on that, confronted by this overwhelming fact of the power of technology, existing notions and practices of art are no longer relevant and that a profound and radical break with the past is being provoked by technology. In detail, the reality and significance of a radically new technologically based art is sustained by the claim that in the present a small number of farsighted artists and scientists are prefiguring a future where more advanced possibilities will be present. In the conventional twentieth-century art historical account it has always been a small and selective avant-garde who have paved the way for new media art. Gere (2004) attempts a history of new technologies in art in the British and American post-war context. This consists of a discussion of artistic ideas and practices that we can take to prefigure the current new media art agenda. This is articulated as a set of practices marked out by their experimental interest in combining different media, using available media technologies, and in performances or events that include interactions with audiences. The underlying interests of such practice are identified by Gere (2004) as a concern for exploring the boundary between art and everything else, music and noise in the work of John Cage, and the role of the audience in defining a work of art. Gere concludes that a post-war avant-garde, through their experiments with mixed or multi-media, set an agenda for, or at least represent an art historical backstop to, contemporary new media computer art. One of the artists cited by Gere as influental in the post-war avant-garde is Roy Ascott, whose writing more than his art operates as a manifesto for the future of art and technology. In his early writings, Ascott (1966) was explicit about the influence of the founding work of Norbert Wiener in cybernetics upon his thinking, and develops the idea that only computer-based art can establish a two-way exchange between the artwork and its audience. In subsequent writing, Ascott promotes a view of art and technology as a new social process in which:

> the convergence of computers, communications, and biotechnologies, is leading to the reinvention of the self, the transformation of the body, and the noetic extension

of mind. In the process, art has shifted its concern from the behaviour of forms to forms of behaviour.

And, in the reverse of this same process:

> Just as intelligence is spreading everywhere, leaking out of our brains and spilling into our homes, our tools, our vehicles, so too is connectivity. We are about to see the environment as a whole come online – a global networking of places, products, ideas, with the Internet as a kind of hypercortex. (Ascott 1966)

The appeal of Ascott's ideas, influenced as they are by McLuhan's notion of expanded and globalised media, is that they promise a transformation of existing relationships between art and the individual. The argument is that technology can liberate human consciousness from existing set patterns and fixed modes of thought. Ascott argues that a 'technoetics', which means an embrace of technology and aesthetics, will be able to connect individual consciousnesses in a new kind of expanded collectivist or, in McLuhan's global village, a tribal consciousness, which will supersede the traditional divisions between art and science, and between the human and the machinic.

The work of art in the age of digital reproduction

The notion that the function of art is challenged by changes in technology was also expounded by Walter Benjamin and his work would have been known to both McLuhan and Ascott working in their different contexts. As Lovejoy (2004) points out, Walter Benjamin's writings from the 1930s were hugely influential to a generation of post-war cultural critics, and several of his essays, including 'The Work of Art in the Age of Mechanical Reproduction', are benchmarks for a contemporary generation of students. Benjamin, himself, was influenced by the historical and dialectical materialism of Marx, with its stress upon analysing the economic and political forces that determine social structures and organise the functions of human exchange. Benjamin saw art and media as deeply tied to the social functions they perform and he explains historical changes in the character of art and media as a direct result of social, political, economic and technological change. Here, Benjamin shares with the Marxist tradition the general concept of historical development propelled by the forces of human production. Late nineteenth-century European society was being shaped by an ever advancing indus-trialisation based upon the private ownership of the means of production and an increasing division of labour brought about by the increasing introduction of mechan-ical machines into all aspects of production, and, of course, reproduction. The social structure of a class society and the rise in the power of the organised working class and, more generally for Benjamin, the emergence of the urban masses, were bound up with the crisis in art and culture provoked by reproduction.

Benjamin's view of the history of art and culture also reflected his acceptance of the concept of the historical development of productive forces and the means of produc-tion. He schematised the history of European art into periods in which art served different social functions tied to the reproductive forces and technologies of those periods. His view of art historical change was, therefore, based upon identifying the complex nexus of forces that propelled changes in the use value of art. This is why Benjamin's sweep of history starts with art serving the function of magic, later ritual, and concludes with mechanical reproduction, which changes the function of art from ritual to exhibition value, or art produced for reproduction. We can schematise this structural history of art's relationship to function and media in the following way:

Technologies	Social/economic system	Function of art
Stone Age	Tribal	Art as magic
Bronze Age	Hunter/gatherers	Art as magic
Iron Age	Feudalism	Art as ritual
Print	Mercantilism	Art as cult of beauty
Machine	Capitalism	Art as art
Electronic	Hyper-capitalism	Art as information

For Benjamin (1937), the advent of photo-mechanical reproduction profoundly changed the function and value of the work of art as well as creating new media for a new age. The photo-mechanical reproduction of the work of art changed the perception and meaning of the work of art because it detached it from its location and context, 'the domain of tradition', and substituted the copy for its previous unique existence, or 'aura'. Benjamin goes on to say that reproduction in general led to a shattering of tradition in art, which subsequently produced a much closer link between art and politics, or we could now say, between the 'new media' and the forms of audience participation. He saw film as the new medium of the twentieth century and of a mass society and culture. He linked the ability of film to reproduce anything and everything and bring things closer spatially to that of the masses' sense of the universal equality of all things. He argued that this had the consequence of the further obliteration of the uniqueness of objects and the establishment of transitoriness over permanence.

This short schematisation of Benjamin's view of art points up the modernist character of his thought, bound-up as it was with linking the new media of film and photography to radical social change. It is this link between new media and social and economic change which is being revisited in the digital moment. It is not hard to see the extension of his argument about the function of art changing again from the mechanical age to an electronic age in which digital reproduction changes the use value of art from art to that of information.

It is the potential insights afforded by the extension of Benjamin's argument in considering art (and media) in the age of electronic reproduction that interests us here and which bears upon our attempts to think about the historical emergence of new media. The most radical insight afforded by the extension of his argument is not, it seems to us, that art is being led by a new avant-garde into a technologically driven future, but that the boundaries of art and all other media are blurring. We might argue from Benjamin that what have hitherto been regarded as the separate spheres of art and media are only maintained institutionally, since their purposes as information are now largely the same.

Michel Foucault – historical archaeologies and genealogies

If we are to be sceptical of the insights afforded by a wholly technological narrative of new media histories and their projections into the future, what method of historical insight should we replace it with? The work of Michel Foucault (1925–84), who held a Chair in the history of systems of thought at the College de France, remains very influential in providing alternative models of history. Foucault was highly critical of the idea of history as a single, measured unfolding of events. He recognised that such a

historical method had no critical means of reflecting upon its own participation in justifying those events (Foucault cited colonialism as the prime example in European written
historical accounts from the nineteenth century). Foucault started from the proposition
that history was written from the point of view of the present and that since the present
is, of necessity, always being transformed, then history is always an account of the past
from the interests, ideas and material arrangements of the present. Having recognised
this he wanted to develop historical approaches that avoided either projecting meaning
into history, or finding first causes (teleologies). His answer to these problems was to
develop both an 'archaeology' and 'genealogy' of historical knowledge. Archaeology
refers to the process of working through historical archives as a means of discovering
the organising principles that produced the field of knowledge, science, art, medicine,
etc. Genealogy is the process of analysing the historical relationships between truth,
knowledge and power. Both genealogical and archaeological approaches involve a

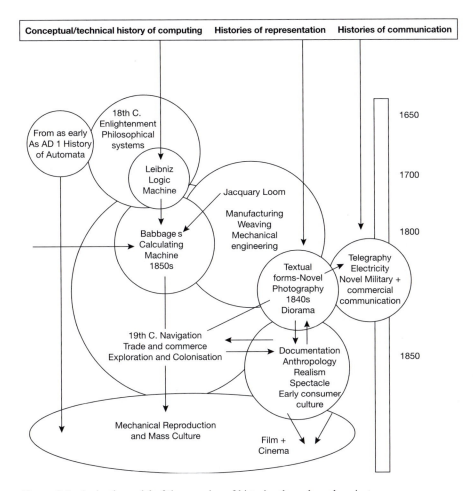

Figure 8.1   A simple model of the complex of histories through, and against
which, new media emerge.
Lister (2003: 52)

process of tracing out and uncovering the multiple beginnings and the complex and chaotic progression over time of knowledge and practices, which, as often as not, involve gaps, leaps, discontinuity and disjunctures.

Genealogies and archaeologies have found a fertile place in studies of new media precisely because they avoid constructing technologically deterministic accounts of the kind we have just rehearsed. Historical affiliations and resonances, rather than origins, are more typically what are looked for in accounting for the characteristic development of emerging new media practices. A number of writers of new media acknowledge their debt to Foucault in their studies of the formation of new media. Bolter and Grusin acknowledge Foucault in terms of looking for affiliations between different media and systems of thought in their development of the concept of 'remediation' (2000). Andy Darley (2000) explicitly embraces a genealogical approach in looking at mechanised spectacle and popular entertainment as sources for thinking about digital animation. John Tagg (1978), in his seminal work on the history of photography, seeks an explanation of photography's 'identity' or nature, in the emerging social and political institutions of social regulation in the rapidly expanding industrial cities of the mid-nineteenth century. Geoffrey Batchen (1999), who explores links between the emergent technologies of photography, mechanical weaving, computing and photo-mechanical printing around the 1800s, also adopts a genealogical approach.

What does an archaeological approach to new media reveal?

Circus and theatre

Interestingly, such approaches to a history of new media take us away from the more obvious history of the computer, robotics, software or the Internet. Instead, they tend to suggest that there are older and longer strands of interest that resurface and are reawakened in new ways in new media. In discussing the origins of digital animation and computer games, Darley (2000: 37) points to the concentration of popular entertainments on fixed sites in London and Paris from the late eighteenth and nineteenth centuries. The circus and theatres were based around live performances of burlesque, pantomime, fairy plays, melodramas, farce and magic shows. Acrobats, conjuring, illusionism, high-wire acts, escape acts, puppetry and ventriloquism provided an intense and visual pleasure. Elaborate props, mechanical and optical-based special effects created sensational and spectacular effects that brought the crowds in. Darley points out that such popular entertainments contained a variety of programmes, including illusion and trickery, which was designed to astonish and astound, stimulate and capture the eye and the gut, rather than the head – qualities and interests that he sees in special effects in contemporary cinema and computer animation. The point of such an archaeological revisiting of early popular entertainments is that it is done from the perspective of a new set of current interests in the present. The comparison between the emergence of popular entertainment in the rapidly expanding industrialised capital cities of Europe in the 1870s and that of the popular forms of new media in computer games, special effects and computer animation now, is a reminder that cultural forms do not develop along set lines. While the circus is just about still with us, live theatrical and dramatic performance has both declined and changed with the advent of other media, notably television. One of the underlying reasons for historically jumping to other periods in which new forms of entertainment and media emerged is to break up and shed new light on the arguments for the linear progression of media and its meanings. By pointing up the continuities between the two distinct periods and their forms of popular entertainment it is possible to both identify common interests in the practices and skills of visual display and illusion, and also to put us in the position of distinguishing the new from the old. One of the most important tasks that Darley set himself in his work on visual digital culture was to examine the new forms and techniques of digital technologies in the aesthetic context of early twenty-first-century culture.

Early cinema and photography

Of course, the aesthetic interest in spectacle and illusion represented by the circus and theatre was, itself, reshaped by the overlapping and emerging new form of film at the beginning of the twentieth century. And this is why there is a similar argument for seeing the relevance to new media of the early experiments in the light projection of images, first in photography and later in the moving image. The current fascination with interactivity, animation, collage and montage in new media has strong affinities with early experiments with the stereoscopic, projected and moving photographic image. Yet in the conventional history of photography and film, these early stages were seen as the relatively unformed experiments, discarded along the way to the fully developed forms of photographic realism and of classical narrative cinema. In both photography and film the general historical development is largely seen as the triumph of realism/naturalism, as it was previously in the history of European painting. But digital technology and new media practices cast a new light on the interests, fascinations and experience of the mid- to late nineteenth century. From the perspective of new media we are able to reconsider the moment when old media were themselves new. Here, the interest in a range of technologies of vision, including the stereoscope, magic lantern, panorama and diorama, were not so many steps towards the inevitability of the codes of narrative cinema but, rather, had their own particular visual and dramatic fascinations. The early histories of both film and photography identify parallel interests in realism and verisimilitude on the one hand, and montage and fantasy on the other. We can put this another way and say that both media contained multiple possibilities for meaning and use with no immediately settled or dominant view. At the same time it is possible to see, as Tagg (1987) does, that within these multiple possibilities of meaning and use, photography is given definition and identity by its constitution within a set of institutional and social relations – a set of relations that set the photograph on the road to being regarded as a certain kind of evidence or truth.

Mechanical technologies

Chemical photography was a mechanical technology of the industrial age, which developed from the 1840s onwards. The camera shutter was operated by levers and springs and, later, roll film was wound on by a simple spindle. The source of energy for forming the captured light image was natural sunlight. The main form for the viewing of photographs was the still print, which required no technology and even the light projection of the photographic image, in the magic lantern, was at first powered by an oil or gas lamp. In contrast to photography, film needed electricity in order to have an audience. Film, which developed from the 1880s, used electricity for motorised film recording and the electric light for film projection. In this last respect the emergence of cinema was as much the result of the electric light bulb and a source of regulated electricity as it was of the principle of film motion. Early applications of electricity and the moving image came together most obviously in the scientific and commercial enterprises of Thomas Edison. It was Edison who put the resources into creating an efficient incandescent light bulb, which he exhibited in New York in 1879, and it was Edison who, seventeen years later, exhibited the Kinetoscope, regarded as the first public demonstration of the moving image. The Kinetoscope passed a strip of film rapidly between a lens and an electric light bulb creating the appearance of movement, which the viewer saw through a peephole at the top. The film was created by a motorised film camera, the Kinetograph, which was also developed in Edison's laboratories by William Dickinson. There were, of course, parallel experiments in recording and projecting moving images in France with the Lumière brothers, and in London Acres and Paul developed a successful machine to project films. By the turn of the century purpose-built cinemas were attracting paying audiences to watch a variety of short, silent films, which in their subject matter emphasised above all the spectacle of movement. By 1898, the Lumières' company had produced a catalogue of over 1,000 short films for screening.

Telegraphy

Film had needed electricity in order to bring large groups of people together in one internal space to watch projected images of the external moving world; telegraphy had also needed electricity to send single text messages rapidly across large expanses of space. Telegraphy was developed in parallel with photography, from the 1830s onwards. The principle that the electromagnet could be used for long-distance communication was demonstrated in the 1830s by sending an electronic current over one mile of wire to activate an electromagnet which caused a bell to strike. Samuel Morse later showed that signals could be transmitted by wire. He used electrical pulses to deflect an electromagnet, which activated a marker to produce written codes on a strip of paper, subsequently modified as embossed dots and dashes. This became known as Morse Code. The telegraph developed in close connection with the advancement of the railways, the telegraph being used to despatch trains, and telegraph wires were built along railway rights of way. Until the development of the telephone from 1877 telegraphy dominated long-distance communication. The general line of historical development in the advancing industrialising countries of Europe and North America from the 1880s onwards was towards a unified, systematic and centralising system of communications, serving the interests of industry and commerce. This pattern of development, with its emphasis upon accurate and reliable information, transmitted at ever faster speeds across greater distances in a spreading network, continued throughout the twentieth century, and today's global communications can be seen to continue many elements of the same demand.

Electricity

The development of a readily available and widely distributed and portable source of electrical energy was an inseparable part of the early development of cinema, telegraphy and telephony. Our current 'information age' is precisely distinguished from its historical predecessor, the 'industrial age', on the basis of the unification of the source of machine power in electrical energy and the replacement of more and more mechanical machines by electronic ones. New media is, therefore, founded upon the scientific discoveries of electricity and the subsequent progress towards establishing a regulated system for the generation, storage and distribution of electricity. Obvious as it may sound, countries or communities without stable and sustainable sources of electricity cannot, by definition, participate in new media. The significance of electricity to new media is not only that it is its obvious source of power, but also that it is deeply shaping of the form and content of the medium itself. The obvious parallel here is between the alternating current of a national electricity grid and the network of networked computers through which electrically charged messages travel. The need for an ever increasing supply of electricity to power the expansion of the global network of networked computers is bringing the debate about the effects of global communications, and that of sustainable sources of energy, into alignment with each other.

Marshall McLuhan was one of the first media theorists to recognise that electricity was the defining feature of television as a medium (1968), just as Walter Benjamin (1937) pointed out that photography and film were, above all, mechanical modes of visual reproduction that had replaced hand production. The instantaneous nature of electrical energy and the ability to control its voltage and current is reflected in the central architecture of the computer. The networking of computers is parallel to that of an electrical grid system. Today, in the US, which has the largest use of high technology, approximately 40 per cent of annual energy consumption goes into the production of electricity. The speed of the application of electric light in the 1880s has striking parallels with the way in which the Internet took off 100 years later. For example, Thomas Edison established the Electric Illuminating Company which built a commercial generator in Manhattan in 1882, capable of producing power for 800 electric light bulbs. Within fourteen months, it had 508 subscribers producing power for 12,732 light bulbs. Early power stations had to be close to the users of electrical power because the system used a direct current (DC) which diminished over distance. It was the development of the alternating current (AC), which could be boosted over distances, that provided the basis for a general system of distribution. The implementation of a widespread system of electric power for public and domestic lighting, heating and the powering of utilities took place over time and differentially across Europe and North America. The early companies were inefficient when demand was small or irregular. Britain, which had a more developed system of coal gas lighting, was slower than the USA to adopt electricity. As the practical uses for electricity grew and multiplied, so did the demand for its production. Growth in distribution led to high voltage transmission and the interconnection of the modern power grid, with power plants able to be located at a distance from consumers. The development of a reliable source of electrical power and the development of utility applications went hand in hand. For media the availability of electrical power decisively altered the direction, scope and applications of the mechanical origins of image and sound recording. Newspapers and publishing, based upon mechanical technologies, dominated nineteenth-century media. The electric motor was subsequently used as a source of powering newspaper presses and electricity was used to transmit telegraphic and telephonic messages, but in the twentieth century television was the first pure electronic medium. The computer and computer networks are an application of electrical energy as well as representing the convergence of previous electrical applications.

Typewriting and the PC

The development of the typewriter and its transformation into the personal computer (PC) is another example of how different technological, communication and commercial interests paralleled each other over a long period before coming together in the computer screen and keyboard. The current networked PC is a digital technological recombination of the previous analogue technologies of the mechanical/electric typewriter, electronic calculator, television receiver, tape-recorder/player, photographic print room and telephone. The main way in which we interact with the networked PC, our interface with electronic information, relies upon a technical combination of the television cathode ray tube and the typewriter keyboard. The arrangement of the computer keyboard, in particular the configuration of the three rows of letters, remains the same as the Qwerty keyboard developed by Thales in 1867 and used in the typewriter he developed with an armament manufacturing company, Remington. The keyboard was termed Qwerty because of the first six letters from the left on the top row.

There is a long pre-history to the development of the typewriter to be found in the development of moveable type and mechanical devices, but for our purposes we can start at the point at which the mechanical portable typewriter was commercially marketed in 1895 with The Underwood No. 1, designed by Franz Xavier Wagner. This was considered to be the first modern typewriter because, unlike earlier models, the type was fully visible as it was being typed. In the space of three years the Underwood Company was producing 200 typewriters per week and, by 1901, was producing the No. 5 model, which sold in millions over the next thirty years. The mass production of the typewriter has the consequence of speeding up the production of writing. In this respect the mechanical typewriter had the same general effect upon hand production as other mechanical reproduction of the time, photography for instance. The basic components of the Underwood No. 1 – the arrangement of the letters of the keyboard, the roller carriage, the ink ribbon cartridge and the mechanical levers – have remained fairly consistent in all subsequent typewriter manufacture and were adapted in the electric typewriter. Just as Edison's 'speaking machine', the phonograph, started off as a mechanical apparatus, without the use of electricity, so too did the 'writing machine' of Thale's typewriter and the 'seeing machine' of Fox Talbot's early camera. As we have already noted, although film cameras could be operated by a mechanical motor, film projection coincided with the electric light bulb. The development of a consolidated system of electricity supply hastened the combinations of previously separate modes of reproduction and representation. The contemporary technical convergence of analogue media in the digital is, in this sense, an outcome of the systematic application of electricity to mechanically based media apparatuses.

The electric typewriter was still being refined and produced for mass use in industry and commerce well into the 1970s, when electronic typewriters which could 'memorise' what was typed became available, and a decade after the first commercial computers were being produced by IBM. Typewriting was a widespread, available and established activity, while word processing had yet to be understood. In 1973 the magazine *Radio Electronics* contained an article outlining a TV Typewriter, designed by Don Lancaster, which provided the first display of alphanumeric information on an ordinary television set. But also in the 1970s, the Personal Computer (PC) was being developed, which would use 'floppy' discs to store files and software. The immediate precursor of the floppy disc for electronic storage was the use of magnetic tape, which allowed typed material to be stored, corrected and edited prior to being printed. Magnetic tape was developed for sound recording purposes for military as well as commercial reasons by the Germans and Americans during the 1930s and 1940s. The fact that magnetic tape was used from the 1950s for storing computer data, also in research projects sponsored by defence funding in the US, points us towards the increasing convergence of technical means within the framework of electronic technologies. The first commercial computer to feature a magnetic tape storage system was the 1951 UNIVAC which had eight tape drives, separated from the central processing unit (CPU) and the control console. Each tape drive was six feet high and three feet wide, and used ½-inch metal tape of nickel-plated bronze 1,200 feet long. The whole computer filled a large room.

The term 'word processing' made an appearance in the marketing of an IBM magnetic tape computer in the late 1960s and had no widespread meaning until the development by IBM of the floppy disc for data storage in the early 1970s. The floppy disc opened up the use of computers for word processing to a much wider group because it was portable and compressed storage capacity. The floppy disc also separated software from hardware, because programmes could be stored on discs, rather than being inseparable from the equipment. Word processing allowed screen type to be understood as the creation of an open-ended document which could be continuously edited. The world of cut and paste had arrived and writing would never be the same again. Word processing conjures up a lot more than typewriting. It involves not only the mechanical production of writing or speech into typography, but also the larger process of composing, editing and even the laying out of text. Thus word processing incorporates processes, skills and practices previously associated with the work of the writer and the publisher. While typewriters were used in the production of writing by some writers, the dominant use of the typewriter was as a means of reproducing handwriting or speech in dictation or recorded speech as a typography. Word processing, made possible by the recording and display of type electrically, extended the entire process of editing and correction, prior to printing. In the present, what we now call text as opposed to type can be seamlessly transmitted, downloaded, stored and reassembled on the networked PC, laptop, palmtop and mobile phone. The impact of these technological changes upon the meaning of writing and the status of texts is still being assessed, but it is likely that the production of on-screen text using word-processing software is changing the ways in which we write. The discussion of mobile phone 'texting' or email text protocols are but two simple examples where there has been considerable debate about the changing use of the written word. The concern for the exponential rise of plagiarism within the academic community, or the status of the author in hypertextual forms, are more complex examples of the impact upon writing of word processing in a networked communication system.

Early sound amplification, transmission and recording

Making historical connections between current new media forms and practices and those of photography, film and, subsequently, television, brings to our attention the increasing primacy of vision in the historical account of media. This emphasis in thinking about new media could be said to privilege the dimension of the visual over that of the textual or auditory. The increasing focus of intellectual interest around the power and influence of visuality in culture, is, itself, a counter to the previous dominance of literature in accounts of significant culture. Without displacing the importance of visual culture for new media, and not wishing to engage in a hierarchy of the human senses and their corresponding cultural forms of transmission and reception, we do need to think about how auditory culture relates to new media. Music is a major cultural and commercial force in the development and marketing of digital products and online services. Sound is very much a part of new media and, therefore, we should at the very least recognise that the history of sound technologies and their cultural uses are important. Our sense of hearing and the cultural traditions of musical and oral communications are being attuned to a digital medium in which the auditory is as algorithmically and electronically captured as the visual and textual.

As with all of the media technologies we are considering, sound recording is best understood as developing over time and in relationship to interests and needs that continually changed as new possibilities were grasped and initial ideas discarded. The principle of the light projected image had been developed in the camera obscura at least 400 years prior to a means of fixing or recording of the image emerged with chemistry in the 1840s. The exact method of producing photographs, from the early experiments using paper and glass positives to the eventual settle method of the celluloid negative, took place over the later part of the nineteenth century. Kodak produced the first negative roll film camera in 1884. A similar historical pattern was followed with the development of sound recording methods.

Sound amplification also has a long history in the development of technological machines for the amplification of sound, but sound needed electricity and the application of physics before it could be transmitted across distances beyond that of the range of the human ear. Alexander Graham Bell working in the US had developed the microphone in relationship to his interest in human deafness and, in 1876, developed an 'electrical speech machine' which was to become the first telephone system. Here was an instrument that transmitted voices across space at the time and speed of speech. In the later part of the nineteenth century, telephony was used for communication between individuals between fixed sites as well as a popular form of public address related to live theatre and musical performances. By 1878, Bell had set up the first telephone exchange and, by 1884, long-distance connections were being made. The early stages of the development of Bell's electrical speech machines demonstrate yet again that technology and its cultural uses do not evolve in a linear fashion. The fact that telephony was conceived as a multiple public address system, rather than its eventual form of person-to-person communication, is a reflection of the nineteenth-century context of social space and cultural communication. Private conversation was still conceived of as something that took place face to face, and private correspondence was fixed within the form of the letter. It is also interesting to note that it is theatre and public performance that again provided the possible cultural content for remote auditory transmission; the telephone as we know it only subsequently developed its own content as an extension of conversation.

In parallel with Bell, Thomas Edison developed his 'speaking phonograph' or 'talking machine', which, as Gitelman (2003: 157) points out, he saw initially as revolutionising print, rather than, as it later became, a major technology for music reproduction. Edison's phonograph consisted of a cylinder covered with tin foil rotated by means of a hand-turned screw, a voice cone, a diaphragm and stylus. The sound waves were converted into pressures through the diaphragm which, in turn, transmitted this to a stylus which made indentations across the surface of the tin foil. It was a crude mechanical device and shared little materially with Bell's speaking machine, which was understood initially to link aural experience and inscribed evidence between talk and some new form of text. What excited nineteenth-century listeners was the idea that the inscribed tin foil cylinders were literally speaking pages in which the exact words and intonation of the author could be reproduced. Like early photographs, each recording was, itself, a unique object, because it was not possible to reproduce multiple copies. In photography it was the development of the celluloid negative that created multiple copies, and in sound it was the 78 rpm disc which extended a popular form of recorded musical sound.

The above accounts of early sound and vision technologies serve to underline a number of important general points that should be borne in mind when considering the current moment of new media. If we regard new media as a new historical moment, then we can equally regard old technologies as having been new once. Even our cursory glance at the early moments of image and sound recording demonstrates that the social context in which they first developed shaped a set of purposes and interests which were not those that eventually came to dominate the twentieth century. Also, it is clear that, as new technologies of their time, they were very much indebted to existing media and cultural forms, in the ways they were used, popular theatre and newspapers being the most obvious examples. It should also be recognised that there was a strong emphasis on novelty and amusement in the demonstration and exhibition of what were, in their time, considered technological marvels.

Television

By the middle of the twentieth century, much of the early experimentation with sound recording and transmission had settled into the patterns we now recognise as the telephone, radio and the record player, all of which were based upon different analogue technologies, each with their own commercial, industrial and institutional organisation. Now we face a new moment in which the recording and transmission of the image and sound has converged through the establishment of a common digital code of sampling and storage. While the technical code of image and sound is common in the digital, the cultural codes remain distinct, which is why the institutions of radio, photography and music recording remain separate. However, it is also important to recognise that radio, music and photography all have an online presence, and image and sound are major constituent elements of online and interactive media.

By the time of the first regular television broadcasts in Britain in the 1950s, listening to the radio, reading newspapers and watching films at a local cinema were regular features of everyday life for millions of people. The technology that made the broadcasting of live pictures and sound possible had evolved in a number of separate developments over the previous fifty years.

Television technology was based upon the development of the cathode ray tube (CRT), which still forms the picture tube of the domestic analogue television set. A cathode ray tube is a glass vacuum tube in which images are produced when an electron beam strikes a phosphorescent surface. The first cathode ray tube scanning device was the outcome of experimental scientist Karl Ferdinand Braun in 1897. Over the next five decades inventors and technicians worked in different countries, often in isolation or in competition with each other, on a range of technical apparatuses with no overall shared concept of what was to become broadcast television. In 1923 in Russia, Zworkin introduced the electronic television camera tube. In the UK, Baird and Jenkins worked upon systems using mechanical scanning devices. In the US, Farnsworth invented the image dissector and Allen Du Mont patented high-speed manufacturing and testing equipment that resulted in dramatic increases in receiving tube production. In 1932, Du Mont developed a cathode ray tube, which he called his 'magic eye'. Such developments were typical of a manufacturing mindset that initially saw the elements of what was, only later, to become television, as prospective technical apparatuses. The early technical experiments in transmitting and receiving images and sound as coded/decoded signals were socially understood as an operational communication system of interest to industrial, governmental or military purposes, rather than as a system of popular entertainment or national broadcast. By the late 1930s test transmissions of broadcast and received television image and sound were being made, but the transition from an organised system of radio broadcasting to that of television was not established until after the Second World War in Europe. In Britain, the BBC had received its Charter as the national organisation for radio broadcasting in 1926. It was the BBC that produced the first national TV transmissions in 1951; British television could be thought of, for some time after its inception, as 'radio with pictures'. As Williams (1974) points out, the development of broadcast television represents a technology of transmission developed before its content was thought of, or, put another way, television was a developed technology looking for social and cultural purposes. Williams also points out that parts of the content of early television transmission were, and have remained, by-products of the technology and that while radio transmission was a highly efficient means of broadcasting sound, television was an inferior means of transmitting images.

The early developments of modern media point again and again to the fact that the material technologies were developed for local and partial manufacturing and commercial reasons of their time and that only over a longer period of time was an organised and systematic set of social communication purposes grasped. Modern media emerged over time through a combination of technological invention, commercial incentive, institutional development and creative content. This recognition is instructive when we come to consider how new technologies are being used in our own period. The video phone is a good example of Williams's point that products can be developed in advance of any social or cultural purpose or content. The low-resolution digital video clips of the latest mobile phones are a by-product of technology. What applications will be found for real-time wireless digital video recording and transmission over the next decade is currently a matter of further speculation and market forces.

The historical development of television is also instructive when considering the rapidly and highly compressed development of the Internet and the World Wide Web. Technically, the Internet originated through the selective and particular interests of scientific groups and military-related government initiatives in the early 1960s in the US, as we detail below. As Castells (2001) points out, by the mid-1990s the WWW had exploded onto the world stage with about 16 million users, but even more phenomenal is the fact that in 2001 there were 400 million users, with predictions of 1 billion users, approximately a sixth of the world's population, by 2005. The extraordinary rapid growth of a global system of one-to-one and many-to-many distributed communication stands in marked contrast to the development of television as a one-to-many, centralised system on communication. Moreover, the Internet and television share a technical history of the televisual transmission screen (CRT), now being overtaken by the application of liquid crystal screens (LCD) and plasma screens, which present the conditions for unprecedented convergence of distribution and reception systems. The question put by Bolter and Grusin (2000) is whether the computer and allied institutions will take over the function of television, or will television broadcast companies take over the function of the Internet.

The actual relationships between technologies and their social uses are, as the example of television suggests, extremely complex. A full understanding of the development of television needs to take account of an historical period of social reconstruction and change after a continental war as Williams outlined. Post-war social and economic change created a new consumer society centred upon the domestic home. The term 'consumer durables' was coined to define a new set of mass-produced products, such as radios, cameras and television sets, which were, in effect, technologies of communication. The important social fact about the use of these post-war communication technologies was that they were consumed privately in the home, by a family unit that was more insular and less extended than previous family organisation. Television thus represented a highly centralised form of communication directed towards the isolated consumer, whereas theatre and cinema in the pre-war period had been popular social entertainments. The larger point here is that television developed in response to a new social organisation of which it performed a shaping role. The habits and patterns of consumption and use established by television are now being worked through the shaping of the popular consumption of new media.

A note about videotape

Early television broadcasting consisted of live material, transmitted as it was produced in the studio or on location. This was because, at the time, there was no means of recording the televised signal. Live broadcasting put a limit on the amount of material that could be transmitted and early television contained intermissions between pro-grammes and a limit to the number of hours of television per day. Early television scheduling and programming was therefore shaped by a system of what, in a post-video age, we now call real-time transmission. Presenters and assembled casts of actors had to perform at the cue of the studio manager, much as actors did in the theatre. As we noted above, analogue sound recording using magnetic tape reels had been developed in the 1930s and 1940s, but no method had been found to record the image and syn-chronised sound of the televised recording. A method was found in 1951, when the first videotape recorder (VTR) captured live images from television cameras by converting the image and sound into electrical impulses and saving the information onto magnetic tape. The further development of the VTR, and its take-up by television companies, radically changed the possibilities for television broadcasting since programmes could now be pre-recorded and edited prior to transmission. The advent of videotape record-ing did more than give television a means of pre-recording and storing televised material, it became a major means for the domestic consumption of feature films, an extension and eventual replacement for Super 8 mm home movie making and an artistic medium in its own right. It is the video image and aesthetic, rather than that of film, that has been incorporated into digital capture and used in new media production. Videotape was also necessary to a generation of video games that used television technology.

Computer games

In seeking to make links between the histories of theatre, photography and film and new media we could be said to be privileging both vision and visual representation in media to the exclusion of the other human senses, their corresponding knowledge and representations and recordings. A rejoinder to this is that the visual (photographic) image has rarely been reproduced without other kinds of textual commentaries, including oral ones in domestic photography, and that film and television are just as much organised by sound as by image. It can also be argued that our participation in, and responses to, photography, film and television are not exclusively organised by an overriding and singular mode of attention to either linear narratives or the realist discourse of repre-sentation. The embedded and lived modes of attention, to television for instance, include the experience of television within a larger social and perceptual field. Specifically, we can include the experience of television as 'background', for instance, as well as modes of attention such as channel flipping which suggests that television can be enjoyed through fragmented, montaged and parallel modes of attention. So, although analogue, terrestrial television is still accessed through a single screen in real time, it can be experi-enced as hypermedia in a combination with other domestic media, for example, watching TV with the sound off while listening to the radio, and by sequencing different channels. Digital television is already offering greater hypermediated experiences, for example on iBBC where programme text information and programme flows can be viewed concurrently on one screen.

The domestic reception of television provides the most recent historical context for the consumption of screen-based computer games. Essentially, the video and computer game is interaction between 'reading' screen-based audio/graphical representations and making programmed responses to the 'rules' or 'conventions' of a game by means of a physical interface (games console, keyboard, etc.). We would expect, therefore, that a history of computer and video games would take into account these two elements, graphical representations on screens and the rules and conventions of games. The former we have already touched upon in discussing the antecedents of film and photography in the visual illusions and tricks of the circus, fairground and arcade. Such amusements contained the fascination with naturalistic projections through which the real could, apparently, be captured and replayed and that the same apparatuses, techniques and technologies, could convincingly conjure up the world of fantasy. These opposing fascinations with the recording of reality and the convincing representation of the obviously unreal, are contained in the history of photography and film, especially in animation and genres of film that rely on special effects. We would also have to add here the long history of narrative illustration, most obviously and recently manifest in comic strips. New media introduces techniques through which the visual conventions of recording the optically real can be seamlessly blended with the graphical representation of the optically impossible. Screen-based computer games make use of graphical conventions to do one of two things. In games such as Tomb Raider, for example, it is important that the graphical representations conjure up a convincing three-dimensional world into which the game player 'enters' through their optical positioning in front of the screen, or through a screen-based avatar. The graphical conventions of this type of game strive towards filmic realism. On the other hand, games such as Sim City and Pokemon still represent or, better, model spatial worlds, and are less concerned with creating verisimilitude than with offering the player a range of views and strategic reconnaissance of the world and the events in play.

Gaming and human play

Computer games are now an integral component of personal and domestic screen-based media. Computer games represent a global industry with an economic turnover rivalling that of Hollywood film production. Computer games are an established part of popular culture, with dedicated websites, international competitions, High Street retail outlets, magazines and related product and merchandising in the toy industry. According to the forecasting firm of DFC Intelligence the worldwide market for video games and interactive entertainment is predicted to grow from $23.2 billion in 2003 to $33.4 billion in 2008.

Because of the scale of the games industry, the study of computer and video games is rapidly becoming an academic subject in its own right, with individuals and groups adopting a variety of points of interest and theoretical perspectives. At present there appear to be three distinct intellectual projects attempting to account for the current ways in which computer games are valued and understood as part of new media. These projects roughly fall into:

- the sociological and cultural interest in studying how children and young people use computers and how this may or may not relate to the wider project of education and play;
- the analysis of games as narrative cultural texts, similar to films, books or television programmes;
- the analysis of games as meeting a deep human interest in mathematical puzzles.

Given the above we would expect a history of computer games to be informed by the wider history of pre-computer games, such as board or card games as well as an even wider history of cultural forms of play. Such a history would also recognise the complex cultural inter-relationship between games and play based on mathematical puzzles and those based upon riddles, rhymes and other narratives. Analogue video games replicated in a different medium older cultural forms of physical games and sports that involved hand–eye co-ordination. The electronic relays of video games, the games consoles, were also reconfigurations of older mechanical interfaces of amusements in the penny arcades. The visual screen interfaces as well as the physical interface of the console of early video games prefigured the graphical user interface (GUI) of the contemporary hypermedia computer. The first version of Spacewar in which two players used a trackball console to 'control' the simple graphic representations of two spaceships, which 'fire' at each other, was developed at the Massachusetts Institute of Technology in the 1960s. The videogame of Pong was developed as an interesting diversion by programmers working for IBM. As Lister *et al.* note (2003: 333), computer games emerged from programmers wanting to know what more could a computer do than crunch numbers. Pong had a very basic screen graphic that used nothing more than a black screen with a white bar on either side representing bats, and a white dot as a ball. The (algorithmic) relationship between the bat, ball and blank screen created 'a game of tennis' in which the speed and angle of ball return was variably programmed to test the 'skill' of the players in predicting the position of the bat. It was introduced in 1972 and was a popular addition to the arcades and could also be plugged into the domestic television set by means of a programmed black box. In 1978, a Japanese company, Taito, introduced Space Invaders which proved to be exceptionally popular in Japan and North America. By the standards of contemporary photo-realistic graphics, Space Invaders used a very simple, schematic form of representation of aliens and humans and used a gravitational metaphor in which the top of the screen represented space and the bottom earth. The small, 'alien' shapes would descend in rows from the top and would 'fire' on the human shapes below, who could 'hide' under four 'shields', graphic dashes, or come out from their 'shields' and 'shoot' back at the 'aliens'. The movement and firing positions of the humans were controlled by a keypad. Pong and Space Invaders involved using the screen as a spatial metaphor and the player–computer interaction simulated rapid anticipation and reaction times through hand–eye co-ordination of schematic on-screen avatars. The replacement of video by digital storage platforms allowed games to use larger memory-hungry graphic files and hence produce today's photo-realistic spatial worlds in which adventure games and shoot-'em-ups can be set.

Automation of manual and intellectual labour

The interests of military organisations in advanced command and control systems, and the application of advanced technology to warfare, are evident influences in the shaping of modern computer functions and applications. But to say that the PC and the Internet are simply spin-offs from military development is only partially true. There has been a much longer civil and commercial set of interests at work in the creation of machines that could repeat human actions, functions and tasks, which have also contributed to our conception of the computer. The most recent historical context for such machines was the European Industrial Revolution. From the late eighteenth century onwards in farming, cottage industries and then in industrial mills, there was an increasing application of machines to activities that had previously been carried out by hand. The textile industry introduced mechanical looms and weaving machines, which allowed cloth to be produced more cheaply and in greater quantities than that of hand production. The Jacquard loom is an early example of the introduction of the automation of weaving whereby sophisticated patterns could be produced by 'programming' the loom using a string of cards with punched holes.

A hundred and fifty years after the Jacquard loom, analogue computers used linear punch-cards to create programmes for processing data. In analogue computers, punched-tape was later replaced by magnetic tape. There is an even longer history of the use of calculating/counting 'machines', devised in order to simplify the complex processes of mental arithmetic, the abacus frame and the slide-rule being but two examples. The externalisation of the programmatic rules of algebraic and algorithmic tasks, previously carried out mentally by learnt formulas, ran in parallel to the industrial conception of programming as the replacement of skilled human labour by the machine. This is demonstrated by the work of Charles Babbage (1791–1871), whose design for a mechanical 'Difference Engine', consisting of cogs, levers and springs, was a dedicated device intended for the calculation and production of mathematical tables for use in nautical navigation. From a contemporary position, such mechanical analogue devices as we have briefly touched upon could all be called programmable machines for the production and manipulation of data. They are typically cited in technologically privileged accounts of the history of the computer as its precursors.

We have already noted that the development of electricity, as a readily available power source at the beginning of the twentieth century, was a condition for the emergence of the technical apparatus of cinema, radio, telegraphy and telephony. The vacuum valve provided the first means of converting an electric current into a system of signals that could have representational values in radio, television and analogue computers. By the 1950s, valves, which were inherently unstable, were replaced by solid state diode technology and magnetic tape was used to store programming information. Such a computer, which needed a large laboratory to be housed, was built by the American National Bureau of Standards and was known as the SEAC (Standards Eastern Automatic Computer) and was used for testing components and systems for setting computer standards. By the standard of today's miniaturised, microchip digital computers, the mainframe research computers of the 1970s were large, complex and cumbersome amalgams of technical apparatuses and required long periods of development and were, therefore, expensive to produce. Computer development in this period was, therefore, governed by large-scale institutions that required functions related to complex information processing. The ILLIAC IV mainframe computer, funded by the Department of Defense Advanced Research Projects Agency (DARPA) and developed by the University of Illinois, was used by the American National Aeronautical Space Agency (NASA) and had a computation speed of 200 million instructions per second – enough, as it was refined, to command and control the Apollo manned flight.

The development of networked computers

From the standpoint of new media we can now consider how the practices associated with the analogue technologies of recording sound, vision and movement and with two-way communications converged in the networked digital computer. The social shaping of the development of the computer and computer networks centres upon a set of interlocking relationships between governmental military and defence departments, armament manufacturers and academic research. In practice, the relationship between these three institutional sites, as we might call them, is most obviously expressed in the form of government funding for research and development projects and defence procurement contracts. This is why it has been said in many contexts that technological development in general is quickened, if not driven, by war, or, in a more complex expression of the argument, by the permanent arms economy. The development of computers from the 1940s clearly reflects such a grouping of interests and participation. In the US and Britain some of the most influential scientists and mathematicians associated with key developments in computing were employed by, or associated with, government military research projects that had been established as a result of the Second World War in Europe. The now well-rehearsed post-war history of the technological development and social shaping of the modern computer and the Internet makes the connection between scientific and military work very clear. The leading figures in the field of early computing, their institutional locations and the funding of their projects came together in a nexus of interests bounded by the Allied war effort against Nazi Germany and later in the US–Soviet axis of the cold war. Vannevar Bush, whose seminal essay, 'As We May Think' (1945), outlined the concept of a multimedia computer, was Director of the US Office of Scientific Research and Development, responsible for the 6,000 scientists involved in the war effort. Norbert Wiener, whose ideas on cybernetics have influenced thinking about the human–machine relationship, worked on a research project on improving anti-aircraft guns. In 1943, Alan Turing, a Cambridge mathematician, was working on the British Colossus for military code decryption.

The development of a computer network, in which computers could 'talk to one another', first took place within the Advanced Research Projects Agency (ARPA), set up in 1957 within the US Department of Defense with the support of Vannevar Bush in order to help the military use computers. In 1972 ARPA became DARPA, the Defense Advanced Research Project. Slevin (2000: 28) argues that the origins of the Internet are firmly rooted in the circumstances of the cold war and the US's fear that the Soviets could launch a long-range nuclear attack with the rocket technology demonstrated by their Sputnik satellite in 1957. ARPANET was established in 1969 in order to develop a communication network for the exchange of research information between centres and to allow scientists and researchers to share information. The ARPANET linked the information carried on computers in different locations, which at the time, we should remember, were large, mainframe analogue computers in a distributed rather than central system.

One of the popular myths surrounding the development of the Internet was that it was purposely developed by US Intelligence during the cold war as a non-centralised command system in the event of a Soviet first strike long-range nuclear missile attack. There is at least a grain of truth in this as Slevin (2000: 29) points out. The US Air Force commissioned research at the RAND Corporation to work on a project to see how the US Air Force could maintain control over its missiles and bombers in the aftermath of a nuclear attack. The answer they came up with was a network of computers that would continue to function even if several of its distributed nodes were destroyed, as against a system with one centralised hub and radial connections, which, if destroyed, would stop all command and control between secondary centres. It is the concept of a distributed network in which all computers inter-linked that constitutes the current network of networked computers, which forms the basis of the Internet and World Wide Web.

The technical objective of the research agencies working for ARPA was to develop computer codes for addressing electronic information in packets, which would allow networked computers to 'talk to one another', which became known as protocols. One of the original research aims, which supported the establishment of ARPANET, was for research centres to be able to share the use of online computer time at a point when mainframe computers were very expensive and needed large physical spaces to accommodate analogue memory. The system of technical networks, which emerged from ARPA's research, became known as the Internet. The system of transmission protocols became known as the Transmission Control Protocol (TCP) and Internet Protocol (IP).

The interests of the military and its allied scientific research organisations continued to influence the development of the Internet through the 1980s as did the wider scientific community through the setting up of NSFNET by the US National Science Foundation (NSF) in 1984. ARPANET was decommissioned in 1990 and the deregulation of the Internet followed. In 1989 the European Laboratory for Particle Physics (CERN) connected to the Internet. It was at CERN that the first server and client software for what was to be known as the World Wide Web (WWW) was formulated by Tim Berners-Lee. He is attributed with solving the technical problem of information flow between networked computers. He wrote a programme that changed the model from passing around containers of information identified by file name, to passing around viewable documents, what we now call webpages. At this time, a standard for the Hypertext Markup Language (HTML) was established by the International Standards Organization (ISO). This is the standard language for hypertext creation on the Internet. The system was first made available in December 1990, and refined over the period until 1993. The early browser Mosaic and, later, Netscape Navigator set the protocols and standards that enabled documents to be stored on web servers anywhere in the world and be viewed on any networked computer using a simple address.

As Castells (2001: 12) points out, the Internet was shaped not only by government defence and scientific institutions but was also the product of a grassroots tradition of computer networking. Here, Castells recognises a constellation of interests combining libertarian scientists in university departments, networked PC users and the larger framework of defence-initiated and supported projects. He formalises the culture of the Internet as being made up from four specific cultures, comprising the techno-meritocratic, the hacker, the virtual communitarian and the entrepreneurial. These are both accurate and evocative terms to describe the grouping of ideas and interest, or, to use one of our other more abstract terms, the discourses which manifested themselves in trends, approaches and beliefs in the Internet's purpose and possibilities. Understanding why we have the Internet as it is now configured needs to take account of the close inter-relationship between the cultural values of the individuals, communities and groups involved in computer science and programming, the institutional purposes for which computers were being built and the historical development of the technical apparatuses.

Back to the future: new technologies and continuous cultural forms

In concluding our survey and discussion of the histories of new media technologies and their evolving uses we return again to the provisional nature of current work in the area. A substantial history of new media will have to disentangle the elements of new media's technological and cultural hybridity. Such a history will be produced by continuous scholarship, research and theory. One such approach, which cautions against the tendency to construct a history of new media as a singular new medium, is evident in *New Media 1740–1915* (Gitelman and Pingree 2003). Here the case is made that the study of new media is not confined to today's new media and that it is important to focus upon historical moments when old technologies were new. In excavating the new moment of old technologies it is possible to juxtapose older and contemporary media and examine continuities and discontinuities between them and take the view that new media is, by definition, the uneven and never finally settled outcome of work upon material technologies in and through particularised social formations. Such a method works in both time directions. Blake (p. 4) uses the contemporary concept of virtual reality in order to show us how the Zograscope (a convex lens through which perspectival drawings could be viewed) was used by the middle classes in the 1740s to construct a simulacrum of polite metropolitan space. Garvey (p. 224) reminds us that domestic scrapbooks in the 1910s employed conventions of bricolage and collage that are prescient of the graphic cut-and-paste repurposed content on today's websites. Such studies as these resist the temptation, which we have already discussed, to construct a teleological history where the early experiments with optical representations, remote communication or analogue sound recording are configured as rehearsals in a seamless history resulting in the inevitable outcome of virtual and immersive media. Instead, by focusing upon media formations that failed to survive for very long, or what might now be deemed dead media, they suggest current new media might also be looked at as in a state of flux and with an uncertain future.

Typically, the history of communication media is seen as dependent upon the history of scientific and technological invention that is most often written as the history of creative individuals who make scientific discoveries, which are subsequently given practical applications. While it is undeniably the case that we would not have the media we do without the dedicated and single-minded efforts of individual technological discovery, their efforts alone cannot account for why and how certain media became established. We discussed above Williams' (1974) seminal analysis of the development of television as being the outcome of a complex and changing set of social patterns, economic modes of production and political needs and values. He makes the startling, but also hard to grasp, point that there was nothing inevitable about the way in which television emerged as the domestic and privatised reception of centralised broadcasting. In other words, we could have had a totally different kind of television, which would therefore have developed a different set of technological possibilities. New media is renewing interests in one-to-one as well as many-to-many forms of interactive telematic communication that are currently being socially explored. The human interest in social communication and interactivity at a distance has a longer history and is not a product of a new technology. Television is an example of the social shaping of technology, which in Britain and Europe in the 1950s emphasised the interests of a strong and centralised system of national communication over and above that of a more distributed, local and two-way mode of interactivity. It follows for us that the same will be true about the social shaping of new media. The networked computer and the Internet have been forged in some key respects in the same social and economic mould of centralised corporate interests as television was. The PC has been produced and marketed as a domestic consumer durable for the family and home, as was television and radio earlier. Greater bandwidth, faster download times and larger file storage are primarily enlisted in the interests of gateway service providers wishing to capture the largest market share – witness the current battle between British Telecom (BT) and America Online (AOL), large corporate providers of 'content' for domestic consumption, in a development similar to the technical refinements of television in gaining greater picture and sound definition. Such developments overwhelmingly reproduce the one-to-many model of television in which the privatised domestic consumer is at a screen at one end and a few large international corporations who provide, and hence control, the 'content' are at the other. This is one scenario that is forcibly illustrated in the digital convergence of television and the computer.

9 'Online Caroline' creating online narrative: Tim Wright

T im Wright is a writer and new media producer who has also worked in games and online content development. In this interview he discusses the evolution of 'Online Caroline', a groundbreaking work of fiction and drama, created for the web. The interview places the project in the historical context of the web as it was beginning to evolve in the late 1990s as a place for entertainment, capable of attracting and building audiences. In addition, he addresses how an online creative work of this sort operates in a cultural context but also has to take into account the commercial agenda of the Internet.

>From: caroline@onlinecaroline.com
>Date: Fri, 21 May 2004 01:00:20 +0100
>Subject: Who are you really, Peter
>To: peter@newmediabook.org.uk
>You are a strange person, Peter.
>Each time I think I've got a perfect picture of you, you do something that turns
>you into someone else. When I stepped into that bath I had a fantastic sense
>of pleasure: the warm water; the music; the oranges; the chocolate; you and
>the mask to watch over me.
>The perfect work environment ;-)
>And then the ansaphone goes. At first I think it's someone in the house. . . . But
>it's YOU on the phone. At least I guess it must be you. You're the only person
>I've given my number out to lately. You haven't given my number out to anyone
>else, have you? I've put the message in the 'Take A Message' section. Tell me
>it's not you. And yet if it's not you, who is it?

The above email is part of 'Online Caroline', an innovative Internet project created by Rob Bevan and Tim Wright. In part a game and a dramatic story, it brings together conventions from a number of different narrative forms to form a complex tale that involves the participation of the viewer on many levels. The project won the British Academy for Film and Television Arts (BAFTA) Award for Interactivity in 2000 and since then has remained online and regularly getting new viewers.

Caroline is a fictitious person with a website who sends her visitors regular emails. She reminds them about something she has done, she exchanges a joke about a friend

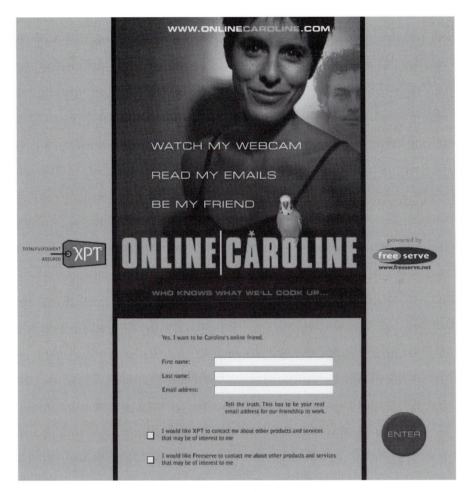

Figure 9.1 Tim Wright and Rob Bevan, 'Online Caroline' (2000)
Detail from the 'sign-up' webpage for participants to subscribe to the project, 'Online Caroline',
which used webcams, email and messages to draw users into a narrative about a young woman.
The project evolved over a number of weeks and depended upon the continued participation of the
online audience. This page was designed to appear like something from a typical website that might
be inviting people to join an online community.

of hers, and cajoles them if they haven't visited her website recently. When visitors go
to her site, there is always a new update on the business of her life and her relationship. Her website opens onto a webcam coming live from her flat. Usually Caroline is
at home, in the kitchen or the living room, sometimes trying on clothes, sometimes with
a friend.

When visitors first log onto the site they are asked if they want to be friends with
Caroline, who has 'just put up her website and wants to meet people'. Each day that
the visitors log on they receive a new 'episode', an increment in the story. Every episode
contains a sequence presented as 'live webcam' footage, which lasts for a couple
of minutes. Other parts of the site include a tour of her flat; a section where the visitor

can pick out clothes for her, 'what shall I wear?'; and, importantly, 'what are you like? (let's talk about you some more)' where she asks visitors to give information about themselves, and they can respond, through a multiple-choice selection.

The narrative evolves over twenty-four episodes and is told through texts, photos and postings on her website and by emails sent direct by Caroline. For over a month, the website 'Online Caroline' keeps up a correspondence with visitors to the site, until the story reaches its conclusion.

The success of 'Online Caroline' is due to the fact that it is more than a story 'told' to an audience, it is a relationship that grows between the subject, Caroline, and her

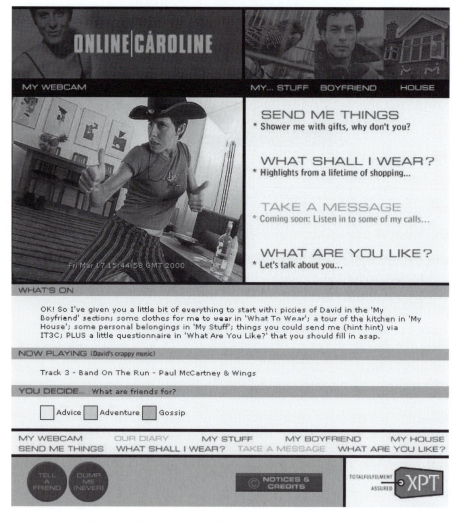

Figure 9.2   Tim Wright and Rob Bevan, 'Online Caroline' (2000)
The homepage of the website showing a still of the 'live' webcam video from Caroline's flat, updated correspondence with the online viewer, and links to the various sections in which they could participate.

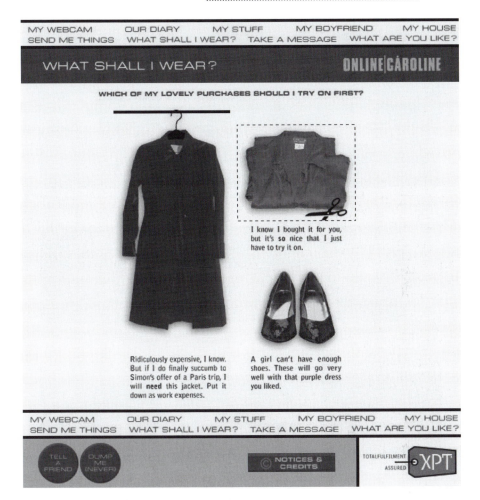

Figure 9.3 Tim Wright and Rob Bevan, 'Online Caroline' (2000)
Detail from 'What shall I wear?' webpage. Caroline would 'respond' in email or her texts on the site to the selections made by the viewer.

new friend, the reader of the website. Visitors to the site answer questions about themselves in response to a 'dialogue' of questions from Caroline. This information is held within a database integral to the website, which also maps how each visitor uses the site and how much they have read. This is then used to generate emails 'from' Caroline. In this way, the experience of visiting the site is personalised for each user so that when they visit Caroline's website they can each receive a slightly different version depending on the information they have contributed. The site is also controlled so that only a certain amount of information can be received each day. It is structured so that it takes a minimum of twenty-four days to experience the drama, though it takes longer if users visit the site less than daily.

The creators of 'Online Caroline', Rob Bevan and Tim Wright, both had considerable experience working with game developers and interactive designers. The format

Simon and I fail to remain sober while waiting for you to turn up.

Lots of food shopping. I'm going to cook you dinner!

I cook you a meal. Simon spoils it. David calls about parcels and babies!

Dressing up for Sophie and you. David's parcels arrive.

Sophie ruins my big night out. The outfit worked though, yes?

Bloody burglars!? Budgie on the loose. What will David say?!

You scare me in the bathroom with your creepy phone message.

Shopping frenzy!! More calls from David about babies.

Simon is very stupid. You don't believe him, do you?

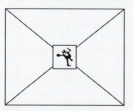

IMAGE DELETED, BY ORDER OF XPT.

Caroline is away. Normal service will resume shortly.

I bring you gifts from Paris. David brings weird stuff from Africa.

Figure 9.4 Tim Wright and Rob Bevan, 'Online Caroline' (2000)
'Our Diary' showing stills from the webcam 'live' video from Caroline's flat. A new short sequence was 'played' on the site each time the online viewer logged on.

they devised for 'Online Caroline' arose from backgrounds in developing projects that explored interactive narrative, online environments and games and brought together different approaches from entertainment and education.

Developing a project for online audiences

'Online Caroline' seemed to click immediately with an online public and it appeared to have come at exactly the right time for an Internet work to become a popular success. Tim, when you look back at the development of the project what do you think were the particular reasons that led to its success?

'Online Caroline' was definitely of its time – you couldn't do something like that now. There was a long gestation period – it was something Rob Bevan and I started talking about in 1997/8. We didn't get it online until the beginning of 2000 and that's when it went a bit crazy, that first six months in the year 2000. Why I think it was of its moment was because it was backed by an Internet service provider, just at the point their share prices were going ballistic and they were taking on subscribers. Suddenly, there was a perception that the Internet was something that was free and accessible to a whole load of people who didn't know anything about the Internet or computers. So there was a very naive audience, potentially mass audience.

I don't think you can talk now about the Internet like that. The whole idea of what Caroline offered at that point was a kind of sci-fi idea. It was about voyeurism and meetings with strangers and all those kinds of things that were very rich for the press to talk abut for a start, but in the imagination of naive users that was very exciting then.

The experience now for many people has been disappointing because it has never lived up to those expectations. So the large number of people coming to the web now come with expectations that, first, they don't really believe what they are seeing – they've become much more sceptical about content on the web. Second, they are being steered more towards mainstream experiences because everyone is using the same ten per cent of websites on the web. The audience is less fragmented in a way so there is less chance for projects like Caroline to get a whole load of people coming out in different directions.

Given that this was a period when many people were exploring new ways of putting content on the web and working online, were there other contexts or interests that were an influence for you?

One other thing about that is that I wrote it specifically to get more women interested in using the web and email. It was inspired by two thoughts: first the Jenny-cam idea – there were people who were putting up webcams and all they were doing was lying in bed under a duvet or waving. Of course there was porn – there'll always be porn. I was interested in that phenomenon and thought why don't we do a webcam where something actually happens?

The second thing was my wife got an email account in 1998 and was very excited by the idea that she could be talking to all her women friends she hadn't spoken to for five or six years. And they were talking about stories about work, about kids and re-kindling their friendships.

I thought that's interesting too and maybe that's a way to get more women interested in computers – to create some kind of drama or connection of characters through email that was personalised by the software. So I wrote it specifically to appeal to women in their mid-twenties and thirties. I figured the boys were going to turn up anyway.

The gender split on the data shows that a lot of women did log in and stay with it and again now I'd say that's something that would still be interesting to do but I don't think there's such a big gender imbalance on the net any more. In about 1999 the split was about 65/35 men to women; now I think there are more women than men online generally. I think a lot of younger women use the net a lot more for chat and community.

Creating a dramatic narrative and analysing data

Were you also interested in the wider context of the way that drama or narrative could work on the web?

I think the world's changed and a drama like Caroline was very much geared to the Internet community that was there at the time. You can't spoof people in the same way now about fake webcams and stuff. Everything's fake. We used to rather pretentiously talk about it being a bit like Orson Welles's *War of the Worlds* when radio was a new phenomenon. You can do that when technology's emerging, people think it's all about giving you the truth and then when suddenly it's not – it's about drama and that's exciting.

Were there other contexts such as education that mattered to you? There were many commercial and cultural projects that were using an interactive narrative format to present educational packages at the same period.

The previous project we'd done was a CD-ROM called 'Mind Gym'. It was about coaching you into problem solving in different ways, but by working with comedy. I'd definitely thought of 'Online Caroline' as an extension of that, in that it was a kind of self-help project where you could get yourself into a relationship with a fictional stranger and then see how that played out for you. I think people lack spaces like that in their adult life. The Internet is a very good place for that.

A large part of the narrative is made possible by the way that you were using the technology: creating a database of information provided by the users and using it to generate supposedly personal correspondence from Caroline. In retrospect do you see that the limitations of the technology you had at hand were a disadvantage? For example, if you were doing the project now you would have access to more sophisticated software that could analyse emails from users to Caroline rather than rely on multiple-choice questionnaires. But it is possible that the restrictions enabled you to have a more manageable relationship with the audience, and therefore control their expectations. In which case, the limitations were something that you could use to your advantage.

There's a whole range of issues associated with that. One of them is cost – anything's possible if you throw enough money at it. We wanted to make it to a limited budget so it had to be based on fairly limited software, which then constrained how the data was captured. If we had the time again I think I would do less form filling and try and make it more like a natural dialogue. Nowadays it would be much easier to do that with the whole business being able to feed databases through emails and it would be much more affordable. But it was very clear to us that we also had to create a system that looked like Caroline herself was capable of managing and almost making it herself.

In part you want the users to be aware that this is a fiction and that they are engaging in a pretence. So I assume the subtler you are with the way your program is operating, the capacity to get it wrong is greater. For example, if the users filled a form which says 'I do or don't have children', when Caroline later mentioned that they had children they would get a twinge of recollection that they had given that information previously.

We didn't want to offer people too many choices. If it became too seamless they wouldn't notice what we had done, they don't see the magic trick, so it has to be slightly clunky for them. The other thing is we didn't want to give the impression that this was some form of artificial intelligence and that it aimed to tell someone about the person taking part – it was just a device to create an entertainment.

In addition, if you get too slick and you gather too much information, and you over-analyse it, you can come up with a profile that is not necessarily accurate anyway. Certainly you can capture too much data – you can build up great profiles of users which then just sit unused in a database.

Developing the project

Can you tell me about the steps you went through to produce 'Online Caroline' and how you went about getting commercial backing for it?

The project went through a whole raft of changes. Rob and I were working at No-Ho Digital, a multimedia production company, and decided that we wanted to do a detective game drama set in London. But it was the kind of project that was going to require millions and the only people who had millions in 1997/98 were games companies and it wasn't a proper game. So we went back to the drawing board and said that there were three elements to the game. One was the story world where the game takes place. We need the characters or the game players and that could be the audience or fictional characters and we were interested in blurring that. And it needed rules. So we bust up that project into different projects: a game playing application; a character development with a relationship development engine; and finally a story world – a back-story sort of thing.

The back-story became XPT.com – the mysterious company that 'employs' Caroline's boyfriend David. For the character aspect we thought we'd try and work out what a relationship with one of our fictional characters would be like and what kind of transactions we would have, and out of that came Caroline.

Then in 1998 we got in contact with a Canadian online entertainment company that was a venture capital start-up that was trying to cash in on the dot com explosion. We pitched them the idea of a webcam drama – which was Caroline – and they gave us some seed money to develop the script and film half a dozen scenes to see what it would be like.

How did they see their relationship with you – were they were expecting to produce and host the project?

It was going to get hosted on their entertainment portal and it would be their exclusive content. But they went bust quite quickly and we managed to get the rights back off them just beforehand. We then went to a television company and suggested that they should be supporting independent content producers for online projects. And they agreed to put money into producing 'Online Caroline', but their remit was they could only do that if there was a TV programme associated with it. So we had to re-jig the project so that not only was it a webcam drama but it had an associated TV series with it, a late night TV series of short five-minute programmes. However, we got lost in development hell with the television company mainly over rights for the web element. They had never had a contract like this – this was long before reality TV – they had never done any combined web and TV broadcasting before this point and they had no models for doing it. We couldn't reach an agreement about the contract – it was really, really difficult.

That was the point when we had a chance lunch with an executive from Freeserve, which was then one of the biggest UK Internet providers, which led to a meeting with the Chief Executive. He absolutely loved it. He said it was the weirdest pitch he'd ever had, he thought we were crazy, and he wanted to invest in it. And they didn't even want to own the rights – they just wanted to borrow them for a year and then revert them back to the company.

An initial aim for Freeserve was that they were very interested in getting more women to subscribe to the service – that they saw this might be sort of a good way in to do that. They liked the way that we were using personalisation of data – that might appeal to sponsors and advertisers if we could show them that people were being drawn in through different ways and their interests were being exposed, as it were.

How did the company view the project? As well as being an entertainment product, and also a marketing device that would give an opportunity for them to build their profile, did they also regard it as a financial exercise?

At that time the company's subscriber accounts were dial-up accounts and the company earned income from BT for every minute that one of their subscribers stayed online. At that time, the average time people were spending online was three minutes a day down-loading their email. We anticipated that we could increase the time being spent online by offering entertainment.

Were you able to complete the production with the funding from Freeserve?

By that point we had the script completely written – we knew exactly what the emails were going to do and what the scenes were and everything and we'd shot nine scenes out of the twenty-four. With the seed money that they had we shot the rest of the stuff over three or four days in Rob's flat – shot all the digital video with the actors, and paid up the programmer whose engine we were using, a guy I used to work with at No-Ho – and basically got the whole thing done with that start-up money. We finished the production in March 2000.

Marketing the project and user statistics

When Caroline was first launched you just released a very innocuous front page inviting people to be Caroline's friend. Did it work mostly by word of mouth and how did you start getting publicity about it?

Freeserve had a PR company but at the launch the only people that turned up were the technical press. But then I don't know how or why, a couple of journalists latched on to it – one was at the *Guardian* and another at the *Sunday Times*. They wrote about it and that's when it went a bit mad and that's also at the time we changed the front end. It suddenly went to a bigger audience and we were getting a thousand people a day signing up for that first month and then it slowed down again, but it went a bit barmy that first month.

How many users did you get when 'Online Caroline' first started?

For the first six months about 35,000 people went through it and those were registered active users. More importantly, people were coming back to the site every day. One of the big problems of the net then, and still today, is that the majority of people visit sites once and only visit the home page. But we had great data which showed we had this significant number of active users who we knew stayed loyal over time.

Now, every time somebody writes about 'Online Caroline' or mentions it to another group the user rate suddenly spikes again. Because the story starts when you register and goes at your pace it means we have months of it just ticking over and then suddenly we get a rush of registrations and people going through it. And we find someone has written a newspaper article in New York or in Brazil. It was interesting that after the initial cost of production there was the cost of hosting but afterwards it's cost free. For an investor, the longer you leave it online, the better the cost per user because it's not costing anything. We don't have to make any new content, we don't really have to moderate it very much. We just have to pay the cost of the server and there it sits gathering more and more people.

We had 35,000 the first year, March to December 2000, and then subsequent to that it's racked up over 60,000. In 2001 we launched the German-language version, Online Caroline.de, and that got 15,000 in its first year and now had about 20,000. So overall there's about 80,000 registered users over three or four years. They're not huge numbers but they were never meant to be. I think we proved a point. We never said we were going to get millions. You can't put up a website and have everyone on the whole Internet come and see it. We all know that now. But in those days people didn't appreciate that and as we know there are whole kind of dot.com shops that put out business plans that said they were going to get millions of people on their site because there are millions of people online. We knew it was going to be a niche project and that what makes a good site work isn't going to be about quantity, it is going to be about quality of the relationship and the quality of the data.

Online community

What other techniques did you use to engage the visitors? For example, you also housed or facilitated a discussion forum for the project. Did you aim to build the notion that the collective audience was a community of users – friends of Caroline?

Freeserve were very keen to have a community site to go alongside it. We thought that people would spoil it for each other – they would tell each other things that would make it fall down like a pack of cards. But Freeserve were committed to the community. Initially to spark that off I thought it would be good if I targeted the most active members of the forum with extra emails that I'd written personally based on what I'd seen them doing from Caroline. The replies were made very personal so that they realised it couldn't be from a database, it had to be human. I thought this would be good and they'd take that back to the forum and go 'Look at what I've got', and stir things up. However, a proportion of the people I mailed replied to me saying, 'I'm disappointed, I was really happy with the idea that I was just playing with a computer simulation but now I think there's some dot.com geek at the other end of the line laughing at me so I don't want to play any more.' They liked the fact that they were experimenting with technology.

Production, responsibilities and costing

How large was your production team and how were the responsibilities divided between people?

Rob Bevan designed and programmed a lot of it, and he had a part-time assistant designer. We had a programmer who did the main capture and email personalisation engine and we licensed that off him with an initial fee and then renewed the licence each year. We had someone who was an executive producer and line producer. I did the scripting and producing.

In addition, for the production, there was a little bit of sound design. For the shoot we hired a two-man crew for the shoot: lighting and camera and sound. We had a cast of three paid actors – everyone else was voluntary. It adds up – so the number of people who got involved in the project at some point is between ten and twenty. Of course, the costs rack up and the programming was not slight. However, we viewed this as something we could reuse in future projects so it was also an investment to an extent.

With all these costs, was the project financially viable and did you have to make economic argument? You have mentioned audience loyalty and being able to get a consistent group of people to come back to a site over a period of time. Was that regarded in the financial justification?

Generally, the project cost over a hundred thousand pounds to make and then there was marketing and the hosting on top of that. You can assess it financially and say that for 35,000 people it has cost £150,000 so that it costs £5 per punter and that is expensive. But we were able to look at other ways of justifying the cost. Freeserve's business end was important because they were also able to look at that in different ways and see how they could get other returns that would make it look palatable. But that's the game: to say '£5 a punter – how am I going to get that back?' It's tough!

Narrative conventions

As a writer you have borrowed lots of different conventions for Caroline that facilitate the audience's loyalty. One is soap opera which is completely different from the way most other websites are constructed – a different way of having and building relation-ships with people. Most interactive media projects use instant response and feedback to capture people's interest. What you've done works differently. But, of course, there are also games that require regular commitment and repay your continued interest. Were these important influences on you?

Games were always an important influence. Rob and I always talk about ideas about games where you don't know the rules. Quite often when we're brainstorming or hang-ing out we'll try and play a game in our conversation or something where we don't know what the rules are. Card playing is great for the banter, the personalities around that and the stories that emerge. I always thought interactivity of that sort is quite interesting.

The second influence is that people really like talking about themselves. So if you can facilitate the mechanism where very quickly instead of being about 'Let me show you my website I've got something really terrific to say', you say, 'But what about you – what's going on in your life?' It's classic sort of affirmation that people do in conversations. The thought behind a lot of what Caroline's doing is, 'I'll tell you a little bit about me but really I want to hear about you'. You can't do that in television –

in any other medium that's really hard to do. It's much easier to simulate that in an interactive environment.

The final thing is also a limitation about technology. If you don't show people things literally – they'll make them up anyway in their own heads – they don't need you really. And if you just create two pegs A and B – they'll draw a line between them and they'll see a relationship between them. So you can second-guess that a bit, intimate it. And definitely with Caroline we found that – if you get an email in the morning but you're not going to see a video until the afternoon, you start thinking about it and your brain goes to work so the story is working away from the computer and away from the technology.

Scripting the project

You have described 'Online Caroline' as being scripted. There are many approaches to scripting and storyboarding websites. How did you got about it?

The most influence in my practice is the fact that I work with Rob, who is a designer and a programmer. We brainstorm things together then I go away and I write a script. But nothing comes without that discussion. Some thoughts might be about images or animation or programming tools or all kinds of stuff. But it always comes back to the idea that I go away and write a script. With Caroline we discussed it on a residency and in the evenings I went to my room and wrote the whole story – all twenty-four episodes – I just wrote the emails and the webcam scenes without any personalisation, just the story.

Do you think of this approach to writing as being more like writing a treatment for a film?

Absolutely. And then it became a kind of improvisation when we filmed because I didn't write dialogue for the actors, I just described the scene and what happened in it. We would try it out a few times and film it, then we'll block it a bit and then we'd go from there. So the actors brought a lot to it as well. After they'd filmed the video I went back over the emails and the site section – I spanned out the site sections based on what I'd seen of the actors, which was really important. For the Caroline emails I got the actress to read them as though they were just speaking so I could hear how that felt even though we didn't use the sound track.

How do you see an Internet project such as 'Online Caroline' in the context of a more traditional writing project?

The main difference is the implication of data and what it means to a narrative if you collect data from people. If you tell me something about yourself, how am I going to weave that back into the story? The second thing is that over the years of working with Rob I've got more sophisticated about the relationship between text and image. Increasingly, I'm not always that bothered about writing now, I spend a lot of time now just using a video camera and improvising stuff, speaking stuff and performing stuff and then stitching that together – then maybe writing a script based on that.

Do you see your ultimate output as being based around a text in spite of the way that you may go about putting the text together?

New media's no different to any other media business in that if you want to get some money out of people you have to have a script. If you don't have that artefact they've got nothing to put a price on and nothing to argue about, and those are two things that producers want to do. Hitchcock said once he wasn't that interested in scripts, he was interested in images and setting up storyboards but he wouldn't have raised any money if he didn't have a script. However, with a lot of new media projects the script doesn't appear in a form that is recognisable – it's the documentation at the end.

Production and management skills

Apart from writing what are the skills that you have needed to carry out the project?

I think it's quite telling that most people refer to me as a producer and not as a writer. I think that's a testimony to the idea that I've managed to acquire producer skills, which were required to get things together. A lot of that comes out of having worked in the commercial environment of No-Ho Digital where I had to manage clients like Microsoft and Orange. I think that really helped when it came to putting together more arts-based projects because I'm quite organised and I'm reasonably good at networking. I can find the right people with the right skills and put together a team. Another important skill is to be good at writing proposals, and creating treatments or documents that will excite people into thinking 'Yeah, I want to do this'. All those skills about thinking carefully about organisation and team building and project management are ones I've definitely acquired through working in multimedia.

On the writing side – whenever I write a script and send it over to Rob he always says, 'I like it but it would be better if it was short, funny and clever'. The key word in all that is short. So I've definitely learned compression in terms of writing text and saying things in less space. It also matters in terms of file sizes, word length, character length, dimension, whatever screen dimension, all those things. It is really critical for writers in this environment to be able to write to any format with very strict discipline. That's definitely an important skill.

Future developments

You are doing many things as a writer and you have developed another Internet project called 'Planet Jenna' with Rob Bevan that builds on some of Online Caroline's very successful aspects, such as an evolving narrative with a central character, but which also has an educational aspect in that it is partly designed to encourage girls to maintain an interest in science. Do you see yourself developing future projects with Rob that continue in this format?

We're still working with broadcasters, ISPs and public bodies on a number of character-led interactive drama projects, and it's amazing how much influence 'Online Caroline' has had on people's thinking in this area. Probably, the formats of the future will be more game-like than Rob and I have been used to – and the personalisation we developed for email will work its way into other areas. In particular, the ability to create personalised colour printouts using audience-generated words and pictures offers very rich potential for storytellers like us.

'Online Caroline' is at www.onlinecaroline.com

Part II

New media practice

10 Who are the new media practitioners?

···

I t is important to resist hard and fast distinctions between producers and consumers of new media. The interactive nature of the new medium requires a consideration that all users are, initially at least, new media practitioners. An instructive parallel can be made here with the historical development and use of photography. In photography there is a very large market supporting domestic, amateur and professional photographic practices. News, fashion, sports and reportage photographers, high street portrait photographers, wedding photographers, fine artists, camera club amateurs and snap-shooters all use photography and they all produce photographs. The products of all these different photographic practices are valued in different contexts and frames of reference. The same can be said for many other media practices, writing would be another good example, where many more people sustain the practice of writing than those whose writing is subsequently published, and far fewer still whose work is given marketing and media prominence.

The Internet is a new form of self-publishing and thousands upon thousands of people maintain personal websites in which they disclose, compose, exhibit, factualise and fictionalise histories, biographies and narratives. Such websites have to be constructed, designed, written, edited and regularly updated. Such activities fall well within a broad definition of a new media practitioner. How well or badly people make their websites is irrelevant to their existence within an unregulated global network of communication. Unlike print the Internet has no publishing house gatekeepers controlling what is considered worthy of publication. The absence of editorial control on the Internet is, of course, a much debated dimension of the new medium which, above all, raises the issue of the quality and provenance of information.

Global use of the Internet

···

Some idea of the scale of the new medium and its use can be glimpsed in current statistics. It is estimated that there are over half a billion users of the Internet globally, 680 million in a world population of 6.4 billion. The world population is predicted to rise to over nine billion by 2050, but the Internet user population is rising at a much faster rate. The worldwide number of Internet users was estimated to have reached one billion by 2005. Currently, the US has the greatest number of Internet users, with approximately

160 million, but the US is falling behind other countries in Internet users per capita. Internet usage is growing rapidly in China, which was expected to have surpassed Japan in late 2003.[1] The phenomenal growth of a new medium has happened in just over a decade; however, the distribution of Internet use is uneven between socio-economic groups within countries as well as between countries. The development of a 'digital divide' between those with knowledge and access to the new medium and those without has been recognised at an international level by researchers and government agencies. Not forgetting the uneven growth, the general world trend in the spread and use of computing and the Internet is uniformly upward. In Europe, Sweden has an Internet penetration rate of 60 per cent and mobile phone penetration rates of 70 per cent (Saines 2000: 8). The picture is decidedly different in 'developing' countries. For example, in Brazil only 11.1 million out of over 160 million are currently online. To counter the slow growth of users the Brazilian government plans to set up Internet terminals at post offices within every major city. Russia's lack of telecommunications infrastructure and stark economic prospects threaten to limit Internet growth, with an estimated 2.9 million adult users in a nation of roughly 122 million. Africa is the most information-poor continent, with the greatest divide between itself and North America. What this snapshot of the continued growth of online and wireless communication technologies indicates, above all, is the sheer global scale of development. No other communication medium in the history of communication media has grown so rapidly at such a scale.

The organisation of new media practice

Remaining with a wide definition of the new media practitioner as someone using computers for expressive and communicative purposes, encompasses the use of the computer at work and in the home. New media practice can involve using the computer to communicate, to access and organise information, to play interactive games, or simply to surf the net. Computer communication importantly crosses the world of work and leisure, or, as it is currently put, the work/life balance. At its largest definition, anyone who uses computers can be defined as a practitioner of some sort. The importance of this inclusive definition of new media practitioners as users relates to the organisation of the self-selecting structure of the various communities of users. Clearly, there is a distinction between professional and amateur practitioners of new media, but that distinction is not necessarily made along the conventional lines: the distinction between professional training and earned income on the one hand, and self-taught amateurs who engage in practice as a leisure pursuit on the other. Many lucrative e-businesses were originally the good ideas of amateurs and many successful websites have been produced by self-taught practitioners. The commercial opportunities presented by the Internet a decade ago, in what is aptly referred to as the 'Internet gold rush', were eagerly seized by many individuals with little or no formal training. However, a greater percentage of new e-commerce is developed along much more conventional business lines, requiring business plans, investment backers and specialist divisions of labour. Another way of putting this is to say that, in the same space of time as the growth of networked, online commerce, a new service industry has emerged to cater for its growing needs. It is an industry that is young enough to still be evolving new roles and forms of labour. It is, more accurately, not one unified industrial sector, just as all photography is not one kind of photography, but a series of separate, related sectors. As we discuss elsewhere, the convergence of media through technologies, distribution and ownership creates an exceptionally complex picture. The older organisation of media, with vertically organised companies, distinct analogue technologies and clearly defined work operations and skills, has given way to cross-media platforms and deregulation of media production. Since the deregulation of television in the 1980s there has been a widening of the base of media production, if not media ownership. Across the spectrum of ownership, media production makes great use of the freelance practitioner. One of the contributory factors that led to the break-up of the older forms of highly concentrated corporate media production in the print and newspaper industry was the introduction of new technologies. New media operates along the 'fault lines' between the old and new modes of production, in the sense that new media is highly present in large corporations, the BBC for example, as well as being a new, relatively low-cost, independent and accessible medium. It is the case that 'professional'-level editing and design software for image, sound and text on the PC is as available to the amateur as it is to the professional. While there is a burgeoning market for 'low-end' amateur digital cameras, 'professional'-level video and still cameras and digital audio recording are within the reach of the graduate student. Bedrooms and bed-sitting rooms are the new recording and editing studios of new media producers. It is possible for a budding film-maker to shoot and edit on low-end digital equipment and send it electronically to a Hollywood producer, just as it is possible for any practitioner to showcase work on their own website. This is not to say that high-end technology sectors in new media don't exist. In the entertainment industries, special effects and animation, for example, remain expensive, involving technically complex computing digital hardware and software. Large corporations and companies run big databases, with the need for system managers and engineers. The point that is being made here is that the new media sector is differentiated along the lines of scale of operation, more than it is along the lines of types of technology. The operational and organisational skills of new media practice are, in this sense, therefore, more generic than those of previous analogue media.

Much of the thinking that limits the idea of the new media practitioner to a narrow industry specialist is based upon the organisation of large-scale and mainstream media production. In the established media forms of newspaper or television production, for instance, there is a rigid division between production and consumption. Millions of people read newspapers, buy magazines, watch television, and a relatively few people, divided into specialist roles – editors, journalists, copywriters, compositors – actually make the products. This model of media production is, within media and cultural studies, understood as that of 'the few talking to the many' and was the model of broadcast media defined more broadly as 'mass media', a term which, in research and study, is now used with caution (Thompson 1999).

The online content and service sector

Another important way of looking at the organisation of the production of online new media is to look at the main types of content and commercial transactions that it organises. The most profitable areas of online content and transaction include travel, retail, recruitment, banking, health, dating, gaming, advertising, pornography and entertainment.[2] In the US, computer dating surpassed both business/investments and entertainment/lifestyles to become the largest paid content category in 2002 with US$302 million in revenues, up from US$72 million in 2001. Of course, there is nothing absolutely settled about the categories of online content and transaction and new areas of content are continually developing. While the current most profitable areas of online content simply reflect their offline equivalent, banking, car sales, travel and entertainment, there are also online content areas that have no direct offline commercial equivalence. Genealogy is an example of a rapidly expanding online content area based upon the popular cultural activity of researching family histories. For instance, www.google.com registers over 15 million results under genealogy. Friendsreunited. co.uk, the website dedicated to helping put old school friends in touch with each other, has been hugely popular and is an example of online content for which a paper-based agency had no previous success. Such examples as these serve to demonstrate the very fluid relationship that online content has to cultural patterns and interests, which are reshaped and extended through the new medium.

Travel and retail are, essentially, forms of shopping that built upon the previous form of home-based product retailing through catalogues and of course eBay can boast thousands of online transactions per day as anyone can sell anything to anyone.

New media advertising

Online advertising takes place on the web or through email. Advertising networks are the online equivalent of agencies selling dedicated advertising space, whether on TV networks, the press or public billboards. Advertising networks represent many websites in selling advertising, and provide a way for media buyers to co-ordinate advertising campaigns sites. Advertising networks vary in size and focus. Large advertising networks may require premium brands and millions of impressions per month. Small advertising networks may accept unbranded sites with thousands of impressions per month. There are broadly three types of online advertising, which are: website advertising, using banner and skyscraper formats (skyscraper ads now account for over 70 per cent of total website advertisements with the standard 468 × 60 pixel banner still the most popular); search engine optimisation, in which key words are embedded in the HTML script for websites in order to gain high ranking; and email advertising which includes directory enhancement posts to moderated discussion lists, newsgroups and forums. Marketers will use combinations of these formats in promoting products and services.

As the web expands to become a major means of reaching larger and more targeted audiences, a greater number of mainstream companies and brands are using the web for campaign advertising, which, in turn, increases the demand for more sophisticated graphic advertising, which has appeal and holds attention. Website advertising has, until relatively recently, been limited to a static graphic image text, rather like newspaper advertising in the early twentieth century. Website advertising has been limited by the need to have small files and high compression ratios in order to increase the speed of uploading. With the technical development of better compression, and, more radically, with the advent of broadband, website advertising is increasingly turning to the use of time-based, animated graphics, known as 'rich media formats'. Rich media formats are seen to enhance the consumer experience through greater sophistication and appeal. Standard graphic formats such as JPEGs and GIFs would not be considered rich media. Some popular formats commonly considered to be rich media include Macromedia Flash and ShockWave, along with various audio and video formats. Rich media formats are regularly being introduced and old formats become part of the mainstream or disappear altogether. What is noticeable in rich media is the underlying drive towards the kind of full motion and 'realistic' graphic animation associated with the sophistication of television advertising. With the greater convergence of broadcast television and online computer communication, it is not hard to predict that advertising will be pervasive and follow on-demand, customised programming.

Entertainment

Online audio-visual entertainment is a major area of Internet content and service provision financially and institutionally linked to existing television and film production and distribution. Here, the Internet can be conceptualised as a digital extension of existing analogue technological distribution systems, a new conduit through which existing media content is delivered. The websites of major media corporations, Time/Warner, CNN and BBC, for instance, will remain adjuncts to cinema and television as long as the Internet does not have the technical capability of carrying the analogue signal of full motion, real-time transmission. The development of broadband allows the delivery of content across the Internet that includes large files, such as video, audio and 3-D, which are the cornerstones of the coming high-speed revolution. Faster connections coupled with always-on access will improve the consumer multimedia experience. With the growth of broadband subscribers, currently around 20 million in the UK, traditional media companies are uncovering opportunities for growth and acquisition in these alternative content categories enabled by the high-speed Internet. The future business organisation of the delivery of online content in relationship to mainstream media formats remains unclear, but culturally we are experiencing the convergence of the domestic computer, the television and the telephone. The future of converged media delivery systems contains both the continued dominance of large media corporate providers of content as well as the potential for a highly deregulated market with a larger number of small media organisations producing networked content.

Video on demand

Sony Pictures, Universal Studios, Paramount Pictures, Metro-Goldwyn-Mayer and Warner Brothers currently provide a movies-on-demand service in the US that allows Internet users to download a limited range of popular films using a broadband connection. The service is known as MovieLink.[3] The compressed files average around 500 megabytes and are viewed using available PC media players. The movie files can be accessed an unlimited number of times over a 24-hour period, on payment of a one day 'rental fee', equivalent in pricing to video rental. All movie files are copy protected, self-delete on expiry of the 24-hour licence, and will not play if sent to another computer. As we have seen above with other online content service provision, MovieLink replicates an existing retail service, in this case video hire. The model of video on demand is a development from pay-as-you-go, satellite television and is very much the precursor of anything-on-demand, online media of the near future. The combination of unlimited access to online archival data, including all media content, and 'intelligent' software programs, will result in a 'digital butler',[4] a machine that knows what kind of media you like – films, music, books, newspapers, programmes and reviews – collects it and arranges your viewing schedule.

Games and gaming

We include the games player as a new media user/practitioner, although conventionally gamers would be described as consumers or hobbyists, rather than creative users. Gaming includes not only the 'shoot-'em-up' video games, but also a wide range of online and wireless group players who engage in long-term role playing games in virtual communities. The scale of gaming makes it an important content area and it is estimated that 145 million Americans play computer and video games, in which '69 per cent of high-frequency players are over 18, and 49 per cent are female'.[5] Interactive video games have rapidly become the largest segment of the entertainment industry, taking in US$6.3–8.8 billion in 1998, compared with US$5.2 billion in Hollywood box office receipts. Video games, which now can be played at home on a computer or a television set, account for 30 per cent of the toy market in America. With 181 million computer games sold in 1998, each home has, on average, two video games (Song and Anderson 2001). According to Nielsen-Netratings, the leading European markets for online gaming are Germany and France. However, in the UK, Europe's second largest online market, just 1.1 million people are gaming via the Internet.

Differentiating types of users/producers

The inclusive definition of the new media user/practitioner discussed so far, which includes the domestic user of the Internet and the routine information worker, could be taken to be confusing the line between professionals, who produce media content, and the audience, who consume the product. Surely, any meaningful definition of the new media practitioner should be limited to the scientists and engineers who conceive, design and build hardware, and the creative designers, editors and planners who produce content. So far, we have resisted this standard definition because it simply reproduces the already well-established organisation of media production and consumption, which new media both does and doesn't follow. We have already proposed that new media practice operates on a kind of fault line between established forms of production and new and different forms of production. We also go on to say that one of the defining features of the medium itself is that the division between author and audience is challenged by new media's interactive quality.

We can move the discussion forward by expressing the relationship of user/producers as a continuum, from the computer scientist, engineer and programmer, to the designer, writer, office worker, college student or school pupil, games player, net surfer and online shopper. At one end of the continuum, the computer scientist is involved in defining what lies 'behind the screen and code', while at the other end, the online shopper is decidedly in front of the screen using a highly prescriptive, coded piece of software. The shopper engages with the surface of the screen, through the graphical user interface (GUI), while the programmer engages with the 50 million-odd lines of code, each with approximately 60 characters, of the Windows Operating System. In between the shopper and the programmer, the designers, writers, photographers, musicians and artists engage somewhere above the code in using the tools of dedicated software to generate, manipulate and organise specific content.

Surface and depth

'On' the screen a graphical interface organises the user's access and control of data, while 'behind' the screen, the blueprint of the computer's memory and processing power lies in electrical impulses based upon mathematical formulas. Surface application and interior code represents a less obvious, but no less significant, digital divide than that

Box 10.1

END USER	⇨	SURFACE
Online shopper		
Net surfer		Invisibility of technology
Games player		
Student/pupil		
Information worker		
Journalists		
Writers		⇧
Photographers		CONTENT GENERATION
Film-makers		
Musicians		⇩
Artists		
Designer		
Programmer		
Engineer		Visibility of technology
Scientist		
PRODUCER	⇨	DEPTH

between those who have access to computers and those who don't. This second order of digital divide is between those who can only use the computer in the ways in which data have been pre-structured and organised and those who can define and achieve new communication purposes for data.

PowerPoint as software and culture

A local example of what is meant by a knowledge divide between a restricted and an open use can be illustrated by the example of Microsoft PowerPoint which was developed for the Microsoft Windows and Mac OS computer operating systems. Bob Gaskins and Dennis Austin worked together to create PowerPoint in a company called Forethought, which was purchased by Microsoft Corporation for US$14 million in 1987. Microsoft released PowerPoint 1.0 in 1987 for the Apple Macintosh and a year later developed a Windows and DOS version. PowerPoint was subsequently incorporated into the Microsoft Office suite of applications.[6]

PowerPoint is a software program, designed primarily as an audio-visual aide in the presentation of information, whether in a lecture, classroom, or corporate event. In this respect PowerPoint is the digital equivalent, or extension of, the flip-chart, whiteboard, slide-projector or overhead projector, which provides for the flexible combination of different forms of information, video, photographs, graphics, text and sound. Power-Point's interface uses the language of the photographic slide in such a way that information can be composed on individual slides using a stripped-down menu of textual and graphic tools and hyperlinks. Individual slides can be ordered into a slide-show using a further menu of timings and animated transitions for the slides and the elements within a slide. The resulting set of slides can then be put into projection mode for presentation purposes either on-screen or printed.

Upon opening a new file, PowerPoint offers the user a choice between a blank presentation and a set of pre-designed formats, based upon business models of planning and marketing. The pre-designed presentations have a graphic style background for each slide, incorporating colours and shapes, with simple hyper-linked cards, to navigate forwards, backward and home. The pre-designed presentations contain various graphic backgrounds, into which information, text, charts, photographs and video clips can be imported. PowerPoint has been organised, and conceptualised, as a sequencer of information. The pre-designed sheets and the menu of tools combine so that the user enters whatever they wish to present within the given structure of hierarchies and sequencing. We could say, then, that the structure of PowerPoint renders all information as the points, the point of course of its trademark title. Knowledge, discourse, pedagogy, communication and exchange in the PowerPoint world of presentation take the form of points, bullet points even, a staccato rendition in which argument and analysis is broken down into a hierarchy of nested points. The widespread availability of PowerPoint within the Microsoft Office Suite has led to its popular use in education and the workplace in North America and Europe. On the positive side, PowerPoint is a useful, simple to use organiser and aide in presentation and marks an improvement upon the whiteboard and overhead projector for a number of reasons. PowerPoint files can be incorporated into any digital electronic communication, such as email attachments or websites, and they share with all other digital files the ability for simultaneous transmission to unlimited receivers. PowerPoint allows for the combination of different information in digital form, so that photographic and moving images, together with sound files, graphics and text can all be displayed. Finally, PowerPoint creates limited animation and navigation which allows any given body of information and ideas to be conceptually controlled. On the negative side, PowerPoint can and often does structure material in a hierarchical and linear cognitive mode, the templates and tools create a 'built-in predisposition' towards any given information, which 'over-determines' the content of any use. The use of titles, captions, clipart inserts, bullet points, charts, logos, combine with the animations and transitions to lock any given content or subject into a pre-set mould of communication. At its simplest, the criticism is that the world of complex and creative thought is reduced to a set of bullet points. Critics of PowerPoint have pointed out that it functions to reassure the presenter, rather than enlighten an audience, that the outliner causes ideas to be arranged in a deep hierarchy which, in turn, reinforces an audience's linear progression through that hierarchy. Tufte (2003) sums up the typical use of PowerPoint thus: 'At a minimum, a presentation format should do no harm. Yet the PowerPoint style routinely disrupts, dominates, and trivialises content. Thus PowerPoint presentations too often resemble a school play – very loud, very slow, and very simple.' While Tufte is right that many of us have sat through crude and simplistic PowerPoint presentations, we have to take care not to see this as exclusively determined by the technology and software. PowerPoint is prefigured in the ways described above, but the quality of a presentation using PowerPoint is also dependent on the context in which it is used and upon the user's understanding of why and how they are using it. Norman responded to Tutfe's critique in precisely this way:

> PowerPoint is not the problem. The problem is bad talks, and in part, this comes about because of so many pointless meetings, where people with – or without – a point to make – have to give pointless talks. The problem is that it is difficult work to give a good talk, and to do so, the presenter has to have learned how to give talks,

has to have practiced, and has to have had good feedback about the quality of the talks – the better to improve them.[7]

The general point is, of course, that any software program, Photoshop would be another example, can be used creatively or routinely. The built-in predispositions of the emergent properties and behaviours of software programs that are structured through the interface menus and tools need to be critically and purposefully understood, rather than simply employed because they are there. The uncritical and routine operation of software does represent one side of a divide, just as the design of software can reinforce limiting epistemologies and paradigms of thought and action.

The user whose knowledge is bounded by and within 'levels' will be limited to their own sphere of operation. In fact, we could usefully label such positions on our continuum as that of the operational. The sphere of the operational holds for all the positions on the continuum, for the scientist just as much as the net surfer. We are not saying that the scientist with the 'deep' code of the machine is in the privileged position of overview. The scientist, or engineer or programmer will not necessarily have access to the know-how of software applications, or that of the languages of hypermediated communication, or, indeed, the reflexes and responses of a gamer twitching in front of the screen.

Previous historical separations of the use of technology

Slater (1999) explores the historical separation between technology and the user in relationship to Kodak and popular snapshot photography. He points out that Kodak's successful marketing, from 1888 onwards, depended on building two features into photographic technology: simplicity and reliability. 'You press the button and we do the rest', Kodak's solution to the early marketing of photography, remains essentially the basis of contemporary popular photography. Kodak based its strategy on divorcing the camera operator from the process of photography, which while making the practice transparent, made the actual process of image manipulation opaque. In making it easy for anyone to pick up and use a camera, Kodak had made the process of photography invisible. As Slater argues, the snapshot camera requires no thought to operate and, therefore, it can be taken for granted and conventionally inserted into everyday social uses. Put another way there is nothing radical or insightful about snapshot photography. The separation of operation from process is the fundamental basis for the current digital divide at all levels. For Slater, discussing photography, it was a partial explanation as to why such a powerful communicative tool, put within the affordable reaches of the European working classes from at least the 1920s, had produced only the privatised, ritual family snapshot. Clearly, there are parallels in the argument about what the networked PC is used for now.

Strategies for dissolving the digital divide

Strategies for crossing the various levels of the digital divide are central to the creative development of new media practice. Without such strategies and the work and struggle that goes with them, we may well face the vision of the digital divide of the future presented by Castells (2001) in his account of the networked society. This is a world that is doubly divided, first into the information rich and the information poor and, second, into users who will only have access to the limited commands of a highly structured market of consumption, and those that have the knowledge to both access and author the full resources and assets of the networked society. Such a divide, with its hierarchical structures of power and control, is not unfamiliar to us when we consider the current organisation of global television, in which a small number of large corporations control the production and distribution of programming for a large (and traditionally passive) audience. There are several arguments wrapped up in the idea of the digital divide, which we discuss in Part II, but it is important, here, when we are discussing the new media practitioner, to grasp that new media has the potential to radically alter the traditional one-way model of transmission and reception. One of the unlooked-for outcomes of the advent of digital code and convergent communication technologies is that they have changed the relationship between producers and consumers by substituting the idea of the enlightened user/author for both of those previously separate positions. Having said this, a large part of the world of commercial new media practice(s) is a world of conventional divisions of labour, most of which have been and are being translated from divisions of tasks performed in existing media industries.

There are areas of new media practice, many of which form the basis of our own examples, where the pressures that drive the digital divide are not so immediate and in which there are various imperatives to cross or expose 'levels'. In such practices as new media art or in research projects the emphasis is to explore both the technology and its use, to be more lateral in thinking and less concerned with immediate outcome. Many new media artists adopt strategies of transgression when working with proprietary software in order to question the ways in which the user has already been programmed to respond, or to confront the ways in which hierarchies of information are thought to be organised.

Private hardware and global manufacturing

The digital divide is one way of expressing a set of experiences and observations that arise from the global organisation of the computer industry and the commercial and institutional contexts in which computer-mediated communication (CMC) is deployed. There are conflicting and opposing interests at work between the economic and the cultural, which the concept of new media can, if we are not vigilant, ignore. At its simplest the argument follows a familiar, yet still relevant, line of analysis, which has been advanced about other powerful communication forms, television for instance (Williams 1974). The argument is looked at in more detail in Part III, but suffice it to say here that the core conflict within the production of media lies within the organisation of media for maximum economic profitability, against the organisation of media for creative communication. The computer industry, like that of Kodak in the case of photography, is organised primarily to drive up its profits by a continual expansion and renewal of its products – selling faster, smaller and more powerful computers to more and more people is a goal in itself. The potential uses of the computer are not as important to the marketing of the technology as the total sale of computers. But as the average lifecycle of a computer decreases, so the number of computers being discarded grows each year. By 2005, the average life-span of a computer will be just two years. An unplanned by-product of this built-in obsolescence is that electronic waste is being recycled in third-world countries where poor regulations threaten the environment and people's health because toxins, lead and mercury will contaminate local water and soil. The US is shipping the majority of its electronic waste to India, Pakistan and China (Markoff 2002: C1). The same phenomenon of mountains of obsolete hardware can be observed with the mobile phone, where handset upgrades are currently running at less than eighteen months. There is a veritable mountain of redundant handsets lying around in millions of desks and drawers across the world. There is nothing intrinsically wrong with a system of technology that creates privately consumed hardware; everyone should and could have mobile phones and laptops with access to WAP. Phones and laptops are objects of practical utility, not items of luxury and status, and their production could be organised along the lines of environmentally safe, sustainable and renewable resources and processes. This is something to aim at, as with all consumer products, but it is far from current practice. The organisation of technological production along the lines of maximising profit reproduces deep divides between people and cultures and it does this within the production of technologies that offer the promise of universal access to the wealth of human knowledge and global communication. This is a stark contradiction which stalks the new media world and tempers the most ardent accounts of the eman-cipatory potential of the phenomenal growth in the use of CMC globally and, especially in the richest countries, is in large part due to making computer hardware affordable to a wider economic group. To produce computers cheaply has meant siting the manufac-turing operation in countries where labour is cheap and stable.

As with cameras and television sets, earlier, new media technologies represent powerful communication tools and systems, which are being organised along the lines of the consumption of products for known and established purposes. Most of the consumption of hardware is organised and marketed around increasing the technical quality of delivery and access to existing entertainment content.

Manovich (2001) touches upon the same problematic of the digital divide in related terms when he advocates the use of the term 'new media object', rather than product, artwork or interactive media, to denote what is made by the new media practitioner. For Manovich, the overall importance of referring to a website or game or digital still as an object is that it relates to experimental models in science and art. In computer science and the computer industry, 'object' is already a standard term, as in the modular nature of object-orientated programming language. 'Object' also has connotations with the Russian Constructivists, who wanted to emphasise the role of design in industrialised mass production, and it invokes the idea of the laboratory experiments practised by the European avant-garde in the 1920s. Manovich wants to hold the new media practitioner to the task of experimentation at a point where he sees the media has yet to develop. In fact, he observes that 'few artists using new media are willing to undertake system-atic, laboratory-like research into its elements and its basic compositional, expressive, and generative strategies'. He goes on to say:

> Today, those few who are able to resist the immediate temptation to create an inter-active CD-ROM, or make a feature-length 'digital film' and instead focus on determining the new media equivalent of a shot, sentence, word or even letter, are rewarded with amazing findings.

> (Manovich 2001: 14–15)

This is a call for critical reflection upon the technology and its software by means of slowing the process down in order to look at each constitutive element of how meaning is formed.

Another strategy aimed at the same problem of over-prescribed programmed choices is identified by Lisa Blackman in the work of a number of artists using interactive soft-ware. Blackman points out, first of all, the notion that the interactivity of proprietary software, while promising 'free choice' or new freedoms to the user, is in fact highly prescribed. One of the principal strategies employed by many of the artists in the exhibition was to disturb the choice offered to the user. The user's expectations were deliberately played around with by introducing into the electronic artwork 'bugs' and 'malfunctions'. In this way, the works not only offer comments upon mainstream views of interactivity, but also attempt to force the user to reflect upon their own preconceived expectations and desires within virtual space (Blackman 1998: 136).

11 CASE STUDY
Commercial web development: Joe Lister

....

Joe Lister is a web developer and works in industry for Internet development companies and for the marketing divisions of large media companies.

Joe works primarily in situations where web development is divided between two areas. On the 'server side', the developers create server-based technology that creates the content to define the workings of the website. On the 'client side', the page content is dynamically created from a database generating content according to the user's request. As a 'client side' developer, Joe is responsible for defining the layout and the visual elements that the user sees on the website.

Joe's work demonstrates how broadly this sort of programming is used and how web-based technology defines and influences a lot of the ways that we are confronted by new media, not only on the Internet.

In this interview Joe discusses the career path he took as a young media arts graduate with a commitment to working with digital technologies. He describes how his skills are used within larger groups and how he operates within the often volatile job market both as a freelancer and as an employee of large companies. He also discusses his approach to specialising in different software packages, in particular Flash and Director, and why specialisms can be an asset to a new media designer.

Developing interactive signage and displays

Can you describe what you are working on at the moment?

At the moment I'm working on something that's not really a web project. I'm working on the system that will control the information shown on screens in mobile phone stores. It will enable them to have big neon interactive displays in the windows that show animations, images and text, as opposed to hanging printed posters in the window. I'm creating a system that allows the shop managers to create the play-lists. This will let them either input texts they type themselves or use pre-created animations that might be created by the designers in an agency. By creating a play-list they decide what will be shown in their shop window throughout the day.

How do you go about developing this sort of programme? Are there particular challenges that you are facing?

I'm using Director to do this. This sort of approach has become the standard way of operating so there are a lot of programs that have play-lists within them, MP3 players for example. What I am creating works in much the same way as they work but the content is custom created. It's a bit different to web design because you are working to a pre-defined output format. The play-lists are managed on a PC but the actual display is a window two metres by four metres with very low resolution, sixteen pixels per metre, whereas normally a computer screen is seventy-two pixels per inch or higher. So we are coming across a lot of problems with getting the text to be clear and to move smoothly, and to adapt huge signs. These are things that don't occur with a website. But though it's a different way of presenting the content, the skills and the basic technologies in creating it are the same.

Background and career path

This sort of work appears to be typical of the new media industry but it is also not something that people are specifically trained to do. What is the career path through which you came to be working in this way and how does it relate to your training?

I can't say that I ever knew that this kind of work existed, but the skills and sensibilities are parallel with what I did at college on some level, even with tape and slide, and the different sorts of work I have done since then.

When I was growing up I was always interested in art and photography but I was also interested in computers and I tried to learn basic programming language when I was a kid. And I liked messing around, but at that time there were less tools to help you programme and less programming languages so I never quite made the leap to be a real computer geek.

After finishing school I thought I might do something that combined being creative and working with computers. I did a photography and multimedia course, but also did all the computing modules I could find and specialised in that.

How much has the theory you learned on your course related to what you have been doing professionally?

The theory on my course was mostly related to understanding how an image is constructed. I always thought it was interesting but wondered how I was going to use this in later life. But later, when I was working in advertising-related web work and I was dealing with briefs coming from advertising companies, I realised that understanding the ways that a message is constructed within an image was quite applicable. Also, within an advertising company the ability to talk about visual ideas is very useful, whether it is solidly based on theory or not.

Developing job skills for the marketplace

How did you translate your educational skills to the workplace? Did you require a lot of further 'on-the-job' training and skills development?

It was very tough coming out of university with no previous commercial experience, because you are only as good as your portfolio so without one it is difficult to convince anyone to give you a break. I think that people who do a placement in industry when they are studying have an important leg-up, especially if they have more experience of working on a team. I was trying to do everything myself and consequently I only had mediocre across the board skills instead of concentrating on one thing like design or programming. But then again that has led me to having the hybrid skills I have now.

In my first job there were some very experienced people, which was very useful because I learned a lot from the others around me. I learned also that the way to be in a good position was to become expert at a software package because that is indispensable. I started building a CD-ROM on my own initiative and when the company realised that I was able to do things on my own they gave me more responsibility.

This was at a time when the web was really taking off and I moved to an agency and worked in the digital marketing department, making banner ads and very small micro sites. It was a fast time for business because all big companies were keen to get websites but weren't sure what to do with them. Marketing was one area which was always needed. Since then I've worked for different companies; sometimes I've been working as a freelancer. I've always known that if you stay still and your skills atrophy you can't get ahead in the industry.

Working in teams

Most of your work has been as part of a team. Does the structure of team work affect the way that you take on new skills and find a role for yourself in the industry?

I've always worked in large companies, or medium to large web design or multimedia companies and it is always team based. As the technology has become more and more complicated it has become almost impossible for one person to make a website all on their own. You need lots of different and complementary skillsets.

Hybrid skills and expertise

Many people talk about themselves as having hybrid skills. Is this the way that you think about your skillset and how you operate? Does it mean that you can find a particular niche?

I used to have a job title of Creative Technologist, which sounds like a title just pulled out of thin air, but it describes that I was midway between a technology department and a design department. People with hybrid skills can be very sought after. Some designers gain technical skills and there is no reason why a designer, if they have the right technical skills, can't learn programming. I have very good programming skills in particular areas.

It's a niche that sometimes seems like it's going to disappear but it never quite has. Straight out of university I found it very difficult to get a job because people couldn't place me, they couldn't put me into either camp, and thought I was a jack of all trades. At the time I didn't have a deep knowledge of the technology but as I've gained deeper knowledge and software skills it's become a more saleable way to be.

When you talk about deeper knowledge how would you describe those kinds of levels in terms of new media?

With programming there are lots of different ways you can programme a given effect and then there are lots of things that have come around in the last few years –

object-orientated programming is, of course, the one that everyone talks about. But ultimately it's to do with the complexity of the problems you can solve. I've never had formal programming training and there are gaps in my knowledge of terminology but I've gained a lot of knowledge because I've read lots of web programming books and worked with clever people.

Programming and knowledge of systems

Much of what you do now is programming knowledge related to software, but do you have to go deeper than that in terms of working with the computer operating system?

Not in the web business; you are totally insulated from that, at least for websites. If you are a client side developer, whatever you create must run inside a web browser and the web browser, for security reasons, isolates you from the operating system. With HTML different browsers would run differently on different systems and that was always the bane of the HTML programmer. What marked out a good HTML programmer was their ability to make a web page look the same across Mac or PC and across different browsers. I felt that this was just a horrendously boring thing to learn because it is the sort of knowledge that is made of little rules, like how to get an image to move this way or that way. I preferred working with programs like Flash, which is another layer on top of a browser and, in principle, it runs the same on any platform. Within Flash there is a lot of depth to which you can programme and it employs a degree of logic and maths that I find interesting.

Do you approach the different pieces of software that you work with as having different paradigms?

They have interface bits that are similar. The overall paradigm is the timeline, with various bits of code that can work with the timeline, stop it or pause it. But on a deeper level, dealing with the way you place things on the stage and manipulate them, they are very different. For example, Flash has a nesting structure that Director doesn't. I started learning Director and worked with it for ten years before I started with Flash. And now that I know Flash, Director seems a very limited environment to me.

Planning and delivering a professional project

Obviously it is possible to describe the sort of work you do in terms of the technology and the technical skills requirements but it is also a creative field. How do you go about approaching a brief or proposal for a piece of work? To what degree does your way of working influence the way that you can interpret that?

There are two sides to this. First, I have to consider whether or not the software is up to the task. Usually you get an idea of how many pixels you are going to be moving about, how much graphics, how much sound, how many elements moving separately. I have to judge what the software is capable of doing mathematically within the limits of the computing power. So that's one side to look at and the other is asking 'How can I do this?', which is imagining how will you get the motion that someone is asking for to actually happen. This may come down to nesting objects within objects and having skeletons of interlinking objects. That takes a certain type of imagination – it's kind of intuitive. I've always been very good at working out how a mechanical object might work. You try and put together in your head the linkages and the code. You have to understand all the different possibilities and to be able to think about different timelines and how they are connected to nested space. What you are creating is a series of nested worlds, and you can go deeper and deeper but you always take into account what is going on higher up.

A lot of what I do is about creating movement through code. It might be about the way in which I bring things onto the screen or it might be the way that planets spin around. Quite often the design calls for a beginning state and an end state, and I'm the guy that makes things bounce around or go between these points. I really enjoy shaping the nature and quality of that movement – making it smooth or bouncy. I've always enjoyed working on the way that the visual elements will respond to the mouse.

When you are defining the visual elements what are the influences that you are drawing on?

I'm not sure where I got my visual language and my aesthetics from – maybe from computer games or maybe from films. What I do is not traditional animation in terms of bounce and stretch or anticipation and weightings. That's not something I'm trained in. But certainly I'm concentrating on the visual quality, especially in the way that it moves.

Lately I've been making interactive animations with dynamically created motion. That takes animation that bit further. It's no longer just putting a bit of whiz onto an interface, the interface is what it's all about. So, the way you are playing with an object, be it a spinning moon or a yo-yo, is a large part of the experience of using those interactive pieces. In a sense the small things that I was originally making to put into sites have now become the larger things that I am concentrating on.

Does this sort of work depend heavily upon understanding the subtleties of user interactivity?

Not as much as you would think. With most of the sites I am talking about, maybe you have two to five seconds to get someone's attention and the user doesn't want to work too hard. After a while they get used to what is happening on screen and how they can work with an interactive piece, but it is very hard to judge how someone will respond. With regular websites you can be more flexible, and often online animations are just supposed to be fun.

Problem solving and furthering knowledge

How do you see your future in a developing market? How do you think your skills will change and grow in response to this?

Generally, people I work with believe that this industry will just become another part of the larger media industry. In the companies I work for, my job is usually within the marketing department and we are paid by the client to promote a product or a brand. It is accepted that digital media will just become just another part of the marketing manager's set of tools.

In a way, it is still easy to learn most of the technologies required. There are actually very few proprietary technologies, unlike other industries, because once it is on the web generally you can hack it, look at it and work out how it was done. So no one keeps a leading edge for very long. Usually if you know the basic technology you can work out how a funky thing has been made. Also there is still a very good tradition amongst designer and programmers of supporting each other. If you've got a problem with Flash or Director there are lots of newsgroups where you can put up a question. You will get a hundred of the best minds on the planet who are doing that kind of work who might read it and will give answers. And it's all done for free. That's how I got really good with Director. That way you get to see every potential pitfall you can have and every possible solution. So when I see a problem that I once had being described by someone, I post my solution to help them out. I doubt if you get that in the aerospace industry or others like that. That's a remnant of the original philosophy of web freedom and those ideas are still important.

12 Programming for design: Rob Saunders

....

Rob Saunders is a programmer and works as a freelance consultant in the media industry with a range of clients. He is also employed on non-commercial projects by people from other areas such as mathematicians, scientists and artists.

With a background in computer science, Rob is a specialist who has considerable expertise in the programming that goes into artificial intelligence and artificial life systems. The work he does often includes developing highly complex programs that use this level of programming knowledge to generate intelligent artworks and complex design systems. In particular, this leads Rob to work as a consultant with design firms where his programming skills contribute to a project alongside the expertise of other new media practitioners and design specialists to create innovative web-based projects. Programming with the sophistication and the depth that he is able to operate at can enable a new form of creativity and visual outcome.

In this interview, Rob discusses how he collaborates with other members of a creative team and develops a project. He also addresses how, as a specialist working with programming and data management at a deep level, he is at a different level from that of his partners and how he manages his contribution to a larger project without allowing what he does to dominate the design or creative concepts.

Background
....

As a programmer, you are closely involved in creative practices. Did this come out of your background and education? What was the pathway through which you got involved in this particular approach to new technologies?

I guess I've always been involved in new technologies. When I was twelve, my parents bought me my first computer; it was a gorgeous little machine called an Oric-1 with a massive 16 k of RAM. Unfortunately, hardly anyone else ever bought one, so in order to play games I had to learn how to program them myself. Pretty soon I found that programming was more fun than playing games.

At school I was always good at science, maths and art; it was obvious that I was going to have to make a choice between studying art or science at university. It was around this time that I decided that what I really wanted to do after university was to develop computational tools for creative people. I had experimented with using my computer, an Atari ST, in my artworks for A-level, and was excited by the creative use of computers by people like John Lasseter who went on to set up Pixar.

Moving on to higher education, I chose to study Artificial Intelligence at Edinburgh University which I saw as the most exciting way for me to continue studying computers. While at Edinburgh I became fascinated by the work of William Latham and Stephen Todd at IBM, using computers to interactively evolve 'virtual sculptures'. After finishing my degree, I decided that I wanted to continue studying evolutionary art and design systems to a doctoral level. Eventually, I became fascinated with the nature of exploration in design and this led me to develop a computational model of curiosity to help me investigate curiosity as a motivating force behind the exploration of design possibilities. The study of curiosity in art and design remains the main topic of my personal research.

What are the areas that you are now particularly interested in working in and that you think have potential for the junction of creativity and high-level programming that you are involved in?

I plan to continue working with artists and designers and hopefully expand to include collaborations with musicians. I'm also very keen to start exploring ways to create intelligent design tools for people who don't think of themselves as designers, e.g. hobbyists.

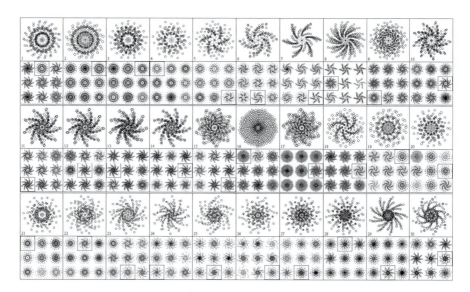

Figure 12.1   Rob Saunders, illustration of the way a curious design agent autonomously explores a space of possible designs (2001)

'A curious design agent was given a simple design tool to allow it to explore the space of possible designs. From top-left to bottom-right the illustration shows a short sequence of the designs that the agent produced. An important thing to note about a sequence produced this way is that the agent moves the exploration process forward by selecting similar-yet-different designs from those that it has seen before. This novelty-seeking behaviour is similar to that observed in human designers as they explore design possibilities during the initial phases of design' (Rob Saunders).

Personally, I continue to research motivations for the creative process including curiosity. I continue to build computational models of curious design systems exploring various design domains.

Collaborations

When you are working on a professional project, what is the basis of the relationship that you have with your client? Has the company usually defined the nature of the project and recognised that they require a level of programming and particular specialism to achieve it, or are they more likely to recognise that you can provide an extra dimension to a project but leave what it might result in up to you?

In general, I'm brought into a project when a team has a good idea of what they want but no idea how to do it. Typically, this means that I'm provided with a brief that lacks a lot of detail and the first thing I have to do is work out what can be achieved in the time available and then start to produce technical demonstrations.

The designers I work with are also skilled programmers, so when they need me to get involved it is because they need something beyond simple computer programming. Typically this will mean that the project requires the development of an intelligent system.

Is there a typical relationship and delineation of skills or is every job or workplace situation different?

I have found that each job is different. In general, I like to delineate my job so that I do not unduly influence artistic or design decisions, but sometimes that isn't possible. Sometimes, there is a natural synergy between the software I develop and the artefacts that are produced, but sometimes the influence that the software I produce has on the creative process is accidental, at least it is so on my part.

Defining 'intelligence'

Terms like 'intelligent system', 'intelligent agents' and 'artificial intelligence' are used broadly and variously in different parts of the media industries, the artistic and research communities, not to mention computer science, where the meanings may be very specific. How are they understood in the professional contexts you work in, such as when you talk about an 'intelligent graphic design system'?

The phrase 'intelligent system' is just shorthand for a system that uses artificial intelligence technology. It is a convenient shorthand for people who work in this field although it must be noted that the term should not be taken too seriously, very few intelligent systems are really intelligent. This is one of the problems that the artificial intelligence community has in general, by choosing such an evocative name the field doomed itself to failure by virtue of people's expectations of what 'intelligent' means.

Intelligent agents are software agents that use artificial intelligence technology. Agents are pieces of software that have some autonomy, in contrast to applications and objects that always do as they are commanded to. I simply use the term 'intelligent graphic design system' to indicate that a system uses artificial intelligence technology to accomplish graphic design tasks.

Using technical demonstration models and prototypes

Projects that operate at the level that you are describing often require the production of a technical demonstration model or a prototype, whereas less complex new media projects developed in the same context, such as product branding, may just have in-house testing before being released. How would you describe the need for a technical demonstration and a prototype and what would you describe as the difference between them?

From my perspective they take the same form but serve different purposes. A technical demonstration shows whether something is technically possible or not. An example could be devising a program for a network layout problem, which might show that a crucial problem could be solved. Another example would be when working with artists I might choose to present a demo that illustrates the problem of something fundamental to the system, in which case it might not try to solve any problems, it simply demonstrates a problem.

One of the reasons that I find technical demonstrations to be useful is that they allow me to show the limits of what is possible in a positive way. I find this to be particularly important because it is often difficult for people who want to use artificial intelligence to separate fact from fiction about what is possible.

In contrast, a prototype is something that attempts to be a partial solution. For example, sometimes I work with artists who are working on projects that use quite rich and complicated data, and my goal is to create a visual model. I might first ask for a specification and from this I would create a first version of the visualisation.

However, my experience working on several projects with artists has made me wary of the disadvantages of developing prototypes, as they can have the unintended effect of setting in stone arbitrary design decisions that I have made whilst programming. Consequently, I try to limit how much effort I put into the look of prototypes so that collaborators don't get too hooked on a particular visual style.

Visualising data and facilitating designs

Visualising data is obviously very important in your field and for many new media practitioners, including artists, the challenge is to find ways to make information that is otherwise to complex to handle, comprehensible and manageable. When you are brought into a collaboration to work in this area how do you go about negotiating what can and can't be achieved in terms of the visual output?

In some cases, I have been contracted to solve a geometric problem, such as in the case of a project to develop software to intelligently lay out complex network diagrams. In cases like these, it is natural that the software I write has a significant impact on the look and feel of the user interface. Ideally, I prefer to create systems that can be easily customised through data files. By using a data-driven approach to the development of creative support software, many artistic and design decisions can be changed without the need for additional involvement on my part.

This was the approach I was recently able to take with the development of an intelligent graphics design system, where I provided a number of different ways that the performance of the system could be changed by editing simple data files. In this case, my client was a small start-up company that saw an opportunity for bringing a new graphical tool to an industry that has to deal with complex data about large networks on a daily basis. Their first product required the founders of the company to produce complex graphics by hand that were then used through a simple user interface.

When the decision was made to produce the second version of their product, the client decided to approach a design firm about redesigning the interface and explore the possibility of generating the graphics automatically. The client brought in a design firm, who were able to determine the initial requirements for the new user interface but they did not know how to specify the intelligent graphic design system.

At this point I was set the challenge of developing an intelligent system that could lay out the complex data in a graphical form. At first this was just an informal challenge set by the lead designer, who is a good friend of mine. Over a couple of free days, I was able to come up with a proof-of-concept that made it clear that the problem could be solved to everyone's satisfaction.

I was then contracted to develop a more complete solution that has been shipped with the second version of the system. Although the original proof-of-concept only took a couple of days to develop, the production version took almost nine months of working one-to-two days a week to complete. The result has been a great success and has helped the company to continue to grow its market.

I am currently working on the second generation of the intelligent design system that will be integrated in the next version of the system, due to be shipped in the second half of this year. Instead of being contracted, however, I have negotiated a share in the company in return for my contribution to the business.

Working with data files

When you are describing 'data files' do you find that different people have a different understanding of what 'data' is even though all interaction with software is based on the management of data? For many practitioners, the dominant metaphor for the way that we work with data is the database, in other words that data is packaged in a modular way so that it can easily be amended, sorted and searched. The experience for most users is one of top-down management of the data using sub-sets or fields and the complexity of data at the bottom level is rarely engaged with. Does this metaphor translate into the programming work that you do?

In general, this understanding of what a program does in terms of processing data is correct, however, not all data is of the same type.

The distinction between different types of data files can be illustrated by considering the difference between a Word template and a Word document. Essentially these are very similar types of data files (almost identical in fact), but a Word template can change how the program works when editing another data file, i.e. a Word document.

So when someone working in my context talks about controlling the behaviour of a program through data files we are talking about data files that fundamentally change what a program is able to do, rather than simply changing the 'raw material' that the program works with. In the case of one project where I created intelligent design agents to generate company logos, I had designers create files that specified the basic shapes, filters and operators that the agents were able to use. Consequently, these data files defined the space of possible logos that the agents were able to create.

The distinction between program and data files can be further blurred when one looks at things like macros commonly used in templates, etc. These are small programs that are written in a language designed to be easier to use than the one used to write the main application so that 'casual programmers' can make more significant changes to the behaviour of a program. Many applications now support some form of embedded programming language.

When you are working on highly complex projects do you find that your partners also need to be very experienced or adept at this way of working to collaborate effectively? Do they need to have a very good sense of what the program could achieve at its deeper levels through the management of data files?

No, this is not necessary. It is often possible to develop computational systems in such a way that a significant amount of the system's behaviour can be controlled through the use of data files without the need for a detailed understanding of the program's inner workings.

Many systems that require collaboration between programmers, artists and designers are developed this way. Good examples can be found in the development of video games. Modern video games often take years to develop and require dozens of people with different backgrounds and skills, so a data-driven approach has become the standard way that such systems are developed.

Rob Saunders' website is www.robsaunders.net

13 Network management: Tim Olden

....

Tim Olden is a network manager. He works within the department of Interaction Design at the Royal College of Art in London, which is one of the most prestigious institutions of higher education in the UK specialising in the arts. Tim also has a background as an artist and develops his own creative work, in particular audio projects.

Being part of a department that includes students, researchers and teachers, Tim is required to oversee the running of the Interaction Design Studio. Key duties are to set systems and standards to ensure that all the resources, hardware and software are kept to the highest standard and can be used appropriately by staff and students alike. He is also responsible for overseeing all the web work that the studio does, maintaining the server and ensuring that all data for the web, and elsewhere, are backed up and maintained. The students at the college are trained on a Master's Degree programme and the work that they create for exhibition often requires specialist support that he makes sure is available. The studios also have an important research component investigating new areas of interaction design, and his job also includes working with researchers to make sure that they have the technical facilities that they require.

In this interview, Tim not only discusses what is needed for him to operate in his position, but also considers how students and professionals now approach working with software in the context of very specialised commercial software applications. He also addresses how people can best learn to problem solve and to negotiate with collaborators.

Necessary skills and expertise for network management

....

Tim, what do you think are the skills you need to work as a network manager? Do you need to have a good grasp of all the software to anticipate all the general software requirements of the students?

The skills that are needed are basically knowledge of software and how it works. These days the critical thing is not so much knowing about software in great depth but about knowing what the software is capable of, so you can point a student in the right direction. You can say it is more about understanding what students and staff require and therefore you have to be able to translate their ideas into practical terms.

Often, people working in similar positions to you talk about the skills of project manage-ment and interpersonal skills as much as they talk about their technical knowledge and software skills. Do you think that in some way this is because they have to mediate between the technological provision and the social environment of the workplace?

The most valuable skills of all are actually not technical, they are about social inter-action: to be very calm and tolerant because people get quite frustrated when they can't get their ideas across. At the end of the day, I think software is just software. All you need to do it is to read a manual and learning it does not actually involve much skill. What matters is obviously how you apply that piece of software.

Keeping up with new areas of knowledge and updating skills

Continuing on that thread how do you contain or develop your knowledge? If you have to be responsive to innovations of systems and software what kind of things are you on the look out for?

This is difficult, because it's very hard for one person to keep up with all the new soft-ware needs, so I choose which bits of software or new technology to get involved with. I try to base my judgement on what I think will be the long-term effect of each piece of new technology. It is important to keep abreast with what is current and how that affects how people think. At the moment there is a lot of interest in programming phones in Java and this is something that I will be looking at because obviously mobile technology is going to increasingly be important.

I train myself mostly, as it is very difficult to get training that works at the level that I am interested in. Also, it is very difficult to find a program that is designed for people who use computers in the way that people in the arts do. I find that in the arts, people have got a huge range of acquired knowledge but it doesn't always exactly overlap, and that the way most training is planned is for people with more predictable sets of knowledge.

Synergy between creative projects and professional duties

Turning to your background and your interests, how much has your interest in music, and your own artistic practice, dovetailed with what you have been doing professionally?

To an extent they are quite similar. I would say that the things I do outside college, which is often not only on computers, is probably more relevant to my work than the music I am involved in. For instance, I made a piece of work with a barrel organ programmed in MIDI a couple of years ago and it refers more to the skills in inter-action and design than it does to any work I have done with computing.

Sometimes you get very aware of the difference between working with computers and working in an analogue way. When I first worked with music I used to do every-thing on open reel and it could literally take a day to make a perfect audio loop by editing manually. Working digitally changed the way I think about producing work but, at the same time, it made me aware that with the speed of being able to make music on computers there was also a hindrance in the fact that you don't have the luxury of sitting back and waiting for things to happen, nor do you get chance outcomes. You can't easily make happy mistakes on computers because they usually do only what you want them to do. Obviously that is quite apparent in music.

Learning a flexible approach to using software

Do you think that there are specific ways in which it is possible to create and support a good learning environment that responds to students' needs and helps them to gain software and technology skills?

Actually, we are not so interested in focusing on teaching software anymore. It is more interesting and more useful talking about how to apply that software and dealing with ideas around the software. We assume people will come onto a course with basic skills. We do give lessons such as refresher courses in Director but it is rather like getting your grandfather to teach younger people to do something that younger people already do.

I don't think anyone nowadays expects to be a master at every single program because there are far too many programs and it doesn't make sense to work that way. In some ways, one program is much the same as another anyway. And they apply what they need to the situation in hand. So if they understand how to work with the Internet and have a good grasp of what they want to do they prefer to move between different bits of knowledge of software to get the result.

The days of technicians in brown coats telling people how to do things are virtually over now because there is a culture now where students have had a lifetime of experience with computers. So understanding HTML just comes naturally – it is a language they have acquired through time. Teaching institutes used to have technicians to show people the 'right way' to do things and there used to be a right and a wrong way, for instance, of writing web pages in HTML. But now students are much more used to using shortcuts than learning a 'proper' way to do things.

Self-directed learning and problem solving

Does it follow that, for students today, an effective way to learn about technology is in self-directed learning? When you are approached with a technical problem where would you suggest that a student should go to find the answer? For example, would they be expected to go onto a discussion group and post questions and get suggestions coming back from other users?

There is an element in which it is best for people to learn like that. There are standard questions that will basically never change, such as, 'What kind of compression is best for DVDs?' or 'What is the best way to go about putting video on the web?'. But students find that it's not just important to find out answers but it's also important to learn to operate a self-diagnostic method when dealing with technology. If someone comes to me with a question I try to fire a question straight back so they find out the answer themselves. In an educational establishment it is valuable to have people realise why things do or don't work instead of having them receive a load of jargon.

Does it follow that for people working in the arts, the most important awareness to develop is the critical approach to technology.

That's because, at the end of the day, computing, in itself, isn't really that important in a department like ours that is centred around interaction design. It is a fundamental background but we regard it as just another tool, just another hammer and chisel. The question is about finding the most appropriate tools for the job. The way the concepts are applied is what is important, rather than focusing on the technology itself.

Supporting projects and facilitating relationships

When you are working with students or researchers at the college are you also helping to facilitate them and to set up the relationships they need to work successfully?

I often act as a bridge between the students and the academic staff or other technical staff within the institution. For instance, some of our students are doing some interesting web-based work but to make their work there are specific things we require from the department that is our service provider. I would never get the students to talk directly to the Computer Services section. The students' projects aren't intended to break regulations, but what the students need the work to do is not going to be conforming to what the Computer Services section thinks of as 'normal use'. I need to be an interpreter to make sure that what they want to achieve is communicated properly. And often you have to be quite shrewd about how to talk to people.

It's fair enough to say that there are many different approaches that people have to computing depending on their professional context, and that what one person thinks of as an 'appropriate use' in one context, another person will not – in the same way as the language that is used by a person in one context, for example in the arts, may be very different from the language used by someone in a different context, such as a service industry.

Probably one of the most important parts of any project management which works across disciplines or divisions is in facilitating communication. In this position, it is necessary that we can deal with a breadth of knowledge and language and, therefore, we may be able to talk to other specialists in terms they actually understand.

14 Interactive design: David Bickerstaff

D avid Bickerstaff is the Creative Director of Newangle Multimedia. The company is a new media design company and specialises in the production of interactive installations for museums and galleries.

Institutions that Newangle has worked with include the Holocaust Memorial Centre, Detroit, where it was commissioned to produce a variety of videos and large-scale installations (2003). At the National Maritime Museum, Cornwall, UK (2003) they designed interactive installations for an enormous, theatrical museum space where exhibits dealt with marine history and included real objects such as boats suspended from the ceiling. Their work wove the stories of nine key boats into a visually powerful and immersive 'title sequence' that could introduce the visitor to the themes explored throughout the rest of the museum. For the Singapore Science Centre (2002) they created animations to tell the story of the discovery of the electron and its impact on modern life. At Thinktank (2002), a hands-on science centre in Birmingham, UK, the interactive displays they created dealt with issues relevant to modern medicine and used a range of presentation forms such as gaming and multi-screen interactivity.

In this interview, David Bickerstaff talks through the stages that lead to the development and the production of interactive installations and displays. He describes how the relationship between the curatorial team, the commissioner and the new media designer is managed, and how the objectives of a particular project are realised.

The role of the interactive designer

Newangle's current project is to develop creative content for the National Waterfront Museum in Swansea, Wales. This is a vast project and the location is a major architectural redevelopment of an old warehouse on the waterfront. Also on this project, Newangle has been working closely with Land Design, which has an impressive reputation for innovative design in the museums and cultural sector. David, can you describe what the starting point is for a project like this and how you work with a lead organisation?

We worked closely with Land Design, the exhibition designers that designed the interior. They were also responsible for the overall concept. Land Design were interested in using

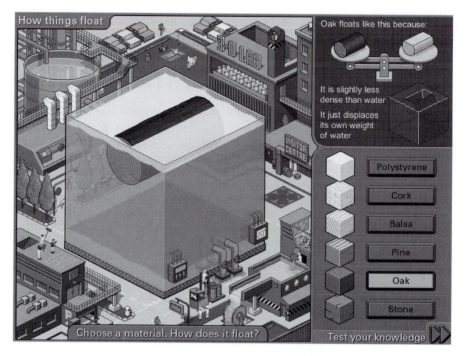

Figure 14.1   Detail from interactive display in the Boatbuilding Gallery, National Maritime Museum, Cornwall, UK (2002). Designed and produced by Newangle
This series of exhibition interactives was designed to explore the complex principles behind boat construction – buoyancy, shape, speed and stability, propulsion, control and design. A strong graphic and animation style was developed to enhance the playfulness and help the interpretation of complex scientific principles in ways that would be understandable, interesting and enjoyable for the visitor.

interactivity as a language and they realised that the best way to make the content work was to actually bring software design on board as early as they could. We were brought in at the development phase. One of the issues with the museum was that, unlike many other museums, they didn't have an extensive collection of objects to draw on for exhibits, so the designers came up with AV and interactive installations to tell a lot of the stories.

And this is where you came in. Would you say that this is typical of the way that inter-active designers become involved in a project? Are projects like this often determined as much by the physical needs of a new building, as by the creative vision of the curatorial or museum experts?

In some situations the starting point is the city planners, who then employ architects to build their museum, who then employ exhibition designers, who then employ software contractors and people who build all the exhibits. The danger can be that the architects create a fabulous building but the exhibition designers are totally constrained by it; this can result in a bad experience. However, for the National Waterfront Museum the planners realised that it was more strategic, and that it would lead to a better visitor experience, if all the partners were brought together early on. As a result, the exhibition designer and the architect were both appointed at a preliminary stage and were in contact at the earliest possible date.

In an example like this, where a range of different people are deciding the structure of the building and at the same time making decisions about the way it will work at a minute level, is it important for you to be able to envisage where the interactive installations are going to be sited and what they will do?

The architect always has the vision of what they are trying to do and how they're constructing the building. The exhibition designers' expertise deals with the way that people flow through the building, how they pick up content, how they interact with the space. They have to consider the priorities of the curators and the museum, what information they are trying to convey what stories need to be told and how they can be told in this journey. They also have to anticipate what the end experience is going to be, what is the balance between straight 'objects in cases' versus a large projection or a single screen interactive exhibit. These are all covered in the planning stages.

At this point the process is passed onto the software designers, in this case Newangle. Our speciality could be seen as marrying the interactive language of software with the physical language of display and providing ways to access content. The first goal we have is to make a presentation, taking on board the initial concepts and developing ways to explore them further. At this point we also aim to try and bring the client into the process and include them in the dialogue.

Planning and assessing the needs of the project

Once you are committed to a project how do you start to design the interactive exhibits? What are the main concerns that determine the sort of technology you are going to propose putting into place?

We start by visiting the site, as a creative team, to discuss in physical terms how it will work and we try to imagine what the visitor would experience. Sometimes this brings up a lot of anomalies, but it also gives us the opportunity to suggest changes that could make the space suit what we think is the best use of interactivity. We also start to consider what hardware is best and look at the hardware interfaces for their robustness and innovative solutions. We are always trying to make things that aren't just operated by pressing a button, but which might use virtual interactivity, gesture, sensors and other options like that. At this point we are trying to determine the best way to use interactive language to access the content, the value of interactivity to understanding content, and the spatial arrangements for each of the exhibits.

You describe the gallery exhibits in terms of an integrated experience both at the point of making and at the point that the visitor experiences them. At the planning stage who is making decisions about content, such as how it will be accessed, what stories are being told and what qualities are being given to them?

We try to define the parameters of the content at an early stage. We usually find that the museum curators have such in-depth knowledge that they want to avoid skimming over subject matter and want to get in as much as possible. However, we are also aware that when visitors experience exhibits they want to get to the content sharply. Therefore, we have to negotiate between these two expectations, and as a result define how much and what sort of information can be included. It needs to be potent information and it needs to be entertaining, something that creates a memory, but also creates a thought process so the information stays in there. It has to have an element of entertainment but also it creates a memory bank of content.

Designing interactive installations – defining the content

What's the process by which you start to design the specific interactive pieces?

We define what we think are the key areas. For the National Waterfront Museum we decided that there were about seventeen stories to be told and that these could be a mixture of video and interactives. Out of these we identified that there were five star items: ones that people would be really interested in. So we focused on these five as a way of getting the right balance between the different types of interactive languages that would be used.

The first is 'The Power of Landscape': a panoramic image with hotspots imbedded in it. This is an image of Swansea that goes across the whole of three projections with a series of embedded hotspots that the visitor can navigate with a joystick. As you click on a hotspot it brings down the data. You can bring data on to the surrounding screens to investigate further. With this process you can go quite deep into the landscape.

The second is 'Power of People'. This consists of three hanging holo-probe screens. These are back projected and you are able to navigate them as a 3-D landscape. This piece is based on information from the 1812 census, and takes you through a 3-D model of old Swansea. As you move across the screens you come to various houses; when you go inside the houses you can explore various objects in a QuickTime VR environment. Each object has stories attached to it, and can be downloaded onto additional screens, so that you can investigate them more and stories get told. It's using a dual-screen relationship for different levels of information.

'Power of Communities', the third section, is a showcase of objects. For this we are using what is called gesture technology. If you put your hand in a virtual plane and point to a 3-D object it will come forward and spin. This enables us to create a 'virtual showcase' where you can actually take the 3-D objects out of the showcase and get a sense that you're actually interacting with them.

The hardware behind this kind of exhibit is actually quite straightforward, tracking movement like a mouse or a touch screen. But the idea that you can move an object around is very effective, and being able to interact with the objects is a way in to discovering a community. It is a very playful process but actually what you are doing is learning: oral histories are downloaded and it is very much like accessing a virtual archive.

The fourth is the 'Power of Organisations'. Once again, this is another database where the information is projected onto a bench, a series of photographs that you can actually move around with your hand. As you move them around they form relationships with each other. It indicates connections within communities: one photograph might show a player of the rugby club and an arrow will then point to another image – one of his mother who runs the hospital. It enables a discovery journey of particular organisations within the community and also the people involved.

The last section is 'Power of your Money'. The intention is to create an immersive space with projections from wall to ceiling. In the centre we will have a shop counter with a modern travelator, a conveyor belt for shopping goods. We will use a real travelator but the objects are digital projections. As the visitor selects an object it comes into their station, but as it does so it goes through various time periods – it goes from what it would have been in the eighteenth century right up to a modern department store. The interactivity with the objects lets you compare what the objects cost in respect to what wages were earned. For example, if you select a bit of butter it will then tell you that in the eighteenth century this cost ten per cent of your daily wage if you were a miner. The aim is to deal with the value of money in a contemporary setting. It's a very tricky combination of atmosphere: getting a sense of an old shop but also having a very contemporary format where visitors can interact with the particular objects coming along the travelator.

Consulting with the client

What is your next step now to produce these exhibits? You are now at the stage when you've done a lot of the content design, and you've obviously mapped out the technological design for them. What do you do to get them made?

Once the proposals have been presented to the client, and they are happy with the way these are operating, we develop them further. At this point we have to address cost and value – what we are spending per item, how much on software and hardware. We need to assess if this is giving value for money or if it is subtracting too much money from the overall budget. At this point we make a further presentation to the client giving our holistic view, and debate whether we think it is worth spending a little bit more money at a certain point because we think it will create more content or if we want to take a different approach.

Does this indicate a different stage in the relationship with the client?

It's a deeper relationship. At this point the client starts to get involved on a much more intimate basis. We've done all our creative, round-the-table brainstorming, now it's time to bring the client on board. We start getting down to the nitty-gritty. The key questions might be about how much content there will be. The client might want twenty stories for something but we might propose using ten in greater depth to find out how that works within this sort of environment.

Stages of production

At this stage are you still in a consultancy role, negotiating with the client on what the final works will be?

Yes, but very rapidly once those decisions have been made we start filming and actually constructing all the software. We will have to do empirical tests of all the hardware, the interactive devices, the joysticks, and all the types of screen we are intending to use. We also have to come up with the exact specifications for the hardware that will actually be used in the exhibit.

What is the next stage in the development of the content? At what point do you define the actual content material such as the textual information or visual detail of the exhibits and the videos?

The interactives and videos all need outline scripts which are written by separate scriptwriters. For the National Waterfront Museum we had writers that had been working with the client for the previous two years to develop the stories. Normally writers will provide content matrices, which are thick volumes of stories and research material, which define who the characters are and what the stories are we are going to tell. These are then used as the basis for the working scripts that we, as AV and software producers, understand. Often, at this point we may have to bounce them back because they are too explicit or descriptive.

Is your aim to allow the interactivity to tell the story and to enable the visitor to learn things by the choices they make rather than by what they are told? If you are aiming to make them learn by selecting information rather than just by receiving it this is very different in approach from a traditional museum exhibit which might be more typically aiming to impart what it sees as necessary information in a much more direct and authoritative way.

Exactly. We have to be planning this from the stage of the outline script so that the details all contribute to the whole effect. What we are aiming at is a combination of documentary story telling and beautiful imagery which creates the sense of being really immersive or engaging. It's very important to get that balance right. So, for example, if there's to be a voiceover then we pass those outline scripts on to proper scriptwriters who know how to write dialogue, to actually hone it down into something very communicable, in a way that visitors are actually going to understand it.

Managing hardware requirements teams and outsourcing to contractors

When the content has been defined, you've hardened down how the content will be delivered and you've struck the right balance with the writers, what then happens to the rest of the physical material and the hardware? When do you make the final decisions about what hardware is being used?

In effect, when we decide on the type of interactivity we are going to use, it has a hardware implication, so having a very big 3-D walk-through implies that we need certain graphics cards and they need to be identified right at the very beginning. Our suppliers have a finite budget and the costing has already been estimated as accurately as possible but there always needs to be horse trading within that budget – such as exchanging a 42-inch plasma screen for a high-end graphic card. It also means that we have to constantly research into new technological innovations for presentations.

How much of the actual production are you responsible for and how much do you outsource?

We make all the image creation and capturing in-house but we contract out specialist programming. For instance, in the 'Power of your Money' section we have objects flowing through several servers, and things like that require specialist programming. Another example would be if we needed a highly sophisticated database, a specialist animator for some graphics work or splitting videos onto different screens. But we control all the aesthetic decisions, and everything would be generated through us, as a creative team.

I see my role as being the person who understands the possibilities or throwing up the possibilities – such as asking if we can get ten screens out of a video, if we can separate each pixel and blow them up. That's the way I work: leading the team to think about it creatively and then allowing a technician or a programmer to come up with a solution. Sometimes out of that comes an alternative solution, which is actually better than the one that I had originally envisaged.

Reflecting upon finished pieces

Obviously there are many different ways of evaluating a finished exhibition piece, and the way that the public responds to it cannot always be completely anticipated. When you are able to see it in operation with the public and you are able to reflect upon the way people interact with it, do you have a sense of it having achieved all that you wanted it to and more?

At the National Maritime Museum, Cornwall, UK, the whole premise of the work we did was about story telling and the human relationship to boats. One thing we have discovered is that management of the speed at which the visitor will interact would be very important, and in a way we used that to good effect in this museum. For one of the exhibits, we decided to abandon some of the more complex digital interfaces we had originally intended and to concentrate on the metaphor of the boat and the winch handle used to bring rope onto a boat. So we came up with the idea of the handle turning and designed the browser scenario so the visitors could scroll through the various interactive choices actually using a physical winch handle.

Figure 14.2   Detail from the Flotilla Gallery, National Maritime Museum, Cornwall, UK (2002). Designed and produced by Newangle

Figure 14.3 Detail from the Boatbuilding Gallery, National Maritime Museum, Cornwall, UK (2002). Designed and produced by Newangle

Figure 14.4 Detail from the design for the Money Gallery, National Waterside Museum, Swansea, UK (2005). Designed and produced by Newangle

It is very playful to be turning the handle and moving the digital interface backwards and forwards, and to get virtual boats coming up and down on the screen. Through this we tried to be aware of managing the entertainment, which was play, and the delivery of content which was the reward, and hopefully the reward was that the visitor would learn something.

It was interesting to watch people use that particular interface because they started off having fun, moving the virtual boats about, and then they would start getting deeper into the content and say, 'I didn't know that' and a conversation would start. It works because there is a dynamic combination between the interactor, the avatar, and the viewers – and there might be two or three other people around. An exhibit like this is successful because it has a seamless quality where technology is not in the way, it is acting as an invitation to get through to the next level. It's that sort of process.

Newangle's projects are documented at www.newangle.co.uk

15 Contexts of new media practice

···

The practices of new media are always, necessarily, embedded and contextualised, by which we mean that new media practice comes out of, and relates to, a given institutional and cultural arrangement. This is true for all of the ways in which the individual becomes involved in new media practice, as well as how new media products are met. The context provides a framework of meaning for the activities of production and consumption. The context is the means by which the practices can be valued by an individual and/or group. The context, therefore, not only has a shaping role in how new media practices are understood and valued, but also stands in a determining relationship to the practices themselves. The contexts of new media can be understood abstractly in terms of certain types of context, wage labour for example, as well as concretely in the local and specific character of any one context, such as working on the *Guardian* picture desk, or in a small new media company in south-west England. The context of practice helps to explain the purposes of production, why practice is organised as it is, and the role of individual practitioners.

At the general level we can distinguish between a private-sector and public-sector context of both production and consumption of new media. The private-sector context of production refers to all commercial activities that are organised on a 'for-profit' basis. The private context of consumption is synonymous with the consumer market for products and services and the activities that are predicated upon them. The public sector of production and consumption refers to all publicly funded institutional uses of new media. The public versus private distinction, at the level of production, is broadly a distinction of for-profit or non-profit organisation, while the public versus private distinction, at the level of consumption, is broadly between institutional and domestic use. This is not a neat and exclusive categorisation because public funding in new media does support production that is privately organised; we are thinking here of the outsourcing, freelancing and franchising operations of government offices, public broadcasting or education, for instance. Commercially organised new media activity is subsidised by, and contributes to, public institutions that procure new media products, which are, in turn, used to deliver services that involve new media. However, the alignment of the distinctions public versus private, non-profit versus for-profit, and institutional versus commercial, does indicate some general characteristics of contexts. A private, commercial, for-profit company will have a culture and organisation that subjects all processes towards the end of increasing profit, through tight cost control and expanded productivity and business. It will typically follow all the norms of business practice, such as the clear identification of itself in a segment of a market, and its competitors. Of course, there is not one monolithic commercial culture and organisation. The private sector of new media production involves different economies of scale, from the individual freelancer, to the large corporation and everything in-between. One would expect to experience differences between the working practices of a three-person start-up company and an established, large corporation.

Old and new media contexts of practice

One of the confusing aspects of the generic phrase 'new media industries' is that it encompasses a diverse set of practices that are differentially related in their real-world contexts. In one sense, the category of new media industries defines precisely new types of businesses that have emerged with the development of the Internet and IT. At the same time new media industries signals a set of new activities and practices that have arisen through the application of digital technologies, within existing business organisations. So at times it is the technology that is seen to be the common link in a chain of otherwise different activities and businesses: banking and newspapers, for instance, both of which use a great deal of IT. At other times it is the forms of new media practice that connect different contexts. Both banks and newspapers have websites, for instance, which need initially to be set up, designed etc. and then managed. In addition there are a wide range of long-established media-related practices of communication, which have been deeply affected by the introduction of new technologies. Film, photography, architectural and graphic design now all use digitally based processes for the generation of image and text, as do television, radio and music production. So the traditional media industries of broadcasting, the press and advertising are also included within the term new media industries, although their institutions and many of their practices are far from new.

Digital distribution

This current complexity in mapping the territory of the new media industries, particularly in relationship to established or old media industries, is a reflection of the different ways in which digital technologies have been applied to existing practices. The traditional media sector has almost universally developed an online presence for their business. The most popularly visited website in the UK is BBC Online, for instance. All of the major Hollywood studios have websites. While at one level a website could be simply a media organisation's calling card, or directory entry, it is also recognised by media organisations that websites are an important direct marketing tool. Additionally traditional media organisations perceive the Internet as a major means of advertising their products, as well as, increasingly, a means of product distribution. The broadband online movie service in parts of the US is an example here. Online publishing is another example where some writers have established a pay-as-you-go instalment of novels. Perhaps the biggest example is music distribution with music downloads disturbing the economic and legal arrangements of existing forms of music reproduction and distribution.

Digital compositing

The established media sector has also adopted digital technologies to carry out the functions previously reproduced by analogue technologies and autographic reproduction, such as non-linear digital editing, music recording, page layout and compositing, graphic design or architectural drafting. This has meant that photographers, editors, musicians, sound engineers, layout artists, graphic designers and architects have acquired the skills of operating computer software programs. There is a generation of 'creatives' working in the traditional media sector who acquired new skills and changed their practices 'on the job', as it were, as new compositing, editing and drafting technologies were introduced. As the software programs and their updates were rolled out across the late 1980s and 1990s, a new technology training sector grew up alongside the industries to provide in-house and short course programmes for workers who needed to adopt computer-mediated communication practices. This was fairly quickly followed by the introduction of formal certified higher level courses in education, which has led to a generation who have acquired a new media knowledge and skills base as a prerequisite for working in a new media sector. The educational organisation of this skills base reflects the complex and differential nature of the new media industries, and education and training in new media are clearly organised along specialist and media-specific lines, which reflect the external organisation of industry. It is not difficult to see the general lines of organisation of education and training in new media matching the organisation and divisions of labour: computer science, computer engineering, software design, software applications and digital technology applications in media production along specialist lines of film, photography, animation and graphic design. Not surprisingly, the organisation of education and training for the new media industries corresponds to our analysis of the 'layers' of computer-mediated communication.

System and support

The near total application of IT systems in advanced manufacturing and service industries has led over a relatively short period of time to the emergence of a large IT technical support sector whose job it is to manage the networks that create a platform of communication and production in different organisations. The traditional media industries not only run information networks, but also require the support of technical production services. The technicians and engineers in film, photography, television and music production, who work alongside the producers and directors, currently work between analogue and digital equipment, often working at complex interfaces that still exist in getting digital and analogue technologies to work together. While traditional media production has developed clear separations and demarcations between production roles, these are less clear in new media production, where there is greater overlap in technical operations, for instance in software manipulation where technical, conceptual and design decisions are closely related.

Digital design

The production of both new media objects, i.e computer-generated programs, and media products that have involved digital processes in their production, video and photography, for instance, require the labour of a variety of specialist practitioners who take on specific roles: producing, planning, directing, designing and technical realisation. The roles can only meaningfully be thought of within the context of the whole production process, and media production has developed traditions of production groups, teams or crews, where each of the separate roles in the stages of production are choreographed and work closely together. Most traditional media production groups have some kind of clearly defined hierarchical structure in the co-ordination of roles and functions inherited from previous modes of production. This is demonstrated by looking at the ways in which new media practices are entering into the production processes of established media.

Film as film and digital techniques

Film, we should remember, is still an analogue medium, celluloid coated with light-sensitive chemicals exposed to light. Film is, essentially, the same mechanical technology it was at the beginning of the twentieth century, although there has been a continuous process of analogue technical developments in the electric motors operating cameras. Mainstream film production remains film based and digital technologies have been introduced primarily in the post-production processes of creating special effects through digital animation and in editing. One group of new media practitioners in the film industry are therefore animators, who produce computer-generated titles and film sequences using digitised elements of film that are scaled and montaged together in the computer before being digitally rendered and out-putted back to a final film form. The computers used for producing special animated film effects have large memories and dedicated software. Computer engineers and software designers work closely with the special effects directors and computer animators to attain the effects that are now an expected part of an audience's enjoyment of mainstream film. Traditional film editing was based upon running actual film sequences backwards and forwards on spools so that they passed through a projection screen which could be paused at individual frames. Editors would mark the beginnings and ends of sequences to be cut, which were then physically assembled in the right order and literally glued together to produce a master copy from which other copies could be made. The development of analogue video meant that film footage could be transferred to a video format with a calibrated time-code and 'video mock-up' of the final editing sequence could be produced on video. This made the editing process quicker and easier, moving backwards and forwards and inserting sequences. Digital editing moves that process further on, making it possible to move the sequences around at will and to control the type of editing technique between sequences and shots, which previously would have had to be shot on film. Like all digital files, they can be cloned, copied and pasted almost at will. The editing process is non-linear since neither the film stock nor the videotape has to be physically moved along a sequence, but instead the computer algorithms render film sequences as so many transferred files. There are two main points to make about the practice of film editing here. First, undoubtedly there is an essential and powerful continuity in the skills of editing, which derive from the knowledge base of film language or, more specifically, film continuity editing. Film editing could be, and still is, taught on any of the technologies of the last hundred years of film. However, the second point is that the introduction of non-linear digital editing is changing how films can be, and are, edited and over time it is likely that new conventions of editing will modify existing continuity editing principles and its variations and become part of the ongoing language of film. The same two points apply to film animation, although in a less obvious way, since computer animation and the traditional forms of 2-D cell and 3-D model film animation are also considered as distinct film forms, unlike digital editing which could be said to be a technique. The equivalent to this difference in film would be the difference between film shot and projected on film and film shot on video or digital video format and broadcast as such. The differences here are primarily of the aesthetics of different mediums. The point for the training of animation practitioners is that, like film, the 'language' of animation can still be derived from the historical stock of techniques, knowledge and practices of animated film. However, digital computer animation has produced spectacular, feature-length products, whose language may stay resolutely within that of film and animation traditions, but whose rendering effects encompass a range of graphics, from the fully realised photographic to that of the virtual rendering of any historical graphic style.

The introduction over time of digital technologies that partially replace previous analogue technologies in a process of production also applies to photography. Contemporary photographic practices remain a mixture of mechanical, chemical and digital processes. It is the very fact of the gradual development of new technologies that led to the mixed economy of processes, with photographers not willing to invest in high-cost, high-end digital cameras until the digital image file had the same image resolution capabilities as chemical negatives. Today, the analogue and digital photographic technologies are interfaced so that a digital file can be transferred to high-end chemical negative or print, and chemical film can be digitised in order that it can be manipulated and distributed in any digital format or outputted to one of a number of high-end laser or di-sublimate print processes. It is possible to say that the photographer remains the photographer, whether they have film in their camera, a digital back on a professional system camera, or a fully electronic digital capture device. By this we mean, again, that the 'language' of photography, being able to control light through shutters and apertures, and being able to compose meaningful images through framing, angle and depth of field, remain the same and can be taught and acquired through either chemical or digital means. Photography, like film, has been mostly affected by the introduction of digital technologies in the post-production process, or in photographic terms, in the developing and printing process. The chemical darkroom has been replaced in many production processes by the digital on-screen 'lightroom'. In photography it is possible to identify the use and development of one software program, Photoshop, as having a marked effect upon how photographic images are stored, processed, edited, manipulated and transmitted digitally. Photography is still photography, with the addition of digital tools replacing the chemical darkrooms of studios and the graphic layout and compositing tables of newspapers and magazines. In this definition photography would barely be included as a new media practice. And yet it is the digital image that was highly visible as a sign, icon even, of the changes signalled by a digital medium. It is differences between the chemical, analogue photograph and the digital image file that have created the most focused debate about the changes a new medium brought about in the language of photography. Digital photography is a distinct medium, but its practices are continuous with mainstream photographic practices.

Video is also a medium that has been transformed by digital technologies, but where the practices are reproduced within traditional production structures. Mini-DV and Digi-Beta are digital video formats used for a variety of professional and amateur productions. Hi-Eight and VHS analogue formats replaced Super8 film stock in the hobbyist and domestic camera and Mini-DV formats are replacing those of analogue video in the miniaturised compact cameras of today. Home movies are now edited with stripped down non-linear editing software on Home PCs and written to CD or DVD discs. Digi-Beta cameras are being used by television and film camera operators, and sound is captured on digital recorders. A complement of digital equipment, capable of producing edited, broadcast-standard full-motion images, is within the affordable reach of a film or media graduate with a bank loan. Such equipment was once only the province of television production companies or even film production companies; now, the camera and editing equipment of many university media departments is on a par with London Soho editing studios. Of course, there are differences in formats and quality across the range of digital equipment, but the principles of the camera and editing remain the same. So, here again we are confronted by the same twin recognitions. At one level, digital video production processes are embedded in the continuous experiences of technical production which support the use of video in documentary, news and outside broadcast, location or studio drama. At another level the use of digital video cameras and computer-based editing by individuals and small production companies is changing not only who can make programmes, but also how they are made.

The point we are making about practitioners' skill sets being both continuous with traditions of medium production, what we are calling the languages of the medium, as well as those languages being changed by the possibilities introduced by digital technologies, is generalisable. The use of computer software for graphical realisation in graphics agencies and architectural practices builds upon a set of visual conventions of autographic practice, often encoded and mimicked in the software tools and menus. Computer graphic programs convert the graphical conventional elements of drawing, lines, curves and tones, into pre-programmed behaviours, which can be combined with the digital typography and digital photography to produce a hybrid digital pixel palette. In addition this electronically combined drawing board, type-setting block, easel and masking frame is also a reprographic process for the duplication, storage and transmission to other forms of realised work. Such hybrid graphical tools can be used in many conventional processes to exactly replicate graphical conventions previously executed using a combination of autograph skills and analogue reprographic processes. Equally, they can be used to produce graphical representations of three-dimensional spaces and structures and to produce seamless photographic and graphical montages that are both conceptually and technically dependent upon the properties of the digital tool. The argument for the emergence of a distinct digital aesthetic is most prominent in the hybrid use of graphics programs. Such a distinct aesthetic as there is has been created by the practitioners of computer-generated graphics programs.

Digital sound

Digital sound architecture, or sonic media, is emerging as a distinct set of practices out of the historical forms of analogue sound engineering and sound recording. Sound as an independent form is, as yet, one of the least explored digital properties of online and interactive media, primarily because of the music and voice reproductive function of the digital medium. Of course, our general argument that new technologies are, in part, an extension of existing technologies, equally applies to the production and reproduction of music and sound. Sound engineering has adapted to the introduction of digital recording and digital transmission in radio for instance. Music production has used analogue recording, mixing and editing and there is an established musical use of electronic instrumentation.

Interactive media

It is, perhaps, only in the new media sector of interactive and online media, for which there is no single traditional set of practices, that the argument for continuity is different. Interactive media is a distinct medium and its language is still being developed. It is not possible to characterise online interactive media as a digital technology applied to an established media, but rather as a new medium that imported an assortment of languages from existing media. This accounts for the hybrid nature of its practices: part graphics, part programming, part scriptwriting, etc. Online screen-based interactive media still display the ways in which the digital simulates the photographic and graphic, and borrows the journalistic conventions of magazines and television. In the early days of new media production small companies working on web development often had a less differentiated division of labour, a culture that encouraged an 'everyone does everything' philosophy, with a 'flat hierarchy' or more collectivist principle of management. The rapid expansion and increasing profitability of the new media online sector has led to the adoption of more conventional divisions of labour and traditional lines of management. With this 'professionalisation' of online media production, the divisions of labour as well as its organisational form reproduces some of its origins in television and print organisation, with editors, features writers, typographers, photographers and graphic designers. It is the interactive or usability designers concerned with the architecture of the interface and hyperlinked navigation whose practice has little obvious precedence. It is user interactivity that represents the most novel element of a new medium and contains the greatest scope for the development of a new medium.

Creativity and the imagination

Media artefacts are looked at in terms of how creative or imaginative they are deemed to be. Arts prizes are awarded, reputations are made, marks are given and jobs are secured precisely on the judgements people make about how creative or imaginative your work, or that of others is. This is equally true of new media work, whether it is a digital montage, an edited video, an animation sequence, the design of a splash page, the interface and navigation of a website, or an elaborate interactive installation. In these examples the issue of creativity and imagination will be translated into specific discussions about how good the concept was and whether it fitted the original brief or aim. In turn, there will be a discussion about how well a concept has been realised. The realisation of a concept will involve very detailed discussion of the ways in which something was put together using particular technologies and software. From broad to detailed, abstract to technical, discussion goes on in relationship to an unspoken body of shared knowledge and experience, which involves judgements about whether the artist(s) or producer(s) have come up with a creative solution, or if the work is an imaginative answer to the project brief. Alongside this regular, embedded discussion and evaluation of new media artefacts and products, usually a discussion among a community of users who have the 'know-how' to consider what alternative possibilities and solutions might have been considered, is a wider discussion of why such objects are made in the first place. The question of 'how' something is achieved will always contain, implicitly, the question of 'why' it was produced. In established and longstanding cultural activities, we rarely ask why and what for. Think of football or feature films; we know they are valuable, that they are supported by large organisations and have extensive audiences and followers who appreciate them; rarely do supporters or audiences have to ask, why football, why cinema, what are they for? New media presents us with a different case, precisely because of its newness and its difference, which leads us to ask not only how well something was done, but why it was done at all and for whom. As we go on to consider, not everything that is new in art and media is easily recognised or accepted by the social and cultural institutions in which it is, or seeks to be, produced. If we accept that there are new media practices that are literally exploring new areas of experience, then it follows that the reception of that work may be uncomprehending and sceptical. Equally, everything that is new is not necessarily going to be eventually valued.

The discussion of what we mean by creativity and the imagination becomes a means of approaching what we understand as the new in new media. By placing the question of what a new media object is and how it was achieved into the context of why it was undertaken we are posing the question, how was it 'thought'? Thinking new media draws attention to the fact that what we do with a medium depends almost exclusively on the values, or sets of values (paradigms), that are inextricably bound up with its organisation and practice. There is then a discussion to be had about how new media is being thought as well as organised and practised, and there is, of course, a crucial connection between all these three elements, between conceptions about what new media is, the conditions under which it is produced and received and what actually stands as the artefact or object.

Know-how

We say that the rules of practice are implicit because they are most often not written down or communicated separately from the making of work. There are plenty of software manuals that are organised procedurally around the functionality of the tools, but have nothing creative or critical to say about what you do with them. It is worth saying here that software manuals do carry an implicit set of assumptions about what the user will be doing with the program, i.e. manuals address a proto-typical user rather than a wayward one. Here, we would say that manuals are just another version of the implicit codes of practice. Practice rules are, by definition, learnt on the job, from show and tell sessions in studios and classrooms, to the culture of the computer and media labs where ways of doing things, shortcuts and achieving effects are demonstrated and tried. In most respects learning-by-doing is how it should be and is the modern equivalent of the medieval guild system of apprenticeship. However, the cautionary note is, as ever, that know-how, that ways of doing something acquired on the job, is not the same as know-why, which is acquired by critical distance and reflexivity, normally associated with the work of theory.

Solutions to practical problems of how to achieve a desired outcome in a new media production can involve a complexity of different orders of applied knowledge and understanding all of which are often subsumed in the idea of creative problem solving. We tend to think of problem solving according to a set of binary analogies, lateral rather than vertical, thinking out-of-the-box rather than confined, non-linear rather than linear, and so forth. Equally the strategies of long-established creative practices are extended to new media, for example the inspired leap, playfulness, non-directed thought, the intelligence of feeling and subjective introspection. These are some of the ways in which the process of creative production has been described by, and about, painters, musicians, writers and architects. The general point to make here is that new media practice(s) are not only building upon the languages and forms of older established media, but also, in doing so, are taking on aspects of their modes of production, which in turn carry with them the know-how we have been discussing. In this respect the small new media production companies that have survived since the Internet 'gold rush' of the mid-1990s have increasingly organised themselves along the lines of either advertising agencies, television companies, film productions or publishing houses. Interestingly enough the first wave of design-and-build web and CD-ROM companies were more chaotic in their divisions of labour and in distinguishing the various orders of function, between technical and creative design. In this first rush to establish business the organisation of new media production tended to reflect the backgrounds of the owners and founders of companies. The major example of new media organising the division of labour along the lines of older media is more clearly seen in the in-house new media production of larger media corporations, such as the BBC or The Guardian Online, where there is a conventional set of editorial and technical functions. Upon reflection, it is hard to imagine any other outcome for mainstream new media than a conventional mode of production and the rapid establishment of a division of labour, since both product and production is being structured and determined by the demands of profitable exchange in the marketplace. The point here is the recognition that new media business has now incorporated the languages, and hence the values, of established media production.

How digital technology is thought about by its practitioners impacts upon what kind of new media is produced. The projects of new media across many different contexts are informed by the ways in which the digital is conceived. If we think of digital technologies being a central feature of the mode of reproduction in our own period, in a similar way as mechanical reproduction formed the basis of the Industrial Age, then we would expect the digital to be a defining logic of post-industrial culture and society.

What 'works' and what doesn't

For most of the time the language of judgement about what is creative and what isn't, what 'works' and what doesn't, what has a 'wow' factor and what is mundane, is assumed and shared among a group working in a common area. Designers know what colours, shapes and proportions 'work together'. Interactive designers can judge whether an interface integrates functionality and feel. Programmers can spot the 'cleverness' in the use of a code, photographers can 'appreciate' the consummate use of Photoshop in a digital image, animators get impressed by the qualities of movement or rendering and so on. Such judgements constitute a routine and everyday practical know-how. Knowing what is good and bad in your field is always based upon an implicit and shared set of rules of the community of practitioners. It should also be considered along the way what various kinds of know-how brought together in new production are. This question has obvious implications for the organisation of the education and training of new media practitioners. The syllabi of the expanding range of further and higher education courses in new media, multimedia, interactive media *et al.*, are themselves expressions of what knowledge and know-how is thought necessary. We can usefully, although not exclusively, think about three distinct discourses or models of new media practice. First, we can say that all of the creative skills and know-how that have been derived from the codes and conventions of developed art and media languages can be defined around the concept of 'the rules of representation'. Second, there is a tradition of practice strongly associated with the avant-garde art movements of the twentieth century which were characterised by breaking the rules and redefining boundaries. Third, there is an emergent approach to new media practice, which is based on a knowledge of computers and how they work, which we might tentatively call 'the logic of systems'.

These models of new media practice can be summarised as:

1 The rules of representation.
2 Breaking the rules and redefining boundaries.
3 The logic of the system.

These are discussed in detail in Part IV.

Industry and culture

Interestingly, new media has been inscribed into ideas about both culture and industry in intensively practical as well as highly abstract ways. Practically, new media is already an established area of employment ranging from large international corporations to the cottage industries of small and medium enterprises, united around a number of section-alised professional journals and sections in the national press. New media can also be identified in the public sector in institutions of government, education and research. New media has become an umbrella term to cover this variety and diversity of sites and activities. New media is a kind of loose collection or sub-category for a range of prac-tices in the more overarching category of the creative and cultural industries. New media applies as a term whether we are discussing web design or digital art. As much as new media is a loose and inclusive term for industrial, commercial and professional practices, still possibly being worked out and claimed by various interest groups, it is also being discussed, as we will see, in much more abstract and theoretical ways as a radically new and distinct medium, as a new cultural and symbolic form.

Health and safety in the human–machine interface

How individuals cope with the immediate physical and psychological effects of spending large amounts of time in front of screens, using keyboards, clicking away at the mouse, varies enormously. In the workplace there may be a positive health and safety culture that promotes good practice, while in others, and we suspect most, the policy is a bureau-cratic paper document filed away somewhere while the culture is one of ignorance.

Trade unions

Trade unions are important organisations to belong to because they support individual members' working conditions and they work with management to improve the overall conditions of work practices, often campaigning for improvements in working hours and working environments. Membership of trade unions and professional associations has declined in the UK over the past two decades as a consequence of changes in govern-ment legislation and deregulation of the public-sector employment. This does not mean, however, that trade unions no longer play an important part in negotiations on work practices with employers and government departments. There are a number of national unions that relate to media workers which, if you are employed in a large company, you should be aware of. The main media-related unions are: BECTU, the Broadcasting, Entertainment, Cinematograph and Theatre Union; NUJ, the National

Union of Journalists; and ACTT, the Association of Cinematograph and Television Technicians. More generally, NUT, the National Union of Teachers, and NATFHE, the National Association of Teachers in Further and Higher Education, cover the interests of teachers and lecturers in new media. Of course, the National Union of Students is a good starting point for participation in a national organisation that campaigns for the interests of people in education.

The body

How we sit at a computer and in what kind of chair is very important to our bodily wellbeing. The height of the screen on the desktop in relationship to our eye level and how the screen is positioned will also have effects upon our posture and eyesight. The position and angle of the keyboard and mouse will affect our arms, wrists and hands. Repetitive strain injury (RSI) can be a long-term, severe disability arising from prolonged use of the mouse and keyboard in unsupported arm and hand positions. The British Health and Safety Regulations (1992), relating to the use of display screen equipment, lay out a code of practice that employers must adhere to. It has been acknowledged that prolonged work with visual display units (VDUs) can create a range of health problems including headaches, stress, eye strain and bodily aches and pains. VDUs give out both visible light and other forms of electromagnetic radiation, which can be harmful above certain levels. However, levels of radiation from VDUs are considered to be well below safe levels as set out in internal regulations. Many people working in new media will be self-employed and unaware of health and safety practices. Many more people are domestic and private users of computers and will be equally unaware of the health and safety executive directives of working with visual display equipment. Common sense should somehow indicate two key things about living and working with computers: first, that we need to consider how we position our bodies in relationship to the workstation and, second, how long we spend at any one time in front of the screen. You should take regular breaks from working at a screen, allowing your body and mind to be temporarily diverted by other activities and tasks. But, in reality, we ignore common sense over and over again as we become absorbed or engrossed in on-screen communication, or as the pressure of increased workloads pushes us towards unreasonable deadlines. Only the conscious establishment of a positive health culture of the office, study or personal space can counteract the built-in tendency within human–computer communication to forget the body, and this is always hard won.

Work/life balance

In addition to the immediate practical health issues related to working with computers, there is a more general question of the balance between work and the rest of our lives. Working in new media can be exciting, is certainly demanding and is often led by tight deadlines which require long hours leading up to the completion of a project. Working in new media can also be very isolating during the long hours spent in front of a computer. Equally, the increased use of online computing both in work and in leisure is increasing the amount of time we spend communicating through the computer inter-face. The results of these changes to our general patterns of living have yet to be studied in any great breadth or depth. Interestingly, the cultural discussion of life in cyberspace is highly aware of the 'redundancy' of the body as we engage with our mind in the various forms of hypermediated and immersive screens. The effects of working with technologies upon the mind, consciousness and our concept of self have also been given attention at the theoretical level as we go on to discuss in Part IV. Reflections upon 'life in cyberspace' seem to be of three orders. At one extreme there is an argument for a full positive 'cyber-embrace', often based upon the inevitability of scientific and technological progress, which suggests that our very notion of what it is to be human is changing as our relationship to computer-mediated communication increases. This view also argues that we have already accepted a great deal of medical technology which 'improves' or maintains the body and that we are therefore at the early stages of the actual merging of the body and machine. The counter to this position is that the application of machines to the body increases our alienation and estrangement from ourselves and each other. Such a view was in evidence in the British trade union AGWU's (Allied and General Workers Union) critical response to the introduction of armband computers for warehouse workers in order to direct them physically through computerised storage systems in order to speed up delivery times. The second position is another kind of positive endorsement of the cyber-embrace, which recognises the separation from machines of what it is to be human but recognises the positive benefits of augmenting and extending our social, psychological and phenomenological reality through an engagement with online communication. Such a position would say that it is great to be part of an online community and to explore our ideas and identities in virtual communities, but then to acknowledge that we need to turn the computer off and engage in face-to-face community activity. The third position is less interesting to us as it is one that does not recognise the creativity of the computer and wishes to limit the use of computers to a range of utility or automated procedures for tedious human activity. There are, no doubt, other more subtle positions than those characterised here, but in all of our understandings about the effects of working with technologies there is a necessary and practical conversation to be had about how we integrate increased computer-mediated communication into our everyday lives. The question for us is one of checks and balances in which the fascinations and benefits of working with technologies also lead us to value and sustain a rich and varied set of social and cultural activities in which we look after our mental and physical health.

Health and safety

A positive culture of physical and mental health in the office, study or personal space is needed to counteract the built-in tendency within human–computer communication to ignore the body.

Useful websites on health and safety

http://www.mda.org.uk/health.htm
http://www.hse.gov.uk
http://www.totaljobs.com/editorial/FLGoingFreelance.html

16

CASE STUDY

Plugincinema.com
– promoting online
cinema:
Ana Kronschnabl

....

Like many new media practitioners, Ana Kronschnabl works across a number of different contexts as a designer, artist and consultant. She can be described as a creative entrepreneur, running her own commercial business and cultural projects. Among her many projects and affiliations is an Internet project that showcases cinema for the web, Plugincinema.com. In this interview, Ana discusses how she draws on her interest in film and her approach to technological innovation to develop a successful creative project.

Plugincinema.com
....

Plugincinema.com is a web-based organisation that shows films made for online presentation. It also advocates and supports digital film-making, giving help and information to would-be film-makers and keeping abreast with the latest debate about digital film practice, reviews and feedback. Plugincinema.com was founded by Ana Kronschnabl in 1999. It is one of a number of organisations and websites that support and promote film on the Internet and digital film-making, others being festivals such as ResCen and One Dot Zero, the websites FiFi and The Bit Screen.

Plugincinema.com is a proactive site, not just a website providing distribution, and its organisers, Ana Kronschnabl, Tomas Rawlings and Armin Elsaesser are interested in attracting and working with a range of new media practitioners from novices to highly skilled technicians, and from 'seasoned' film-makers to those just starting out. For this reason the site includes a film school with interactive exercises, a glossary explaining all the technical aspects and links to suppliers for equipment and books. They also provide information on how to translate traditional analogue practice into digital film-making.

The idea that there can be unique style of film-making, made for and using the Internet, is the fundamental concern of Plugincinema.com. The philosophy and approach of Plugincinema.com is expressed in a key document on its website, the Plugin Manifesto. It argues that there is an interest and a need for film-works that are specifically designed for the Internet.

The Plugin Manifesto states:

Filmmaking on the Internet is at a truly exciting time. Currently, very little exists that has been designed for viewing on the Net. Much has been carried across from

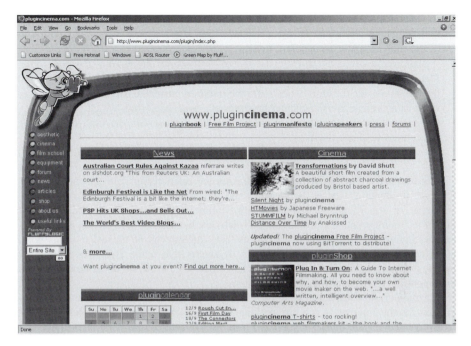

Figure 16.1   Detail from Plugincinema.com website (2005)

Plugincinema.com supports film-making for the Internet by presenting works specifically made for online viewing, gives technical information for film-makers and media artists, discusses aesthetic issues about Internet film-making and maintains links to current articles and sites of interest.

other mediums e.g. TV and film. This is not good. It means that the work being shown cannot be appreciated in the form it was originally intended. It also does web films a disservice because audiences complain about the lack of 'quality': their expectations are for the traditional film, seen in its familiar context.

In the same way that film found its own form in relation to the theatre, and TV in relation to film, the web filmmaker needs to search for the appropriate form for films on the Internet. It is incumbent upon the independent filmmaker to be at the forefront of these new technologies lest they be subsumed by the media conglomerates. Independent filmmakers, geeks and artists have an ideal opportunity to experiment and push these technologies creatively.

(Plugin Manifesto v.1.3)

Plugincinema.com argues for greater experimentation in film-making and sees that the opportunity to make and deliver film online gives fresh opportunities for film-makers who may be interested in new ways of working. Above all it recognises that working digitally and online gives a potential for a 'new form' of work. Forget Hollywood, it says, 'film can be art'.

It was decided very early on in Hollywood that films were products and not art. Independent filmmakers and artists have always known this to be wrong and have made films with genuine artistic merit. This usually takes place outside of the traditional studio system, although sometimes it happens from within. Film was hijacked very early on in its career. Claim it back! The difference is in the overt aim of the film: to communicate and inform as well as entertain, or to make money.

Narrative evolved as an intrinsic part of Hollywood filmmaking. Examine other filmmakers such as Deren, Vertov, Godard and Brakhage to see how they structured their films outside the Hollywood narrative tradition. Structure can be created in many ways using colour, music, chapter headings etc. as a shape from which you can hang the images. Or the structure can simply emerge from within the film, by allowing the content to shape itself.

(Plugin Manifesto v.1.3)

Fundamentally, Plugincinema.com addresses the relationship between the technical forms of production used in digital work and the creativity of film-making. It emphasises that an important part of making films online is not only in understanding how digital technology enables production and delivery but also in recognising the characteristics it supports and enables. It suggests that structure can be created in many ways using colour, music and chapter headings. It asserts that while Hollywood films are largely products, independent film-makers and artists have always found alternative ways to respond to the possibilities of the medium.

In particular, they advocate using the tools that are appropriate for the job, since film-making for the Internet is not film-making for the cinema. They emphasise using the tools invented for the medium, such as Flash, HTML and compression algorithms, and pushing them to see what they can do in creative terms.

Founding Plugincinema.com

Ana, can you describe the career path that led you to Plugincinema.com?

I studied film drama and art at Reading University. After I graduated I set up a video production company, a co-op, which also took on commercial work. In addition, I set up and taught film courses at a private college. Later, I decided I was interested in going into TV and so I worked at the BBC in Wales. Shortly afterwards, I began an MA in Manchester which led me to write on gender and technology. I became very much interested in the way that technology is perceived and used by men and women in different ways. After completing the MA I got a job at the University of the West of England as a Research Fellow in Creative Technology.

At this point, the various areas I had been working in drew together. I became interested in how Internet could be used as a delivery medium for films. Around this time, which was 1997 and 98, the Internet for most people was a slow means of delivery for anything more than conventional websites. I was thinking about putting my own films online and I realised that it wasn't possible for me then. But I've always enjoyed working within available confines or limiting factors and so I saw that as a challenge.

What kind of work do you now do in new media? How would you describe how Plugincinema.com fits into your practice?

I am doing many things, all of them tie in with each other though. I think that's typical of lots of people working in this industry. First, I am running Plugincinema.com. Second, I am making films for the Internet. I have also written a book, *Plug In & Turn On: A Guide to Internet Filmmaking*, with Tomas Rawlings. And continuing with the educational side, I am completing a PhD which is on the delivery of films over the Internet and also over restrictive bandwidths such as delivering to mobiles and other hand-held devices.

I am also running a multimedia consultancy, 'Fluffy Logic', which specialises in making games for hand-held and mobile devices. In addition to that, I am doing a lot of VJ'ing. I am really interested in exploring this more. I like the way that video can be mixed with music to make more of a performance.

Placing films online

There are a lot of considerations that you have to deal with in managing a site that presents innovative work. Some of these must be technical, such as making the work accessible to the widest number of people, but some of these must also be curatorial, because you are making a selection and devising a context in which it is presented. How do you determine what work you include?

The Plugincinema.com website invites contributions from film-makers. It presents a range of works of different styles and themes, which gives an indication of the range of approaches that a film-maker might take to making work for the Internet. Typically, the works shown are no more than a few minutes long, and are linear in structure. They will all open with a conventional plug-in such as Quicktime or RealPlayer.

Do you think of Plugincinema.com as primarily being an exhibiting site that houses and exhibits experimental work? Do you also see it having a discursive role by taking part in a wider cultural debate and stimulating discussion about the kind of work it shows?

Although the Plugincinema site mostly talks about, and shows, short films it is also interested more broadly in the way that the Internet can be used as a delivery medium. We are concerned with exploring digital content creation when applied to new delivery platforms such as the Internet, mobile phones etc. We see restricted bandwidth content creation and its distribution as not simply squashing TV or Hollywood cinema into a smaller screen or bit-rate, but as a new form, with its own emerging aesthetic, conventions and viewing context.

The dynamic nature of digital media, coupled with computer technology, allows for a reassessment of the relationship between media producer and consumer. The stark boundaries that existed in the past no longer apply today and will be further eroded in the future. This re-defining of the producer/consumer relationship is a fundamental paradigm shift and its importance cannot be understated.

Do you think that it is necessary for Plugincinema.com to make a distinction between the different roles that the Internet has as a delivery mechanism and simultaneously as a creative medium?

Essentially, I am interested in the Internet as a form of distribution, but one that has very unique characteristics and possibilities. What people are only just coming to realise is that the Internet doesn't deliver everything that they thought it would when it first became such a phenomenon. And that applies to film as much as anything else. It is a perfect device for trailers, fan-sites, screen-savers etc., but it isn't ideal for watching half-hour dramas. It's not just about length of duration or about screen size, it's also about the situation we are in when we watch things online. The way that we choose to view them is usually different from the way we look at TV. This could mean that we download films that sit on our desktop and loop, and when we feel like a break we just 'look in', or a five-minute animation. Or this could involve pieces that last for only thirty seconds at a time but are delivered to the desktop over a period of a week.

Defining new approaches to structure and narrative

In the Plugin Manifesto you talk about the need to find new forms of structure that provide an alternative to conventional film and that this may mean a period of experimentation, of feeling around in the dark. You also talk about this being an opportunity to make work outside the traditional values and means of production because online delivery gives a chance to make films for specific, minority audiences. Do you think that you have seen different approaches to film-making through the films that are shown on the Plugincinema.com site?

I'm particularly interested in the way that film-makers are exploring how you can structure film without using traditional narrative. Of course narrative has been the main thrust of Hollywood, so it's what most people expect. But if it's taken away, what else can be used? It's not that you can't use narrative with short film, of course you can, and advertisements and film trailers show ways to do that all the time. But there are alternatives. There are a lot of precedents for experiments in structure and form in both film and video, and many of the things that were being explored by early practitioners are appropriate to look at from the point of view of digital production.

What is your approach to making a film for the Internet? Is there a difference in the processes, conceptual or technical, from the way you would work with a conventional short film?

I see it as being exactly the same approach. Structuring comes down to similar things: having an overview then moving into detail and seeing a progression through segments. For me, it is the same as developing any other creative plan or storyboard. Through teaching I have acquired a love of systems, and I see how important they are when it comes to planning. In my own film 'Distance Over Time' I used specd and the idea of movement and travelling and a sense of colour to structure the film.

But having said that, it is very important that you bear in mind the effects and restraints of the Internet because that affects the conceptual development. I am constantly experimenting and using different compression techniques and processes.

Experimentation with process

When you talk about experimentation are you referring to exploring new software or technical resources?

It's not always necessary to use software to create experimental work: there are more general forms of experimentation. 'Distance Over Time' is about movement through space. I experimented with moving myself, moving the camera, with my small baby moving in the bath, and with lots of forms of transport. The film starts slowly and the movement gradually builds up. This was my basis for experiment and I then matched it with an appropriate filming technique. The film was shot on a stills camera, which could capture twenty-second clips of video. Therefore, I was using a simple device with astounding compression that was already taking place in the camera and that leaves little way to go for compressing later. So I could describe that as an experiment that paid off. I also like to experiment with players and editing. I edit a lot in After Effects, using layering and effects – exploiting what compression does.

Another film of mine, called 'George the Mewvie', which is about my twenty-year-old cat, was inspired by the movement of her fur as it was being blown by the wind. With movement, the pixelation produced by the compression algorithm resulted in a very particular visual quality. It was this effect that I concentrated on stylistically while making the film, and it created a definite style and feel to the piece.

Sometimes I use the technique I have developed for one piece and re-explore it for another. Currently I am also working on a sound and dance piece, working with a dancer, a musician and a DJ all operating together in a performance. This is essentially a genesis of the same idea that was seen in 'Distance Over Time' but it will take it in different directions.

Collaborations with technologists

Plugincinema.com advocates in its manifesto that 'filmmakers and Geeks should be friends'. Are you arguing that in order to facilitate collaborations, technologists and film-makers should learn to work more closely together?

Although many of the short films appearing on the Internet have been made by those familiar with the technology, rather than traditional film-makers, there would be more interesting films resulting if people who had spent their lives learning the craft of film-making got together with people who could make the technology work for them. Film-makers, in order to be good at their craft, have always had to have a certain level of technical knowledge and are perfectly positioned to collaborate with technologists. As a result, the clash of assumptions and of traditional ways of doing things produces surprising and challenging new work.

An example of this is film-makers who work with techies from the games industry. The games industry produces lots of moving images, and there is huge potential for people to create exciting stuff that way. One of the emerging new forms we feature on plugincinema.com is 'Machinima', which involves taking apart 3-D games engines to create films.

Illusions and innovations

What other technical approaches are demonstrated by other pieces in the site?

A lot of people experiment with the material of digital video and the different ways that outputting can produce. One of the film-makers, for example, Chris Savage, takes existing footage and puts it through a process that turns the image into ASCII. You wouldn't know that it was ASCII text, it appears to be an abstraction of some form, you just see it as being visual.

The Plugincinema.com site doesn't emphasise interactive works or non-linear pieces that might enable the viewer to navigate them in different ways. Do you think that there is an important distinction between a linear work and a work that might conform more to the design of a game and involve the viewer interactively?

There's a fine line between different approaches and eventually it comes down to individual preference. People get seduced by technology and excited by what they can do with it. I am not excited by the idea of interactivity per se, since computers are by nature interactive, but that doesn't mean that interactivity is not in itself interesting, or indeed essential for new media artworks. What I love is being transported into someone else's world, and that's why I love cinema, film and visual entertainment. I appreciate someone else's shaping and I'm not interested in shaping an ending myself. I find games interesting for other reasons. Ultimately they have a narrative with the illusion of choice. They give choice but the player can only go so far, as every choice has a result, so actually the concept of choice is an illusion. But I don't want to play a game in the context of online cinema: I want to have a creative work delivered to me that I can watch, enjoy and contemplate.

Plugincinema.com website and the Plugin Manifesto are at www.plugincinema.com

17

CASE STUDY

Advertising and marketing: Vivienne Stone

V ivienne Stone is a producer working within the advertising and marketing industry on large-scale new media projects. Her jobs have included working with one of the leading international agencies with a focus on new media, Saatchi & Saatchi, New Zealand, where she was responsible for their Interactive Team. Integrating a new media arm into a traditional advertising agency was a critical role for the future vision and success of the agency, and she played a part in all aspects of its strategic, creative and media services. Saatchi & Saatchi, New Zealand, describes itself as an 'ideas company', dedicated to transforming the businesses, brands and reputations of its clients, and it sees new media as an important part of this engagement.

At Saatchi & Saatchi, one of the many projects that Vivienne Stone was responsible for was the adidas 'Institute of Footballitis'. This was the official website for adidas for the FIFA World Cup 2002. This was a hugely successful and record-breaking site. It created an increase of over 900 per cent to adidas' football site and the registrations almost doubled adidas' database of online registered users.

Later, after leaving the agency and establishing herself as an independent producer, she began developing a website for an important breast cancer service provider, Breastlink, a medical company in the US.

In this case study, Vivienne Stone discusses these two projects, outlining roles that different people took and how, as producer, she co-ordinates the work. In addition she reflects on the way a company can work at a geographic distance from its client, and considers what the advantages and disadvantages are of remote servicing, and how to build relationships with clients. She also addresses the importance of working with the online community in projects of this nature, and how understanding an online audience's needs, behaviours and interests is a crucial part of the success of a project, and therefore of the producer's role.

Commencing the adidas FIFA World Cup campaign

Can you describe what skills you have gained from your background that have contributed to the way that you work in advertising and in particular on the adidas campaign?

Before I worked in the corporate sector I came from an arts background which gave me a lot of experience in working with limited resources. I think it also gave me a good experience in developing ideas and creative processes, as well as an excellent network of artists and musicians and so on available for contract work. I'd also worked for Terabyte, a multimedia production company where we had often had to work alongside a client's advertising agency. This made me really aware of the need for integrated communications, and the importance of different teams who were working on the same job to communicate with each other. It sounds incredibly basic, but it is often quite hard to achieve.

Prior to winning the adidas World Cup work we had developed an earlier project, 'Beat Rugby', which had been incredibly successful for adidas, and really stressful for us to deliver as a team (we were under-resourced as game developers). When we won the World Cup work I knew that in order to deliver a project of this size, we needed to create immediate scale and volume. I went looking for contractors and partners to work with us who already had developed products or projects that our vision for the adidas campaign required. For instance, we had pitched to adidas an online PlayStation-style game and an online auction. So I looked for partners who had expertise as game developers and who had already created robust online auction software.

In order to successfully integrate these partners into the creative vision of the project we spent a lot of time briefing them, and talking about the ideas and desired outcomes. One of the reasons why I think the project was as successful as it was is because we spent so much time integrating our partners, so that we were working as one team.

Commencing the project – creating an online community

....

How was the concept for the World Cup website developed? Was your team responsible for the creative concept or were you working with a key market concept provided by adidas?

We were following a concept that had already been developed by adidas and their Amsterdam-based advertising agency, based around the idea of the 'Institute of Footballitis'. The idea was that over a six-month period fans would display symptoms of footballitis, starting with football fever where people started getting excited about the upcoming World Cup. It then progressed to 'football mania' and ultimately into a fully blown case of 'footballitis', where fans were just living and breathing football. The entire adidas, advertising campaign, including TV and print ads, was all around the 'Institute of Footballitis'. Our job was to use this concept on the web and build a community around it. In that sense we were responsible for developing creative ideas that would work online, and to substantiate the 'Institute of Footballitis' concept.

How did you use the web to build the community and give it a more complex aspect?

We came up with three core ideas that were going to demonstrate footballitis. The first was to represent the world as being made up of units of football enthusiasts, the second was an auction and the third was a game. With these three ideas, fans could partici-pate on different levels. To show the infection of footballitis around the world we divided the planet up into hexagons. There were approximately two million hexagons so essentially if you were a fan you could click on anywhere on the world and scroll down to your town. You could then decorate as many hexagons, in as many parts of the world as you wanted with your team colours.

In the virtual community huge numbers of people were promoting their teams, and every time a registered fan interacted with the site they added to an individual score that gave them 'adidas points'. Fans could acquire points by being football maniacs on the adidas site. The more time they spent online they worked out that there were all kinds of things planted around the site that if found gave them bonus points. They could get points by decorating hexagons in their team colours, and by playing the online game and so on. So it became almost compulsive fun, which is exactly what it was supposed to be.

Was there a tangible connection between the virtual and the real world?

Fans could use their points to bid in online auctions for authentic football gear, some of which was signed by adidas players (such as Beckham, del Piero and Raoul). We held auctions three times a day in three time zones and in eight languages. The third idea of footballitis was the online game. This was a Playstation 1-style game, which was free to play. There were three phases, medium, intermediate and hard levels, at which they could play the game. It was a single-player game so fans played it on their PCs and uploaded their scores to receive their points. In three weeks, 34,000 people from 116 countries downloaded it. The four winners of the game won tickets to the real World Cup final in Yokohama, Japan.

The role of the Executive Producer and team building

Let's talk about what it takes to put a team like this together and to realise this kind of project. Can you outline what your responsibilities are as Executive Producer?

The initial responsibility is to define the project and the working relationships. At the next level down, the main responsibilities are managing the client, identifying and managing the contractors, working closely with the creative director on the development of the concepts and essentially managing the production of the content. So it covers a lot of ground! In setting up the project, the Executive Producer has to identify what talents are needed and when we need to bring in specialist contractors. For the adidas site it was also important to decide how much software needed to be written from scratch. For example, for the adidas auctions we knew we needed eBay-quality software, and that if no existing software existed that we could customise we would need to build it. We also needed to have an online game that could meet a very sophisticated set of demands and we knew that this would need to be produced by a specialist games development company. Both of these had to be delivered within a very tight time frame and we needed to be sure that all the software components interacted with each other as they should. All of these areas have issues about intellectual property rights, so the Executive Producer needs to establish the parameters within which the software is being used.

When you've established the working relationships, and planned your approach the project, how do you go about setting up your team? Were you using an existing team or were you bringing in outside expertise?

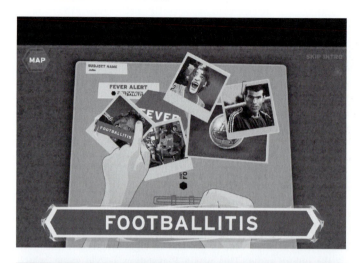

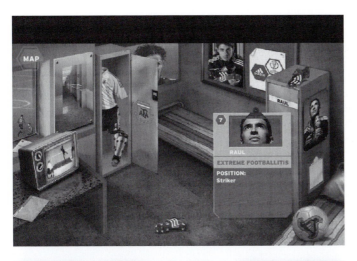

Figure 17.1 'Institute for the Study of Footballitis' (2002). Designed for adidas for its FIFA World Cup 2002 campaign, and produced by Saatchi & Saatchi, this was the most successful web-based campaign in adidas' history. The website was based on the idea of 'footballitis', in which fans become completely consumed by football during World Cup time, and created a fictitious institute that recognised the players' symptoms and gave them rewards. Details from the website show: (a) the entry to the website, (b) the Observation Room, (c) the Sign the Planet game, (d) the Players' Dormitory, (e) the Playstation-style game.
Images courtesy of adidas International and Saatchi & Saatchi.

At Saatchi & Saatchi our team designed all the creative aspects of the project, the look of the auction, the game and the planet. But I knew that our technical needs were great because this would become a massive online community. If it was as successful as we anticipated, based on the Beat Rugby statistics, and what we had therefore told the client, I knew that we would need external expertise in writing software. We anticipated that we would use existing software as much as possible but build other things from scratch. (The auction software and database were built by a company named e-centric who at the time were owners of a New Zealand online auction, Trade Me, and the game was developed by another New Zealand company, Sidhe.)

Security and management of the website

On top of your responsibility to the client to create a site which fulfilled their creative requirements, were you also responsible for ensuring that it was secure enough to with-stand any interference?

This is one of the reasons why we had to be very rigorous in researching the software that we needed to ensure that the site was as robust as it needed to be to withstand the millions of visitors and the many hackers that would want to have a go at hitting us. Anyone who has made sites that target a youth audience knows that hacking is a major challenge. And if you develop a campaign that is based on a competition with people winning prizes like trips to the World Cup finals which are hotly contested items, then there are kids out there who are as clever, or cleverer, than your team. One of the big responsibilities in developing a project like this is to maintain the corporate needs of the client as a market leader. So on one hand it has to be technically reputable but, in addition, it has to be technically accomplished to operate as an Internet leader in a media youth sports category. If the site falls over or people hack it, the client very quickly loses credibility with its audience.

Defining the relationships with clients and creative content producers

You said that as Executive Producer you worked closely on the development of the concept and the way it was realised through the content of the site. Is there an issue about defining how much you can do with an Internet project?

I think it is important for the producer to have integrity about what is happening through the content and defining the fine line between the possibilities of technology and the purpose of the campaign. The creative director will have really strong ideas about how it can be delivered but will probably not be a subject expert and won't necessarily want to be. The client is often really concerned about the finer points of the subject matter, like the details of a boot, which are very important to them. For me, the role of producer is kind of finding the moment of truth between the client's subject expertise and the creative director's conceptual ideas. A great project, regardless of whether it's on the Internet or not, has always really worked through the content and found the position from which it operates. I think that getting that balance right has often been overlooked on Internet projects. I think it is really important to make sure that no single aspect is over-developed.

Understanding the audience

How much do you rely on formal feedback, such as statistics, and how much on intuitive assessment? Do you rely on user testing to get a sense of whether or not you are fulfilling expectations?

Yes we do but the other side of user testing is being really clear about who the audience is and what do they want to see. To develop a project successfully you have to be able to answer, from a user's point of view, 'What story are you telling me?' and 'Are you taking me on a journey I want to go on – do I like the story?'

User testing also plays an important part in ensuring that the content is working. For us, user testing on the campaign was really important because we were developing it in eight languages and we needed to know that the content would work for all those different communities. We had to make sure it was user tested by really proficient gamers because the game was such an important part of the credibility of the site for its target market. And because the World Cup was being hosted in Japan and Korea we had to have a particular focus on Asian languages. So on top of the other contractors that we worked with there was a translation centre, and native speakers in eight worldwide offices who were user testing it, so we were working at a very high level of subtlety of language, which was incredible.

Project evaluation

At the other end of a project is the evaluation when it is completed. How did you go about assessing the success of the project? As a producer how do you measure the success of something so complicated and multi-level in terms as this? Do you depend upon statistics such as user hits or are there other criteria that you consider to be important?

When we look at it from a company point of view we delivered an amazingly successful campaign for adidas where we increased the traffic to the website by 960 per cent and we delivered over 2 million unique visitors over the three-month duration of the campaign. We increased their customer user database significantly and we blew their main competitors out of the water in terms of the comparative campaigns.

At the same time, there are always personal challenges that mean the most to you. No two projects are ever the same and so it is always a challenge to be working in a new territory – which is essentially what the interactive space is. Every time I am involved in an interactive project I want my team to do something that hasn't been done on the Internet before, like delivering a Playstation-style game to be played over the Internet and not on a Playstation box. There is always a major technical challenge that we set ourselves – in this case one such challenge was figuring out how to divide the world into 2 million hexagons as opposed to squares (which would have been a lot easier!). It's important to keep pushing the boundaries and that can make it quite hard work for the client. You are wanting the client to take a lot of risks, and the clients will generally say that they are happy to take risks . . . but not too many.

Developing the Breastlink site

Let's turn now to another project, which as we speak is currently in progress: the website commissioned by Breastlink, a medical centre based in California. How did this project come about and what is your role?

The project commenced in 2002 and I am working on it as an independent producer, with a former colleague who had previously worked with me at Saatchi & Saatchi, New Zealand.

The proposal for the site came out of a meeting between my colleague and Dr John Link, an oncologist and author who advocated a new approach to breast cancer care and emphasised that women with breast cancer should have optimal care from multidisciplinary teams of experts. The aim of the website was not only to give information about Breastlink, a group of medical centres in California where John was based and where this treatment philosophy was practised, but also to be an online service to women. First, I have to say that I became involved in this project because I thought it was really worthwhile. Yes, it is a commercial project but it's also something that I believe is important. In the US alone 180,000 women a year are newly diagnosed with breast cancer. There is a lot of activity in the health sector around breast cancer and a need for good information.

Commencing the project – initial research

You began the project with a field review of existing websites about breast cancer. How did you go about this?

We developed a 'top 10' criteria of what a good breast cancer site would cover. This included things such as how it could support an online community, what kind of services it could offer to women, the tone and manner of the site, and the 'uniqueness' of its content. When we did online searches into breast cancer we found that a search engine returned several million possibilities. We conducted an extensive review of breast cancer sites ranking those that we looked at against the criteria we had proposed.

One of the things we were looking for was how different websites might give specific information or a specific angle on breast cancer, because the topic was so broad. In our opinion an important criterion was that sites needed to be clear in what they were offering to women. We applied the same criterion to the existing website of Breastlink in California. We then presented this information to the clients. This wasn't a formal competitive pitch, but a report, which led to a proposal from us for a new comprehensive website.

Why did the company decide to take up the proposal for a new website and not just extend the site they already had?

What they had was typical of a small business and how it operates with its web presence. Often a business starts out doing something and does it really well and before they know it they have grown. In this case, until this point they were giving information to patients, or future patients, of the four breast cancer centres in Southern California but they weren't following any strategy to provide for a broader online community of women. What often happens in the second stage of evolution in a business is that once it has some traction and knows its audience or market, it has to reassess how it positions itself in the market. A website enables it to really use and build on its reputation and take a position and give messages that reflect where it is now.

Role of producer

Moving now to the production of the site, can you describe how your role differs from the one you had as an Executive Producer in projects for Saatchi & Saatchi?

In many ways it's not dissimilar. As with Saatchi & Saatchi, my role has been managing the relationships between all the partners and providers, and working alongside each of the medical and psycho-social specialists. I've also been working with women who are part of the community of breast cancer survivors. Being familiar with their interests is a necessary way to develop the content. Again, finding the integrity of the content, the position from which Breastlink communicates. In a world full of breast cancer information what value is the Breastlink website adding to women? I guess this touches on a fundamental requisite of what makes a good producer in my opinion. Yes, you need to be able to manage clients, teams, timelines and budgets but you must never forget about the content. At the end of the day it is the simplicity and strength, or otherwise, of the content and how it communicates with its audience that will make your project successful.

Defining content and visual design

You have described yourself as the editor-in-chief of the content. Are you responsible for defining the scope of the content and how it will be represented through the interface and the opportunities of the website?

I wrote a creative brief for each of the contributors which very clearly defined the key idea for the site as optimal care. First of all we worked with the company to define 'optimal care' because, prior to that, 'optimal care' was just a term that was used but there was never a very clear definition of what it actually constituted. It was important that users of the site understood what it meant and if, for example, a woman got optimal care treatment, what did that mean for her, what should she expect. Out of that I wrote a brief for each of the writers which discussed optimal care from their particular angle. Also, I worked with women who were breast cancer survivors to review and critique the content and to tell me if they thought it was successful or where it could be more useful.

As the producer have you also been responsible for overseeing the visual aspect of the site and the interactive design, and defining how it reflects or works with the content? With the World Cup site many of those choices had been made, but it also needed to be quite different: highly visual and very sophisticated in its use of animations and navigation. I am interested in the choice that has been made to keep illustrations and large design elements to a minimum and to let it seem very informational.

The brief for the look and feel of Breastlink was that it needed to look like part of the breast cancer community but we didn't want it to have any clichéd images. In part, we wanted women to feel good about coming to the site, like they were taking good care of themselves by being there, but the design couldn't be over-dominant, because women were there for information and we needed to respect that. We didn't want to

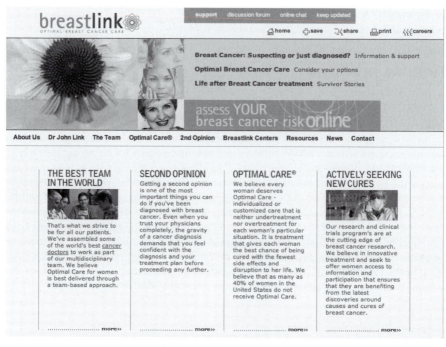

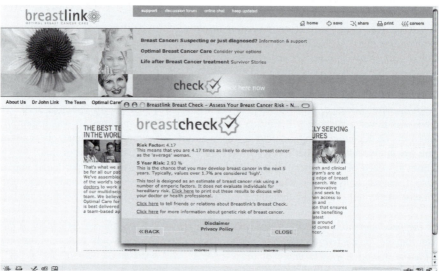

Figure 17.2   Breastlink.com (2004)

Designed for Breastlink Medical Group, a California-based breast cancer company, Breastlink is a breast cancer service site that gives information about optimal care for women with breast cancer. Details from the website show: (a) the homepage, and (b) Breastcheck: an interactive tool whereby women can take an online test that assesses the risk of their developing breast cancer. The Breastcheck software uses family history and medical history to give a general estimate of risk. Users are also advised that it should be accompanied by annual mammograms and consultations with a doctor.

Figure 17.3   Doris Mitsch, 'Lily' (2005)
One of the images commissioned by Breastlink and created by digital artist Doris Mitsch to use
for online artwork.
Image courtesy of Breastlink and Doris Mitsch.

make a huge graphic experience of the site because that wouldn't help our aim to deliver
the information as swiftly as possible, and we also appreciated that a lot of the time
users would be printing out the articles to read them. In our planning we thought of our
typical user as a woman who might be in crisis and all she wanted was information but
nonetheless she wanted an elegant, handsome site.

For the Breastlink project we have also been working with US artist Doris Mitsch.
Doris is a digital artist who creates artwork by using a scanner. She's been described
by *Wired* magazine as 'Georgia O'Keefe with a high res scanner'. Her still-life images
capture the movement of light over an object. We have commissioned her to create
images that Breastlink can use in education and marketing materials, as well as artworks
that hang in the Breastlink centres.

Supporting an online community dealing with breast cancer

*Another aspect of the contributors' content are the sections of the site where women
will be able to contribute their own experiences. Why was that level of user participation important for this project?*

One of the things that I am really interested in is including survivors' stories that we will review every six months and the women will be re-interviewed. The idea is that living with breast cancer is an ongoing thing and each story is like a work in progress. I like the idea that people will read stories about survivors and think, 'Their story is like mine' and 'I wonder what happened to them and if they are still alive'. We hope that the website becomes an ongoing story.

Managing the relationship with the client

How do you deal with quality issues in terms of your relationship with the client? You described the complexity of your relationship with adidas and that, because it was international, it created issues in the way you could communicate with each other. Have you been able to build on what you learned in that experience?

The key learning I took from the adidas relationship was when you work remotely you can be very efficient in your production because you don't get caught up in the daily operational business and you can just focus on delivering the project. You can use that to your advantage but the major disadvantage of distance is that you don't have eye contact and you are not together in real time. That makes it hard to have a subtle and responsive relationship. So our strategy with Breastlink is that every three months we meet with the client, either in LA or in New Zealand. Having a great relationship with your client is critical to doing great work. Often you'll be trying to steer the project in new directions; for this to occur the client needs to trust you. Whilst you can create a good long-distance relationship, it takes time, and it is never as good as one-to-one real time.

Setting goals and measuring value

Are there any other issues about the kind of milestones, or the sorts of goals that you set for yourself in this project? When you look at these do you recognise that you are coming up to your expectations or not?

Thus far we have only been live for about three and a half weeks. I feel really pleased with the extent of the information that is available on the website. Everybody says how important good pathology and mammography are, but very rarely does anyone deconstruct what that means for the user and this website does that. I am working really hard on the linking strategy and I feel confident that we can achieve our goal of making Breastlink a top-ten website. I am happy with the way I am working with the client to ensure that they commit to the ongoing publishing of new content and building the Breastlink community. The online community is the challenge that I now face.

It sounds as if when you evaluate the project you are involving the client as collaborator.

A successful project like this really is about managing the whole education trajectory of the client. You can't just build a website and then sit back and think 'Fantastic, I have done it'. It requires ongoing commitment to the relationship, continuing to build content, and to evaluate how we communicate with our audience. I do feel that all the checks *are* in place and we have got a really fantastic relationship with Breastlink. I believe that this bodes well for long-term project development.

Also, through the process we are making a really meaningful and useful piece. It feels really exciting that we are using the great potential of the Internet and spreading information that will hopefully be useful to women with breast cancer. This knowledge is very satisfying for me.

Projects and websites referred to in the case study are at: www.saatchi.com, www.frontier-network.net.nz, and www.breastlink.com

18

The creative laboratory: Anne Nigten

....

Anne Nigten is manager of a creative laboratory, the V2_Lab, which is part of one of the leading international centres for creative new media, V2_Institute for the Unstable Media, in the Netherlands. Working with a team of approximately twelve people she directs projects that cover a wide range of artistic and technical areas.

V2_Institute for the Unstable Media is an interdisciplinary centre for art and media technology founded in 1981. V2 concerns itself with research and development in the field of art and media technology. V2's activities include developing new projects of artistic work, organising public exhibitions and presentations, conducting research, publishing and developing online archives.

V2 has a reputation for developing a number of very complex projects with some of the most significant media arts organisations in Europe. When a project is produced at V2 it can have come to them from a variety of sources, such as an institutional consortium that has put it together through a major funding application and has developed it over time. But it can also come from an independent individual artist as a unique gem of an idea.

V2 has developed an extensive network with a large base of partners and resources. Many of the scientists and researchers who approach them have a knowledge based on their previous work, and as a result they are often interested in developing a project in partnership with them. Artists also approach them because of their knowledge and skills, and because of the technical resources V2 can offer them. V2 also has an open 'artists in residence' programme to which artists can apply.

In this case study, Anne discusses how she works with a team of specialists to develop often hugely complex projects with artists and how she structures the collaborations to gain the most effective use of people's skills and abilities.

Selecting projects
....

Anne, how does a project come to the V2_Lab? What are the criteria you use when you select the projects you work on? Is there a specific criterion that you use?

When we receive applications for our research and development or our residency projects the first thing we look at when making our selection is whether they are suitable for our field of expertise. This is because it does not make any sense to commission a project or to invite artists for a residency when they are looking for technical facilities or support with which we are not familiar. On the other hand, we also try to take into account the artistic value or qualities of the project, and we try to keep the possibility open that when a project has been developed successfully it could be shown in one of our public events.

We act both as initiator of research projects and facilitator for artistic projects but also as a match-maker between people from different fields. Sometimes when an artist comes in we see that there are possibilities for them to benefit from a scientific or a technological research project. In this situation, we try to embed their objectives within ongoing research so they can benefit from the resources available outside our lab as well as our engineers and designers. We are constantly making adjustments to the skills and directions we have within the Labs so they have good coverage and we know we have specialists working in all significant areas. For example, some years ago we recognised that we would want to work with open source software, and so we developed our expertise in this area and this gave us a lot of resources to draw from.

Obviously every project is different, but is it possible to generalise at all about the process a project goes through when it is developed by the labs, after it has been selected, and what your role is in this process?

One of my first roles is to help people with fundraising, so I assist them to make applications to different funding bodies and talk with our international partners to see if there are appropriate exchange programmes. From then it is mainly my role to supervise the development and we have project managers on each project who I supervise. I have to keep the balance. Every now and then, especially in the beginning during the meetings, I find I have to guard the artistic concepts and also to see how we can best deal with the group dynamics. Sometimes my role is to assist in facilitation and sometimes it is much more a collaboration, and in this case everything from the concept up involves the whole team.

Working with group dynamics and different disciplines

The artistic process can always be very complicated to manage but in the context of a lab it must be further complicated because there are many different issues covered by different members of the team, all of whom might have their own way of working. For a lot of artists it must be very different from the way they are used to working in small collaborations or with a single partner. How do you help them to adapt to other group dynamics and learn their colleagues' working methods which come from traditions different from their own?

It is very important to be able to handle this. Particularly in collaborations, you really have to juggle around with hierarchies and structures. We did several experiments with the group dynamics of projects in very transparent ways. We would propose to the whole group of collaborators new ways of working and often just by having them think through the proposal there would be a new awareness and a real change in their attitudes. Sometimes it is necessary to get people to understand each other's way of working before a project can go forward.

For example, an engineer's approach is often based on problem solving. However, artists do not necessarily approach their project as being something to solve. Instead, they are searching for the best way to create and may be thinking conceptually about the role of the audience and the participants. But that is often very remote from an engineering point of view, as engineers may be much more interested in addressing a problem from a technical perspective. What people want to do, or can do, with it is on a secondary level. So there is quite often a clash between objectives as well as ways of working. In several projects where we have experimented we have taken a hypothetical position: this is to say that we recognise there is no problem to solve from an artistic perspective but if we could just problematise some of the issues and reframe them as problems this could make one part of the development more easy for the engineers to collaborate on.

In this sense could you say that you analyse what the project is about from an artistic point of view and then give it clear unified goals or questions to respond to that are dealt with by others on the team?

Yes, and the basic architecture of software is usually a nice way to deal with it because with this you have a clear set of goals set in the beginning. You usually develop that in a modular fashion so you can always extend it, but to create the main software you are trying to look for the basic objective, or a set of problems to be solved in the first instance. From there you start to build and then you can devise an early prototype, involve the audience and gain feedback from the audience and so on.

Managing communication between partners

You have suggested that one of the issues in working with media artists and techni-cians, engineers and other practitioners is that communication between them needs to be properly managed. This is on top of defining goals and questions for the project in a way that both parties can agree to. It must be important to make sure that media artists are not restrained because they may work with language in a more abstract way than engineers or technicians who may use language more precisely. People don't often talk about the way that media practitioners use language and are more likely to talk about what they achieve technically. But conceptualising a work and expressing this to a team is a very important part of the development process. How do you see your role in this as a manager so that this doesn't just happen on its own accord and that, if there is conflict, it can be developed interestingly and not result in a collision of points of view?

In part, my role is kind of a broker or a mediator and every now and then I also find myself in a slightly schizophrenic position because I have an artist's background but I am increasingly more familiar with the scientific approach. In that sense, explaining and helping people understand each other is one part of my daily job. Often, the linguistic skills of artists are quite impressive but their facility is one of using creativity and poetics of language to explain a concept because they want to leave options open rather than narrow it down too early.

Skills, expertise and technical knowledge

A lot of the things that you are describing that you would do are things that a general curator would describe they do in terms of managing, developing and producing work starting from the ideas. But you have considerable technical knowledge and experience too. What are the skills you have brought to your work?

I started with an unusual range of expertise. I had a background in theatre design, including the technical side of theatre and, as well as that, expertise in television and video, animation, but also in interaction design and technology. So it was a very eclectic kind of background. Over the years I started to work more closely with the engineers on the technical level, knowing that you cannot learn everything at the same time. But having a broad basic understanding turned out to be extremely useful, and I think of it in a way like having a bird's-eye view on the broader context of technology. Often programmers have the tendency to zoom in to one thing to the exclusion of others. This often applies to working with code, and they focus on their particular piece of code only and tend to forget quite often that there is a larger context, and that the research is being carried out by other people.

This sounds like you have had a classic mixed learning curve, from learning specific hands-on technical skills for whatever the job you are in requires, to learning organisational and management skills along the way. Over time have you gained more technical specialisms?

I read a lot of technical research papers to really understand the different approaches, the methods for research and especially the protocols that have been chosen for different kinds of languages. It is important for me to know what the disadvantage or the advantage of each approach might be, what can you do with, what can you not do with another. I need to be able to provide this kind of basic research and understanding when I bring a project into the labs before proposing a particular approach to the programmers.

I think it's also necessary to emphasise my personal motivation, because I ended up in a place like V2 for a reason, not just because there was a sequence of opportunities. My own motivation started with V2_Lab years ago, and was driven by the fact that I saw that it was important to improve the possibilities for media artists who were not accepted into galleries or museums. I figured there could be quite a different model for this practice. On top of that I also wanted to move the artists' practice into other domains and into other areas. And so my main goal has been to see how we can collaborate with, or infiltrate, other organisations or institutions and to get them to take on interactive or participatory works.

Helping to define an existing project: 'Whisper'

One of the recent V2 projects is 'Whisper' which was devised by Thecla Schiphorst and Susan Kozel; it originated in Canada and was developed in Rotterdam at V2_Labs. The project is an environment in which participants wear responsive garments that visualise their bodily energy forces and it also enables them to link to and respond to other participants in the space.

Whisper is a very complex project which had a number of different goals, some of which were technical and some artistic, and many of the things it wanted to achieve had not been attempted before. How did you go about managing its development and what were the greatest issues that confronted you?

Figure 18.1 'Whisper' is a real-time interactive media installation, based on small wearable devices, wireless computer communication, and hand-held technologies which are embedded in evocative and playful garments worn by the participants. 'Whisper' involves collecting data from the bodies of participants (such as heartbeat and breath) and, through visualisation techniques, interpreting that data so it can be projected as an image and shared by the participants. Action research performance presented at Cambridge Drama Centre as part of 'Future Physical' (2003) following the development at V2_Labs. Thecla Schiphorst and Susan Kozel experiment with gestures with collaborator Kristina Andersen.

Photograph by John Chapman.

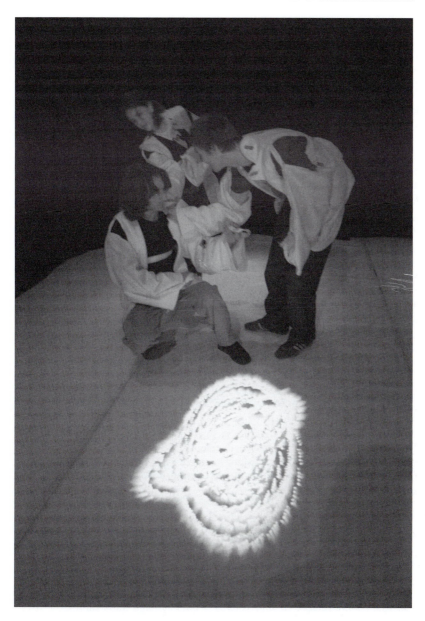

Figure 18.2 Thecla Schiphorst and Susan Kozel, 'Whisper' (2003). Public participants work with each other to create and influence the patterns of light that respond to their body data. Action research performance for 'Future Physical' (2003).

Photograph by John Chapman.

The challenge with the 'Whisper' project was that at the beginning there were too many experts participating. It was a very exciting proposal but like many complicated projects it had many concepts. So from the beginning a concern of ours was to enable it to focus down. Firstly we provided a residency space in the Labs so the group could really work together, as there was a team made up of the artists and the software developers. So as well as working with two of our team members, it was essential that we could provide them the space to really meet, discuss, rehearse things. That was followed up later on with a show of early prototype which was followed by some evaluation and mediation and led to another show of the same early prototype.

On the technical level our hardware developers developed the hardware interface and central system. We had all their collaborators present at V2 and they worked together for several weeks to really understand the different bits of the system, and how they could be put together. One of the main important aspects of this collaboration was in getting people face to face in the same space. This was particularly interesting for the developers because what it showed was that sometimes they had misinterpreted each other's work in the first phase of the project.

In the end the work that resulted was very exciting and very innovative, and the outcomes have led onto other projects as well. We all learned a lot from the experience.

This reflects back on what you were saying earlier about getting people to understand each other's intentions and ways of operating. Earlier you were referring to artists and technicians or engineers, but in this case it can obviously apply just as much to technical specialists from different areas.

This kind of thing really starts to happen when you put parts of a project together — especially when it involves hardware. It's also crucial to be able to try it out to see if it really does what it should do, and to enable a space for artistic reflection up on it. So we worked through to the stage of an early prototype which had several, kind of, iterations. Then those were reviewed and again adjusted by our hardware developer. This is more than strictly hardware development because the hardware in this case needed to be interfaced with software. So there was a very strong communication link between the max programmer and our hardware developer. That was the first prototype.

Milestones and evaluations

We've talked about projects having successful outcomes, and you've also talked about the stages that projects go through in their development. With each project you obviously define what the milestones and targets will be for each stage. Can you describe how you measure and evaluate each project as it goes through these stages?

I think you need to be able do that from the very beginning onwards. We are very keen on evaluating each part of the development or research process so usually we have evaluation meetings of the team after each milestone. If I haven't been working with that part of the team that is the moment I join them again. Sometimes when we have an evaluation we see that things are not working according to the aims of the project, or the results are not actually what we were hoping for. This is exactly the moment I have to be able to propose another approach. Having an alternative strategy is one thing I think you should always keep in mind.

Prototypes and user-testing

How do you go about defining at what points in a production you can user-test it? Some people might try to develop a limited form of a prototype or a demonstration model so that they can test and feed the results back into production. But in the projects you are describing understanding the results you are getting from testing can presumably be quite complicated too?

If you look at the dramaturgy of a project it is really hard to isolate one single little bit, test it and take the test results into account on a larger scale. All those different kind of partial events are part of the total dramaturgy of a project so if you isolate one bit it is unrepresentative and still really hard to estimate what the value of that test is in a larger context. On the other hand, if you are having to test a prototype or a work in progress, you also have to be very careful to involve people who are not aware of the value of testing but have the ability to look upon what they do as a finished art project. Sometimes they will criticise the art piece as if it is a finished piece so that you also have to filter out some of what they say. But sometimes also they just want to have a good experience and they are so disappointed when they don't have it because the work is not finished.

Is there a difference in the way that you work with prototypes and the way that a more commercial lab might use them? For example, some of the projects that V2_Labs develops are taken on to a commercial level. Do you see the projects you develop as having commercial possibilities that can be explored through the development and proto-type process?

I think that we also have to admit that sometimes we are really good in making func-tional prototypes, but this is not necessarily the same as finished marketable products. With several of the projects we have been involved in we have decided not to go through the phase of commercial development of the project even though we might believe that they might be a commercial success. You need other organisational skills for that and in that sense we are much more research oriented.

For example, there is a project that we worked on a few years ago that has the poten-tial to turn out to be a 'killer applications' for education. But after detailed talks with the artist we decided not to participate in the commercial development of that piece as a final marketable product for several reasons. I think in retrospect we can see that it was a crucial part of the project and we helped to convince potential investors. However, I would really like it if investors were willing to invest in early research and then help move it on to another segment of the field.

Providing a cultural context for experimentation and a safe place to fail

Do you think that the way the V2 operates, and your role within it, are unique or are there comparable places operating in similar ways?

One of the remarkable things about V2 is that in Western Europe, North America or Australasia there are very few places which have a laboratory context in which media artists are able to make work with such a high level of expertise to support and enable them. Of those that exist very few would be outside educational institutions, and educational institutions have a completely different research directive. What V2 also provides is a cultural context and actually, in very real terms, there is a context where a work can be shown at the V2 centre or in the festivals. But exhibiting the work isn't essential, unlike residencies or labs that are attached to big events or organisations, where a specified product is required. This must enable a much freer chance for artists to make their work and to focus on the experience that they can get out of this.

I think that we can conclude from the way that you have described your structures and organisational methods that what you offer artists is a very rare possibility to develop beyond their original expectations. Also, importantly, that practitioners not only have the space to grow at V2_Labs but they have the space to fail if needed, in an environment that isn't aggressive or competitive. This is, indeed, very desirable for new media practice.

Information on the activities of V2_Institute for the Unstable Media and V2_Lab is at http://lab.v2.nl and at www.v2.nl.

Further documentation on the project 'Whisper', by Thecla Schiphorst and Susan Kozel, is at http://whisper.surrey.sfu.ca/

Part III

New media forms

19 Human–computer interface

···

The human–computer interface can be thought of as three layers, which refer to the ways in which meaning is controlled in the relationship between user and machine. In this section we will look at each of these layers in turn and discuss the relationship between them, but, first, they can be summarised as:

1 the physical apparatus by which the user is able to operate the machine (and its operating system, the OS);
2 the software programs that organise the users' access and navigation of a database;
3 the cultural codes and conventions through which the user understands what data is and how they access and navigate it.

It is important to remember that the user encounters these three layers of the interface as one thing and that at the level of practice it is unnecessary to make what are, after all, analytical distinctions. Such distinctions become important in reflecting upon practice. It is here, often in theoretically informed writing, that we understand that the human–computer interface (HCI) is not simply an outcome of a technology, but a complex outcome of technological development and cultural modes of communication. This leads us to say that there is no necessary relationship between computer technology and the design and function of interfaces and that the relationship between them is a matter of convention and preference. New media practitioners do not always use a software application for the purposes it was designed and graphical user interfaces can also 'get in the way' of the user's needs.

It is also possible in theory to envisage the HCI as consisting of only two layers: the computer layer and the cultural layer. Computer technology is young enough for more than one generation to be able to remember various stages of the progression of the three aspects of the HCI. In the short history of the PC, there are users who can easily recall the screen interface as exclusively based on text and in which navigation required memorising and typing long strings of commands in order to change applications or files, to copy or format a disk. The graphical user interface (GUI) of the 1980s, i.e. the Apple Desktop and, later, Windows, changed all of that, but the recognition of the visible and invisible layers of command between the machine and the user's desired goal remains. A contemporary example comes from Harvey L. Molloy, from the Scholars Programme, National University of Singapore.

[How many interfaces do I use to check my mail?]

Here are some of the interfaces I negotiate with a cursory nod to the respective debates, issues and histories that lie behind the design:

Press switch on PC to switch it on. This switch seems perfectly natural to many users, although some do keep their PCs and Macs in sleep mode, yet some early computers, such as the Canon Cat, had no on switches but ran all the time! This was to reduce start-up time. Raskin (2000) argues that few interface designers acknowledge the frustration of start-up time. Ideally, there should be no start-up and a machine should be immediately ready when the user is ready to begin.

See flash of DOS screen. Remember that at one time computer languages were the only interface between users – who were then known only as 'programmers'. Many users don't even think of their desktop as being a visual metaphor that allows them to find, store and create files. For many users the metaphor is the computer. Type in my password. Three different interfaces are at work here: (a) the keyboard, which is the great grandchild of the QWERTY typewriter developed and patented by Remmington in 1874, (b) the computer screen window which was first conceived of by Alan Kay at Xero PARC and (c) the data input screen whose origins lie in the development of forms. Forms first appeared in World War I. Use the mouse to click on browser icon. The mouse was first developed by Douglas Englebart. The difference between the single-click mouse, developed by Jef Raskin at Apple and the PC's 'double click' is notorious. And finally: Open browser and go to Asiaone.com.sg. Once I arrive at Asiaone.com to check my mail I face an illustrated page. The origins of this page are clearly in print media, especially newspapers and magazine. We read 'web pages', rather than 'files', and build home pages about our family and pets. So within the space of one interaction I have negotiated many interfaces.

The dream machine

In most of the historical accounts of the emerging subject of new media, reference is made to how humans have envisioned the creative potential of machines. In such accounts we recognise the central fact that humans have dreamt of making machines that are extensions of the human mind and body, in advance of an available technology to realise such dreams. Such discussion raises the issue of what we mean by the word human, in the human, computer and interface, because it is a cultural and historical concept of human capabilities that guides machine 'intelligence'. The current collective concept of computer interface is the result of diverse human enquiry, intention and desire; it is the product of human knowledge and skill. Obvious as this is, it is an important addition to Molloy's point above that the human–computer interface is not the result of one unified design concept and realisation, but rather the temporary outcome of many strands of human interest and intention. Ted Nelson, whose seminal publication of 1974, *Computer Liberation/Dream Machines*, constituted a 'revolution' in thinking about the possibilities of interface, was very explicit about putting the 'human' at the centre of HCI.

> The exhilaration and excitement of the coming time is hard to convey on paper. Our screen displays will be alive with animation in their separate segments of activity, and will respond to our actions as if alive physically too. The question is, then: HOW WILL WE USE THEM? The design of screen performances and environments, and of transactions and transmission systems, is of the highest priority.
>
> (Nelson 1974)

Nelson, more than many others, recognised that the computer industry of the 1970s, dominated as it was by industry specialists and the academic computer programming laboratories, represented an orthodoxy which controlled access to the increasing amount of information held on computer databases. His vision and his project were directed towards making computers more responsive to human needs. In *Dream Machines* Nelson's view was that 'responsive computer display systems can, should and will restructure and light up the mental life of mankind'. This was visionary thinking, coming as it did ten years before Apple Macintosh launched its first version of the Desktop in 1984.

A key phrase in Nelson's view of future HCI reveals his conception of the screen interface needing to be responsive to our actions, 'as if alive physically too'. Here we see the dream of the machine that is ultimately interactive, in which the layer upon layer of control functions have been erased so that, 'when the real media of the future arrives, the smallest child will know it right away' (1974: 317). Nelson was not alone in wanting machines that 'augment', 'extend' or 'facilitate' human thought and action. Nelson's vision owes a lot to Vannevar Bush who, earlier, working for the American government as the Director of Scientific Research and Development, wrote 'As We May Think' which was published in *Atlantic Monthly* in 1945. In this article he sketches the possibility of a machine, the 'Memex', which, using supermicrofilm, would be able to bring files and materials on any subject rapidly up on screens mounted in an office desk. Both Bush and Nelson saw the development of such machines as dedicated to a great human goal: 'Presumably man's spirits should be elevated if he can better review his shady past and analyse more completely and objectively his present problems (1974: 47).'

We can see in this history a dualism, written deeply into HCI development, of creating interfaces. On the one hand there is a keen desire to minimalise, or erase completely, the layers of mediating technology and operating code, in order to maximise the immediate, intuitive and sensuous relationship with the content and data, and, on the other hand, there is an equally strong impulse to maximise the access to the control and manipulation of data through making the mediating layers of code visible to the user. This tension lies at the heart of interface design and development and is an important aspect of the cultural analysis of the use of computer interfaces. Bolter and Grusin's (2000) concept of remediation precisely expresses the tension between the immediacy of the transparent interface and the hypermediacy of multiple access.[1]

Physical interface

At the level of physical interface design and development the issues of immediacy and hypermediacy are embodied in the design and realisation of the material devices and technical apparatuses by and through which human communication with data takes place.

Screen, mouse and keyboard

The screen, the keyboard and the mouse comprise the physical interface of the PC, operated by the computer hard drive and its operating system, usually housed in some sort of grey rectangular plastic box sitting adjacent to a colour monitor. The desktop PC is typically hardwired into the electrical power and data network connections. This is the arrangement of the physical computer interface both at work and in the home. We sit at a desk, facing the monitor, with the keyboard and mouse in front of us. There are alternatives to the desktop mains computer and the interface could also be a laptop powered by battery with a wireless modem network connection, or, as is increasingly the case, the example of further miniaturisation of technology, a palmtop or mobile phone. At present all these applications still use either the liquid crystal grid screen or plasma as the information terminal and the keyboard as the means of control.

Screens

The computer monitor developed with the first PCs in the 1970s. The computer monitor was an adaptation of the television monitor using a cathode ray vacuum tube to transmit electrical triode scanlines. The first PC monitors only transmitted text and numerals to the screen and all commands were by text keyboard. The development of the graphical user interfaces (GUI) from the mid-1980s meant that the monitor could be used to represent a series of windows with graphic icons. The subsequent development of GUI has moved ever more to the animation of the screen in photographic, filmic and stereoscopic image and sound. The graphical screen is also a multi-windowed screen in which it is possible to run a number of programs simultaneously. However, the computer screen belies its origins in the television monitor and still provides the cultural location of looking at screens. Of course, we don't normally watch television sat leaning forward at a desk, which has given rise to the popular distinction between PC as a lean-forward technology, whilst the television is characterised as lean-back. Little stays still in the converging world of new media and the new generation of plasma television screens are being marketed as home cinema, just as the flat screens of the PC are promoted as the new place to watch TV. The development of liquid crystal (plasma) display and greater resolution and miniaturised data projectors all point to a greater 'flexibility' and detachment of the screen from the computers that drive them. Screens are now portable and scaleable, and, linked with recent developments in wireless technology, screens are moving towards even more fluid and flexible interfaces. Screens are becoming part of the general material fabric of everyday life, in architecture, town planning, clothing and fashion accessories and in domestic appliances.

Mouse, online presence and point and click

The mouse was developed at Stanford Research Laboratory (now SRI) in 1965 to be a cheap replacement for light pens, which had been used at least since 1954. The mouse was made famous as a practical input device by Xerox PARC in the 1970s. It first appeared commercially as part of the Xerox Star (1981) and Apple Macintosh (1984). The mouse is a peripheral control device of the HCI, which creates the 'point and click' culture of the graphical user interface. The advent of the mouse heightened the sense of the user's screen presence, which previously had been embodied in the blinking cursor. The graphical interface introduced an additional spatial dimension to the screen and the mouse provided the location and command tool in the form of the now universal pointing arrow or finger, or customised as another graphical avatar.

Avatar

The pointing arrow is the user's screen presence which within new media is also referred to as an avatar. An avatar is, therefore, a control interface between the user and the program. Historically, the word avatar refers to the incarnation (bodily manifestation) of an immortal being, or of the Ultimate Being. It derives from the Sanskrit word 'Avatara' which means 'descent' and usually implies a deliberate descent into mortal realms for special purposes. Among people working on virtual reality and cyberspace interfaces, an avatar is an icon or representation of a user in a shared virtual reality. In multi-user domains (MUDS) and multi-user object-orientated environments (MOOS), players perform text-based characters which explore environments and encounter other characters which are also defined as avatars. The most highly developed graphical avatars reside in computer games, where an animated figure is controlled by the user to navigate graphically represented spaces and engage in contact with other graphically represented objects. Avatars focus attention upon the virtual dimension of computer-mediated communication (CMC). At its most minimal level, the pointing arrow is the user's virtual presence in the computer's hard drive, i.e. systems and applications. The graphic icon is the user's virtual presence within the network of networked computers and, specifically, within the online portals, browsers and domains, collectively known as cyberspace. In moving to describe the interface control established by avatars as the user's virtual presence in cyberspace, or, more fully, remote human presence in virtual reality, a much wider and more philosophical set of ideas becomes entailed. This subject is discussed more fully in Part IV, but here it is worth looking briefly at how the avatar is thought about in the current range of GUIs. As we will see, the advent of the GUI brought with it the graphical spatialisation of the computer screen. This became the defining metaphor for thinking about communication through and with computers. Prior to GUIs, computer systems and operations were interfaced numerically, textually and sequentially; after GUIs the interface presented the computer as a shallow spatial domain with layers, compartments, windows, files, menus and tools. This metaphorical spatial-isation of data, as an office or desktop controlled by pointing and clicking, more than invited the corresponding metaphor of the user in the space. But what is meant by the user being 'in' the space? Canny and Paulos take up the argument when they say that, 'when entering cyberspace it is the mind that enters, whilst the body remains outside as the mere transducer, moving text or audio data in through keyboard or microphone, and catching data from monitor and speakers' (Goldberg 2003: 277). The division of body and mind is established here as a problem or limit, rather than recognition that CMC is primarily an intellectual engagement with a medium whose interface is currently visual and auditory. The desire for greater embodiment in and of the interface is part of the cybernetic discourse in which the human–machine relationship is constructed around machine as an extension of the mind–body. Such interests lead inevitably to a frustration with the current limit of the screen interface because it contains the rela-tionship between the whole human mind–body–environment experience and the online world in a restricted channel of reception. The desire for greater embodiment and pres-ence in virtual worlds leads Canny and Paulos to ask, 'If we build avatars that "look" realistic enough, shouldn't the virtual experience be equivalent, or possibly better than the real?' (Goldberg 2003: 277). In practice, it leads them and many other cybernetic scientists and researchers to develop physical interfaces and computer programming that can 'match', 'imitate' or, in their terms, embody the richer sensorium of human-to-human communication. For the present, though, the online presence of the user remains firmly in the realms of the screen and the mind, while we do need to think about the slumped body.

Health and safety

While the future of physical interfaces with computers may involve us in a much fuller spatio-body interaction, we should not forget the body in the present. Not enough atten-tion is paid to what is happening to our body while we are sat in front of a screen,

tapping and clicking away on keyboard and mouse. Employers are required by government regulation to consider the health and safety of employees working with computer
technology. Guidance and advice is available from many sources on health and safety
when working with computers (see pp. 153–5).

Graphical user interface (GUI)

For new media the development of the GUI represented a dramatic step forward for all
computer users. Prior to the development of GUIs from the late 1980s, the means of
controlling a computer was by lengthy commands and text-based operations.

A detailed history of computer interfaces development would show us a complex set
of separate developments and interests that were eventually drawn together. This is not
unlike the history of other media technologies. For instance, neither photography, film
nor television can be understood as being 'discovered' or 'invented' in a single uniform
process. The actual histories reveal that people were working on separate ideas, problems and approaches, which only over time and in relationship to complex purposes and
outcomes came together to form what we now recognise as a fully formed medium. The
same is true of computer-mediated communication and the specific development of the
GUI. However, a shorter summary of key events in that development would include the
invention of the basics of the point-and-click interface, the mouse, windows and menus
in the 1970s by researchers at Xerox's Palo Alto Research Centre. It would also include
the landmark product of the Apple Macintosh graphical desktop in 1984. The subsequent development, some ten years later, of Microsoft Windows 95 was seen as a copy
of the Macintosh and new systems such as Windows XP, Mac OS X, and KDE or
Gnome on Linux are more or less variations on the original Mac interface.

With the introduction of full-screen graphical interfaces from the mid-1980s, the space
of interface design was enlarged from one to two dimensions. This meant that it was
possible for the user to directly manipulate graphical objects, including grabbing objects,
moving them, cutting and pasting, changing size, and using constraints. Many of the
interaction techniques popular in direct manipulation interfaces, such as how objects and
text are selected, opened and manipulated, were researched at Xerox PARC in the 1970s.
In addition to graphical menus, full-screen interfaces often apply the function keys on
the keyboard as a primary means of interaction. The two main advantages of function
keys are that they serve as interaction accelerators and that there are so few of them
that users often are able to learn them by heart. The introduction of the GUI and direct
manipulation were responsible for a massive expansion in the number of users since it
made manipulation of data more immediate and straightforward and removed the need
for learning complex keyboard commands. It also sped-up and simplified moving from
one application to another, since they could be graphically represented as windows with
their corresponding menu bars. For many of the earlier new media practitioners, in particular photographers, typographers, layout and graphic artists, the graphical interface
represented the user-friendly toolkit, which allowed for the immediate display and direct
manipulation of visual elements.

Beyond the screen

The physical interface of screen, keyboard and mouse have been seen by many (Ascott,
1990, 1999 and Stelarc) as a limit upon the human–computer interface in which the
machine technology restricts the potential forms of interaction. Physical interfaces have

been envisioned that are responsive to a more complete human spatial/temporal sensorium, involving movement, sound and light. There are two strands of interface development and application involving more immersive interface environments. The first of these is represented by the development of virtual environments, in which the use of headsets and bodysuits renders it possible for the user to perceptually 'enter' simulated spatial environments, and the second is augmented realities, in which a graphical interface is part of the body and environment relationship. Current research is on the use of interface glasses, which relay graphical information as part of visual sighting. Intelligent Architecture represents a dimension of augmented reality interface insofar as spatial structures can include remote sensors linked to programming in order to offer the building user control of the physical environment.

If the screen has been seen to mark one limit of the physical interface, then the keyboard and mouse mark another. The development of whiteboards, touch screens, light pens, sketchpads and voice-activated software offers limited alternatives to the current control of the user's on-screen presence by the keyboard and mouse. In the same way that the computer monitor is an adaptation of the television monitor, so the keyboard is an adaptation of the typewriter. It is an odd image to think of the computer as a combination of a television and a typewriter. First-generation PCs, of course, were not much more than typewriters, calculating machines and textual and numerical databases. Today's PCs incorporate the functions of television, radio and telephone. In looking through current research at MIT[2] it appears that the future of user interfaces is in the direction of larger, information-abundant displays that will utilise to a much greater degree the extended human perceptual skills in rich information spaces (Negroponte 2003). A broader survey of interface development shows two trends: one towards a greater differentiation of users according to culture, age and occupation, with a strong emphasis upon learning communities; and the second towards interfaces that are more spatial, immersive, responsive and intuitive. Researchers are exploring systems that have the ability to perceive, communicate and interact with the user using speech and vision. There is an interest in the development of highly interactive and information-rich virtual environments, which would have multi-modal input (visual, tactile, auditory and olfactory) to increase the user's sense of presence. Such research reinforces our view that the drive is for greater verisimilitude, greater immediacy if not spontaneity; in short, to build machines that behave more like us. How such developments will eventuate in applications across the work–leisure use of CMC is hard to predict beyond the obvious interest in more immersive games environments and more layered screen-based interfaces. The development of physical interfaces based upon the human voice, facial or other body languages remains a frontier inhabited by those researching the development of deep, immersive virtual environments.

Returning to the current limits of mainstream screen interface design the emphasis remains essentially functional and goal orientated. The common wisdom of human–computer interface design is that it seeks to discover the most efficient way to design understandable electronic messages. The World Wide Web contains voluminous information on the design of menus, icons and forms, as well as data display and entry screens as published guides to interface design. Various principles have been devised, among them Schneiderman's eight principles of human–computer interface design. It is worth summarising them here, not because they are ultimately correct, but because they illustrate two important points: first, that there is a striving for consensus and, in a new medium, the principles are there to establish agreement and order; and, second, because the principles represent, rightly or wrongly, a set of rules or conventions around a common conception of the purpose of CMC.

1 Recognise diversity.

Make your main navigation area fast loading. For repeat users provide a detailed explanation of your topics, symbols and navigation options. For new users provide a text index for quick access to all pages of the site. Ensure your pages are readable in many formats, to accommodate users who are blind or deaf, users with old versions of browsers, lynx users, users on slow modems or those with graphics turned off.

2 Strive for consistency in menus, help screens, colour layout, capitalisation, fonts, sequences of actions.

3 Offer informative feedback – rollover buttons, sounds when clicked.

4 Build in error prevention in online forms.

5 Give users as much control as possible.

6 Reduce short-term memory load by providing menus, buttons or icons. If you use icons, make sure you have a section which explains what they mean. Make things obvious by using constraints – greyed-out items in menus for options not available in that page.

7 Make use of web conventions such as underlined links, colour change in links for visited pages, common terminology.

8 Provide a conceptual model of your site using a site map or an index.

(Schniederman, 1997)

Cultural interface

The cultural interface is the means by which we make sense of GUIs and computer operating systems. The cultural interface is the cultural language of computer-mediated communication. The cultural interface consists of the codes and conventions derived from cultural interaction and communication. Another way of saying this is that the cultural interface is the physical interface, the computer operating system and the programming languages as they have been conceived at the practical cultural level. The GUI of Microsoft Windows would be meaningless to anyone who is not already culturally familiar with communication that relies upon arranging and framing objects and icons within the spatial layout of frames. Indeed, if there are still human cultures where people have had no contact with desktops, books, texts and files, or screens with graphic, photographic and moving image representation, then a computer screen would make little sense at all. This is an extreme way of making the case for the cultural dependency of knowledge and understanding. But it is also the beginning of accounting for the cultural layer of the HCI as a hybrid of previous media forms and interfaces. Not that we were accustomed, prior to computing, to thinking of a painting or a book as an interface, although we have discussed how we imaginatively interface with books and paintings. In recognising the cultural dependency of the computer interface on previous media we can also say that, like other media, the cultural interface is itself a code that carries cultural messages in a variety of media.

20

CASE STUDY

'Vectorial Elevation' – public arts project: Rafael Lozano-Hemmer

Rafael Lozano-Hemmer is an artist whose practice crosses a number of fields and approaches, but who often works with new media on a large and spectacular scale. In this case study he discusses a large-scale interactive art work, 'Vectorial Elevation', which was created as an interactive installation for the Zócalo Square in Mexico City for Mexico's Millennium New Year celebrations.

The interface between computers and users is demonstrated in this case study as a complex form of histories and conventions. In this project the interface is spoken of as not only being a point at which people and computers meet, but also a point at which ethics, politics and expectations all inform the way that the artist makes choices about the appropriate way to construct an interface. These decisions are as much informed by the histories of different ways of working, such as theatre and architecture, as they are about technology.

In this case study, Rafael discusses the various roles of the artist and shows them to be a complex group of functions and positions. They include the artist as the creative motivator and the visionary of the project. They also include the artist as the producer, in this case operating at a very senior level with extremely large budgets, negotiating with the city and government at very senior levels, at the same time as managing a large team of practitioners. Last, they include the role of the artist as having a social mandate or social responsibility to develop work in a public context that addresses what the artist may define as his responsibilities.

Through his discussion, Rafael illustrates that this is substantially more than the way that, in another context, an artist might identify himself as having a responsibility only to himself or to further the technology he is working on.

'Vectorial Elevation'

Rafael Lozano-Hemmer's large-scale public art work 'Vectorial Elevation' was created as an interactive installation for the Zócalo Square in Mexico City for Mexico's Millennium New Year celebrations. It ran from 26 December 1999 until 7 January 2000 and has since been repeated in other locations.

'Vectorial Elevation' was a massive light display in which eighteen giant Xenon searchlights were situated around the perimeter of the square, placed on the roofs of the buildings, and used to create a constantly changing array of patterns. From dusk to dawn over the period that it was in operation, the robotic-controlled searchlights moved into a new configuration every six seconds to present a new light design. These 'fingers of light' made designs that ranged from grids to cathedral-like domes over the city square and which appeared to change with the fluidity of a choreographed perform-ance. Reaching over a half a mile into the airspace above the city square, the lights could be seen by the surrounding urban area for a distance of up to a fifteen-kilometre radius.

The lights were controlled and synchronised through a website with public access so that any visitor could design a light display. The website featured a 3-D Java interface that allowed participants to make a vectorial design of lights over the city and see it virtually from any point of view. Using a 'drag and drop' format with a series of simple options for people unfamiliar with design as well as more complex options for the more confident, the website enabled participants to make a design, see a model of how it would look in space, from various points of view, and to add their dedication before it was submitted.

When the project server in Mexico received a submission, it was numbered and entered into a queue. Every eight seconds the searchlights would orient themselves auto-matically and three webcams would take pictures to document a participant's design. The site had a streaming video of the square to enable remote users to view the way that the designs were presented and, in addition, a design archive page was made for each participant with comments, information and watermarked photos of their design. Once the archive web page was set up the participant was emailed the specific address so they could view or save the documentation.

'Vectorial Elevation' was conceived as a massive public participation project as well as a public spectacle. So, to facilitate access, free terminals were set up in public libraries and museums across the country where volunteers could explain to people how to use the site. In addition, the site received contributions from participants from ninety coun-tries and all the regions of Mexico.

'Vectorial Elevation' was awarded one of the leading international awards for new media art, the Golden Nica award, at the international festival Ars Electronica in Linz, Austria, in 2001.

Figure 20.1   Rafael Lozano-Hemmer, 'Vectorial Elevation', Zócalo Square, Mexico City (1999–2000)
'Vectorial Elevation' was an interactive art project originally designed to celebrate the arrival of the year 2000 in Mexico City's Zócalo Square. Using a design tool on a website, members of the public were able to design immense light sculptures over the historic centre of the city. The designs were rendered by eighteen robotic searchlights placed around the square and could be seen from a fifteen-kilometre radius. A personalised web page was made for every participant with comments, statistics and virtual and real images of their design from three perspectives.

Photograph by Martin Vargas.

Figure 20.2   Rafael Lozano-Hemmer, 'Vectorial Elevation', (1999–2000); view of the municipal palaces.
Photograph by Martin Vargas.

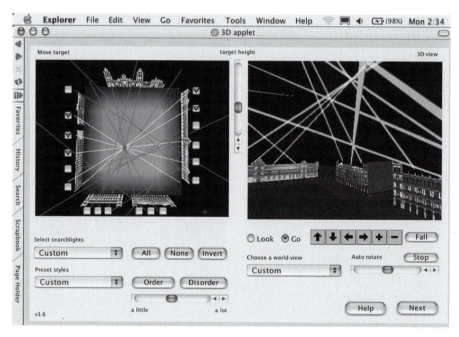

Figure 20.3   Rafael Lozano-Hemmer, 'Vectorial Elevation' (1999–2000).
Detail from the online interface with 3-D java applet that enabled participants to contribute designs for the presentation in Zócalo Square, Mexico City.

Background and interest in new media as performance

Rafael, how did your background in arts practice lead you to make new media pieces in the public space and also to work on such a massive scale as you have often done?

I started working in radio and performance arts, with live music. I would utilise available technology to create new sorts of instruments and use live sensors so that dancers and actors could control their own dynamic set design. Later my preference became to make performance into a 'theatre of the streets', which is to say that at any given point the city has embedded within it specific narratives, and what we wanted to do was disturb these stories. This way we would bring out tangents and subtexts to the narratives, or establish new relationships in public space.

Later on you gravitated towards working with new media technology from more conventional forms of performance in the public space. Was it an obvious progression to work in the public arena with technology?

When it comes to working with electronic media, I've always said it was closer to performing arts than to visual arts. It fitted in well to my approach to the 'theatre of the streets' which is a very theatrical approach to public space and one in which the

Figure 20.4   Rafael Lozano-Hemmer, 'Vectorial Elevation' (2004)
A 3-D rendering of a contributed light design in O'Connell Street, Dublin, Ireland, submitted while 'Vectorial Elevation' was presented during the celebrations for the EU expansion in 2004.

staging operates like a series of connective platforms within the city itself. I don't think of working with electronic media really as a collective object, but it is more of a process or a dialogue. Museums or galleries did not seem to be the best place to experience that, but to work in public space was the best way to get directness and dis-intermediation into work.

Working with scale

Creating work in public space also implies that the scale of the work is large, or that it can be expanded as necessary to take on the challenge of a big space. And your works have been very large, sometimes spectacularly so. How important has it been to you to work on this scale?

I have often said that my work is only as big as my insecurities! Though it is true that I am interested in working with technological amplification. It gives a new way of thinking about the concept of virtuality which makes us seem very small, often almost non-existent in the face of the complexities of the machine and the network. In virtual environments, like an architectural walk-through, data is presented through encumbering interfaces like VR helmets, and your body is left behind, and the virtual environment asks you to suspend disbelief and believe in the simulation. In contrast to this, in a public space, the difference in scale between us and massive public architecture is such

Figure 20.5   Rafael Lozano-Hemmer, 'Body Movies', Rotterdam (2001)
In 'Body Movies', photographic images of people standing in the street were projected onto the wall of a public square in Rotterdam. Passers-by could interact with the projections by casting their own shadow onto the building using the beam of large spotlights. Once they made their own shadow correspond exactly with that of one of the photographic images the program would then move onto another frame and introduce the image of a different person.

that we are made to seem tiny, almost to the point of negation of our own bodies. With relational architecture, which is what I have called my series of urban works, we do the opposite and amplify the human gesture so that it transforms the buildings around it.

One of the things that seem significant about all your works is that there is a real sense of people joyously performing alongside each other. There is rarely the sense that there is one individual participant who has a priority in the piece while others can only be spectators.

Yes, and my objective is not necessarily to have everybody take part in a managed way. Of course, there are limits to what they can do but I'm interested in setting up a platform that can still get out of control.

It is very important that in a public space no one will tell you how to act, and with media art including my own you are often given instructions telling you to press a button or move in a particular way around the space. This is something I have tried to avoid. For example, with an earlier work, 'Body Movies', which was created for a public square in Rotterdam in 2001, the interface was 'operated' by having people play with their own shadows, which is really very intuitive. I think the reason why a piece like this succeeds is because we all already have a intuitive understanding of what we can do with our shadows.

Collaborations and team operations

Can you describe how you work with collaborators? You've worked with a regular group of people over several years, some of whom share creative credits with you on the projects, including Will Bauer and Conroy Badger. How do you find that these sorts of collaborations affect the creative process?

I've been working with Will Bauer, who is an engineer and composer, for a dozen years or even more – we started working with theatre and interactive installations. Later, I started working with Conroy Badger who is an electrical engineer and a programmer. I also programme – but enough to know that I am terrible compared to Conroy. From the earliest projects we've never had a precious division between the development and the production of the piece. It's usually generated through both the invention of the tools and the conceptual framework.

The model of collaboration that we started to work with was one based a bit in cinema or performing arts. It uses the idea that there should be a director with a lead voice, and very clearly defined roles for other people involved in the piece. This way we could still keep the eccentricities and the biases and the nightmares that make a good work of art. Prior to us deciding to work this way, I had worked in a bigger theatre group in which everybody had an opinion and the final result was work that was just a result of consensus – which is not good for art. Now most of the time our collaborations have a core team and take on other people with different skills depending on the specific nature of the piece. For example, in 'Body Movies', which uses a very large number of photographs taken on the street, I worked with five photographers.

Today we live in an era of collaboration. I don't think the popular notion of the artist mostly working alone is often true with new media. Even if you are a solo artist working with Photoshop you have to be aware of the fact that your work is influenced by the programmers who built certain tools. I think when you are working with interactive art you are always working with a collaborative context and dialogue.

Necessary skills and expertise

We've talked about the other collaborators. What are the skills that you bring to the table as director and key creative visionary which enable a project like 'Vectorial Elevation' to take place?

The first thing I think is the capability to understand the context and also to study the precedents and what other people are doing. Being a generalist is something that is extremely useful. I actually studied chemistry and art history and then I worked in performance, so I am the kind of person who hovers over several disciplines. It helps to be able to move between different disciplines, and to feel comfortable with the languages of those disciplines, when you aim to produce a project. Sometimes I call my function the lubricating glue. On the one hand you can lubricate to make things happen and take the path of least resistance so a project can go ahead. And on the other hand you 'conglomerate' people who would not otherwise be together, like programmers and producers, or funders and press people. I think that this kind of work requires that directorial capability to comprehend the multiple entry points and to present it to the general public, so that they can see it as something valuable. To do this you have to be rigorous with the kind of conceptual or ideological background you have for the piece and you have to understand the ways in which the technology can be made to work in your project.

The evolution of 'Vectorial Elevation'

How did 'Vectorial Elevation' evolve as a project? Did you have a very fixed sense, from early on, of what it was going to be, and what your approach to it would be?

The commission for 'Vectorial Elevation' was for the Millennium celebrations in Mexico City and so I studied what other cities were doing to celebrate the Millennium. I got outraged over the kind of pedagogical 'sol et lumière' spectacles that are so often used and which try to represent the richness of a culture in an exhaustive way through icons and stereotypes. If you are trying to represent a culture, what is often most salient is what you are actually omitting. The Minister of Culture in Mexico was very accepting of my criticisms but said that the proposal needed to stem from an episode in Mexican history. I then nominated as a starting point the fact that cybernetics was first postulated in Mexico City at the National Centre for Cardiology in 1946, where Mexican cardiologist Arturo Rosenbleuth was working with Norbert Wiener to try to understand self-regulation of the heart. They hypothesised the theory of messages and feedback in order to understand this phenomenon. Based on this I proposed cybernetics as a part of Mexican history and thus 'Vectorial Elevation' as a project, which was accepted.

The site nominated for the project was Zócalo Square. The space is so large that the architectural scale swamps an individual. There could be a demonstration of 30,000 people but the numbers would seem tiny in the whole square. So I proposed that in order to work with such a space we needed to work with technologies of amplification that would not make it into a little ghetto but that somehow the whole square could be personalised. On top of that we had the fascination of working with the most powerful lights in the world, which are of course associated with military spectacles and victory parades and all of that, so we had to consider how we could turn around technology and make it into something that the people could use.

Conceptual basis to developing an online project

One of the very notable things about 'Vectorial Elevation' was that it united people of different communities in the one experience. There was an online community and an offline community, each in very different contexts and not necessarily working together but experiencing it together. For people online, designing light patterns made sense knowing that they would be realised in the public space with a live audience. For people in the square, knowing that the designs they were observing were sent in by the public was an important aspect that made the work more than just a spectacle. Was the online aspect of 'Vectorial Elevation' a fundamental part of the project from the beginning, as a way of enabling large-scale public participation?

We agreed that we needed tools that could allow us to disseminate this project not only through the city but also through the whole world. So we aimed to use this as an opportunity to make a high-tech project in which people could be represented through their own creativity. In Mexico in 1999 only 1 million people had Internet access and they were mostly the elite so we also ensured that there were also public-sited Internet stations so that other people could go online.

The role of the non-interactive subjects was also an important part of the piece. You don't need to have everybody who participates in a piece to be going online or working with the interface. I was always inspired by the work by Sol le Witt, in which instructions are an important part of the conceptual aspect of the work. It is wrong to say that the moment of contemplation is not an active moment. The physical response to the way you react with the work affects your perception in an active way. Your body reacts to it and to an extent that is exactly what is happening in 'Vectorial Elevation'. When you are standing under the canopy of light, the entire field of view overhead is in motion. You feel a sense of motion, you feel a sense of displacement or dynamism, and those feelings are active so there is nothing passive about just contemplating.

Did 'Vectorial Elevation' develop the way you originally wanted it to, or did you have to adapt it as you progressed with the development?

Absolutely. One of the things I find fascinating is that, when you are making this kind of work, there is a large degree of improvisation in the actual development of the piece. As with most media artists I did not have access to the equipment that I would eventually use. When you're working with this scale, your understanding of the effect that these powerful lights will have on the square is entirely reliant on your imagination. When you finally do get to have all the technology together in the space and all of your decisions have to be compressed in that tiny little window of time, your capability to improvise, to make sound aesthetic decisions, has to go into high gear.

One of the examples of how that worked out in 'Vectorial Elevation' is that in my original concept I assumed that in order to process and present a fairly large number of designs the lights were going to have to render patterns in the sky every second or, at most, every two seconds. I wanted, as much as possible, the tempo of the piece to be like a heartbeat. I wanted almost constant motion. It was not until we started working with the lights that we realised that for the lights to move 180 degrees we needed eight seconds and that was, therefore, the maximum speed that we could have for the change of designs. The decision was made to bring down the tempo of the piece to eight or ten seconds. Upon seeing it I decided that we had to make it even longer. I realised that we had to work with a space of contemplation.

Presumably, you were also having to deal with problem solving on a technical level as well as an aesthetic one. Did you have to make compromises?

In this sort of project you are constantly having to deal with large, unexpected obstacles. The difficulties happen in the very last minute. Finally, you've got the technology in place and then a number of directorial decisions have to be made right then and there. And that's at the level of aesthetics but also with practical issues. We almost had to cancel the project because we put the lights up and turned them on and then all of a sudden we got a call from the airport telling us that we were shining into the landing trajectory of the aeroplanes and blinding the pilots. So, on one hand, we had to deploy an immense amount of bureaucratic negotiations, and, on the other, we had to come up with a technological solution. We ended up modifying the program so that whenever the lights were directed towards the landing path of the planes they automatically dimmed by 30 per cent and the beam was opened more. So by the time that it could hit an aeroplane five kilometres away it would not actually be so bright. This kind of thing is totally overwhelming – you're about to be shut down for something which you didn't think of when you were first conceptualising the project and you've got to be able to respond very quickly.

I don't recommend making a work like 'Vectorial Elevation' to anybody who wants to have a peaceful and quiet time. This kind of problem happens all the time with projects and now, at least, when we show 'Vectorial Elevation' we know which are likely to be the problem issues. We know how to deal with censorship, with possible corporate takeover by sponsors, we know about air traffic control, we know about safety in terms of search lights, we know about dealing with the noise of generators, we know about the bandwidth we can get from the Internet – stuff like that. And now it is a lot easier to set up a project like this but definitely when you're first working on one of them it is like having to become something like a production manager for a rock opera.

Earlier you discussed that you were interested in the narratives within different public spaces. On one hand we might talk of these as master narratives of power and history, but they are also about public ownership, expectation and understanding. 'Vectorial Elevation' demonstrates a work that is presented in a public context and has to negotiate the consent of the public on different levels. Sometimes it might be official, through formal channels, and sometimes it is much more subtle and about being respectful. Were there particular ways in which you had to approach these issues?

One example of consent is political and about freedom of expression, and one of the really interesting political discussions we had was to do with censorship. In Mexico when we did the project, the Zapatista movement was very active. There were a lot of extremely media aware Zapatista activists who were carrying out all sorts of electronic disturbances online and then along came my project which was going to take place in the most emblematic part of the city and in which people would be able to express their opinions through this method without any censorship. It created a very interesting debate because the Minister of Culture of Mexico totally defended the freedom of people to say whatever they wanted. However, there were a lot of other bureaucratic characters in the background who were advocating that we should censor the texts that were being sent in online. So it was a very fascinating discussion to have, and of course all of this happened just at the very last minute. Just while we were trying to figure out how not to disturb the aeroplanes, we were also having to deal with political issues of censorship and practical and technological issues.

Perhaps it helps to think about the sorts of projects that we are talking about as oper-ating through evolving processes, not fixed. Often new media artists don't talk in terms of specific goals and outcomes when describing the works that they are aiming to make. Maybe this is about keeping the possible outcomes unrestricted but it may also help to keep creative opportunities open to them, which is something that new media artists are often most interested in. Does this matter to you?

That's true, and if you know what the outcome is going to be, then why do it? It has to be alive – you have to create a space for the public to express their involvement. We have to trust that the public has a very sophisticated behaviour that will emerge, rather than treat them with a paternalistic attitude. Often you find in museums or other insti-tutions that you are given a didactic linear reading of how to interpret a work, but this makes it boring. People are able to respond with much more ingenuity than some author-ities think they are. With interactive art you depend on the public to participate, otherwise the piece does not exist. It's a really humbling decision as an artist because there's nothing you can do to control how the public will react. And the celebration of that is something that makes interactive art very strong.

Rafael Lozano-Hemmer's website is www.lozano-hemmer.com

21 **Interactivity**

How are we to understand the term interactivity?

'Interactivity' has become a familiar and overused word in the everyday language of new media, which for some theorists renders it vague and unhelpful (Manovich 2001: 55). But it is hard to ignore, let alone dismiss, the word 'interactivity', because there is not as yet another word to describe how the user is 'positioned' in the human computer interface (HCI), and because interactivity focuses attention on the engagement of the user of computer-mediated communication. Interactivity is also a central concept in the further development and design of all graphical user interfaces (GUIs), and is therefore central to computer architecture and computer design. In addition, interactivity is an important concept because of the comparison it provokes with previous media communication, encouraging new thinking about old media. Because interactivity has become one of the naturalised everyday terms of new media, it has currency across a wide range of practices and productions. Interactivity is common to any discussion of the computer user's experience and, hence, the design and development of both the physical and metaphorical interface with the computer and the data it allows us to access.

Interactivity remains a key concept in new media. It is a concept that marks out a set of defining and characteristic differences between analogue and digital media. Interactivity has been hailed as both the founding principle of a new medium as well as its defining myth. Interactivity is the bedrock of the claim for the radical newness of digital media in two important senses. First, the idea that new ways of accessing and manipulating data through HCI and GUI extend the human mind and create new ways of thinking. Second, that interactivity creates a new set of communication tools, which change the relationship between author and audience and hence offer new freedoms of expression. While there is substance in both of these claims, the major criticism is that new media's transformative and emancipatory nature has not been borne out by the experience of most users of interactive computer products. On this critical view, computer interactivity is characterised as displaying limited choice and navigation within fixed and bounded programs.

A concrete way of approaching interactivity in computer-mediated communication is to focus upon the programming languages that establish the baseline possibilities of interactivity in the first place. The first principle of computer interactivity is that the user can interrupt a sequence of programmed information, whether in the form of image, sound or text, and then choose to make a link to another part of the same sequence or jump to a new and different sequence. The user is able to move through the data-set in a branching structure, depending on the (hyper)links that have been programmed. The branching structure presents itself culturally as a mental structure of choices in which the user has to ask her/himself which path in the fork they wish to take. The interactive designer has to build in to the data-set a structure of forking paths according to some concept or logic, even if the logic is randomness. The multiple linking of messages, or parts of a message, was made technically possible by the creation of a system of labelling and addressing electronic information within discrete packages which could then be stored and accessed within a network of computers.

Hypertext

Computer interactivity is based upon programming 'languages' which get computers to 'talk to each other' in a common way so that pages of text, graphics and images stored on computers can be accessed and displayed across the network of computers. The basis for this 'language' is the hyperlink, which is an element in an electronic document that links to another place in the same document or to an entirely different document. HTML is the universal language for publishing hypertext on the World Wide Web. It is a non-proprietary format and can be created and processed by a wide range of tools. The original concept of hypertext was developed by Ted Nelson in the 1960s, who also acknowledged the earlier writing of Vannevar Bush (1945) in applying a concept of how the human mind works through the linking of ideas and thoughts by association to the computer. Nelson (1974) coined the term 'hypertext' to refer to a form of electronic text based upon non-sequential writing that branches and allows choices to the reader. Elaborating on Nelson's account, Bolter (1991) defined hypertext as having 'no canonical order' and that 'every path defines an equally convincing reading'. A (hyper)text, now seen as a network of possible texts, cannot be taken as univocal since it is a multiplicity, and it is in this fact that Nelson argued that hypertext changed the reader's relationship to the text and the relationship between author and reader since it gave the reader the ability to write back into the text. Later exponents of the radical potential of hypertext argue that hypertext frees the reader from the hierarchical and fixed thought inscribed in the linear text (Landow 1992). Hypertext allows the reader to make lateral connections by mental association and deliberation through the branching structure. This, it is argued, encourages the reader to make novel connections and promotes a creative, more active and independent problem-solving approach. On the other side of the argument, it is evident that hyper-linking and hypertexts create problems of coherence and definition for the 'reader' within a text or sustained train of thought as well as broader problems of the lineage and authenticity of the intellectual sources of texts.

Hypermedia

While the arguments about hypertext as a radically new form of writing and conscious-ness continue to be explored, there is more general agreement that the interactive nature of hyper-linking can, and does, augment intellectual capacity and give greater and more immediate access to bodies of knowledge and media tools. The graphical computer interface presents a hypermediated environment that extends the notion of the text in hypertext to include visual, sound, animation and graphic content and these hypermedia texts are extended beyond the written or linguistic text.

It is the underlying numerical coding of digital media and the modular structure of the media object that allows an infinite number of different interfaces to be generated from the same data. Digital media objects are not hardwired together as in analogue media which have closed elements within a fixed structure. Digital media objects have an open and fluid state, as so many bits, and it is this that shifts the emphasis in communication towards the procedures of programming. The customising of data in user interfaces represents a major arena of such programming development, since the elements remain separable and are only brought together by the programming of hyperlinks.

Hypertext Mark-Up Language (HTML)

Hypertext Mark-up Language is a universal and networked application of hyperlinking. HTML is now the simplest way of adding human-readable data onto the web, which was developed to allow unidirectional links to be made between documents. Tim Berners-Lee wrote the first HTML language and defined the URL and HTTP specifications, which established the World Wide Web. His first program was later developed into Mosaic at the National Centre for Supercomputing Applications (NCSA) and, subsequently, Marc Andreessen, who had developed Mosaic, left NCSA to found the Netscape Corporation, which in turn set the stage for Microsoft. While Tim Berners-Lee, working at CERN, had developed HTML as a non-proprietary piece of software that could be used and developed freely, Netscape and Microsoft were established commercial corporations looking to maximise investment, turn-over and profit. The division between these two institutional forms of software have given rise to the politics of the free software movement, and computer hackers who regard the Internet as a universal language beyond ownership. Conversely, the interests of Microsoft and other large corporations are in code encryption and policing their legal rights to sell licences to their software.

In terms of our discussion here on the practice of interactivity, it is the access, understanding and manipulation of the code upon which the software is written that is seen to guarantee greater control of the medium.

> I liked the idea that a piece of information is really defined only by what it's related to, and how it is related. There really is little else to meaning. The structure is everything . . . The brain has no knowledge until connections are made between neurons. All that we know, all that we are, comes from the way our neurons are connected.
>
> (Berners-Lee 1999)

Linear v. non-linear

The problem with the arguments about the limits or possibilities of interactivity in new media is that the tendency in some writing and thinking has been to set up binary oppositions in which the interactive features of new (digital) media are all too easily set against the apparent non-interactive nature of previous (analogue) media forms. On this view, watching television or film becomes an essentially non-interactive experience, whereas clicking around the Internet, playing a computer game or using a CD-ROM is interactive, because it requires user participation to make links between the discrete parts. The extension of the same argument is that computer programs enable new structures in which the user can move through the (data) content at will: old media, film for instance, is a preset programme, which cannot be altered by the viewer.

Another way in which this binary conceptualisation of interactivity has been employed is to say that new media is non-linear, whereas old media, film and television, are essentially linear. The film will run its ninety-minute course whether you stay and watch it or not. You can't intervene in the cinema performance or a broadcast television programme, all you can do is walk out of the cinema or turn the TV off, whereas the computer program allows the user to interrupt and branch. This difference is increasingly being eroded by digital television and DVD, which do allow for a greater degree of manipulation of pre-recorded material and, of course, freeze-framing, fast-forwarding and rewinding are long-established features of the experience of analogue video watching. We will look at what is entailed by the idea of non-linearity in more depth, but the point about interactivity being made here relates to technology. Computer interactivity is, first and foremost, the ability of the user to interrupt a 'data-set' and to be able to 'jump' from, or 'link', any one discrete point to another. As we have established, video, like all analogue media, is a continuous recording of information, rather than being made up from the discrete unit of digital code, so moving around a videotape requires the mechanical time to move the tape across the playback/recording cylinder. Digital information is constantly being reassembled in the much faster electronic time.

An extension of the claim for the liberating qualities of non-linear and interactive media is that the audience is put in a radically new position of active engagement, in contrast to old (linear) media, in which reception is essentially passive. This is one basis for the vogue definition of new media as 'lean-forward media' as opposed to old media as 'lean-back media'.

Most critics of the claim for the new freedoms of new media have gone to great lengths to demonstrate the actual continuities between old and new media forms in order to show that much of what was being claimed for new media was present in old media. A very obvious example is the printed book where, while the conventional organisation of text is from left to right and front to back, in the sequential order set out by the author, it is perfectly possible to physically and intellectually move around the text by turning pages and holding in the mind what you have read. Most comparisons of old and new media establish that all media, from the printing press to television, borrow and reframe many aspects of previous and parallel media. On examination, the current stage of the development of new media has been shown to contain obvious continuities with the forms and conventions of analogue media, while at the same time, re-ordering, re-composing their meaning and significance.

Binary opposites

As we have alluded to above, one of the recurrent ways of expressing the defining qualities of new media is to say what they are not. This has been done, as we have discussed elsewhere, by contrasting the operational qualities and possibilities of new media with those of so-called old or established media. In this way, for instance, it has been possible to contrast the digital photographic image with the chemical photographic image, or the previous editing methods of film and video with those of digital editing. Through such comparisons it has been possible to discuss the similarities and the differences in the cultural codes and conventions, or what we have previously summarised as the languages of analogue and digital media. At the point of extreme difference a set of binary opposites can be posited which, if nothing else, demonstrates how, at an earlier stage in the development of new media, the argument and the promise of a radical departure from old media was formulated.

Analogue	*Digital*
Transparency	Opacity
Realism	Montage/collage
Linear	Non-linear
Non-interactive	Interactive
Passive	Active
Window on the world	Windowed worlds
Perspective	Surface
Proscenium	Permeable space
Old media	*New media*

One of the useful things about this exercise in defining binary differences is that it produces a group of related terms that operate at the descriptive level of computer-mediated communication. The list of words in the left-hand column does resonate with what we have come to expect of film or photography. In their mainstream development, film and photography have asserted media transparency and been commonly understood as windows on the world precisely in order to bring us realistic depictions of the outside world. In contrast, words in the right-hand column of the above list have to be more speculative of the characteristics of a new media, now defined in opposition to that which is old. But at a descriptive level we can have no quarrel with the fact that computer programs with screen and keyboard interfaces have established conventions in which the screen is subdivided into a number of frames/windows, any one of which can be active at any one time. And we can go on to say that the screen interface is a surface, and although digital code can simulate spatial perspective, so that any one window can be arranged in a Cartesian spatial perspective, it remains a surface to be replaced at will by another surface. In this sense the surface is opaque and the collection of windows is a collage. It is also true that while there is always a hierarchy of program commands, we can move within and between windows in a non-linear way insofar as we can 'jump' or move from point to point within an almost infinite network of points. But the point of the binary exercise is not to characterise old media as in some way limited and historically redundant against a forward-looking and dynamic new set of achieved media possibilities. We have acknowledged that so-called old media has many of the qualities of new media – our discussion of interactivity, for instance, and that new media has yet to demonstrate that it delivers the new qualities in all of those ways indicated by the list. In contrast to the tendency to use the binary exercise to uncritically reject old media as limited and applaud new media as unlimited, is its use in exploring the dynamic tension between each of the formal oppositional elements. In effect, applying such formal oppositions becomes a fruitful way of examining old media from the vantage point of new media and vice versa. As has been pointed out, all old media was new once and it is possible to reconstruct the historical formation of any medium where many more possibilities of use were present than those that subsequently became settled. If we can see in those older formations of media the undeveloped, unsettled and unformed uses, then we can apply such an understanding to the current moment of new media. On the basis of such historical insights we can conclude that current interests and fashions in new media will give way to others and that some interests will predominate over others.

Technological interface

Interactivity in computer-mediated communication (CMC) is currently governed by the manufacturing limits of the human–computer interface (HCI), which in its current and dominant form is that of the screen, keyboard and mouse of the PC. There are, of course, other material interfaces or peripheral devices which, when combined with software, create interfaces using the human voice or, with whiteboards and pens, using hand-writing and drawing. More experimentally, HCI can be through the whole body, using data-gloves and vision helmets or with remote sensors, but generally, interactivity is, for most people, limited to the interface of the screen and the devices (keyboard and mouse) for screen command.

The current limits of interface hardware and software are reflected in the idea of the impatient user in front of the screen, constantly clicking, waiting for screens to refresh, images to be rendered, files to be saved, or of the frustrated user, who typically experiences the system crash or failed link. The experience of slowness or error in digital media is measured, not against the time taken in older media, but against an expectation of a technology which promises fluid and flexible connections in a near timeless (virtual) time. In any comparison of the time taken to perform similar functions in analogue media, searching a card index or the library shelves, writing a letter or developing and printing chemical film, it would be pointed out that digital media is super-fast.

In industrialised cultures the time spent in front of screens continues to expand, both at work and in leisure. The amount of information that is received on-screen, publicly and privately, increases correspondingly. The time spent in front of screens, whether in the lean-forward or lean-back mode, presents us with a range of physical, social and intellectual issues related to the replacement of human-to-human communication with human-to-machine communication. 'Life on the screen', as Sherry Turkle (1995) has put it, produces effects both upon the human body, now considered redundant or useless, and on social identity or the self, which in cyberspace is no longer considered unitary.

Interface analogies

The analogies with other human activities that have sprung up around the use of the Internet and the World Wide Web reflect some of the different dimensions of the inter-active experience. We will examine the cultural meaning of such analogies in the specific discussion of interface metaphors when we discuss navigation, but here analogies operate simply as the attempt to define the interactive experience. The experience of waiting for the next thing to happen is reflected in the intervals between the next big wave, in the 'surfing' metaphor. An openness to mental changes of direction, interest and occupation is reflected in the bookshop or library 'browsing' metaphor. The low-level, partially distracted character of Internet browsing is often down-graded in the analogy of 'grazing'. The games player, whose rapid thumb pressing of the games handset acts as an interface to her screen presence, is also an 'impatient user', ultimately frustrated by the physical limits of the interface. All of these modes of attention and engagement with computers suggest that there is a general striving for greater instantaneity, spontaneity, fluidity and intuition in the HCI relationship. This suppressed desire for greater freedom in the HCI is reflected in ongoing research and development, whether in the telematics of space robots, or ever more responsive games. It is also part of the discourse of the deep, immersive dream of virtual reality, which contains the desire for a limitless knowledge machine or simulated realities. Developments in artificial intelligence, robotics and nanotechnology also push at the frontiers of the human–machine interface. All of these discourses contain, in different registers, the belief that current communicative tools could be extended by forms of increased end-user interactivity, characterised by the idea of greater freedoms or capacities of thought and communication.

Interactivity and the non-hierarchical

The value of non-linearity in data access, retrieval and composition is further advanced by the recognition that digital programs, systems and networks are potentially non-hierarchical. In the place of traditional hierarchies of knowledge or information, reflected in the library, museum, archive and academy, the knowledge embedded in cyberspace is no longer seen as territorialised or governed. Knowledge in cyberspace is imagined as horizontal rather than vertical and connections between objects and information are pictured as random until they are given meaning by the user, who 'authors' their own set, route or collection. The user is placed in the position of making novel connections between bits of data and the information and ideas they contain, and hence can operate outside of the ways in which knowledge and understanding hierarchical organisation is governed. Such modes of interactivity are seen to credit greater human agency to the user within these changing forms of communication: making new and novel connections. Having greater agency in a space that is conceptualised as horizontal is closely associated with established notions of human creativity and play.

The counter arguments are, once again, not against the principle or potential of CMC and HCI for greater freedom of thought or communication for the artist, scientist or the population at large, but against the claim that it is an established fact. Early pioneers of cyberspace have long pointed to the increasingly prescribed organisation of Internet portals and the dominance of large corporations. Those scientists, programmers and artists who have advocated the development of free software have developed incisive critiques of the new hierarchies and ideologies of software. More broadly, studies of the cultural and social uses of cyberspace/CMC/HCI demonstrate that the qualities of greater human agency, freedom and play are counterpoised by greater human surveillance, exploitation and cultural exclusion and narrow forms of end-user consumption.

Control, automation, variability and interactivity

At the operational level of the HCI, interactivity can simply be equated with control of a technology and the short history of the development of HCIs can be understood as one of increasing and improving human access to, and control of, data storage, retrieval and manipulation. However, the discussion of, and interest in, interactivity stretches beyond the technical organisation of HCIs into culturally embedded applications and uses in which programmed interactivity is increasingly discussed in relationship to thought, knowledge, imagination and representation. These are, after all, the terms in which we approach the discussion of analogue media, precisely because the material and technical apparatuses have been subsumed within patterns of settled use. In film, for instance, the medium of light-sensitive chemicals exposed on continuous strips of celluloid is no longer the point of interest, but rather what can be said or expressed through shooting film. The recent revival of interest in analogue film apparatus and its relationship to meaning has been re-invoked precisely because of the potential developments of digital, interactive moving-image technologies. This is another aspect of saying that one of the unlooked-for cultural outcomes of the development of new media is that it has provoked interest in re-examining the settled relationship we have to old media.

The interactivity of old media

The differences between old and new media, set in binary opposition, become much more problematic as a view of analogue media, because they define analogue media as historically closed. It is not possible to cast old media simply as non-interactive or linear just because the user does not physically, literally, navigate the order in which data are presented. A painting on the gallery wall is a static object, a flat framed surface, which is viewed at once, and yet there is a physical interaction as the viewer scrutinises the surface at different distances. In reading the painted image the viewer's eye travels across the surface and her/his mind is actively seeking to interpret the given information. The mind will fill in elements where the visual information is incomplete in order to make sense of a figure-ground relationship or an implied spatial-scale relationship. Put another way, for as long as the viewer is held looking at the painting the mind is deciphering elements of visual information in an interactive way in order to build up a set of meanings for the whole. The same model of the interactive viewer having to complete the image can be said about photography and film. The recognition that old media also contain a physical and mental interactivity should lead us to delineate carefully in descriptive accounts of new media as exclusively interactive, and question accounts of old media that suggest the viewer is passive or inactive.

It is important, therefore, to insist that interactivity, as such, is not new, it is just new to electronic media. We interact physically and psychologically with our environment and with each other as a defining aspect of our humanity and culture. At its most general, the term 'interactivity' applies to a multitude of human activities, encompassing such things as sex, reading a book, watching a play, conversation or playing games. At root, interactivity defines a certain kind of relationship between humans and/or objects within an environment. Interactivity is a relationship in which the actions and behaviours of people and/or objects are co-determinate. A working definition of interactivity might be, 'that which promotes or influences reciprocal action, or, that quality which involves or encourages response'. Further, interactivity has been summed up as, 'the mutual and simultaneous activity on the part of both participants, usually working towards some goal, but not necessarily'. Both of these attempts to define interactivity involve the basic idea that an action on the part of one person or thing creates a reaction in or upon another, and so on. Conversation is a social interaction as the utterances of the participants are reciprocal. Culturally, interactivity has been applied to contexts in which individuals are actively participating and immersed in a constructed relationship to an environment. Education is a very good example of where interactivity has been deployed in argument. Traditional educational pedagogy, derived historically in different ways from scriptural iteration, can be seen as placing the learner in a passive position in which the student receives and copies that which the teacher transmits. Against this traditional pedagogic account, modern activity-based learning stresses that learning is enhanced by an interaction between the learner and the objects of learning. While Victorian pedagogy conjures up the image of the mute pupil rote learning by copying, the twentieth-century, enlightened teacher encouraged pupils to question and discuss. Today, there are still arguments among educationalists about how we learn and the best ways of learning. Liberal and progressive pedagogy underlines how increased pupil involvement and interaction encourages greater depth of understanding, while traditional pedagogy stresses the importance of teacher authority in defining the right orders of knowledge. It is no accident that computers have been increasingly deployed in education, not only because information communication technology (ICT) is recognised as central to the knowledge economy and information society in general, but also because interactive computer programming has been seen to provide interactive or programmed learning experiences.

It should be clear by now that interactivity is a general human quality and that technologies are not inherently or automatically interactive, quite the reverse in fact. In any history of machines, we would have to note that automation, not interaction, was the goal of development. This is demonstrable in the historical trajectory of the industrial revolution, in which tools and operations were first mechanised and driven by steam power, and later in the more complex stages of mechanisation, powered by electricity. In each successive stage of industrial advancement, machines were produced that reduced the mental and manual labour of the machine operative. Today, aircraft are piloted automatically by machines and the role of the pilot is to watch the instruments which show the progress of the machine flying the aircraft. Workers in automated industrialised plants watch machines, periodically inspecting dials, levels, meters and carrying out certain manual operations thought uneconomic to programme machines to do.

Automation brings about a relationship between human and machine not only of replacing human labour but also of putting human labour into the position of watching and waiting. It has long been pointed out that automation represents a deskilling of human labour in such machine/computer automated operations, rather than the development of higher-order skills involving creativity and thought. However, the discourse, which posits either the eventual dominance of machines over humans (the dystopian future) or humans over machines (the utopian future), is not the issue here, because humanity is not faced with a deterministic either/or situation. Computer/machine complexes have been developed that undertake a range of routine and repetitive tasks previously requiring the mental and manual labour of countless thousands of people. Equally, countless thousands of people now routinely interact with computer/machine complexes in the labour of creating, tracking and, crucially, consuming data.

While such macro observations of the characteristic organisation of labour in the Information Age are sanguine reminders of the routine and repetitive nature of our interaction with computers, they should not detract us from looking, in some detail, at HCI interactivity in both its achieved and potential forms. It is important here to remember that we interact with computers in both wage labour and leisure time and, therefore, our relationship to the computer is typically one of both production and consumption. For most people this relationship might be experienced as one in which routine and repetition is the primary experience of computers in wage labour, while novelty, entertainment and choice are the experiences of the use of computers in leisure. Certainly, the marketing of computer-based domestic and personal digital media stresses again and again the increased choice and freedom afforded by computers, digital television, mobile phones and broadband access to the Internet. The numerically smaller number of people who use computers as professional producers, designers, architects, artists, photographers, film-makers, musicians and programmers predominantly experience interactivity in terms of the use of the computer as a tool. But clearly interactivity increasingly and seamlessly crosses and re-crosses the boundaries of production and consumption, work and leisure, in ways which bring into question previous divisions of producer and consumer, author and reader or storyteller and listener.

The promise of a radical shift of the relationship between producer and consumer because of computer interactivity is, as we have noted before, typically couched in terms of an as yet unrealised future potential, rather than any actual achieved modes. Commentators point to the relatively limited forms of programmed interactivity, rather than to any major area where the interactive potential of autonomous programmable links between data points has transformed art, communication or modes of thinking. The Internet does represent the first truly new media of the twentieth century which has been taken up and applied on a global scale and in a short space of time that has to be recognised as nothing short of astonishing. And yet at the same time as we can marvel at the scale of this vast network and the speed with which it has been established, the ways in which it has become embedded in everyday life are mundane. There is, however, something sterile in the rehearsal of the intellectual 'stand-off' between techno-sceptics and techno-utopians over the issue of current achievement and future potential. The arguments are not reducible to either an ideology of a technological (determined) future, as the techno-sceptics have it, or simply a matter of the next technological (Romantic) leap forward, as the techno-utopians typically frame it. Interactivity is in the here and now as all of the following; as ideology (discourse), as instrumentality (control), and as cultural products (objects). All three aspects are bound up with understanding, use and production.

We can ground these arguments about interactivity by seeing how they are entailed in cultural projects involving the human–machine relationship. The term 'project' is used here to signal how social and cultural applications of technological development, and intellectual reflection of such uses, are grouped and related in practice, i.e. how ideology, control and product are inter-related. There is a case for saying that what we are signalling as cultural projects of technology are the material-social manifestations of specific discourse or ideology. Developing the science and technology of putting a human on the moon can easily be seen as an example of a project of ideology as much as technology. The larger project of space travel is not simply a practical application of science and technology, but also a discourse about the future of humanity. The same will be true of the projects of human–computer communication which form the discursive and practical framework of new media.

In Part IV we illustrate how the larger cultural framework of new media operates by identifying two persistent technological discourses that many new media productions fit within. The first discourse is about the relationship between the human mind and memory and the machinic extension of consciousness. The second discourse we identify as the relationship between human perception, representation and language and how machines can extend our perceptual and communicative world. Our distinction in discourse is comparable to Peter Lunenfield's characterisation of systems and operations for accessing the database as 'extractive' and interfaces which invite us to navigate the database in graphic representational worlds as 'immersive'.

Summary of interactivity

- Interactivity is a naturalised everyday term in new media.
- Interactivity has been hailed as both the founding principle of a new medium as well as its defining myth.

- Interactivity focuses attention on the engagement of the user of computer-mediated communication.
- Interactivity is a central concept in the design of the graphical user interface (GUI).
- Interactivity is an important concept because of the comparison it provokes with previous media communication, encouraging new thinking about old media.
- Interactivity marks out a set of defining and characteristic differences between analogue and digital media.
- Interactivity changes the relationship between author and audience.
- Interactivity is characterised as displaying limited choice and navigation within fixed and bounded programs.
- The interactive features of new (digital) media are all too easily set against the apparent non-interactive nature of previous (analogue) media forms in binary opposition.
- Interactivity for most people is limited to the interface of the screen and the devices (keyboard and mouse) for screen command.
- Technological interfaces promise fluid and flexible connections to and between data in a near timeless (virtual) time.
- Interactivity is not new, it is just new to electronic media.
- Interactivity applies to a multitude of human activities.
- Interactivity is a relationship in which the actions and behaviours of people and/or objects are co-determinate.
- Interactivity promotes or influences reciprocal action, or that quality which involves or encourages response.
- Interactivity is the mutual and simultaneous activity on the part of two or more participants.
- Interactivity is a general human quality and technologies are not inherently or automatically interactive.

22

CASE STUDY

Interactive installations: David Rokeby

....

D avid Rokeby is an artist whose work is largely in the form of installations that use a software system that he has devised. Since the mid-1980s he has been one of the leading international practitioners in new media, exploring the possibilities of computer systems as well as finding new ways to create interactive artworks. One of the most important things about his works is that they demonstrate that interactivity can create highly complex environments because it brings together the intelligence of the machine with the knowledge, assumptions and perceptions of its audience. As a result, his system actively demonstrates how the users are key participants in the work and shape its possibilities at a range of levels.

Based in Canada, Rokeby's work has been internationally acclaimed. Among the prestigious awards he has won are: the British Academy for Film and Television Arts (BAFTA) for Interactive Art in 2000, the Prix Ars Electronica in 1991 and 1997, the Golden Nica in 2002 and the Canadian Governor General's Award in Visual and Media Arts in 2002.

David Rokeby argues that interactivity is a medium through which we communicate with ourselves. It provides us with a reflection of our actions and decisions, like a mirror. Rokeby speaks of technology as something that at a very fundamental level works for us because it addresses how we conceptualise our place in the world.

As an artist, Rokeby is keenly aware of the difference between his point of view and that of an engineer who strives to maintain the illusion of transparency of the process. The engineer may emphasise interactivity as being a series of processes, activated and controlled through an interface, and that through design and refinement his or her goal may be to maintain the illusion of apparent transparency. In comparison, Rokeby sees the role of an artist as being to explore the meaning of the interface itself, and through that to ask questions about the way we understand the world.

Rokeby's installations are frequently based on a software system he has created, the 'Very Nervous System'. The system enables complex ways in which the computer analyses the participant's, or user's, actions and feeds back data that can result in a variety of forms. Typically, in his work, Rokeby questions how we construct 'meanings' by making the outcomes of his work a little unexpected, so that we think about our cognitive processes as well as those of the machine's activities.

Figure 22.1   David Rokeby, montage demonstrating the operation of the 'Very Nervous System'
(VNS) software (1990)
'Very Nervous System' is an interactive sound installation using video cameras, image processors,
computers, synthesisers and a sound system to create a space in which the movements of the participant's body create sound and/or music. The installation uses a complex but quick feedback loop
and the interface is invisible and very diffuse, occupying a large volume of space, unlike most interfaces which are focused and definite. 'Very Nervous System' has been primarily presented as an
installation in galleries but has also been installed in public outdoor spaces, and has been used in
a number of performances.

In this case study, Rokeby discusses his approach to software and making work in
which people interact with machines. He reflects upon the way that we comprehend
computer intelligence and the possibilities it offers to the artist to experiment and explore.

The 'Very Nervous System' – developing software

*David, let's talk about the 'Very Nervous System' (VNS) because it is the first of your
artworks and one you are now returning to work on again. It is also the work through
which you initially developed the software program 'VNS' which you have used consistently through your work. Can you start off by distinguishing between the artwork 'Very
Nervous System' and 'VNS'?*

Literally 'VNS' is an evolving set of tools that grew out of the artwork 'Very Nervous
System'. I use 'VNS' as a short term for 'Very Nervous System' sometimes but actually 'VNS' refers to the technological substrate, and 'Very Nervous System' is the
installation. As time has gone on this has become an evolving set of tools that just keeps
expanding and expanding.

*In the installation 'Very Nervous System' the audience, or participants, are in an inter-
active environment in which their movements and gestures are read and interpreted by
the computer and generate music or an audio output. As people start to play with the
space it becomes obvious that the computer is reading even very subtle gestures and
that the sound that is created is not just the product of translating movement into sound,
as if the human actions were being interpreted as moving across a grid, but that it is
evolving a complex response to the movement. Is it reasonable to describe 'VNS' as
being the fundamental software, or the operating system, of your work? Maybe we could
also say that the concepts that underlie 'Very Nervous System' seem to thread their way
through most of your works.*

I've always been fascinated in using gesture as a tool in this medium. I've been trying to develop it in a way that avoids obvious trip-ups because they can almost become a self-parody through the over-use of certain techniques. But there is a very lovely state that my work's got to recently in terms of the process of the practice itself. As a result of the series of works, I have developed a large body of tools and I can make very focused additions to it in order to make each new piece. And yet it is also quite malleable – I can respond to new ideas and questions and thoughts quite quickly. That's exciting.

Of course, in the beginning, 'Very Nervous System' didn't start that way at all – it started with no operating system, and it was only about six or seven years into the project that I started to formalise the tools. The tools rose out of that piece. But I would not say that every other piece has risen out of the tools, but instead that they have floated on the support of that tool set.

Dealing with machine intelligence

Another constant thread through your work is the subject of machine intelligence. It frequently questions what that might be, and how we might respond to it as an audience – or less specifically, how we respond just as humans. There are many different ways in which people talk about machine intelligence. Can you talk about the way that you approach it?

There are two different aspects of this for me now. The key original one, which really led to the development of works like the 'Giver of Names', was a question about what was happening to our concept of intelligence now that we use it to apply to machines; and recognising that in continuous encounters with machines, if there is an intense feedback loop, we tend to shift. There's a convergence of things once we find what we can both agree on: what things I'm doing that the computer will support, and what things I have to do in order to earn that support. This generates a kind of convergence of ideas and behaviours.

There's a quote from Alan Turing that implies that he recognised that the meaning of the word 'intelligence' was going to shift as quickly as machine capability increased. That's exactly the kind of convergence in context, a convergence that means that both things are slipping. Even if you say at the end of an exploration that machines are intelligent, you aren't meaning the same thing as when you started with the experiment. So from my point of view it is important to consider what the concept of a machine intelligence means at a particular point in time. I might ask what is it to design something that we might be tempted to call intelligence? On one level it is a critique of what's credited to machine intelligence, on another level, as a tool to understand human intelligence.

I think that there is a certain kind of relationship between a human and a computer that makes ideal use of human sentimentality and machine rigour. I think it's a very delicate balance but it's a very special one. There are times when the machine's absolute punishing rigour is useful, not as something turned against ourselves but actually as something towards ourselves. There are times when our lack of rigour means that we misunderstand ourselves. In a curious way, the computer's rigour helps us understand ourselves and helps us understand how we think we understand ourselves. It helps us to unravel some of the mistakes we make through the fact that we are so invested in ourselves that we can't really see ourselves.

It is sometimes hard for us to recognise what is intelligent and logical in the machine and what expectations we are investing in it. One of the things that is fascinating in works like the 'Giver of Names' is that it is not obvious at first how the computer is thinking. In the 'Giver of Names' the audience is confronted by a series of objects in front of a plinth, such as a rubber duck, a toy gun or a wine glass. When they place one or a combination of the objects on the plinth the computer 'observes' them and starts to 'name' what it sees. The language the computer uses is often very descriptive, some-times appearing to be missing the point of what the objects are completely, but making very plausible assumptions, and sometimes creating strangely evocative associations and suggesting odd meanings. Of course, it is obvious for us to combine our own facility for visual analysis with word associations and to verbalise them. When we observe a machine do this, or not do it completely, what is taking place becomes fascinating.

It's a way of making what's so familiar unfamiliar enough that we can look at it. One side to the discussions about the way computers can work, which is a really interesting one, is the importance of machine intelligence as something separate, as something inde-cipherable and profound in its indecipherability in a sense. There's something about the alien perspective, the profoundly alien perspective, not invested with humanity, that is interesting. This is an aspect of pieces like the 'Giver of Names' which I've only started in the past few years to appreciate. It's kind of a hopeful thing in a way. There are extreme limitations and constraints on how machines can think in ways like humans, largely because they haven't a human life and therefore can't put anything into context. On the other hand, there is a powerful creative energy that's possible because of the lacks of constraints. In a more general way in the case of using a computer to look at yourself, it becomes a new kind of sense and sense-making organ.

This is also demonstrated in one of your later works, 'n-Cha(n)t', which extends upon the way that the 'Giver of Names' operates. In 'n-Cha(n)t' the audience enters a room of computers suspended in space. Each monitor shows the image of a human ear. If the visitor speaks to the computer the ear may 'listen', cupping its ear to concentrate. When it appears to have 'listened' enough it seems to start 'thinking' and, with a finger pressed into the ear, shows that it has stopped listening. It then starts to verbalise the mean-ings and associations to what it has heard, or misheard, in a manner similar to the 'Giver of Names'. The result is a stream of oddly poetic riffs.

The installation has a further stage: it becomes apparent that the computers can operate as a network and share the verbal associations between themselves. In time they start to find a common 'stream' of language and their chattering falls into unison as one collective chant. A clap of the hands by the audience and the chorus will break and the computers will separate again into separate, listening, units. Is this an addi-tional demonstration of 'making sense'?

Constructing meaning

Recently, whilst setting up 'n-Cha(n)t', I realised for the first time that what is emotion-ally powerful for me about the piece is that it rides on a substrate of nonsense. What the computers are saying is structured nonsense. It really is nonsense, it's not grounded in anything, but it's shared. Even if the machine doesn't know what it means when it talks about 'killing', it's sharing that with the other machines – there is a communica-tion, they're working from a shared reference, a kind of culture you might say. So this meaningless token takes on meaning in that context. It is the nonsense that makes the community itself visible. This places the focus not so much on what is being said but on the way that meaning comes out of a shared reference, and on the nature of the struggle to come to share a reference.

I've come to realise that I'm thinking a lot about meanings, not meanings in the sense of 'the meaning of life', but in relation to how do we construct meaning? Does it have persistence, is it ephemeral, is it an accident of a moment? It begs the question: is meaning in the connections or in the things that are connected, or in some combination thereof? A very simple question in a sense, but it was interesting that the writing of the code that manages the connections drew me into thinking about meaning in a way I hadn't expected.

Obviously we can say that we read a meaning into whatever it is the machine is doing but there's also a certain quality to the construction of meaning that we get from the machine which is very distinctive. I think you've talked about this in relation to your installation 'Watch', in which the computer takes a video feed from a camera that is usually pointing to the street outside the gallery and splits it into two side-by-side projections, in one of which only things that are moving are pictured and in the other only things that are still.

Something that happens with this installation is similar to how photographic and film technology has given us a way of seeing the world, a visual vocabulary of close-up, zooming, panning and editing, which are things that our visual processes can do but we are not necessarily aware of. In 'Watch' we are aware of the way that the computer is data sorting or selecting from the video feed, and it seems to give us a way of seeing that we cannot otherwise have, even though probably deep within the layers of our cognitive processes we are processing the same sort of information.

We don't see them on the level at which all the processes are drawn together into a coherent visual representation of the world but we are doing motion detection and all these things at levels of the visual cortex. I am often reminded of a quote from Merleau-Ponty, 'human beings are condemned to meaning', which reflects his phenomenological perspective. It suggests that just by having an eye placed in space we cannot help but find meaning because of the partiality of our experience and that meaning comes out of the partiality and the specificity of our devices of acquisition.

Figure 22.2   David Rokeby, 'Watch' (1996)
Still taken from the live processed video stream of 'Watch' at InterAccess Media Arts Centre, Toronto, Canada. In the image on the left only moving figures are visible, such as cyclists, and on the right only stationary objects are visible, such as cars waiting at the traffic lights.

'Watch' condemns us to a certain set of meanings by just carrying out some simple processes. I cannot help but feel romantic by looking at one side of the images on the screen. The computer allows us to play those sorts of experiments with aspects and fragments of human experience and make the results tangible – these little introspections, these little wayward loops of self-consciousness, ways we can see ourselves.

Evolving projects and open-ended practice
....

One of the other key issues that comes up in relation to your work is the issue of the ever-evolving project. Obviously we've been talking about the way that ideas develop or have a consistency across work over a number of years. In some cases this is reflected in the way that some projects clearly build on what has been done previously, starting with the 'Very Nervous System' and using the same software substrate. In some cases you have gone back to re-explore and re-develop previous projects and extend the way that they can perform. Do you have the sense that sometimes the artwork is itself never finished?

I think there are two things going on. One is that my practice, in some ways, is better framed as a research practice. I rarely start with an absolutely clear end point in mind

Figure 22.3   David Rokeby, 'n-Cha(n)t' (2001)
Installation at the Walter Phillips Gallery, Banff Centre for the Arts, Canada, illustrating computers in a state of readiness to 'hear' words from the audience.

n-Cha(n)t is a community of computers with the facility to recognise and respond to language and which are linked by a network. The computers intercommunicate and, through doing so, 'synchronise' their individual internal 'states of mind'. When left uninterrupted to communicate among themselves, they eventually fall into chanting, a shared stream of verbal association, until finally achieving unison.

when I'm working on a project, so how can I know when I am done when I don't have a coherent goal? That probably comes from my commitment to following my curiosity in engaging with the materials of my culture with as open a mind and as rigorous a questioning and process as I can have, and to following in the course of doing a project the strongest intuitive tugs and the strangest questions that arise. So when a piece starts with a couple of questions it's not going to end with a finished piece. It's going to contain a dialogue within itself.

The second thing is of course is that the medium, the means, is changing all the time. As the technologies develop you can express the same thing at different levels of mentality, viscerality, tactility, etc. and that can lead a piece to different places. It is especially so when your process of working is to develop a technology, develop a set of ideas, a way of thinking. I've often talked of 'VNS' as being a medium and that there are pieces within that medium. You could say that there are a lot of finished 'VNS' pieces but the medium itself is constantly evolving and shifting. I like layering, too, and the process of presenting each phase of a work is a learning process which often points out another layer, another angle, that can be added in a way that doesn't destroy the coherence of the piece but adds to the experience.

Commercial exploitation of software by artists

I also want to ask you about the way that you also use 'VNS' as commercial software and receive an income through selling or licensing it. What are you licensing?

The right to use the software. There are many different ways to talk about what actually happens when someone buys a piece of software from me. Most of it is just legal gobbledegook but people have the right with the tools to do whatever they want with what they produce with the tools. There's no restriction.

So you're not actually modifying it or creating a kind of bespoke use of the software for the client?

No. One of the things that is a key part of my engagement in this stuff is a love of the generation of possibilities and developing software is a very powerful way to produce possibilities, to construct possibilities. I'm fascinated when I see people use these things in ways that I hadn't imagined. I'd prefer it that they don't use it in ways that I would find morally reprehensible. When you are working with a tool that is pretty much used entirely within the art community that's not too much of a danger but I've talked a lot about the dangers of leakage from the art world out into the public realm. You produce something innocently for an artwork knowing that it's almost impossible to really abuse it because people going into an art context are coming in with a certain set of frames of reference, but when you take that same technology and put it into a household device, there's a shift in the meaning of that interface. So far it hasn't been successful enough to be that problematic.

Background and skills

Your practice suggests that you have a very broad base of expertise. Can you talk about your background and training that's got you to where you are now and how much is self-taught or acquired along the way as different situations present themselves?

My background training originally comes from a long-term early interest in synthesisers. I got access to a local university's sound synthesis lab when I was thirteen. I built little electronic circuits early on and gained access to computers, also when I was in my teens, by working for an engineering firm where I taught myself to programme. At that point the technology was relatively simple, so my knowledge has grown with the technology, which has been a real advantage. I've been able on each project to say 'what do I need to know to do this project?' and set out doing experiments or finding a book, or whatever to deal with that.

In terms of informal training, it has been on a need-to-know basis and that's meant that I have weird holes in my knowledge base. It has an interesting scatter-gun character because I know a lot about infra-red illumination and a lot about a particular kind of programming because those have been important to me. There have been times when I've really wished I had more formal education in one or another of those areas because I've wasted a lot of time re-inventing the wheel but, on the other hand, thinking my way through each process has been very valuable. There's always been a part of me that's been interested in knowing what I'm doing from the ground up, knowing what I'm dealing with. It is also a reflection on the way I do projects, trying to be involved in each layer. I try to have a coherent understanding of the whole of the piece, from down at the logic and silicon level to right up to the overall behaviour.

Operating as an artist, technologist and researcher

As you describe it, your background has been varied but your practice has taken you into the arts sector which has responded very positively to your work. Obviously there are many people in the international arts community who draw simultaneously on different levels of expertise, being responsible for the programming at a deep level as well as developing the concept for their installations. But it is not an obvious combination of skills and approaches. How do you find that this has affected your practice?

I think it's an interesting and tricky balance. It is not easy to balance technical expertise, especially in the computational area, with art making because they do encourage substantially different modes of thinking. For all the talk about the convergence of art and science, or art and technology, it is a rich and complicated battle, though sometimes a loving combat. I don't always find myself doing these two things in a complete sense of integration. I'm now pretty good at moving back and forth between those areas but they are different spaces. It took me a long time to learn to make commissioned artworks because I did not know how to provide for myself the kind of creative distance that I would need to walk into an environment, a context, and let an idea come to me. I learned this skill over time but it was a very precious thing that I didn't intuitively know to start with. I knew how to construct the pieces but it took time for me to find the critical and imaginative space necessary for them to evolve.

A further complicating aspect to this must be that, as you have earlier said, you can think of your work also as an ongoing research as well as making individual artistic pieces. Is there a tension between the desire to question and explore possibilities and to make a specific work?

There's a pleasure in the completeness of a piece which is positive. I like to have incredibly long-term open-ended projects going at the same time as doing more specific

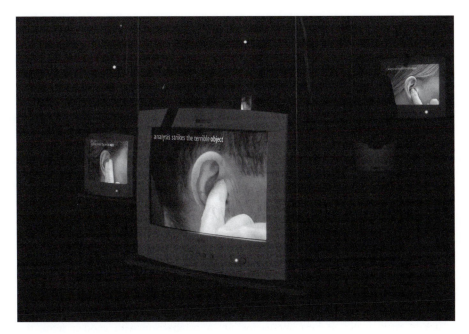

Figure 22.4   David Rokeby, 'n-Cha(n)t' (2001)
Detail of the installation at the Walter Phillips Gallery, Banff Centre for the Arts, Canada, illustrating the computers processing the verbal information.

pieces, but there's a nice balance there. Keeping a balance has been an important thing
for me as an artist in this sense; recognising that there is conflict between those two
states of mind and learning to navigate back and forth. Learning not to put the expectations supported by one onto the other and vice versa has been very important to my
maturing as an artist.

David Rokeby's website is at http://homepage.mac.com/davidrokeby/home.html

23 Digital code

....

At the centre of discussion about new media language and the wider debate over the impact of new technologies on media, stand two key concepts or terms, 'code' and 'digital'. Understanding new media crucially involves an understanding of what is entailed in the digital and its code. Such an understanding of the digital, as it relates to new media, is best approached by a comparison with another term, the 'analogue'. This comparative approach has been adopted by a number of different writers when discussing the impact of digital technology upon specific mediums. Film and photography, in particular, have been analysed and discussed in terms of the historical shift from analogue to digital code.

The terms 'post-photography' or 'digital photography' are markers of a set of differences identified between the analogue medium of photography, based in chemistry, optics and mechanics, and the new digital medium of photography based on optics, electricity and computing (Lister 2003). Likewise, film has also been approached through a contrast of analogue and digital technologies in discussing the technical form of digitised film and the cultural form of film language (Manovich 2001). To a lesser extent, computer animation has also been explored through a comparison with previous forms of drawn and cell film animation (Darley 1999). In all three cases cited here digital media has been contrasted with a previous analogue form. In all three cases digital code is seen as the fundamental basis for considering changes in the nature and use of the specific mediums of photography, film and animation.

Analogue media

....

All recording media prior to the advent of digital encoding can be defined as analogue. Photography, film, magnetic sound tape, vinyl recordings and videotape are all analogue in nature, as are drawing, painting and sculpture. All of these media contain material processes in which continuous physical inscriptions of some kind are made in or on surfaces. The brush marks on a canvas, ink rubbed into scored lines on an etching, the silver salts of the photographic print or the electronic magnetic signal on a piece of tape are all material equivalents. In all these examples, one set of physical properties, light patterns, sound waves etc., are being registered and ultimately inscribed into another physical medium. The sound waves of the human voice, spoken or sung, over the duration of time, are translated into patterns of signals on electro-magnetic tape. The light, cast across a rough wooden tabletop, becomes an analogous set of tonal differences registered by the light-sensitive silver salt crystals held in suspension on the emulsion of the unexposed film in the camera. Both are transcriptions of one set of properties, light and sound, into another, chemicals and electromagnetic tape, which over time were developed as part of the technologies and mediums of sound recording and photography respectively. Another way of putting this is to say that the technological medium has reconstituted or transcribed the original voice or visual scene.

Analogue is a term used to define some thing or property as 'being like' or resembling something else. In the case of the photograph the light and dark tones of the chemical grain of the negative are similar to the reflected light pattern of what was framed in the lens of the camera. In the case of television the light and sound of a scene is analogous to the audio-visual signals that are recorded continuously on electromagnetic tape. An analogue sound recording on tape can be displayed on an oscilloscope as a complex mixture of constantly changing wavy lines – the lines show all the different aspects of the signal. Simplistically the line pattern or wavelength represents the characteristic pattern, whilst the number of these cycles represents their frequency.

An easy, everyday example of an analogue recording would be a photocopy – the copy is analogous, but not identical, to the original; the image is always slightly degraded. If the photocopy is then copied and this copy is copied the quality of the image gets worse and worse. The same applies to analogue video and audio recordings. So analogue media record and store 'information' through some kind of material transcription, which transfers the configuration of one physical material into an analogous arrangement in another. The photographic negative is analogous to the light pattern, the videotape is analogous to sound and image recorded over time. One hour of unedited videotape equals one hour of real time. The physically recorded material is culturally and technologically coded, so that the machines and their materials, together with our knowledge of seeing and listening, reconstitute the original through the analogy.

The continuous nature of analogue media marks a crucial moment of difference with the digital. Electro-magnetic tape is a continuous surface upon which sounds are transcribed. The relationship between the sound and its recording is also continuous. The same is true for photography in the image-forming properties of light-sensitive film and papers. The photographic negative records the latent image of reflected light in a continuous relationship to the light as it strikes the surface of the film in different intensities. Putting this another way, we can say that neither magnetic tape nor photographic film record or transcribe the original signals by breaking them down systematically into units or bits. In analogue media there is no code as such, only the continuous medium of transcription.

Analogue media developed as part of the Industrial Revolution and the mass production of artefacts by a system of the division of labour and the replacement of human labour by machines. As such, analogue media reflect the processes of standardisation in which production was divided into separate, simple, sequential activities, which could be endlessly repeatable, such as the frames of a film or the dots of the half-tone process of newspaper photographs. However, analogue media were not interchangeable and each developed its own materials, properties and apparatuses. A camera could not be used for recording speech, just as the newspaper could not reproduce movement. Of course, film could reproduce visual moment and sound but only by combining or synchronising the separate analogue media of film and magnetic tape.

Analogue media can now be defined retrospectively from the vantage point of the digital as continuous data or information in which the axis or dimension that is measured has no apparent indivisible unit from which it is composed. Conversely, we can understand that converting continuous data into a numerical representation is digitisation.

Digital code

In contrast to the analogue, the digital medium is not a transcription but a conversion of information. Digital media store information as formal mathematical relationships in abstract electronic forms. Digital is the generic term used for the processing and recording of information using binary code, the digits 1 and 0 which are represented in the registration of two different voltage levels in electronic circuits, or in transit as electronic impulses. A digital file, whether it is a text, image or sound file, is effectively a mathematical set of instructions, a long string of zeros and ones, written in computer code. The digital medium is defined precisely by that fact: that it creates a systematic, intermediate code of discrete units. Digital code breaks everything down into uniform and exchangeable bits (or bytes). The full significance of this difference between analogue and digital takes time to appreciate, but it is this single fact of digital code that accounts for most of the radical possibilities in the convergence of media and the creation of new media.

The strings of binary digits are founded as mathematical formulas or algorithms, which constitute the digital code. It is this feature of digitisation which has meant that images can now be thought to exist as electronic data and not as the physical medium. Digital data are created by capturing and sampling at regular intervals.

Digital capture

Capturing is achieved through interface devices with single or networked computers. The keyboard and mouse, for instance, are a means whereby a computer software program can capture the typing of this text. If I was in a drawing program right now I would be using the mouse and its screen avatar (an icon) to designate shape and colour which would be captured, or using a whiteboard with a 'pen'. More easily grasped would be the example of image capture through a digital recording device. In the case of the light-formed image of photography, a digital camera has a CCD (charge-coupled device) image sensor in the place of the older analogue film which captures an intensity and gives it a numerical, binary value. The analogue characteristic of chemical photography – the grain, tone and colour of an image – is simulated by assigning a value to a pixel in a digital image. With video it is the software that grabs frames which can be streamed as video.

Sampling

The frequency of sampling determines the resolution of the data. Sampling turns continuous data into discrete data which are quantified by being assigned a numerical value. Each sample intensity is converted to an integer number value.

Storage

It is the translation of the analogue image or sound into a numerical code that now enables them to be electronically stored and transmitted. What happens to any analogue media work once it has been digitally captured and electronically stored within the network of networked computers radically changes the ways in which we regard the work, how it can be used, who owns it and how it is controlled. Digital photographs circulating freely on websites and attached to emails are now regarded as 'information' along with everything else. Most obviously, the digital image can be manipulated, combined and re-contextualised in any number of ways, as can textual and sound files.

Code

It is the coded nature of digitised media that has resulted in a photography or sound recording being understood as 'information'. A digitally produced or reproduced media object becomes subject to algorithmic manipulation and it is the system of algorithmic coding that allows us to now think of media as conforming to programmable rules. The importance of digital code is underlined by Manovich (2001: 27–48) who describes five principles of new media as numerical representation, modularity, automation, variability and transcoding. This is a useful taxonomy in which each term describes how digital coding treats a surface or a frequency as a set of separate elements that retain their separate identity while being able to be combined into more complex structures and functions. The above account of digital code functions well at a technical level. It is the account of the technical transcription or encryption of one form into another. Manovich's taxonomy goes some way to helping us see that digital media artefacts are products/outcomes of a specifically technical set of possibilities. Modularity creates the ability of digital media to clone any part of its code and make new combinations, for example, while variability creates the characteristics of mutability and change and so on. What a technical account of digital code doesn't do is help us understand how any digital media artefact means anything, other than at the very abstract level of saying all digital media is information. In order to understand how digital media artefacts mean anything we are thrown back into the cultural realm of language and it is here that we find the term 'code' given precisely the role of explaining how meaning in language operates.

Cultural code

We have indicated how binary code is an essential technical characteristic of electronic digital media and computational systems, but code is also a central part of the analysis of cultural systems of communication. The concept of code is not new to thinking about digital technology. Code has been a broader way of thinking about communication throughout the twentieth century, both technically in analogue apparatuses and culturally in the analysis of meaning in language. The very idea of a media message involves the concept of code. Media messages are encoded by a sender and decoded by a receiver. In media and cultural studies, code is generalised as the rules or conventions by which communication takes place within a given medium. The coding and decoding of messages in newspapers, photographs, or Hollywood cinema are understood to have developed over time and are subject to change because cultural rules can be broken and new rules learned. Here, code is being used as a collection of rules at any one time which govern the overall construction of film genres such as the Western, thriller, comedy or those of a television soap-opera. In all of these cultural forms, codes and conventions organise the structuring of the story, plot, characters, acting, lighting and camera positions.

Linguistic code

The specific analysis of linguistic code owes its origins to the foundational work of Ferdinand de Saussure (1857–1913) who developed the systematic study of signs. The study of sign systems was later taken up and applied to a wider range of ideas and objects, which could be said to be sign systems. Claude Lévi-Strauss (1958) applied a structuralist approach in anthropology to the study of totems and taboos. Roland Barthes (1973) applied a semiotic analysis to photography and cultural activities such as writing, fashion, exhibitions and film. The theoretical work of Jacques Lacan (1901–81) was an application of structural linguistics to Freudian psychoanalysis. But it was Ferdinand de Saussure who first developed the concept of language as a system of signs, in which the sign, composed of the signifier and signified, is the basic unit of meaning.

Language as a system of signs

Conceptually, the sign is the smallest unit of meaning in a system and is composed of the signifier and the signified in which the signifier is the material existence of the sign, while the signified is the mental concept to which the signifier refers. The relationship between the signifier and signified is arbitrary because there is no necessary relationship between the two terms. The relationship between the sign and its referent, the object or idea to which it refers, is arbitrary within the system and is governed by cultural rules and conventions.

Sign =

signifier	+	signified
sign's image as perceived		the mental concept to which it refers

The arbitrariness of the sign

In the writing of Roland Barthes we can see the application of a semiotic analysis to the medium of photography. Barthes' analysis of the photograph returns us to the analogical nature of the medium of photography. On the surface the photograph does record, or sample and store in digital terminology, visible reality into the discrete grain of the negative. On closer inspection, literally by physical enlargement, the grains of the photograph cannot be meaningfully identified as units in a larger system, which could be defined as a code. This is why Barthes calls the photograph the perfect analogon and why he went on famously to analyse the photograph as a message without a code. In 'The photographic message', Barthes develops a structural analysis of photographic meaning and, in doing so, identifies what he calls 'the photographic paradox'. The photograph, unlike language, has no systematic structural code because the analogue medium of light-sensitive chemicals on the celluloid negative which forms the image cannot be broken down into discrete units. In the photograph there is the scene, which is a reduction but not a transformation of the literal reality. It is not necessary to divide the photographic message into units and signs, which are different from the object, as in language; there is no relay, no code – the photograph is an analogon. This is why Barthes says that the photograph is, at this level, message without a code, it is a continuous message. Yes, there are other messages (analogue media) without a code, drawing, painting, cinema, TV, theatre, but they have an immediate and recognisable supplementary message which is the treatment and style. Barthes introduces a way to distinguish between the order of these messages:

- the analogon itself is the *denoted* message – the literal scene – the continuous message;
- the cultural message is the *connoted* message.

However, this duality of messages is not evident in the photograph. In the photograph the mechanical analogon, the light-formed image, fills its substance leaving no room for a second message. He calls this 'analogical plenitude', however this purely denotative status of the photograph is mythical, i.e. its objectivity. The analogue photograph is not a transcription but a direct inscription of light which makes it a message that is continuous with its referent. Barthes says that since meaning cannot proceed from this 'first order' of the photographic message, because the photograph has no code, then meaning has to develop through a 'second order', which is a cultural code of associative, or connoted meanings. The paradox is thus the co-existence of two messages, the one without a code (the photographic analogue), the other with a code (writing, treatment, rhetoric of the image). This is a paradox not because of a collusion of the two messages, but because the connoted messages develop on the basis of a message without a code. The reason why it is important to understand the photographic paradox is because digital technology introduces a discrete technical code into the photographic image. As we have said the digital camera samples light values and converts them into a binary code, which are then given discrete values as pixels. The 'death' of analogue photography and the

---

Box 23.1

Analogue	Digital
Transcription: the transfer of one set of physical properties into another set.	*Conversion*: physical properties symbolised by an arbitrary analogous numerical code.
Continuous: representation occurs through variations in a continuous field of tone, sound etc.	*Unitised*: qualities divided into discrete, measurable and exactly reproducible elements.
Material inscription: signs inseparable from the surface that carries them.	*Abstract signals*: numbers or electronic pulses detachable from material source.
Medium-specific: each analogue medium, bounded by its physical properties and its specific techniques.	*Generic*: one binary code for all media enabling convergence and materials conversion between them.

ushering in of the post-photographic era is based precisely upon the substitution of a digital code for the perfect analogon which was the chemical photographic negative. Mitchell argues that 'an image revolution in the formalisation and diffusion of computer generated imagery heralds the ubiquitous implantation of fabricated visual spaces radically different from the mimetic capacities of film, photography and television' (Mitchell 1992: 225). Much of the general argument that the photographic image could no longer be trusted ignored the fact that the photograph has always been a selective and constructed document that gains meaning in its passage through technical mediation and cultural context. The fact that the digital image does have a technical code has led to changes in photographic practice and a culture's reception of digital images. The digital code of the photographic image destabilises the relatively fixed analogue image and adjusts us to the mutability of code. This adjustment is still taking place in the emergent practices of digital image production which make the intentional processes of image creation more apparent and compel us to be more knowing about how images are created.

Digitisation is also the effective precondition for the entry of photographic images into the flow of information that circulates within the contemporary global communications network. It is the translation of the photographic image into a numerical code that now enables it to be electronically transmitted and, effectively, become electronic data.

24

CASE STUDY

'In Conversation' – public participation: Susan Collins

....

Susan Collins is a new media artist whose projects have often worked with an online public and enabled them to engage with a 'real' space. She creates the unexpected in her works and presents them in ways, or places, that offer humorous interjections into daily life. In her early video works she would frequently position images that were surreal or slightly off-key into a public space, such as a walkway or a public meeting area. These projections would disrupt the logical everyday flow of life, the patina of normal routines, in simple but beguiling ways. The result might be that people would talk with each other about the work that they had seen.

For her project 'In Conversation' (1997–2001) Collins used the Internet to take this one step further and to create a portal between worlds. The work enabled a community in a town to communicate with an online group of visitors to a website. The work had two distinct parts, an online component and a physical site, and worked with two different populations. It also brought them both together in the same 'real' space and aimed to have people engage with each other by giving participants the opportunity for a two-way dialogue.

'In Conversation' was first staged in Brighton in 1997, and was updated and repeated in other locations around the world in subsequent years. In this project, people passing by in a street would find an image of a large animated mouth projected onto the pavement, which would appear to be talking to them in a distinctive computer audio voice. If they stayed and seemed to be curious, the voice might ask them a question directly, such as 'What's your name?' or 'What are you doing today?'. If they replied, they might start up a conversation. It would soon emerge that the voice was speaking dialogue sent from people who were visiting a website. Conversations would spring up between the people on the street and the people online, being mouthed through the projected image of the mouth.

The website presented a live video feed of the action on the street and a concealed microphone picked up the local sound. The online participants could type their comments or questions into a simple text-entry box. After hitting 'send' the texts would be queued and 'spoken' in the street. Participants could not read each other's contributions but only hear them, voiced on the street and relayed to them through the video stream.

As a result, extraordinary conversations often sprung up, with people in Chicago, Sydney and Berlin chatting to bemused locals in the city where the installation was

taking place. Once it became clear what was happening, people in the street would begin to congregate around the mouth projected onto the pavement and chat back to the international personalities 'through' the mouth almost as though it were a medium in a séance. It soon became clear that where people were from, or how many people were contributing online at any time, was largely irrelevant. What mattered was that there was a totally surprising link between two places, and between the very real world of the street and the rather un-real world of the Internet site.

In this interview Susan Collins discusses the issues she confronted in making an experimental work in a public space and working with diverse groups of users. She also addresses what challenges she was faced in making work in which she was not only the creative producer but also a facilitator who was creating a system for others to use.

Developing the work

Firstly I'd like to ask you about the concept of 'In Conversation' and its development. What was the background to the work?

For a few years I had been encouraging students and other artists to explore the Internet and web as an opportunity for collaborative and distributed work, and yet in terms of my own work I was more interested in making work that occupied or intervened in 'real' space. By 'real' space I mean a non-gallery space, therefore a space that is part of everyday life, public or private. I was also not that interested in work that only occupied the space of the screen or could only be experienced and explored through sitting down at a computer.

'In Conversation' was preceded by works in a train station and on streets where I provided content, both audio and video projection, which was then randomly triggered by viewers. I was already looking for ways to develop the work beyond response-based interactivity – where a passer-by might be more meaningfully involved in contributing to the content of the work itself within a given structure. 'In Conversation' was commissioned as part of a series of Internet art projects about the city. When the invitation to apply for it arrived in my email inbox I had a real 'aha' moment. The call for proposals catalysed something where I realised precisely how I could combine both interests, and somehow link the distributed, international, collaborative structure of the Internet with the type of interventions that I had been doing on the street.

Figure 24.1   Susan Collins, 'In Conversation' (1997)
Detail from the website of the initial presentation of 'In Conversation' in Brighton, UK, showing the streaming video and the text box for online participants.

'In Conversation' was an online and public installation that provided the means for individuals in the street and on the Internet to engage in a live dialogue with each other. This work aimed to examine the boundaries and social customs of distinctly different kinds of public spaces – the street and the Internet chatroom – each with its own established rules of engagement.

Figure 24.2   Susan Collins, 'In Conversation' (1998)
Still from the streaming video showing passers-by gathering to listen and talk back to the online participants. This presentation was in Amsterdam, the Netherlands, as part of an exhibition 'Avatar' in the Oude Kerk, in Amsterdam's red light district.

Dealing with limitations of technology

Were there any issues about the technology that you needed to make the piece being available to you at the time? Sometimes artists speak about having to deal with the limitations of the available technology. They suggest that they start with original concepts for their projects that are highly ambitious and seamless but have to modify these to fit the available means and resources. Was this the case for you?

Actually, this was a case when the technology was there, at a level to enable me to make the work I wanted to make. As far as I know 'In Conversation' was one of the first examples of an artist using live video and audio streaming, and the free version of Realplayer software that enabled it came out just in time. But the whole project was a high-risk learning process where we grabbed emerging technologies and moulded them for the work.

It would not be the same work if the technology was already out there to make it seamless. I think I would not have been interested or inspired to make it. There was definitely a pioneering feeling that made the work more exciting because of the newness – especially at a time (which seems hard to remember) when not that many people were online. One aspect of the work was finding a way of introducing pedestrians to the concept of international connectivity from the street without any kind of visible computer interface.

There was seamless high-bandwidth technology available already at that time, for example in universities and the corporate sector, that I could have used had I chosen to have a smaller online audience pool (i.e. university users). However, I deliberately chose to limit the stream for 28.8 k dial-up so that as many home-users as possible were able to participate, so broadening the viewer and audience demographic beyond specialist or university users.

Material quality and limitations of the work

Was it a concern for you to find a balance between technical limitations, of things like bandwidth and free software, and the quality that these might have brought to the work, even if sometimes they gave it a 'clunkiness'? Looking back do you see the time-lapses and the disjointedness as an important quality of the experience of the work?

The material quality of the work, in particular the time delay, which gave rise to some wonderful collective sentences and parallel conversations, became essential as part of the fabric of the work. Also, I like the fact that the process was exposed through its own material, you could almost feel the pixels being squeezed down the ether. I explored this further in my recent pixel works – including 'Fenlandia' – and also in the installation 'Transporting Skies'. This work is very much of its time and a moment in emerging technology. I would not be interested in re-staging it with perfect unclunky technology; it would not be the same work.

On its first outing in Brighton, in 1997, the work definitely had a magical quality partly brought on by the unfamiliarity by many people in terms of direct contact with the Internet. Pedestrians were also still at a point where a street projection was interesting and unusual though it has since become more commonplace through logo projections and advertising. By the time of its last outing in Berlin in 2001, already what the work was offering was not so surprising, and passers-by were becoming less

Figure 24.3   Susan Collins, 'Fenlandia' (2004)
'Fenlandia' is an Internet work in which images are drawn from webcams in various locations in the UK.

The webcams harvest images pixel by pixel, recording at different rates over the course of the year. Each image is collected from top to bottom and left to right in horizontal bands continuously, marking visible fluctuations in light and movement throughout the day and being archived at two-hour intervals. The images can be viewed live and are also updated regularly on the archive section of the artist's website.

This image, of Sutton Gault in Cambridgeshire, UK, was built up at the rate of a pixel every second via the Internet in horizontal bands. It depicts the 21 hours and 20 minutes leading up to 18:43 on 5 July 2004.

amazed both by the connectivity of the Internet and also less likely to stop and wonder at an animated projection on the street.

So I think the limitations of using emerging technologies can be advantagous if one catches them at that moment before they become ubiquitous or commonplace, and before they are already associated with any kind of industry, such as advertising or nightclubs.

Creating open or participatory systems

Can we address how you position yourself as an artist making the work? I am very interested in the way you talk about work as being an 'open system', and the artist as the creator of a conduit through which content flows. Can you elaborate on that a bit because the technology of the system itself isn't 'open' in the way that one talks about open source or to a program that can respond to users? Is this the same as saying that you are creating a space for engagement?

Yes, in a sense, in a work like this it could be seen as a form of architectural space, a crafted or designed space with given parameters where the artist could also be seen as architect. It is, though, in a sense important, for me, to remember where this work actually came from and how it evolved through the previous series of 'street' works where I had placed pre-made sounds and images in a space that responded or reacted to the viewer's presence and movement. With 'In Conversation' I created an opportunity for people to 'inhabit' the work, to a limited extent, with their own language and to contribute to it. This ability to make the work grow is what leads to it being an 'open system'. And this is combined with the expansion of audience opportunities made possible by the web.

Described in this way, the content of the work was obviously the virtual and real social engagement that was taking place. But it's also not as though what it offered was just a system, as 'In Conversation' was a very crafted space, or two spaces, and very precisely visual. It seems to me that 'In Conversation' is very different from many other projects that invite user participation and performance because it is so layered and with a 'real' site involved.

The 'realness' of the site, I think, made it quite compulsive viewing as not only could net-users witness what was happening elsewhere (the compulsive viewing of webcams, for instance, I think is probably well documented by now) but were able to actually influence its outcome, interfere with it in some way (as well as communicate). People didn't only send messages, they also tried to subvert the chat aspect to make it musical, using letters and punctuation as percussive instruments.

I think I used the hiccups in the system and the dislocations inherent in streaming media (and the unpredictability of any public space over time) as fundamental to the fabric of the work – such as the delays having a direct influence on the fluency or confusion of the resulting conversations, or of rain leaving the street empty of physical pedestrians and allowing the net-users to take it over as a chat space.

Defining responsibility

You've talked about there being a fragile balance between freedom and control and between responsibility and censorship in works like this. This could be taken more broadly to look at the relationship the artist has to the work. Maybe these questions are an inevitable outcome, and maybe the deliberation that takes place at the point of development of the work – deciding where one stands in terms of authorial control – is almost a signature to this kind of work. Can you describe the way you decided how much you would manage this work and how much you would leave open to unknown possibilities? Over time and repeated showings how did you decide if there were things you needed to manage for practical reasons or others you decided you could let be?

On the first showing I saw the work very much as a one-off experiment, honestly not knowing firstly if it would work and, secondly, if I could get it to work technically, whether it would function socially and be taken up as an instrument by users and viewers. From memory my expectation was that I could probably get it to work technically but doubted very much that it would function socially.

I definitely knew I wanted control of the images both on-screen and on the pavement. I considered whether we needed a language filter, and then realised there were many ways for people to be abusive and this wasn't something I would factor into the software. In the first showing in Brighton someone came online when they saw a nun in the street and became abusive, and the curators just made a snap decision to turn down the volume until the online abuser got bored and went away. After this happened this became what I would suggest for counteracting this potential for abuse, but as far as I know none of the subsequent venues needed to take this action. In some footage I looked at of Amsterdam the work has a way of self-censoring. One man became very engaged in conversation, and stayed for some time, and then it seemed that a new much more aggressive person appeared online. (I should point out that it is hard to tell how many people are online as they all share the same computer voice.) The man in the street left once the online person started using sexual language and he appeared to be quite disappointed as until then the communication had been quite gentle and charming.

Engaging the audience

Regarding the audience, how proactive did you have to be to get an audience to the website and to the street? Was it easy to publicise?

I knew that I didn't want the work restricted to art viewers or expert computer users (hence going for a low-bandwidth streaming option that would be accessible for home users). I didn't know of any other artworks at that time using live video streaming. The only live video streaming that included audio, at that time, were live news channels, otherwise it was mostly real-audio or video only (with no audio) such as porn or strip channels, or global services such as the American Stock Exchange or news feeds such as C-Span. If you look back at the Yahoo events guides at the time you can see that it was quite limited.

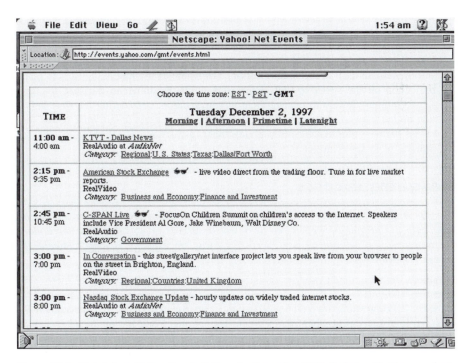

Figure 24.4   Detail from Yahoo Events listings for December 1997, featuring 'In Conversation'.

I was very lucky as because there were so few live webcasts at the time, Realplayer were keen to promote any live events taking place to encourage people to use its software – and ran a listings guide called Timecast. Someone from Realplayer picked up on what I was doing, probably because I had been in touch with them with technical questions, and let the Timecast people know about it. The next thing I knew it was being depicted as a cartoon on the home page of Timecast and suddenly my online viewer figures jumped to 1,000 or so a day which was a lot at that time, and the viewers were very international and, from the feedback I received, seemed to cover a broad cross-section of society. I encouraged people to email me if they wanted to know when and where 'In Conversation' was happening and there was a loyal following who would come online at the opening of subsequent installations.

It also helped that there was a lot of national press interest in the daily papers, on TV, including BBC News 24, and World News, on radio, including BBC World Service. The BBC made a 5-minute TV documentary when the work was shown in Helsinki which was repeated several times on both BBC 2 and BBC World, and German TV and radio covered the piece when it was installed in Berlin.

Artists as facilitators and promoters of projects

Did you see it as part of your role that you would be the facilitator, or did you antici-pate that it would find its own audiences by people passing on information to each other?

There was a lot of 'word of mouth' information about the project, and the interest grew over the years rather than being a single 'hit'. As far as the street goes, I was very clear that the sites where I chose to show were those where pedestrians would be passing, and so hopefully come across the work by surprise. My strategy was to spread the word to online users by email and see where that went and for street viewers to come across the work during the course of the day or evening.

I kept the information about the work to a minimum, and deliberately did not include any information about it at the street location. The extent of my facilitation was to place the projection on the street so that street users might be drawn to the spot for long enough for online viewers to engage them in conversation, considering the time lag. It was the online viewers that generally informed the street users about what it was that they were participating in, and often giving them instructions as to where to look for the camera, or to speak up, etc.

Measuring success

Was the traffic of users both online and in real space important to you as a criterion you could use to gauge whether the work was a success or not? Or were there more qualitative ways of measuring how successful it was, for example, if some audiences or groups seemed to engage more 'interestingly' than others?

I couldn't define a single user-group as behaving in a significant way, but there were definitely individuals, both on the street and online, that became very involved in the work – regular users. I would regard that as a criterion of success . . . I also personally regarded it as successful when things would happen that I had not predicted – such as the percussive use of the speech device, and also when online users would persuade street users to do things for them such as sing a song or dance, which often they did. Online traffic obviously was one criterion – it meant the site was of interest to a significant number of people. I also felt it was successful if the audience was made up of a largely non-art or non-net art audience as it meant it was actually having an impact in the 'real world' and not just talking to itself.

I hoped that the work would encourage people to question communications tools and what we actually choose to do with them when we have them. I expected much of the communication to be banal. For me this was not a criterion for success or failure. I wasn't setting out to make a piece that would increase our appetite for meaningful communications, rather, to hold a mirror up to what we actually do with the increasingly sophisticated tools that we do have.

One art reviewer referred, slightly disparagingly, to the banality of the communication having seen only the texts archived in the textlog on the site without actually having experienced using the work directly himself. He seemed to be missing the point of the work entirely.

Providing support for the audience

In projects like 'In Conversation' artists often say that they had to spend time educating users and giving support and feedback. In your case was this mostly technical support or did you find that you also had to educate people to understand why this had been made as an 'art project'?

The support I gave was mostly online and technical, and to be expected given that most people hadn't yet installed Realplayer on their machines and this work required them to download it. On the street it was users that educated other users in terms of what was actually going on and how to make the best use of the (invisible) microphone and camera interface.

The venues took a lot of educating, though, in different ways. With the exception of the initiating venue, Brighton, who participated fully in the R & D aspects of the work, each new venue presented fresh technical challenges.

I view the work as an art project, and it has obviously been presented in this context and funded this way. However, I have never particularly flagged this up online – even hiding behind the inconversation.com tag which removes it slightly from the 'hand of the artist'.

Getting feedback

Did you get direct feedback on the project or was most of the user experience something that you had to deduce from observation and by watching tens of hours of video footage?

The great thing about online projects is that people do give you feedback via email. It's not scientific of course, but many observations and suggestions flowed in from online users. I often logged on and observed the work live so I could check regularly on how it was going in different venues.

I still haven't watched all the videos, and I now have many more than tens of hours' worth – more like hundreds!

Susan Collins's work is at www.susan-collins.net

25 CASE STUDY
Designing sound: Justin Bennett

J ustin Bennett is a sound artist. His work usually takes the form of audio installations, which contain sound sampled from real spaces and which are then placed
into a sonic landscape of sound. In this case study he describes how he works with
sound and his approach to devising and constructing his installations.

Justin Bennett writes that:

> I spend a lot of time listening to places and recording them. A place, whether experi-
> enced or remembered, is defined by its ambience, or 'sense of place'. This can be a
> physical or an emotional response to the space itself, the objects and activities
> contained within it, or to its acoustic manifestation; its soundscape.
>
> Listening to a place gives us spatial and temporal information not necessarily deter-
> mined by our point-of-view. Architectural or natural acoustics and ambient sound
> contribute to the soundscape as much as the sonic details and intentional sounds.
> Listening to a recording of a place thickens the plot. It stimulates immersion in the
> soundscape by removing visual cues, but creates distance through its transposition
> of space and time. Making a spatial soundwork is, for me, creating a place ... By
> placing a number of loudspeakers in the exhibition space, this conceptual place can
> manifest itself within real space and real time.
>
> (From the catalogue of the exhibition 'Just About Now'
at TENT, Rotterdam, July 2000)

Justin Bennett's installation 'Site', which he discusses in this case study, was exhibited in Rotterdam in 2000. The piece is a series of spatial soundworks where sonic
details from one location are mapped onto another. In this work the sound moves in
patterns, curving lines, as if someone is constantly moving objects from one place to
another. As the audience moves through it, the character of the underlying invisible
space is slowly revealed.

Approach to working with digital media

*Firstly, as a sound artist, how do you see your relationship with the computer? Does
it provide you with a tool that enables the highly specific production of your works or
do you think of the way you work with it as part of the creative content?*

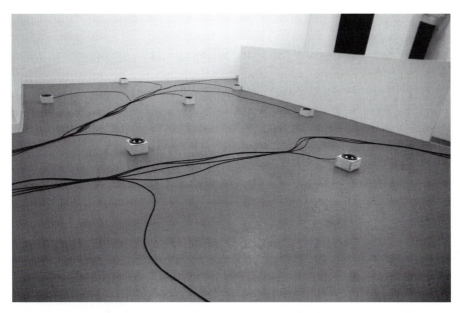

Figure 25.1   Justin Bennett, 'Site' (2000)
Detail of a computer-generated audio installation made for the gallery exhibition 'Just About Now'
at TENT, Rotterdam, showing the layout of speakers. The sound moved in patterns and curving
lines, as if someone was constantly moving objects from one place to another.

It is more of a tool, but it is a tool that I can re-design each time I use it for a new
piece. To some extent the creation of the program and the piece are identical. Still, I
tend to have the shape and sound of the piece in my head before I begin.

Defining the scope of an audio installation

*Is what you are creating a 'fixed' or pre-defined composition that the audience discovers
by interacting with it, for example, through a system like motion detection? Or is it that
the sound is more 'dynamic' and the audio landscape is being created live by the
computer program?*

The piece is 'live' and not interactive. The sound is produced by a kind of 'drawing
machine'. The machine (a computer program) knows the shape and size of the
space. Certain points in the space are defined as 'attractors' which modify the movement. The machine makes choices about movement, rhythm of drawing, length and
shape of the lines, but because the limiting parameters are strict, the behaviour doesn't
appear random.

Can you explain more about the 'attractors' – what does this term mean?

In this case it means a point in space which has a kind of gravitational pull on the movements occurring – bending and distorting the movements. 'Attractor' is a term from
mathematics: an equation can produce a very complex movement which tends to circle
around an 'attractor'.

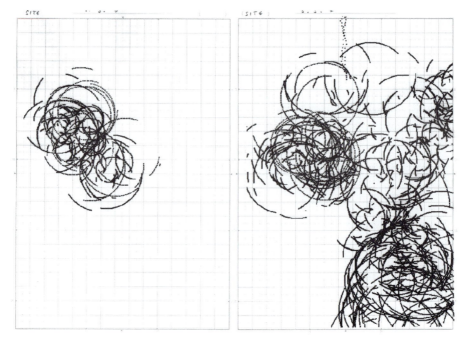

Figure 25.2 Justin Bennett, 'Site' (2000)
Drawings produced by the computer software. As well as drawing lines with sound, the computer software also produced drawings that described the space and the movements within it.

As the machine draws an imaginary line, it moves through defined areas which have different 'sound-types' assigned to them – banks of 'samples' which it can choose from. Each area has a very distinct sound-type – footsteps on gravel, shells, glass, or breaking twigs, rustling leaves etc. I rely on the unpredictability of the machine to hold the interest of the audience, rather than using interaction.

How do you organise the space? Can we assume that you divide the room into a 3-D grid to create the different areas and give them a library of different sounds, in the way you have just described? And that the drawing goes through this grid with different lines being simultaneously drawn?

Yes, though it is a 2-D grid. There are only two lines being drawn at any one time – like the movement of a person's feet or arms through the space.

Audience experience of the work

Tell me what it is like when the audience or users are in the space. Are they 'hearing' the lines being drawn so that sound is moving spatially around them? At what speed is this happening?

The audience hears the sound moving around them, or past them, depending on where they are standing. The method of spatialisation creates very stable images, so you can really walk around or through the sound. The speed depends on the behaviour of the program – it can move very fast sometimes.

Can you tell me what the ideal scenario is for you of the audience and the way they respond to and hear the space?

Ideally, I would show the piece on its own in a large space. Then there is the possibility to get different 'perspectives' on the sound. You get the most out of the piece by staying a few minutes. This is always something I have to consider a lot: how long will people stay, and how is it possible to make a balance between creating a sense of variation (so that the piece doesn't get boring) and consistency (so that people can get an idea of what the piece is about quickly). This has very much to do with the internal timing of the piece, but also the type of space, whether it leads to other spaces, whether the space has another function apart from being an 'exhibition' space etc.

Making a piece 'alive'

It would appear that you are having to make a lot of choices that are determined by what we can actually perceive and locate as audio signal. If it all happened too fast there would, presumably, be a blur of sound and that might not be the desired effect. And similarly it would happen if there were too many lines being drawn at any time.

Yes, I want to give the feeling that some kind of 'performance' is taking place – that the movements could be perceived as coming from some 'natural' cause, rather than flying round the room. That would be another piece entirely.

And following on from that, how important is it for you that they know what is happening? Could they just come into the space and hear sound and not know anything about the way it is being triggered and created? Is the fact that it is being constructed live an important concept for them to be aware of?

It's not important to know technical details. I think that the piece itself should create its own feeling of 'alive-ness'.

The idea of 'lines' of sound being created through space of the installation is such an evocative metaphor. What creates them? Is this enabled by the organisation of acoustics and the projection of sound or is it something else?

The sound moves between the loudspeakers arranged on the floor, following the imaginary lines drawn by the drawing program. Because the sounds are sharp, high-frequency sounds from natural materials we can localise them very accurately and follow the movement with our ears. It's a kind of choreography. The 'drawing' is built up slowly in the memory of the listener. Meanwhile the division of space into different types of sound also gradually reveals itself.

Taking fragments or samples of sounds

When you describe your installations you talk about taking incidental sound or fragments. Is a 'fragment' the same as saying a 'sample' – or are there other distinctions that need to be borne in mind?

The approach to the installation 'Site' is unusual for me. I usually use long pieces of recorded sound which have a shape, duration, space or rhythm. Here, I'm zooming in to the details. Michel Chion (in Audio Vision) talks of 'Materialising Indices' in film soundtracks: the crunch of a footstep on gravel which suddenly grounds the film in reality, or rather materiality. Here I use hundreds of these tiny moments which, although very short, still carry information about material, action, weight. They are strung together in random sequences by the computer which turns them into a kind of flow again. I think the word 'sample' is confusing because it means different things in different contexts. These sound fragments are perhaps closer to 'grains' which build into a texture. Heard singly they are pretty meaningless.

Can you say a bit more about this – one thing that I am interested in is the way that the term randomness is frequently used but can mean so many different things. Some random actions in computers aren't that random but are partly prescribed. And others might be extraordinarily complex and they may have multiple pre-conditions or things that affect the selection going on (for example in an A-life program).

The program is not very intelligent – it doesn't really know what the sounds are. The composition here is really created by spatially laying out the sounds and choreographing the movements. There are relationships between the movements and the sounds of course, but they are set out in the composition rather than being 'generated'.

In this piece I use randomness in a lot of different ways. At the micro-level I use a non-repeating random number generator to create the sound sequences. You'd have to listen very hard to hear a sound repeat. Typically for each sound-type I use about thirty different fragments which are strung together in different random orders. At the macro-level there are random variations in the length and shape of the movements, but these have strict limits (including the attractors mentioned above) which cause types of gesture to be repeated and the changes in behaviour are quite slow. I did this so that I could create the feeling of a unique gesture for each movement. Our ears are very sensitive to repetition, and I wanted to avoid that.

Composition

Maybe this is the best time to ask you to talk a bit about your approach to composition. Because that is very important to the philosophy that underscores this kind of work. How do you see yourself in relation to the control of the content? Do you see yourself as a 'composer'? Do you think of yourself as an artist working with sound as your material? Do you 'create' or do you 'enable' or are these terms irrelevant?

I used to think that I knew the difference! Often my relationship to the material and the space comes more out of sculpture and the visual art tradition, but when I start dealing with time I am composing to a certain extent. It depends on the sound material and the way that I want the audience to listen – some sound material lends itself to be used in a more narrative or spatial way than a musical way. In 'Site', I think there's a kind of balance. In a way it's sometimes closer to dance (although choreographers may not agree here!)

Is working with captured sound different in this way from creating synthetic sound? I know, of course, that it's an artistic choice and that 'real' sound is your millieu. But are they essentially the same thing and one is captured and the other generated, or are they different?

In this particular case there isn't a big difference. To use generated sound would mean only a very small change to the program. These are 'natural' sounds recorded through microphones, onto tape, and played by a computer through loudspeakers, so their perceived source is more complex and maybe more indirect than if they were generated by the computer. In the end though, what counts is what it sounds like and I think that this piece 'feels' physical by using the recorded sound.

One possible problem of working with recorded sound in installations is that you already have something 'fixed' – and here I get around that by fragmenting and re-assembling the sounds into new 'streams'. Generating sound can increase flexibility but you're limited by the possibilities of the synthesis techniques you use. Processing live sound, which lies technically somewhere in between the two, can be a very flexible and sensitive way of working – especially because you can make a piece which 'listens' to its environment and responds.

Development and testing

Can you tell me something about the way you set about making an installation like this? Do you work spatially in a studio or workshop? Do you test it with audiences as you develop it?

I often begin by making a 'model' of the piece in the computer. I can get it working, add controls for parameters that I know I will want to 'tweak' and build up libraries of sounds, with some alternatives. Sometimes I can really try out the piece in my own studio, but normally it doesn't really get built up until I'm actually in the final space. In this case, I can choose how many loudspeakers there will be and where – determined visually, which means I have to adjust the spatialisation to get the sound working properly. Then, I tune the sound to the space by changing volumes and filters, maybe even changing some of the sounds completely. If I can stick around, I will change it sometimes when I see the audience responding, e.g. at an exhibition opening the settings have to be very different from a normal day!

Using software

How much do you work with a specific piece of software? Do you find that some software allows you to work with sound with greater fluidity than another program would?

I work with Max/MSP, which is the version of Max that allows you to work directly with audio. The difference between Max/MSP and other programs is that it is a program-ming environment, almost a programming language. This means that working with Max/MSP is anything but fluid! However, it allows me to develop tools to create specific pieces and lets me define the starting point from which I want to work, rather than having to rely on a commercial paradigm for music-making. For instance, 'Site' is a machine which draws into a 2-D space and translates this into sound. Another piece, 'Sound Mirror', is a listening, monitoring sculpture which builds up a database of sound. 'Ezekiel' is an interface for live mixing and spatialising recorded sound. These pieces could have been made with another program, or combination of programs or hardware, but I found this way the most flexible and straightforward.

Do you build upon the way you have used the software previously for each new work or is every piece completely new?

I try to make my programs modular so that I can re-use parts of the software. At the moment I am making a piece which uses a similar way of organising sound and rhythm, but with a different approach to spatialisation. Some of the timing algorithms used in 'Site' appear in the new program, which also treats image fragments in a similar way to the sound. It will end up as a 5.1 video DVD and so won't be run live. Hopefully, I will be able to check it in the space before burning the DVD itself.

Justin Bennett's work can be seen at http://this.is/justin

Part IV

New media
theory and
practice

26 Convergence

···

Digital code is the technological basis for media convergence, enshrined in Nicolas Negroponte's (1995) phrase, 'from atoms to bits', in which he recognised the transformative power of converting words, sounds and images into bits of electrically stored information. The potential of digitally converged media technologies has been an object of widespread attention for over a decade and has been most specifically focused upon the convergence of broadcast television and the networked computer. The possibility of merging the domestic television and PC became a battle between the TV companies, who were content rich but did not have the digital delivery technology in place, and the Internet Service Providers, who had the digital means of transmission but not the content. In the 1990s the TV/PC convergence was largely seen as being based upon the optical fibre cable TV network, which could also be used to receive fast connections to the Internet. This was, in fact, the dream ticket envisaged in the AOL–Time Warner merger, since at the time the latter controlled twenty per cent of the US cable TV market. However, we need to remind ourselves that there is much more at stake in convergence of television and the Internet than technology. Television is both a medium of communication and a technical transmission and receiving system, which is to stress that television is a cultural medium, with developed institutions of programming and control and forms for the production of content. The domestic television receiver was developed specifically to receive that content. The Internet, on the other hand, like the telephone, developed as a transmission system without any institutionally produced fixed content. It is the World Wide Web, which has developed HTML pages with graphics, images and texts, that can be said to be the content of the Internet. The Internet is an electronic network designed to transmit code to computers that contain software programs, which can convert the technical code into human-readable documents. In all likelihood the future convergence of the TV and the Internet will require some other kind of domestic electronic device, or appliance, for receiving in digital form the content of both historical forms of television and the hyperlinked pages of the WWW.

In 2000 the American film and publishing production conglomerate Time Warner combined forces with the Internet Service Provider America On-Line (AOL) to create the world's largest media corporation. This merger represented an important new level in the convergence of the industrial and economic organisation of media production and distribution. At the time of the merger Time Warner controlled 20 per cent of the US cable market, which was a major factor in AOL's decision to merge, because it would allow fast connections for their subscribers. After the merger AOL–Time Warner's brands included AOL, Time, CNN, CompuServe, Warner Bros, Netscape, Sports Illustrated, People, HBO, ICQ, AOL Instant Messenger, AOL MovieFone, TBS, TNT, Cartoon Network, Digital City, Warner Music Group, Spinner, Winamp, Fortune, AOL.COM, Entertainment Weekly and Looney Tunes. This was a media corporation that could have the vision to provide a total integrated system of technical communication services and media entertainment content for a domestic market across all media platforms.

In the 1990s the concept of the convergence of television and the Internet ran ahead of the technological ability to deliver a unified media system, if that was indeed what was being collectively aimed at. At the present moment the meaning and potential of digital media convergence is regaining interest because of further technological developments in digital video compression, higher definition image capture and broadcast formats and greater bandwidth. However, while the actual technologies for producing an integrated system for the delivery of high-definition, multi-media and hypermedia digital media now exist, the short-term economic imperatives of differentiated media ownership make it unlikely. Indeed, the idea of 'one black box' through which households receive all news, entertainment and two-way communications is an extremely unlikely outcome of convergence, since the proliferation of media products in a digital form suggests a multiplicity of systems and devices. However, the common deployment of digital technologies across a wide range of applications continues to expand the processing and transmission of digital information. This suggests that further digital convergence is highly likely for a number of reasons. The technologies for digital capture, encryption, storage, transmission and display are increasingly cheap and ubiquitous with prices falling as markets increase. Workstations, laptops, palmtops, cameras, mobile phones, music players, digital televisions and digital converters are part of everyday life in the Western world and continue to replace analogue domestic technologies. The quality of digital objects and materials continues to match the cultural fascination with verisimilitude and hyper-sensate representations in all media. It would appear that we want media to be fully equivalent to, if not surpass, the reality to which our senses give us access. In addition digital technology is making it possible to transmit higher definition video streamed material from anywhere to anywhere in real time. For these reasons alone technological convergence in the transmission and reception of media is likely to increase. It is important, however, not to confuse what are real differences between technologies and media and, within the latter, between media forms and media economics. What the Time Warner–AOL merger indicates is that convergence needs to be thought of in more than the technological dimension. Media ownership has been converging for most of the twentieth century in the print, television and film production industries as Time Warner, prior to its merger with AOL, exemplifies.

Henry Jenkins (2001) distinguishes five distinct kinds of convergence which allow him to predict that 'no single medium is going to win the battle for our ears and eyeballs'. Jenkins' distinctions are more refined categorisations of the distinction between technological, economic and cultural convergence. Jenkins would agree with the technological and economic levels of convergence mentioned here, but he goes on to distinguish three types of cultural convergence. First, there is social or organic convergence, which can be defined as social practices in which we are engaged in more than one level of media attention. Multi-tasking in the workplace would be an equivalent to the organic convergence of watching TV and texting a friend at the same time. Convergence here is one way of discussing new patterns and modes of attention to, and engagement with, mediated realities. Second, Jenkins defines cultural convergence as new forms of cultural creativity at the intersections of media technologies. Here, he is pointing to the emerging forms of participatory culture in which users can 'work upon' media content and digital information through annotation and so on. Third, global convergence recognises that there is two-way 'cultural traffic' in a global communication network, which leads to cultural hybridity. However, such two-way traffic is not equal and the domination by major transnational corporations, who are 'content rich' and have the means of transmission, outweighs small and emerging local and national producers and providers. This structural inequality in globalised communication networks ensures the cultural dominance of the West or, even more specifically, the cultural norms and products of Hollywood. While such Western dominance of globalised media is evidently the case, digital media convergence has made this process of cultural imperialism more globally visible and given local communities 'plugged into' the network a means of 'acting back' upon dominant values as well as using it for their own purposes.

The discussion of convergence is, at one level, inimicable to all aspects and dimensions of new media in the sense that convergence is technologically written into digital media. But as we and others have indicated, convergence does not mean an irreversible tendency towards all media becoming one medium, nor all broadcasting and communication systems becoming one global corporation. Both of these scenarios are dystopian and technologically determinist and, while convergence is a real fact of the media landscape, there is historical and current evidence as well as theoretical perspectives to support the view that we will continue to have differentiated and heterogeneous forms of communication. One of the most simple yet powerful reminders of this is that media, of whatever kind, are more than their means of transmission. Media are deeply coded forms of human communication, meaning and value which emerge and change over time. Technical changes to the means of transmission of a particular medium clearly have affects and effects upon what is and can be communicated or expressed – in effect, how a cultural message is technically coded. Digital technologies are the latest in a long line of technical developments that have been applied to specific media forms: radio, television, film, photography, music and the contemporary arts. One limited version of this understanding of technology suggests that digital media applications are simply new tools for longstanding and established human purposes of communication. This is, at many levels, hard to deny and is a kind of truism illustrated by the fact that typing this text on a laptop, rather than on a portable typewriter, is, for example, simply swapping one tool for another. On the other hand, the more complex point lies in the recognition that the tool is a 'mediator' between the intended message – to follow the example, the thought in my head, formulated through language – which I then type into the laptop, which is eventually read and interpreted by a reader. The ways in which computer-generated type mediates the process of writing are hard to fathom, but in some obvious respects it is clear that the digital tool proliferates versions of text. The electronic 'cutting and pasting' of sentences and paragraphs on a VDU screen is seamless and fluid. The copying and 'saving as' of text to different files, formats and other computers gives on-screen text a temporary, unfixed and ultimately more relative feel which changes the status of text itself. The impact of digital technology upon the cultural forms of writing is clearly evident in how email has changed the institutional memorandum and the personal letter, how weblogs are changing forms of journalism and how text messaging is changing language. We should also note here the highly developed discussion and debate about the relationship between hypertext and forms of literature.

The argument about whether digital media are simply a collection of technical tools or a new cultural medium is an important one that runs throughout this book, but another way of looking at the problem is to say digital media are both a set of tools and a new medium. Technical convergence has re-ordered the toolbox, recasting the separate tools of analogue media into a common digital matrix, allowing sound, image and text to be captured, encoded, edited and outputted in the same technical 'studio' using the same 'apparatus'. Of course, this does not mean that what is being worked upon is necessarily experienced as converged media. Film is still film whether it has been digitally edited or not. Music is still music and novels are still novels and so on. The cultural forms of media persist, but in the converged world of the digital toolbox, we also know that changes are taking place within the cultural media forms themselves. Hybridity is one of the obvious outcomes of convergence and this is evident in the content, structure and language of particular forms. Digital 'special effects' are an example of how the digital toolbox is creating hybrid styles and types of animated film sequences in feature animations, live action films and computer games. Photoshop is also a part of the digital toolbox, which has produced a new typology of montage in photographic images across art and advertising. Interestingly enough the application of skills using the digital toolbox in the digital workshops of the world remain highly differentiated and specialist. The application of software skills follows the media forms in film editing or sound mixing, for example, and even in the new areas of online media services the preservation of specialism and demarcation of specialist skills is maintained.

CASE STUDY

Training for the games industry: Maria Stukoff

....

M aria Stukoff is a new media artist and producer with an interest in creative approaches to gaming. As the manager of a training initiative she ran a scheme that brought people with a wide range of interests and skills into the gaming industry, 'The Game Plan'.

Media Training North West, the agency for which Maria set up the scheme, was based at the BBC in Manchester. It aimed to identify ways to develop new creative media knowledge in the North-West of England and provide new pathways to employment covering the latest creative technologies, such as mobile phones, music technology, inter-active TV and writing skills, and, in particular, to bring these skills into the computer and video games industry.

Originally the agency was established to provide the TV and film industry with the emerging new skills. Media Training North West (MTNW) provided training programmes to enhance the skills of media technicians. The programme then extended to look at the convergence between the media sectors, such as radio and TV and film. Developing upon its early successes, it broadened its remit to address the needs of the games industry. Unlike a training agency the organisation did not provide training programmes directly but worked with industry partners to set up schemes which they brokered.

Through their unique scheme 'The Game Plan', the agency devised a way to provide an entry point into the games industry for people whose work experience was broader or maybe unrelated to games development, but who had skills that could be diversified to be used in the sector. The agency worked with a mixture of people who had new media training and expertise, and people who had none. In addition, it aimed to bring a more culturally diverse workforce to the games industry.

In this interview Maria Stukoff addresses how 'The Game Plan' operated and discusses how new media industries such as game development can draw on a wide range of skills from unexpected groups of people. Through her experience, she makes it clear how wide-ranging expertise in creative areas can cross-over into very specific new media practices.

Figure 27.1   Maria Stukoff and Jon Wetherall, 'Blubox' (2005)
A visualisation of a bluetooth-enabled game system for wireless devices. Designed and developed by Maria Stukoff and Jon Wetherall, ONTECA, Liverpool. (Commissioned by the MMU Regional Office, Manchester Metropolitan University.) The image shows the phones, cables and the map of the local area covered by the tourist/history trails.

Finding new areas of creative talent

Did the initiative to set up a training scheme come from the games development industry as a way for them to access new creative talent from the community or was there a different starting point?

It actually came in the other way round. Part of my job as a project manager was to excite the industry to ask how new talent could come to them. 'The Game Plan' project was based on the hypothesis that we could make employment routes visible and accessible so that there was a viable use of this talent resource. And, of course, this is not the stereotype of the young male geek that people usually associate with the games industry.

There have been many training initiatives supported with public funding which have enabled people from the community to gain new media skills and to set themselves up as practitioners working in the industry. Sometimes they have had very impressive results, for example the training provided by Artec in London for long-term unemployed people where they worked with people who often had little educational background but who had great potential in terms of being media producers. Schemes like this resulted not only in people entering the industry but also in people setting up their own companies and groups and working in very unconventional and exciting ways. They were coming up with design ideas that might have been unlikely to come from people with a more conventional training background. Did the same pattern emerge within the games industry? Since the training that you were enabling was not the same as generic, entry-level skills but much more targeted, did this have an effect on people's eventual interests?

It is interesting that all our participants' groups wanted to work in this industry regardless of who they were and came from. What we provided was different because it was not about coming out with skills that might lead people to be independent producers or freelancers. An important part of 'The Game Plan' was that the games industry provided the training by bringing their professionals to the table for training workshops. So all our workshops were delivered by people working in the industry who made their skillsets available. We also had closed workshops which were a significant way of operating because our participants included people like career advisers, script writers and producers of film and television programmes. Their interest was in creating new employment opportunities because they recognised that the traditional media sectors were converging with the increasingly visible game development industry. The game development studios were also beginning to recognise that they were in need of new talent and expertise from those media sectors to create better game-play narratives or special effects.

Skills specialisms

Often when people talk about the games industry, and the kind of skills that people need to operate within it, they talk about very well-defined and specialised areas of expertise, for example, working with certain kinds of coding or certain kinds of graphics. Was there a place in the industry for people without that sort of expertise that takes years of training to develop?

This issue of specialisation is a tough one and often gets thrown about at game development conferences I attend. There is often a concern that the industry itself is becoming stagnant because the skills are so specialised, with people doing very specific design applications that they do for years and years even though games themselves, and the technology associated with them, might change. It can be so very focused and a game designer for a PS2 console, for example, might suddenly find their special abilities are not needed when the new PS3 development kits arrive. But with the advancement of technology the industry also recognises that it always needs new skills, for example, with special effects like making reflections on glass work better or creating more realistic textures. So they may decide they need to look towards the film industry to bring in other specialists to work with their teams and facilitate a convergence between the different skill-sets.

One of the issues of game development is that there is no single way of entering it. Did you also work with people at the point where they were already in education, to supplement their skills?

If you look at education there are a lot of graduates who have already completed an animation degree or have an art and design background before choosing a course in game design. Following direct routes into game development is more typical from people with computer science degrees. However, there are issues with courses offering game design degrees. Often graduates come out with a degree that is far too broad and not

Figure 27.2 Maria Stukoff and Stardotstar, 'Sussed' (2002)
Gallery installation at Oldham Art Gallery, UK. The game-
based interactive installation that allows up to four players to
learn sustainable issues centred around the artworks shown in
the gallery. This artwork was conceived and developed by
Maria Stukoff and Stardotstar, Manchester.

specialised enough for the industry to employ them. For example, though they may have
relevant programming skills these may be to an academic curriculum where they may
have learned little about programming for creative applications. In these situations just
having programming skills alone isn't enough. What isn't always taught is the importance of teamwork, and this is a key issue for game design teams.

So the question is do you become specialised and focused or can you broaden people's
skill-set out to be more knowledgeable? In our training model we approached the idea
about working in the game industry very differently. Every workshop was designed to
reflect and enhance the cultural interests of the group we were working with regardless
of gender or the age group.

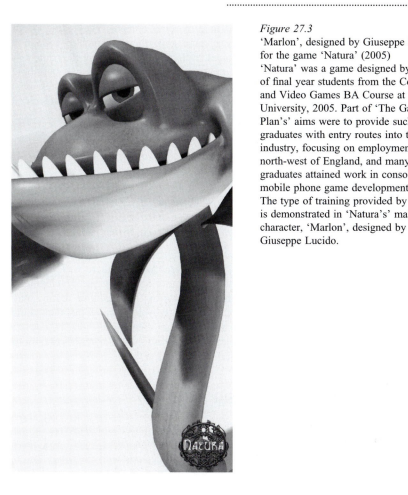

Figure 27.3
'Marlon', designed by Giuseppe Lucido, for the game 'Natura' (2005) 'Natura' was a game designed by a group of final year students from the Computer and Video Games BA Course at Salford University, 2005. Part of 'The Game Plan's' aims were to provide such recent graduates with entry routes into the industry, focusing on employment in the north-west of England, and many graduates attained work in console and mobile phone game development studios. The type of training provided by Salford is demonstrated in 'Natura's' main character, 'Marlon', designed by artist Giuseppe Lucido.

When we worked with young South Asian women in Manchester we found it was very clear that the mobile phone was an important technology and they used it continuously to interact with their favourite Asian TV music channels by phoning in to select tracks. However, they didn't relate to the mobile phone or interactive TV as a creative media. Our study revealed that all their boyfriends or brothers had Gameboys or Playstation 2 consoles at home and though they don't actually play themselves, the girls would often watch it being played. So what we tried to do is introduce to them an idea of creative game-play and interactive exploration, something they otherwise thought of as being just 'everyday' and not really about media or creative arts.

We devised an eight-week course that looked at interactive TV enabling them to write their own game program and explore what type of interactive content would interest them to become media creators themselves. As a result we have had several young women change from studying law to media studies.

With another group we actually worked with university students still in their second and third years. These students were very frustrated with the fact that they had no access to game studios or exposure to industry professionals because lecturers came from an unrelated field and had not worked in game development. They came to our workshops to meet industry people. This exchange gave them a level of validation they needed, and, most importantly, they gained skills in communicating their interests from a professional context. The important thing wasn't just about content, but about the information they were exposed to being expressed in the language of a professional as opposed to an academic lecturer. We know this worked because we tracked several people and those who got jobs reported that the information given was the key for them getting into a development studio.

Building on existing skills

If you are providing training for this diverse range of people do you find that all the training workshops and opportunities have to be designed as bespoke courses, specifically tailored for the cultural context or particular experience of that group?

We tailored all the training programmes on the skill gaps that were identified from the industry. For example, our industry steering group identified that there was a lack of scriptwriters in the industry to bring a wealth of new story ideas to game development. However, people who might have skills such as scriptwriting and dialogue writing may not even consider applying to a game developer because they don't know that their skills are needed and because the game industry, being a rather closed shop as it is, doesn't often seek to mention this skill gap. We organised a workshop with a scriptwriter from the game industry who designed a specialised course with us.

Communication as essential skill

From what you say I assume there are some generic skills or abilities that are important. If you are doing this, what are the kind of skills that you identify that you think are most useful across the board for people to get an entry point into the games development industry? Are they technological skills or ones to do with the nature of the sector?

One of the things we learned from all our projects, whether they were with students, people with previous employment histories, recent graduates and even teenagers, was the major point that professionals from the games industry highlighted again and again, that good communication skills were critical. Frequently the young men we met could not effectively communicate why they liked a video game or why they wanted work as a game designer. Most producers explained to me that essential interview techniques are to ask about what game they are currently playing, wanting to hear them articulate several key concepts like game play or level design issues, offer an understanding of 3-D design features. Many failed at this first basic hurdle regardless of how good their portfolio was.

One of the gaps that were highlighted during 'The Game Plan' was the poor communication existing already within game development teams. The main thing that we tried to pass on to our trainees was that they could be a great designer or programmer but if they couldn't communicate it would be very hard for them to find employment because the nature of game development is now so specialised in different areas, professionals need to be able to talk effectively with all their team members in order to successfully work through all the levels of game creation.

You have been identifying conceptual skills as the skills which were most important to impart, but also that it is crucially important that people understand the nature of team-work, collaborative endeavour, and also critical thinking. However, you haven't described any particular transferable skill-set as essential, for example, skills relating to graphics or coding. Are they less important than getting people to think in a partic-ular way?

Depending on where people want to work in the industry technological skills are of course essential. However, there are many different university courses dealing with game design concepts, expecting to get their students into the industry. But if you had two graduates being interviewed and one had also been doing their own work separately at home, could show a good portfolio and could converse about the elements and the conceptual ideas of gaming, I think that he or she would probably have a much better chance to work in the industry than someone coming out of a three-year degree who couldn't demonstrate this commitment or breadth.

Size and approach of companies

Presumably one of the other issues about communication is that games developers may need to communicate with others about the work since the games market is very volatile and the way a typical company will operate changes according to economic moods. What sort of companies were you working with?

We are particularly working with independent game development studios that are actu-ally quite small. A company with sixty people would be considered reasonably large. Teams in the north-west of England can be small because they provide a development service to large publishers who mostly decide on the projects. One studio might be designing planes or asteroids for a particular game and another might be creating the characters. There will be internal producers with each studio and external producers working for the publishers and co-ordinating the various contributing development studios.

A different model is where a small company is developing a game in its entirety. It is the publisher's responsibility to market and promote it. And then there are the game retailers but that is another story.

As an artist, much of your own work has drawn on the technology, forms of participa-tion or metaphors from games culture. Also, you have been creatively experimenting and researching for some time into the way that people participate in this sort of creative project. Did this expertise and knowledge help you to decide on the approach you used in setting up 'The Game Plan', as this type of game-based learning project did not have any precedents within the public sector?

Much of the creative management decisions for 'The Game Plan' were closely related to how I approach my own artwork. As an artist exploring interactive media, I am always fascinated about how people learn to be creative with new media communication tools. I would say that my work is about building interactive situations, providing new perspec-tives of an environment the public can engage with in a playful and interactive way. It's important to me to inspire teamwork, such as the installation of the multi-user game at Oldham Gallery or the wireless 'Blubox' system. Console games or interactive TV are not inaccessible artistic tools when given the creative freedom to make your own content and to locate those within a cultural and social context.

28 Information

Data

As more and more knowledge, in its representational forms, is converted into digital bytes, so it becomes an enlarged collection of data. We would not commonly think of a piece of music, the complete works of Shakespeare, the facts contained in an encyclopaedia, a photograph or a poem as data, other than as the way in which they become stored in a computer or transmitted through the network of computers. We ordinarily distinguish data from knowledge as the prior, raw or untreated state of information. Data are a product of various procedural systems, as in a quantitative collection of material, the results of a survey for example, which is also understood as a body of information when it is applied in some context or situation. A computer operating system processes data of a different kind, the algorithmically stored electrical impulses, coded as sequences of '0's and '1's. Data reside in the materiality of microchips of the CPU, in the switching between two states of electrical impulses which create the combinations of coded instructions. A computer database stores information through the additional procedural programming and code of software which carries the instructions and choices for accessing data in a readable form. The distinction we are making may be regarded as quibbling, since 'data' and 'information' are often used synonymously. However, the distinction is important when we relate our understandings of data, information and knowledge to the question of computer language and the preoccupation new media practice has with databases, networks and software. We need to go further with this line of thought.

Database

The shift from analogue to digital encoding, recording and transmission renders all manner of knowledge, facts, records, files, archives, text, numerical tables, images, sounds and films, all previously held in different material forms, Negroponte's 'atoms', into a common digital code, sequences of bits, '0's and '1's, stored in the electrical stasis of computer microprocessing 'chips'. Such material, now encrypted as digital code, is collected, stored and retrieved through files and databases, which structure data according to institutional or individual categorisations of subject, type or procedure, i.e. financial, medical, historical, legal, etc. The organisation of binary code in a database is subject to the classification of data by the different needs of access and retrieval, so in one sense we cannot abstract primary 'data' from its specific structural organisation, which is also a binary code. Database programming has been developmental in computer science over the last twenty-five years and database models have shifted from simple 'flat file' databases, which had only one record structure, rather like a spreadsheet and with no links between separate records, to contemporary 'relational' and 'object-orientated' databases, which separate the rules of access from those of the structure of data. This, as Schmidt and Zimmermann (1994) points out, 'allows combinations of data to be retrieved that were never anticipated at the time the database was initially designed'. The general point to reflect upon is that databases are designed using mathematical and logical rules according to the perceived needs of the users, to store and retrieve data. The general development of database design has been away from fixed structures and towards ever more fluid relationships between all data sequences. The reason why database design continues to develop ever more fluid characteristics can be glimpsed in the uses to which data are put. The idea of 'data mining'. in which any given body of 'raw' data can be trawled through in different ways to reveal or uncover new and potentially useful or profitable information depending upon what you are looking for, is a prime example.

Databases as a platform for new media

Databases constitute one of the fundamental platforms upon which new media practice takes place, because accessible databases are used in new media to construct interfaces to and multiple pathways through searchable data. The new media object is, in this sense, to be thought of more as a conceptual map, made manifest through a designed set of instructions for navigating a database, than it is a traditional finite work. But here we must be clear, once again, that in the cultural practice of new media, the definition of technical databases used in computer science, to model and program hierarchical, relational and object orientated structures of data retrieval, is being extended and given a metaphoric, if not symbolic, extension of meaning. This is most clearly explained in relationship to the significance accorded to databases within the discussion of digital art. Lovejoy (2004) states that 'the database itself and the three dimensional virtual space it exists in can be thought of as "true" cultural forms'. This is a reference to the World Wide Web and the Internet, seen, metaphorically, as a new form for structuring of cultural experience. Seeing the WWW and Internet as 'the database' amounts to a theoretical leap in which the specificity of different technical databases, scientific, financial and institutional, each with their own codes of access, are collectivised as a unified cultural form. Clearly, the WWW is a major new cultural medium whose forms are, as we write, being worked out through the convergence and remediation of existing media, writing, photography, film-making, games, economic transactions, etc. The remediation argument (Bolter and Grusin 2000) stresses the continuities between, as well as the transformation of, the digital extensions of analogue technologies and their corresponding outcomes in media forms. Lovejoy's desire to cast the database and its navigability as a 'true' cultural form builds upon Manovich's argument that the abstract paradigm of a database stands as a new model for the organisation of thought, hence as a new symbolic form of the computer age (2001: 219). The unfolding of this argument is important to grasp because it helps us understand much of the preoccupation in new media with databases. The reasoning is based, as we have seen, in the discussion of code and on explaining the structurally linked hierarchy of computer levels. Digital code is the basis of computer data and how computers operate (CPU, ROM and RAM), and is therefore the foundational, or underlying, level upon which the communicable level of human-readable files is built. The total collection of items digitally encoded on computers and made available through Internet browsers and search engines (the non proprietary software of HTML as well as the proprietary software of AOL, Windows, Netscape, etc.) share the logic of binary code. It is the abstract total of all computer-stored data and its networked organisation that is being called the cultural form of the database, and it is the binary logic, its code, that is being understood as the paradigm through which meaning is organised. The 'true' nature of this new paradigm of communication is to be found in the characteristics of the organisation of computer procedures. Digital code consists of non-continuous, separable and distinct sequences, which can be cloned and combined in any order. The relationship between the sequences is technically arbitrary, since there is no necessary relationship between elements of the system. A database is a collection, or a list, in which each item possesses the same significance as any other. Such a system can be characterised, therefore, as non-hierarchical and non-linear and it is these two characteristics, above all, that are defining of the new paradigm. Manovich (2001: 218), Lovejoy, Paul and Rush make the argument that the digital database is a new symbolic form for a new age, by opposing the digital data network to the fixed, linear and hierarchical mould of the older analogue forms which, it is argued, tended towards the cultural paradigm of narrative.

Narrative

Narrative symbolic form is the underlying structure of linear perspective in painting, and naturalist and realist representation in the novel, theatre, photography and film. The essence of narrative form is that it establishes a set of fixed relationships between people, objects and events in time and space, which are organised into linear or pictorial structures that are then read or seen as corresponding to reality. In visual narrative forms, objects obey the rule of consistent perspectival diminishment towards a vanishing point on the horizon as they do in optical vision. In narrative film, the spatial world or the viewer is 'mirrored' in the spatial editing of film sequences so that the events portrayed operate coherently in front of the camera. In the narrative novel, characters relate to one another and events unfold in consistent time frames. The frame of the painting, the frame of the cinema screen, the proscenium arch of the theatre, are all devices through which a reality is represented. The narrative structure of the painting, novel, film or drama allows us to view the dynamic unfolding of events and relationships within the reality framing device. In creating the representational window onto constructed realities, narrative form also establishes the position of the viewer/reader in their own separate contingent reality outside of the narrative frame. Narrative form thus formalises two realities, one of the body in time and space and the other of the mind that is engaged or occupied in the representation. The representational reality of narrative form is often described as 'illusional' since it is not contingent in time and space with the body, although an audience or reader is rarely, if ever, confused about the difference between the contingent reality of their immediate senses and the constructed reality of the narrative they 'enter' when watching a film or reading a fiction. However, it is precisely the fixing of the two 'realities' and the 'suspension of disbelief' necessary to enter the narrative that has been seen by the European avant-garde in art and literature as a rejection of the immediate reality and its replacement by illusion. This argument becomes more than a matter of pointing out technical differences in styles of art or genres of media when it is framed by the wider debate about the relationship between representation and reality. The new paradigm of the database as the new cultural form, brought about by the development of networked computers, is one powerful position in this debate, which holds that representation can no longer give us any meaningful truths about or encapsulate current reality. Lovejoy makes this explicit: 'The computer shattered the existing paradigm of visual representation by converting visual information about reality into digital information about its structure' (2004: 223). There are, as we have noted, those who counter this argument by pointing out that the predominant cultural languages of new media built upon the database have been continuously adapted from the narrative forms of analogue media (Jenkins, Bolter and Grusin, Lister *et al*.) It is also important to recognise that narrative forms are not monolithic and have been subject to continual development, manipulation and stylistic variation over time, through the invention of stylistic and rhetorical devices within the language of whatever medium. Thus, for instance, the US soap operas 'Six Feet Under' and 'Desperate Housewives' break with nineteenth-century naturalism by including dead characters within the action. But, as Manovich argues, while a database can support narrative, there is nothing in the logic of the medium itself that would foster its generation. Once again we are returned to the question of whether there is a digital cultural language to be found in the paradigm of the database. However, the question of a new formal language is formulated, not for the first time, through a stark binary choice in which the narrative paradigm is cast as an older and ultimately historical ordering of experience, while the digital database paradigm is grasped as the new, current and forward-looking order. Why is this argument so compelling and far reaching? The analytical purchase of the argument is the powerful degree to which it unifies a whole set of observations of the technological and cultural characteristics of digital technology, with a much wider set of systemic changes at the social and economic level. We will return to the argument that narrative is a barrier to reality in the next section on digital aesthetics, but first we need to complete the wider argument for the ascendancy of the digital paradigm in the computer age.

Binary opposites used to characterise difference

Narrative	*Database*
Representation	Information
Linear	Non-linear
Fiction	Reality
Illusion	Control
Fixed	Relational
Object	Process
Author	User
Old media	*New media*

Information

The argument that the computer database represents a new symbolic and cultural form contains two related but different strands. The first part of the argument states that because the database is the primary structure and mode of the computer it is conceptually as well as technically its essential form. It is then argued that the Internet and the WWW are the social embodiment of a global database, which functions as a network containing a limitless amount of information in digitally coded (database) form.

The digital encryption of potentially anything and everything, whether that be the digital scanning of historical archives, telematic remote surveillance in real time, the constant additions and revisions of texts, sounds and images on hyperlinked websites, or the updating of stockmarket indexes, now constitutes a common currency as digital information. The difficulty with the argument, as ever, lies in what status or meaning is given to this recognition, what significance can be given to computer data, understood culturally as information.

Knowledge in the information age

One of the bases for the 'information age' lies in the economic investment in, and practical expansion of, computer and telecommunication systems by both public institutions and private companies over the past twenty-five years. It is now widely accepted that networked computers and mobile telecommunication devices are central to many economic, industrial and social functions of the globalised world. The growth and centrality of the computer in the economic sector has been linked to the decline of manufacturing industry and the growth of the service sector in North America and Western Europe during the post-war period. For Castells (1999) the 'information revolution' represents a new kind of economic organisation in which information processing has superseded manufacturing as the dominant mode of production. In this new economic organisation, information becomes a commodity and a form of 'leading edge' economic power. Castells' view of an information economy builds upon the wider analysis of a shift from production-led capitalism in the Western democracies to commodity-led capitalism in which communication technologies are centrally entailed. Both Jameson and Harvey elaborate upon the decline of a manufacturing economy and the rise of a commodity economy with a larger service sector as central elements in defining 'the condition of post-modernity'. Commodity-led capitalism is also the economic basis for the term hyper-capitalism, upon which Baudrillard established his analysis of the new 'era of simulation'. While there are significant differences in the detailed arguments and the conclusions drawn by these theorists, there is a general consensus that a profound set of social, economic and cultural changes in the organisation of production and exchange have taken place since the 1980s, whose effects are still being felt. They and others (e.g. Lyotard 1979) conclude that the mass increase in the use of computer technology and the application of increased scientific knowledge has also been central to the ways in which we think about knowledge, science and learning. That information is now regarded as the universal commodity of the computer age is now taken as a fact. But it is this very fact of regarding information as a universal common currency, a new commodity that can be stored, processed, transmitted and received through computer databases and networks, that raises the issue with which we began this discussion, by asking what are the differences between data, information and knowledge. Lyotard (1979) argues that the 'computerisation of society' has changed the nature and function of knowledge such that it can only survive if learning is translated into quantities of information. Toffler (1990) says something similar when he points out that in a computerised society knowledge now encompasses data, information, images, symbols, culture, ideology and values, to become not only intellectual capital but also a commodity.

Tactical media

Such perspectives are important for new media practice, because they alert us to a whole set of problems related to the access, control and meaning of digital information. Hackers have already decided upon a strategy of resistance and activism in what they see as the global dominance of information. Here, the global networked database is pictured as a new repository of (total) information, and cyberspace is seen as the new territory in which gophers, crawlers and search engines contain the all important algorithms of network 'intelligence'.

The tactical media movement started in the US in the 1990s. Gregg Bordowitz, theorist/practitioner, is one of the group's founding members. Geert Lovink is a member of Adilkno, the Foundation for the Advancement of Illegal Knowledge, which is a free association of media-related intellectuals that has also developed tactical media perspectives. Tactical media distinguishes itself from radical 'alternative' media of the 1960s and 1970s on the basis that it is no longer possible to adhere to strict ideological positions, or even to support the analysis of ideology, moving instead to what Lovink defines as 'pluriform'. Tactical media are engaged in an informational power struggle through gaining control over the informational bases of instrumental, structural and symbolic forms of power. The Free Software Foundation (FSF), established in 1985, campaigns against the corporate proprietorial ownership of access to digital information and believes instead in the computer users' rights to use, study, copy, modify, and redistribute computer programs. Those academics and researchers who support the perspective that technology is 'socially shaped' argue that the 'black box' or technology contains social and economic values which have become invisible and naturalised and can only be revealed by analysis (Williams and Edge 1996). The notion of information as some kind of raw material and the database as its repository misses the point that data have already been 'worked upon', 'shaped' and hence given value in the process of becoming data. Such value is, as has been suggested above, ultimately its exchange value, knowledge as commodity, in which there are new procedures for tracking and auditing its acquisition. This, as Lyotard and others have subsequently elaborated, has profound effects upon the educational establishment in which the functions of knowledge, as research and as acquisition, are located. New media practice that does not recognise the transformation represented by data processing misses the structuring power of information and the emerging character of cyberspace.

CASE STUDY

Innovation and media institutions: Matt Locke

....

Matt Locke is head of New Media Innovation at the BBC and a writer on new media. Originally having trained as an artist he was formerly the Creative Director of a new media arts organisation in the north of England.

In this case study he addresses how new media is constantly creating new opportunities for users and audiences, and how this will increasingly impact on the way that traditional institutions see their role. In particular, he suggests that new economic models have to be considered by broadcasters, and considers how successful dot.com initiatives such as Amazon and eBay suggest that there are new ways that people can access, and create, cultural products.

Matt, I would like to talk with you about the future of new media. I am interested to know where you think media innovation is going. I'm not talking about the development of applications or computer programming, but of the shifts in the way that media impacts on people's lives. One of the things that we discuss in this book is how new media can be seen in relation to the history and broader context of older media practices and the way that they have shaped our understanding of the world. In some ways it has taken a while for these older media, certainly in their highly organised corporate forms as broadcast, film distribution and newspaper or music production, to respond to the innovations that have been taking place at the grass roots level with practitioners. But there have been deep changes occurring in the way that those industries understand their relationship to their products and their public. What do you think are some of the key concerns?

One of the things that is very apparent in talking with people involved in all levels of work with new media is that there has been a shift in understanding of the impact of new media. In the 1990s the debate was largely about finding ways to develop new forms of content, new art forms, and new types of practice. This has now been superseded by an understanding that what is most significant is mining existing data, having multiple or plural interconnecting networks through that data, and expanding access to data through these networks.

Within creative practice, one of the themes that has been explored by artists and theorists, if not by industry, has been the openness, availability and mutability of existing material. So, drawing on archive material has often been more important than creating new artefacts. This, of course, ties into discourse and practice that comes out of post-modernism exploring how to work creatively in a cultural context that is post mass-narratives.

Mass amateurisation and making visible

The focus now is on processes of 'making visible', which is a phrase that is being used in current debates around classifications and taxonomies. What technology has done over the last twenty years is make visible a lot of the process of creating meaning, the process of cultural production, and make it live and dynamic, and in this way the tools of production become more accessible. I think that one of the most interesting discussions of late is that the trends in technology over the last century, and over the last twenty years in particular, have been towards 'mass amateurisation'. For example, technology challenges the idea of professionals as the unquestioned owners of truth and knowledge. Technology has, increasingly in the last ten years or so, led to the amateurisation of professional fields so that people can get information, for example about their healthcare, on the net. They can then use this information to build cases against health policy or institutional science, often by sharing user-generated information.

Another way of seeing this might be the growth of the open source movement as a viable and legitimate alternative to corporately controlled software.

Yes, this is definitely the case, and this also illustrates the importance of scale in user-generated production. I am not interested in a kind of glorification of the amateur but in how this can be seen as a new trend in user-led innovation. It is no longer a case that it is somehow naive or folksy for people outside professional institutions and professional organisations to have a major impact on their sector. This is because of the incredible scale that digital technologies give to user networks. For a broadcaster like the BBC, this scale has huge ramifications on our relationship with our audiences.

Notions of innovation

Can you contextualise how media organisations like the BBC have understood innovation?

The fundamental driver for innovation in the BBC's eighty-year history has been the producer. Innovation has been about individuals with great ideas, professionals essentially, coming up with programme ideas and content ideas and then driving them through the organisation. The BBC, through its commissioning processes, has developed a way of dealing with producers of innovation, enabling people with great ideas to make, for example, documentaries like 'Blue Planet'. Originally that would have always been solely within the organisation, but increasingly, over the last twenty or so years, we have commissioned more ideas from outside. As a result of this history, the BBC is very good with dealing with individual producers of innovation.

And over the last ten years had that approach also been taken to its relationship with new media?

Yes, definitely. Organisations like the BBC, in the first flush of the new media boom, first asked where would they find the producer-led content and unique ideas that could come from new media. I think that was the first organisational response to the Internet. For some, exploring this space was essentially about cheaper broadcasting. But a lot of people who were involved in the web from its early days had more radical ideas about what it could mean. When the dot.com boom began and when money started flowing into the web people initially tried to graft existing economic and broadcast models onto it. Many people presumed that we were going to go through a hybrid period, but that the Internet was basically a dynamic broadcast platform waiting to be filled with new media content. They expected that all broadcasters had to do was to find the new formats for content, in the same way that television eventually developed its own formats for dramas that were different from radio.

Disintermediation and eBay

What you are describing is parallel to what went on within the arts sector where it was expected that the Internet might develop another platform, and that it would develop its own artistic network with unique creative forms. Many interesting experiments took place. However, this of course presumes that there is a new audience for this work.

What was not really happening at that time was an appreciation from a user point of view, and whether these formats could reflect all the value people might get from the web. In retrospect, nearly all the business models in the economic sector that have actually succeeded on the web include some form of disintermediation of existing institutions. These aren't the conventional models with a producer, broadcaster and mostly passive receiver. They involve some form of transaction which gives the user the control, passing the audience member or the consumer more power than was traditionally in those relationships.

eBay is possibly the most radical version of disintermediation, in that they have no stock, they have no inventory, all they do is basically intermediate between individuals. They have done something that is constantly being analysed in studies of new media, to do with building trust in relationships. The trust system of eBay is based on feedback for individual transactions from buyers and sellers, which is a very efficient system, in that feedback is linked to real transactions between people. It is often being analysed by people who want to build trust-based models online because it seems to work very well. eBay is an enabler. It is a kind of passive cog in that it operates with only a bare minimum of rules, but maintains a huge amount of successful relationships in its communities. Media organisations like the BBC are starting to ask questions about whether we can provide similar enabling roles.

Can you expand on the way that disintermediation affects a broadcaster?

Broadcasters like the BBC used to have a lot of control of the supply chain. In other words, they defined the analogue TV standards, invested in the infrastructure, had experts in broadcast spectrum planning, and in that way it delivered its content directly to its audience. Now when people switch on the television they may get Sky or a cable network. The direct relationship between the producer and the audience has been broken.

Could we extrapolate this to say that a potential power of digital networks is essentially to disintermediate existing media organisations so users can now download content in ways that they choose, rather than in ways that are controlled by the producers?

Users are interested in exploiting the power of digital networks to define the relationship that they want with content. People are going to expect to get the content they want without having to worry about any organisation, its branding and, crucially, its economic models. This is a major issue for commercial broadcasting, because their existing brand and economic model is based on the fact that they control the context, how the content is received, so for example they can place adverts in the content stream. Obviously this has been challenged by products such as PVRs [digital personal video recorders like Sky+ or Tivo] where people skim through the adverts. And now something far more radical is challenging the economic models of all broadcast organisations, where the content is distributed directly between users: peer-to-peer networks.

Amazon and the 'long tail' model

In thinking about these arguments, and thinking about something like eBay as a model, we stop conceptualising a broadcaster as being primarily the provider of new content but as a holder of a vast amount of available material, an archive.

One very important current economic debate is about the 'long tail' argument. If you look at any content available in the market, whether books, music, TV, whatever, 80 per cent of the volume of sales will be generated by 20 per cent of the available product. Now, in markets where there are fixed barriers to the amount of products you can make available at any one time, for example a broadcast TV channel with its limited spectrum, you are economically only interested in the head of the tail – the hit shows. What digital technology has done is make the remainder of the tail economically viable. Amazon is the best example of this. There is basically no additional cost in making available all the products on the market at the same time, because Amazon do not have physical superstores; it takes just extra server space to list 20 million books rather than 20 thousand books. What they have seen happen, which is really interesting, is they are getting more and more of their business now in the 'long tail'. A considerable amount of their sales are generated by stock which previously wouldn't have even been available in a bookstore.

Is this what they are doing by offering recommendations based on the user's latest purchase and the history of other people's purchasing.

Yes, this creates a very simple way to enable people to find their way into this 'long tail'. Within a couple of clicks, maybe on the same screen, you can display content which previously you would have not seen in a bookstore. Users start to buy things they never would have, the extra transaction costs are minimal for Amazon, and it adds significant value to their consumers' experience. So digging out a really obscure dub reggae CD from the 1960s or 1970s, for example, has been made considerably easier by the power of digital networks – it's just clicking on a few recommendation links.

It also provides a different way of accessing information, because you are rarely in a position where you are trawling through a huge list of titles. The 'push' from the server end has become very a pervasive and important way of operating.

Traditionally, most economic models have been about concentrating what is available. So if you know what the next big movie is, what the next book is, then you are going to be more economically successful. You could describe this as purifying the signal from the noise. To make content production viable, it is in your interest to keep the signal as pure as you can – to find the most 'hits'. What is interesting in 'long tail' environments is that digital networks actually make noise viable again. They throw noise back into the signal and this makes lots of niches suddenly economically successful. Digital networks enable you to do that.

Amazon is sometimes uncannily good at suggesting content to you because it can mine a database of millions of users. In a way Amazon noise is the millions of bits of data they get from their users, and rather than creating a master signal for all users what they try to do is create dynamic signal just for you.

Historically, a broadcaster like the BBC could be described as an attempt to create a master signal for the whole of the UK population, and its aim is to represent the interests of the whole of the UK population. Amazon does not have to worry about that because it is not trying to sell to the whole of the UK at the same time. It can create all the stuff that you want, create something that is highly personalised because it does not have to deal with the scale of a broadcast model.

Increasing choice and the institutional challenge

Are you suggesting that we will need to deal with a shift in people's relationship to media because they are expecting to operate with a more intelligent and dynamic model? Therefore, they are expecting access to a broader range of output that gives them more choice?

I think it is not so much that they are expecting it in every single transaction but increasingly the value models that have succeeded online are ones where people get a more personalised service. In a way the question for all institutions is 'what is the value proposition?'. Amazon and eBay have come up with new models which create value for the user whilst also answering those needs for personalisation and more choice. For organisations that currently have a remit to represent audiences on a national scale, for example a political party or organisations like the BBC, that is potentially really radical. How can a traditional organisation move to a model where it is trying to address those questions about personalisation and choice, without fundamentally questioning the broader narratives that have always surrounded it?

So part of an approach to this would be to work with existing material, and find a strategy whereby the resources of a broadcaster could be more available?

I think what would catalyse a new creative renaissance in the UK would be for the broadcasters to get content out there, and let people access the archives and devise their own means of working and experimenting with it. That is really what the creative future is all about. But this presents huge challenges in terms of business models, because no one really understands what the value of archive material actually is. I think there are values in the new forms of intermediation you can put on top of archive materials. So if we can create tools that encourage people to easily source that material and share it with their friends to build on it, and then to share those newly built products with their friends again, then that's a new kind of value created.

Again, if we look at the long tail model probably only 20 per cent of material in any media archive will ever be commercially valued by a large audience to justify releasing as DVDs. So the question again becomes what do we do with that long tail to make it valuable? I think that the only thing we can do is make it as openly available as possible, to encourage new forms of creativity, to encourage the kind of boom that we saw in the 1980s with the first cheap, easily programmable computers.

User-generated product

Of course, we are not only talking about archives when we are talking about content, but we also need to think about current material being generated, for example news feeds, or current websites. If we want to look at arts projects for an indication of future uses, we can see a number of artists who are making work that is entirely constructed by pointing to, or re-purposing, work that is live and online.

Most of the art works that work with these concepts have operated at a much smaller scale than the products of mass entertainment, though. There can be a substantial time difference between something having value in a cultural sector, such as artists making online diaries or personalising their mobile phones, to things that have major public and commercial take-up, such as blogs or downloadable ring-tones.

It won't be until we have seen a user-generated piece of content that suddenly gets a major audience, goes on BBC1 or ITV for example, that we will understand how broadcasters will have to react. Especially if one of their users has taken a piece of content or functionality and created a much better product than the broadcasters could have created themselves. That is the big challenge of user innovation. One approach is to suggest that it's actually the kind of relationship that broadcasters *should* have with their audiences. They should encourage their audiences to create excellent products, to have the benefit of working with new technologies, and to distribute their own content to their own existing networks. What we have not yet seen is this happening on any great scale. My projection will be that soon there will be a service generated by users which becomes a very visible and highly discussed cultural event, and broadcasters will have to think about how it exists within the parameters of what we now call broadcasting. It is fascinating and very challenging, and it is going to change the way that people see the broadcaster's role.

The extension to that debate must be to ask what role institutions play in enabling that process? To refer to the long tail and the importance of scale, the issue will not be just about users accessing material and re-working it so that it can cross over to a national audience. Instead, it could be that this is an opportunity for people to use information at a very local level, just for their local communities or local interest groups. As we have seen with photoblogs, a vast number of personal initiatives operating on a small scale can become a huge phenomenon collectively, and the Internet allows projects to shift scale unpredictably.

In this scenario, it can follow that there is an important role for institutions to play as a catalyst in these kind of debates and to help determine what things are going to add value to our experience. And in what direction to help take the debates.

The shift we have had in understanding the impact of new media has been from a relatively dumb assumption that it was merely a series of pipes – it was another way of just chucking content out there – to the realisation that it fundamentally destabilises a number of our roles as organisations in the broadcast world. What we really need to understand is where the new opportunities are. And the answer is that there are likely to be many, and they are likely to be on a number of different scales.

BBC New Media Innovation website is at www.bbc.co.uk.

Matt Locke's personal website is at www.test.org.uk

30 The location of new media in culture

···

Digital culture and global economies

···

The exponential expansion of computer networks and applications of digital technologies over the past two decades have been central to the development of the concept of globalisation, the networked society and the information revolution. All of these concepts and the issues and debates they raise are familiar territory in the discussion and practice of new media. There is no one correct theory or explanation for the enormous global changes that have taken place, but rather a number of competing positions and prescriptions. The concept of globalisation is centrally about recognising that the world economy has undergone a fundamental restructuring and reorganisation. The new global information superhighway can be seen either as a progressive force for future world peace and prosperity, or as a new form of media and cultural imperialism that maintains the divide between rich and poor. One of the things that most accounts of globalisation agree upon is the emphasis upon the structuring power of technological and economic systems in determining social and cultural change (Kellner 1995).

New technologies and computer networks have quickened the possibilities for flexible systems of production which, in turn, have created new transnational labour markets. The older, vertical organisation of production, recognised most clearly in the image of Henry Ford's motor company, in which cars were made in one place in a single ownership factory, has given way to a more spatially distributed (horizontal) system organised around sub-contracting, just-in-time delivery systems and consumer-led markets (Harvey 1989). Globalisation also describes how industrial production historically concentrated in the older industrial countries of Europe and North America has declined and been redeveloped in the emergent industrial economies in South America, South East Asia and China. Related to this shift in industrial production, new technologies have created the computer and information industries, which now employ increasing numbers of information workers on a global scale. It is these very same technologies and computer networks that transnational media corporations are using for instantaneous twenty-four-hour global broadcasting, thus increasing the cycle of globalisation (Morley and Robins 1995).

Post-modernity

The arguments and ideas surrounding post-modernity and post-modernism and the intellectual writers associated with them are entailed in most accounts of contemporary new media practice and the discussion of digital technology. The social and cultural dimension of globalised economic activity has been fruitfully defined as 'the condition of post-modernity' (Jameson 1984). The condition of post-modernity is another way of accounting for the relationship between technology and social and cultural development. Post-modernity is, as Jameson points out, a periodising concept, which connects the emergence of new aspects of culture with changes in social life and the new, globalised economic order. Post-modernism, as distinct from the condition of post-modernity, identifies trends or distinct movements in theoretical thinking, art, architecture and cultural life. Post-modernism, in all its forms, argues that the changes in the world over the past fifty years have been of such a magnitude that we can no longer continue with the rationalist modernist paradigm of thought and action and that a radical re-organisation of philosophical thought and cultural activity is needed. Post-modernists typically pointed to such cataclysmic events as the Second World War in Europe, the Holocaust, the collapse of the Soviet Union, the Aids pandemic and Chernobyl, which rationalist science and technological progress did nothing to stop.

Harvey (1989) gives a very concrete and still relevant image of the experience of the post-modern condition in his account of 'time-space compression'. He argues that the transition from Fordism (vertical organisation of production) to 'flexible accumulation', has brought with it two decades of time-space compression. Time-space compression has a disorientating and disruptive impact upon political and economic practice, class power and social and cultural life. Flexible accumulation has the characteristics of accelerated turnover time, a speeding up in labour process and an accelerating of de-skilling and re-skilling. Interestingly enough, these characteristics are now normal features of the informational workplace. In parallel with acceleration in production, Harvey points to acceleration in exchange and consumption where commodities circulate faster with a corresponding shift from goods to services. This account of the condition of post-modernity, speculative in the 1980s, has been a normal description of the culture of urban life at the beginning of the twenty-first century. What is more challenging is Harvey's analysis of the individual and social experience of the post-modern condition. Here, he talks about a world that has become volatile and in which everything is more ephemeral; a society in which the values of instantaneity, disposability, novelty and obsolescence have become naturalised; a throwaway society, where we have little attachment to anything, including idealism and people. This is a society in which permanence has been replaced by temporariness. The accumulative consequence of these features of time-space compression is a more fragmented or diversified society in which we experience sensory overload and in which we have less sense of future continuity. How individuals and whole cultures understand and cope with the effects of time-space compression is varied, according to Harvey and Jameson.

A typical set of cultural responses to acceleration and information overload has been to simply deny or block out the new experience and instead to revert to images of a lost past. Other 'negative' responses, including excessive simplification and myopic specialism, are set against the more positive response of being adaptable and fast moving. Such features were also noted by Simmel at the turn of the twentieth century in Vienna and by Alvin Toffler in the 1970s (cited in Harvey 1989).

1. Increasing power and sophistication of machines:

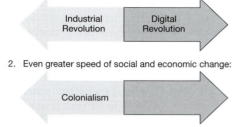

2. Even greater speed of social and economic change:

Figure 30.1   1984–2005: two aspects of change

The cultural industries

The emergence of the 'cultural industries' since the 1980s can also be understood as a reflection of an economy based upon consumption and information. The cultural industries include many cultural activities and social occupations that would not previously have been thought of together. At the conceptual level the cultural industries now encompass everything from opera to online shopping, even though at the practical level they are still reproduced through different institutions. The key linguistic attribute of this new definition of a cultural industry, or, more accurately, a collection of industries, revolves around a recent formation of ideas about 'creativity' and 'culture'. In the United Kingdom during the 1980s, the Greater London Council (GLC) developed cultural policies that connected creative and economic activity in a new way. The GLC argument was distinct from the discourse that arose within industrial capitalism, and is still residually present, that economic activity guaranteed work and prosperity, while culture was non-profitable and relied upon the support of the industrial and economic wealth makers. A society that regarded industry as the necessary economic base and culture as the contingent superstructure can now be seen clearly as belonging to an earlier period of capitalist organisation. In the wealthy countries of the globalised economy it is consumption that leads production and in a market of over-abundance there is no longer a hierarchy of needs, which in turn erodes distinctions between fashion, art and all other needs. GLC cultural policy reflected the erosion of structural difference between elite and popular culture at an institutional and political level by funding a wider range of contemporary and community activity previously considered to be outside of the remit of serious culture. The current concept of the cultural industries does contain two competing ideas of creativity: on the one hand, creativity is a necessary condition of a culture of consumption, in which creativity has become a feature of commodification, and, on the other hand, creativity is seen as central to a culture based upon the free rein of human agency. The extension of these arguments can be recognised in a variety of ways within new media practice, first as a continued challenge to settled, linear notions of nation, community and identity and to established notions of the institutional location of culture, and second as opening up and driving new cultures of diverse production and consumption.

Thinking about culture

Between the nineteenth-century tradition of thinking about culture and society as vertical hierarchies, and recent contemporary thinking about culture and production as horizontal and networked, the concept of culture as 'a whole way of life' has had a significant impact. The concept of culture as a whole way of life is a complex one, because it now begs the question of whose culture, and the idea has been the subject of criticism in post-colonialist writings as potentially mono-cultural, nationalistic and Eurocentric. Culture as 'a whole way of life' was also eclipsed by the post-modernist emphasis upon fragmentation and the rejection of any attempt to define a unified homogeneous culture and society. But the thinking of Raymond Williams, whose work does most to elaborate the idea of culture as a whole way of life, still contains several useful and pertinent concepts for the analysis of cultural change, and hence is relevant to the current moment of new media, which we examine below.

The lineage of the idea of culture as a whole way of life is sketched by Stuart Hall (1997) following the seminal work of Williams (1975) in which Williams outlined the historical etymology of both culture and society. 'Culture', according to Hall (1997: 2), is one of the most difficult concepts in the human and social sciences to define. In most cultural studies accounts of culture the modern point of departure is the definition of culture offered by Mathew Arnold as, 'the best that has been thought and said' in a society. Here the idea of culture is that of the summation of the greatest ideas repre-sented in classic works of literature, painting, music and philosophy. Williams (1965) moved to define culture as 'a whole way of life', or as refined by Hall (1997), 'what-ever is distinctive about a way of life'. Academic work in the social and human sciences from the mid-1970s in Europe, North America and Australia, moved to what Hall called the 'cultural turn, in which the very idea and work of culture became more central in accounts of human social production and reproduction. Culture became not a debate about what should or shouldn't be included in the cultural list of hallowed objects, arte-facts and works, i.e. should we include Bob Dylan's songs as great works of an age, or 'Super Mario' for that matter, but rather culture was grasped as a process, a set of prac-tices. Here, culture becomes identified with the processes by and through which people produce and exchange meanings. In Hall's account he goes on to say that culture is 'what distinguishes the "human" element in social life from what is simply biologically driven'. Culture here underscores and includes the symbolic domain of social life. Culture is participation in the construction and reproduction of meaning in all its forms.

The analysis of culture

In helping students grasp a model of culture as the communication of meaning within a whole way of life, the Open University Popular Culture Course Team, led by Stuart Hall, represented culture as a circuit (Du Gay *et al.* 1997). This diagrammatic model was used to indicate the whole social process by which meaning is achieved. It was used in the practical analysis of the Sony Walkman (1997). In their different ways these practical and analytical accounts extend the thinking of Raymond Williams, who dis-cussed the history of the idea of culture in terms of three definitions: the Ideal, in which culture is the process of human perfection or universal values; the documentary, where culture is the body of intellectual and imaginative work; and the social, in which culture is the description of a particular way of life. While Williams and his followers developed the later model, he also said that all three definitions of culture continued to operate and should not be considered mutually exclusive. In dealing with the problem of these three different ways of regarding culture Williams identified two operational levels of culture: the lived culture of time and place, and the recorded culture as represented in language and artefacts. These two operational levels are actively connected by (a) the operation of a selective tradition, which at any one time defined what was worked upon and included within the documentary, and (b) a structure of feeling, in which the lived culture operated upon and was reflected by the documentary.

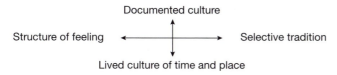

Figure 30.2   'Dimensions of Culture'
Williams (1975)

New media's cultural location

Given the short history of new media practices we would reasonably expect its account to be at the level of 'the lived culture of time and place', with much less emphasis placed upon a documented culture. However, there is evidence of an increasing interest in the documentation and archiving of new media artefacts, objects and products, and there is a growing body of academic literature involved in defining histories, genealogies and a canon. In Williams's model we would characterise attempts to define a new media canon as the shaping of a future 'selective tradition'. As yet the archiving and evaluation of new media is relatively uncharted, although it is clear that some major art institutions, the Whitney and Tate Modern for example, are beginning to assemble a selective canon, and the histories of new media emanating from the Massachusetts Institute Press are also constructing a selective tradition. In our terms a more important task in 'the lived culture' involves engaging with and looking at what people are actually doing with, and in relationship to, new media. New media practice can be defined concurrently as art, as part of wage labour and as entertainment and the impact and reception of all these activities and the work they produce in culture has yet to be fully received, let alone evaluated in any measured way. This heterogeneity of experience does need to be described if we are to begin to have a substantial account of the lived culture of new media. There is an argument here for case studies, descriptions and phenomenological accounts to be carried out in order to build a larger picture of what the practice of new media amounts to. This is, in effect, the argument for organising this book around case studies. But to account for new media within Williams's model of a lived culture and a structure of feeling presents theoretical as well as practical problems. Williams was writing significantly before the network of networked computers had started to develop. Williams was writing in and about a culture in which the organisation of media

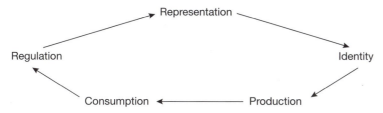

Figure 30.3   'The Circuit of Culture'
Hall (1997: 1)

was highly centralised, something he analysed in detail in account of television (Williams 1974). Williams was also of a generation of intellectuals who were struggling to account for change within a class society based on an unequal distribution of power, while retaining the importance of the idea of a common and shared culture, deeply rooted in community and settled ways of life. This project of accounting for continuity as well as breaks in cultural and media communication still has agency in the discussion of new media and remains the legacy of Williams in the British Cultural Studies tradition (Lister *et al*. 2003).

Creativity and new media

Williams's tracing of the European tradition of thinking about art and creativity remains an important, yet overlooked, framework for considering new media, precisely because new media practices re-engage the central debates about the relationship between culture and nature, humans and machines and art and reality. The development of computers and networks has refocused attention upon whether we should understand our use of machines as an extension of the human body through new powers of sensory perception, remote operation and modes of thought. In itself this is not a new idea as we have seen, and in one general sense all tools can be considered as extensions of the body. The point of departure for new media lies in the claim that computational power calls forth and demands a radically new kind of creative paradigm, one that requires us to break with the aesthetic aims and representational interests of previous media forms. Allied to the idea of a new creative paradigm for a new media are a related set of positions which posit that we have already reached a stage in our relationship with computers, their networks and interfaces in which the human mind and imagination can be liberated from the constraints placed upon them by the modes of previous expressive and communicative media (Minsky 1996). We need to be able to follow the argument for a paradigm shift in order to understand better what is actually being achieved across a range of new media practices and how different practitioners formulate and understand their own aims.

   Williams's account of the creative mind starts by pointing out how our modern use of the terms creativity and imagination can be traced back to Renaissance thinking where there was a renewed interest in the work of Plato and Aristotle who both employed the idea of imitation (mimesis), although in different ways, to define the function of art. For Plato, art (imitation or appearances) was a means to the expression of The Divine Idea, whereas for Aristotle, art (imitation) was a means of revealing what was universal.

   Williams schematises four competing and overlapping models of art that were operating from the Renaissance and which continued partially into the modern period. These, he said, were art as the revelation of a hidden reality, art as the perpetual imitation and embodiment of the idea of beauty, art as the idealisation of nature and art as a form of human energy that vies with nature. It is the last definition, Williams argues, that became the basis of the Romantic view of art from the late eighteenth century onwards and which formed the basis for the modern view that imaginative activity is uniquely human and not part of nature.

   Williams was very good at providing synoptic overviews of highly abstract histories of ideas. In the following we have put his schema in a diagrammatic form to show how he summarised the theoretical shift from classical to modernist conceptions of the relationship between art and reality. We have added the final section in order to update and extend the debate, of which we don't know whether he would have approved.

Platonist

Man	natural seeing	appearances
Artist	exceptional seeing	reality

Romantic

Man	natural seeing	reality
Artist	exceptional seeing	superior reality

Modernist

Man	natural seeing	reality
Artist	exceptional seeing	art

Post-modernist
[our addition]

Man	constructed seeing	simulation/information
Artist	deconstructed seeing	art/knowledge

Figure 30.4 'The Role of Art and the Artist in Society'
Williams (1961: 32)

Williams refines his schema when considering the modern period. Here, he says that art does one of three things: it is either a reflection of reality, a representation of a superior reality, or an organisation and synthesis of reality. The realist discourse embraced art as a reflection, while the Romantics and Idealists considered art as a superior reality. The idea of art as the organisation and synthesis of reality was distinctly modernist in tendency and, as Williams points out, was able to embrace the psychological models of Freud and Jung in seeing the artist as the emotional explorer in contrast to the scientist as the rational explorer. Like many other critics and commentators of the day, Williams accepts, although he wants to move beyond, a classification of twentieth-century artistic activity in terms of nominalist categories. The conventional account of the modernist aesthetic establishes three categories of human imaginative exploration: representational objectivity; emotional subjectivity; and formal abstraction.

The major shift in Williams's own thinking about creativity in 'The Creative Mind' chapter (1961: 19–56) comes with his attempt to move beyond the dualism, or binaries, inherent in the traditions of thinking about art, artists and creativity. He does this by turning to the biological science of his day. He looked to the developing fields of the psychology of perception and the biology of the human brain for understandings about how seeing, or, more abstractly, perception, worked. Using the work of J.Z. Young and Russell Brain, Williams developed a model of creativity in which he was able to reject the human subject v. natural object dichotomy by recognising that seeing, or sense perception, was an active process of interpretation in which each individual has to learn to see. For Williams this was a fundamentally new starting point in thinking about art and reality as it allowed him to place creativity as an essential and necessary means by which every individual interprets the world, arguing that 'there is no reality experienced by humans into which our own observation and interpretations do not enter'. Experience and understanding of the external world has to be grasped as a continual process of learning and re-learning in 'a whole process of social learning'. Williams seeks a unity of purpose between art and science. Both, he argues, are inextricably linked parts of a general human process of creative discovery and communication. In his model of the process, 'consciousness is part of the reality and the reality is part of the consciousness'. This is, of course, a highly abstract formulation of human creativity and Williams goes on to attempt to detail the process. For our purposes the most important part of the account considers how the creative process, in a period of rapid social change and disturbance, requires us to construct new rules of communication, new languages or forms, in order to grasp new experience.

Art is an intense form of general communication and can quite literally lead to an enlargement of vision and an extension of our ways of seeing the world. But art not only serves the frontiers of knowledge but also encompasses that which is known and familiar. Williams sums up this profoundly social definition of the creative process in the following way:

> To succeed in art is to convey an experience to others in such a form that the experience is actively re-created, not contemplated not examined not passively received, but by response to the means, actually lived through, by those to whom it is offered.
>
> (Williams 1961)

Williams schematised the kinds of response a society can make to any form of a new language or medium which has relevance for new media practice:

- Artists' new language initial resistance eventual acceptance.
- Artists' new language initial acceptance continued acceptance.
- Artists' new language initial acceptance eventual rejection.
- Artists' new language initial resistance eventual rejection.

Marxism

In addition to the intellectual tradition of thinking about culture marked out by British Cultural Studies we also need to reference particular aspects of the intellectual tradition stemming from the European mainland. Williams was attempting to account for the creative cultural process in terms of the material organisation of things and in this he shared in, and was influenced by, the European tradition that can, very briefly and broadly, be understood as stemming from the theories of dialectical and historical materialism developed by Karl Marx (1832–94). In post-war Europe, the work of Marx had been developed into much wider schools of critical thought. Although Marxism is primarily associated with a political critique of capitalism and with the revolutionary movements of communism, it was also very influential in a much broader academic intellectual tradition of thinking about media and culture. Within this Marxist tradition, attention focused upon the question of how the economic base of society determined an unequal and oppressive social and cultural superstructure. How culture in any one period or epoch operated to secure the dominance of ruling ideas became a matter of intense analysis (Althusser 1971; Barthes 1957). The hierarchical and fixed relationship between base and superstructure, in orthodox Marxist accounts, in which the economy determined and culture reflected, was challenged as failing to grasp the determining role of culture in reproducing a dominant or ruling set of ideas or ideologies (Althusser 1971 and Williams 1961). The Frankfurt School in Germany, associated with the work of Theodor W. Adorno, Walter Benjamin, Herbert Marcuse, Max Horkheimer and, later, Jürgen Habermas, continued to develop the relevance of Marx's historical materialism to problems of the post-war division of Europe along capitalist and communist lines. This body of work, later known as 'critical theory', directly addressed the role of media and media technologies and continues to be a reference point in the discussion of new media. So, too, does the work of Foucault (1994), whom we discussed in Part I in relation to new media histories, whose ideas of power-knowledge precisely address the process through which individuals come to occupy structured social and subjective positions.

Freud and psychoanalysis

In thinking about media in general, and new media in particular, it would be impossible to leave out of the intellectual account the importance of the work of Freud (1856–1939). This is because the notion of the self has been central to the content of media and artistic communication. How an individual represents herself and her reality has, until relatively recently, relied upon the established notion of a stable autonomous self, the individual, who is both a sender and a receiver of communicable experience. In Enlightenment thinking, founded upon the physical sciences, reality is an external, knowable entity which the autonomous individual has direct knowledge of and within which she projects herself. Up until the end of the nineteenth century, science and philosophy had conceived of the rational and conscious human mind, while religion and theology maintained the concept of the human soul. The relationship of the individual to reality establishes the difference between subject and object, which confirms both the external reality and the coherent separate self.

Freud's radical contribution to the understanding of the human mind is based upon his elaboration of the concept of the unconscious. Prior to Freud, philosophy had equated the human mind with consciousness founded upon reason. Freud argued that only a small part of mental activity was conscious and that the unconscious consisted of inadmissible and involuntary ideas, which also motivate behaviour. Reason was no longer to be regarded as the given order of the mind, but had to be struggled for in an otherwise ungovernable and irrational unconscious. Because the unconscious is, by definition, not open to direct inspection by the mind itself, its content and structure has to be inferred. Freud developed a theory of the unconscious based upon his treatment of neurosis and his analysis of the content of dreams. Freud argued that the unconscious is made up of impulses, desires or wishes, which get their energy from the primary physical instincts, of which sexuality was primary.

The unconscious and representation

Psychoanalytical concepts have been influential in the analysis of representation because they address the subject and the self. Psychoanalysis applied to art and cultural studies opened up the possibility that representation operated at the level of the unconscious as well as the conscious, both in its content and reception. Such a perspective led to an understanding that seeking satisfaction to unconscious pleasures could not be excluded from the account of representation. Freud's account of the unconscious is based upon his theory of polymorphous perverse infantile sexuality and the subsequent repression of unacceptable sexual wishes. Repression of unacceptable wishes leads to feelings of guilt, loss and anxiety, which become visible in clinical neurosis. Freud's sexual theory was also based upon the symbolic primacy of the male phallus, which structured sexual identity. The subordinated place of female sexuality in the symbolic order was criticised by feminist intellectuals but also used to analyse how patriarchy structured the sexual power of looking. This was famously applied in the analysis of Hollywood cinema by Mulvey (1973), who used Freud's theory to demonstrate how men and women appear in cinema and how they are 'unconsciously' structured by 'the male gaze'.

The application of psychoanalytic ideas to new media focuses upon three main ideas. First, how the unconscious operates to position the fragmented subject/user in cyberspace;

second, on the fusion of human and machine in the creation of the cyborg; and third, the projection of unconscious wishes onto technology in the technological imaginary. Ideas about the relationship between the body, mind and technology continue to draw upon the psychoanalytic tradition's emphasis upon the role of the unconscious and in determining how we make associations between things. The importance of the symbolic and the imaginary in psychoanalysis was developed by Jacques Lacan (1901–81) who applied a structural linguistic analysis to the elements and operations of the unconscious, arguing that wishes and desires form a symbolic signifying chain. Lacan's structuralist reworking of Freud included what he called a 'mirror phase' in which the infant child identifies itself with an image outside of itself and, in the process, mis-recognises itself, creating the idea of 'the other'. Lacan calls the mirror stage the realm of the imaginary, which is a pre-linguistic realm of images, whether conscious or unconscious, based in visual perception, or what Lacan calls specular imaging. Lacan's idea of the incomplete and fragmented self, generated by the misrecognition that takes place through the image of 'the other' as self in the imaginary, can also be applied to technology in a way that gives technology the power of creating a realm of wholeness. Cyberspace and the Internet have been conceived as potentially spaces for the creation of new identities and freedoms (Blackman 1998; Turkle 1995). Technology is also thought capable of extending and changing the nature of consciousness and the body, as we explore further on.

Marx and Freud created a theoretical legacy that has dominated post-war European thinking about individual experience and collective life, 'whole ways of life', and how they are structured by forms of economic and political power and the unconscious. The central endeavour of structuralism, semiology and post-structuralism, culminating in the various writings grouped around the idea of post-modernism, has been to give an adequate account of the structure, organisation and mechanisms by and through which individual consciousness and communication take place within a given historical order. The effort within this intellectual project has been, overwhelmingly, to understand the unequal relationship(s) individuals and groups have to power, and one of the central threads of this work has been the articulation of the structuring and organising power of difference in seeing 'the other'. The importance of these theoretical traditions to an understanding of new media practice cannot be underestimated because we cannot detach the question of (differential) power relations from how power, in all its forms, is communicated and mediated, and with what representational outcomes. Media and cultural symbolic forms and their technological apparatuses are deeply bound up with the articulation as well as disarticulation of power. Media forms are, in a sense, the agents of power and hence an individual's relationship to media is also a relationship within the articulation of power relations.

In practice, 'media power relations' means many things, from the direct question of who has material access to the production and reception of media, which is, as we know, highly differential in the digital divide, through to the more indirect ways in which power relations are embodied in any media form and with what representational outcomes in media artefacts. The question of whether new media constitutes a new cultural form or paradigm also contains the question of what power relations are structured in and by that form. We only have to look at the cultural politics of the Internet and its cultural forms of the WWW in such writers as Rheingold, Castells, Croker and many others, to see that the Internet is a 'contested arena' and a 'site of struggle' in which individuals, groups and institutions engage unequally, in competition not only for specific voices, to get their message out there, but also for the very definition and regulation of what cyberspace or, more practically, online communication, is and should be.

31 A framework for considering new media in contemporary culture

··

How, in detail, do these discussions about culture bear upon new media and its practices? In what follows we discuss three ways in which we think new media engages with as well as contributes to our current understanding of wider contemporary cultures. First, we discuss new media as an extension of existing media forms and institutions in which we account for new media as the result of the application of digital technologies to existing cultural practices. Here, new media is, as might be expected, thought of as a continuous extension of, rather than a radical break with, the current landscape of media culture. Second, we discuss new media as it has been taken up and framed by the institutions of contemporary artistic cultures. This, we assert, has become largely a matter of the way in which new media is argued as the latest extension of the European modernist avant-garde with its typical stance of rejecting the established modes of artistic language and representation. Third, and much more speculatively, we discuss some of the ways in which new media, now in its widest sense as the world of information and data, has been seen as challenging fundamental notions of thought and human nature. We have defined these three areas of discussion as follows and will look at each one in turn:

A New media as a continuous extension of existing media culture in which the rules of representation are maintained.

B New media as an avant-garde within art institutions in which the rules of representation are playfully broken.

C New media thought of as provoking a crisis in culture in which the rules of representation are abandoned in favour of the logic of the system.

A New media as a continuous extension of existing media culture and the rules of representation

··

> The reassuring smell and touch of book pages, the anticipatory crackle of opening a new music CD, the cosy comfort of surrendering oneself to broadcast television's scheduling, the magical darkness of an audience

watching a cinema, the warm community feeling of listening to radio –
these aesthetics of media might now be forgotten. And the politics that
accompanies them – the liberal, autonomous individual of print and film, the
pacified consumer of broadcast media – might also now gradually dissipate
with the advent of new media, with their different aesthetics and politics.

Poster (2002)

Within this redolent image of our familiar media one can already detect a compression
of different cultural periods. The warm community feeling of listening to the radio is,
perhaps, a nostalgic reference to the use of radio during the Second World War when
it so successfully bonded the people and the state against the threat of German invasion,
and later during the reconstruction of the 1950s, before television was established. And
the experience of surrendering to scheduled TV from the limited number of broadcast
channels is already an older experience that has been mixed with video, satellite and
cable channels for at least two decades. Both of these cultural forms have been seen,
in their turn, to dissipate or change a previous set of cultural habits and responses.
The book was thought defunct with the advent of mass television, and video was hailed
as the end of cinema. Now, Poster gently posits the question of whether we are on
the brink of witnessing a wholesale disappearance of the familiar landscape of media.
In doing so he reflects upon the character of individual aesthetic response, at a particular historical moment of change, to the material and cultural media that make up the
media-sphere. The magic of cinema is to be found in a unique combination of its technical and cultural development. First, the aesthetic of cinema lies in the technical
apparatus for projecting light through the exposed frames of film to create the grainy,
flickering cinema screen image. Second, the aesthetic of cinema lies in the development
of narrative film story-telling. Finally, the aesthetic of cinema lies in the social organisation of entertainment in which large groups of people, who previously may have
attended dance halls, music halls or theatres, sit collectively in the dark, entranced by
the silver screen. The aesthetic experience of cinema has taken just over 100 years to
develop to its present day form of the Multiplex with its wide-screen, Dolby surround-
sound qualities projecting digitally manipulated and mastered film. The same could be
said of the fifty-odd years of television broadcasting, which started with the limited
scheduling of live programmes from the BBC, often received with poor-quality signal
reception, on the original nine-inch black and white domestic receiver. Technically, the
media of film and television have continued to develop along the cultural line of greater
verisimilitude or visual and auditory plenitude to the point where our domestic living
rooms can be turned into a home cinema or concert hall.

It is upon this contemporary landscape of domestic and public media choice that we
have so far been considering what the likely impact of the computer and digital technologies will be. Digital technologies have been entailed in newspaper, film, television,
radio and music production for some time now and we can already experience some of
their characteristic effects. At one level the engagement of digital technologies with
existing media remains, behind the scenes as it were. The broadcasting of 'The Archers'
or any other longstanding radio drama on a digital signal will not alter the familiar cast
of characters or the storylines, but technically, digital radio will allow a listener who
missed the beginning of a programme to 'replay' that section and 'catch-up' again during
the broadcast, and of course that is only the beginning of the possibilities for digital
reception and storage. But the point being made here is that at the level of the technical
transmission, relay and reception of media, digital technologies enmesh with analogue
counterparts to deliver the same content. But, as with our example of digital radio, this

is only true up to a point, because it is, as we have previously discussed, the common code of the digital that allows for new ways of receiving, storing and copying material which have, as yet, to develop new patterns and cultural habits. Do we care that photographs in newspapers have been digitally treated before their conversion back to the analogue ink on the half-tone printer's plates, or that books have been word-processed and laid-out on a computer screen, or that a favourite piece of music has been digitally re-mastered?

These examples demonstrate that digital technologies and computing have been introduced into existing media forms in a process that is continuous with other historical developments. Of course, people do care when it occasionally comes to light that digital code has been responsible for an unacknowledged alteration to some aspect of an analogue original, which they can't themselves detect. But such examples as there have been of digital skulduggery in the press have remained a marginal social concern and it is largely assumed that it is business as usual in media production houses, with editors exercising judgement and control.

In other areas of existing media, particularly in advertising, television, film animation and music production the digital has had obvious and dramatic effects upon the style and conventions of content. It is precisely in advertising that digital manipulation is most aesthetically visible, paradoxically through the invisibility of the seamless joining of separate elements of photographic or filmic images. If digital manipulation has been disapproved of in a class of photographic imagery considered factual or documentary, it has been applauded for creating the seemingly 'impossible' illusions in photographic and film imagery that are classified as fictional, fanciful or fantastic. The invisibility of the digital in one cultural register of 'information', in press and news coverage for example, is as culturally conventional as the visibility of the invisible in another, in advertising, in art or domestic photography. This acceptance of the digital simulating different photographic types, or genres, is a clear extension of a cultural dualism that has differentiated the genres of analogue photography over the past 150 years.

As with digital photography, audiences have come to aesthetically recognise the digital in film production in both its invisible technical mode, in digital editing for instance, and in its spectacularly visible visual effects. The 'special effects' of digital animation and montage, which have been widely applauded in mainstream cinema, build directly upon the traditions of analogue post-production techniques stretching back to the earliest film animation experiments of George Meliese (1864–1903). Since the widespread use of three-dimensional mapping and rendering software in post-production, audiences have quickly come to expect film to be able to create credible and 'realistic' scenes of anything humanly imaginable, however fantastic. Our pleasure and delight in 'sleight-of-hand' and convincing illusion also has a prehistory in painting, architecture, fairgrounds and the circus.

Much has been made of the radical change represented by the digital simulation of the photographic and film image (Mitchell 1995; Lister 1995). This has been discussed in terms of the digital fundamentally changing the relationship the photographic image has to its referent in the real world. This is because the digital replaces the material, continuous link between the light reflected from objects and the latent image formed by the camera and fixed by chemical action, with electronic sampling registered by binary code. Much of the early discussion of the radical nature of the digital image was couched in terms of undermining photographic truth, but, as we have noted above and elsewhere, analogue photography also relied upon a constructed cultural rhetoric to establish legibility and meaning. More recent attention has focused upon the convergence of the

graphic and photographic, represented by the digital image, because digital code processes the sampling of light through the lens of a camera in the same way as it does
the sampling of any other visual source and hence essentially gives the same values to
both. The merging of photography with graphics and film with animation, where the
same principle applies, is a fruitful way of identifying the visual aspect of a digital
aesthetic. However, when we marvel at the combination of epic-scale fantasy with photo-
realistic effects in many recent films, *Lord of the Rings* (Jackson 2002) for example, or
the digital recreation of the gladiatorial games in the Roman Coliseum in *Gladiator*
(Scott 2000), we are experiencing the established pleasure of cinema of which the digital
effects are part.

   Because the digital simulates its analogue source it is not possible to easily aesthetically distinguish, or separate, a digital as opposed to analogue part of the experience
and so the experience is more one of registering what the digital makes possible within
the conventions of analogue media, i.e. the special as opposed to normal, or ordinary,
effect. Audiences recognise and measure the scale of difference of the effect made
possible by the digital, from those they have come to expect, or register, as previously
analogue. The measurement and recognition of such changes, in effect, are tempered by
the different ages of the audiences and their familiarity with digital technology. But the
ability of the audience to simultaneously be taken in by a digital rendering of a photo-
realistic effect, and recognise and appreciate it as an effect, is a contradiction in the
filmic experience, or a binary characteristic of digital media, which is extensively
discussed by Bolter and Grusin (2000) in their account of remediation. Bolter and Grusin
argue, as we discussed elsewhere, that remediation represents the competing interests
in our attention to both immediacy, i.e. to be immersed in the digital film effect and not
notice how it is achieved, as well as what they call hypermediacy, which is the opposite fascination in precisely noticing how an effect is achieved and sustained. In our
sustained interest in immediacy and hypermediacy in media, we often switch between
the two modes within media experiences, which could be said to be two kinds of attention to detail. In media where the visibility of the means would detract from our
immediate pleasure of suspended disbelief, in which we are immersed in the moment
by detail of the world/reality/story, we have to diminish, but cannot completely eradi-
cate, our attention to the details of construction. At moments of obvious (special) effects,
or, alternatively, where the illusion fails to hold us 'in suspension', then our attention
to the detail of construction comes to the foreground.

   It could, therefore, be said that the mode of attention to all media is one of an 'oscil-
lation' between the detailed effect of transparency and that of technical mediation. It is
in the detail of these two alternating modes that we can begin to distinguish a specifically digital set of effects and it is a collection of such digital effects that have been
generalised as a digital aesthetic. What has been most often noticed in cultural forms
that have adapted to, or are based upon, digital technologies (photography, music, film,
games and the Internet), are a number of common and characteristic responses to the
way digital code changes, or simulates a previous analogue register. Our attention here
is, interestingly enough, upon noticing differences between technical aesthetics and
looking for bigger patterns and structures that would form the linguistic syntax of digital
technical mediations. The digital image, sound and/or text, on a computer, television or
projected screen are still experienced as an analogue flow that is digitally simulated.
This flow can be algorithmically programmed to be at the speed of speech and the persistence of vision, or static, or anywhere either side of those two states. At many points
the digital is a straightforward simulation of the effects of analogue recording, but at
other points it is noticeably different from them, and is, therefore, a registered digital

effect. Such digital effects have been defined, often in opposition to the analogue, as the replacement of a surface by layers, the analogue surface being unilinear and fixed whereas the digital is layered and mutable. The digital aesthetic is most often defined against the analogue, while, in practice, being continuously entailed with it.

Television is currently on the cusp of digital technological change, which is having powerful effects upon its design, programming, scheduling, transmission and domestic reception. The introduction of digital software in graphics and animation has already changed the design and amount of on-screen material. The computer has interposed itself between the screen of the television camera and the screen of the television receiver so that we can no longer think of the two in a direct connected way in time, space or place. Of course, the introduction of video recording in television changed any original historical notion of real-time correspondence in television broadcasting, so that television has to caption material as 'live' coverage. However, the control of on-screen material by a computer is, in part, an extension of the previous analogue practice of inserting pre-recorded video sequences into real-time studio broadcast. But the digital computer, as the compositing and editorial control centre of televisual sequences, has made the space of the television screen closer to the multi-layer, simulated screen of the computer screen itself. The effects operating within the rectangular frame of the domestic television screen already incorporate computer-generated 3-D studio sets for news and current affairs programmes, studio sets which include teleconferencing and multi-screen displays, the mixing of live and recorded animation sequences, and the inclusion of subtitling and running text.

In these ways the television screen is partially mirroring the windowed multi-application screen of the computer. What the broadcast, cable and satellite television screen can only do in a limited way at present is to allow the viewer to act back, or interact, with the material. Currently, the digital signal allows those who can receive it to have a number of limited options within programmes. But the speed of the convergence of the television and computer is, as we have discussed previously, as much a matter of resolving competing commercial interests in media ownership as it is of technical application at this point in time. The convergence of the networked PC and domestic television reception is a complex example of remediation in which, at one level, the content of television, largely news and entertainment, remains culturally continuous, but delivered and received through digital technologies, while at another, the content of television, both discrete programmes and flows, is being reconfigured by the computer.

Television is characteristically a 'lean-back' medium while the computer and Internet is a 'lean-forward' medium. As a way of characterising the typical difference between the viewer of television and the user of the computer, it is a highly successful analogy and conveys the dominant way in which the viewer or user is 'positioned' or structured by particular media. Lean-back carries that sense of passivity involved in a common cultural habit of watching television, while lean-forward accurately indicates a work ethic associated with using a computer. We have discussed elsewhere the suggestion that television is distant and passive, while the networked PC is close and (inter)active, and recognised that this is a much overused simplification for the types of response to both media. But what the contrast between lean-back and lean-forward media does is to remind us, not only of what is significantly different between television and computing, but also what they have in common. While our bodily posture may be typically different, we can also recognise television's undoubted ability to sustain attention and involvement and recognise distracted states of being in front of a computer. Both are screen media that deliver overlapping content but in different ways. Indeed, many of the uses of the Internet are highly conventional: shopping, corresponding, and a repurposing of much of existing media content. This is what has led commentators to say that in its current form the Internet offers nothing new. As we have said, the Internet is closely bound up with existing media because existing broadcast and print media have developed closely associated ancillary websites. In this respect the Internet is rapidly reflecting the dominance of major media producers and distributors. The most visited website in the UK is the BBC Online, for example.

The arguments of Turkle (1995), Rheingold (1993) and others, writing in the 1990s about the radical, subversive or liberationist possibilities of cyberspace, stand in stark contrast to the WWW today, which is structured along highly commercial and conventional lines of commodity consumption and private communication. This is a very good example of how existing media forms, news and feature journalism, advertising, broadcasting and the retail and service industries have 'acted-back' upon, or 'colonised', the potential of a digital medium to create new cultural forms, and shaped cyberspace along familiar lines of the one-to-many forms of communication. The recognition that the WWW has recently developed along dominant lines should not blind us to the many ways in which, as a medium, it has extended and built upon private and personal forms of communication and exchange and that these are 'exposed', because of the non-hierarchical networked database, to mainstream media, for example as journalists pick-up on personal weblogs such as the 'Bagdad Blogger' as a source of information. Such examples, while framed within the conventional structure of news journalism, are examples of the Internet's potential of greater access for a much wider range of people to produce media on the web. In this description of the Internet and cyberspace, new media is clearly developing in a close and continuous relationship to existing cultural forms of communication in which the media languages are modified and extended, rather than radically transposed. Against this description of converged media as familiar and continuous we need to bear in mind the case made for the interactive and networked, in effect, the lean-forward, dimensions of new media.

The rules of representation

Looked at as a continuation of existing media forms, new media reinforces, as one would expect, established traditions of thinking and analysis of media. The widely accepted underlying paradigm within the established media and cultural studies tradition is that of representational form in which media (technology plus cultural language) is seen in complex and problematic ways, to mediate between an external reality – society, nature, culture – and the position and interests of individuals and groups within and towards that reality. The concern within this paradigm is upon what view of reality is contained in media representations and how any given representation constructs views of reality. While it has long been argued that media has a problematic relationship to the real and that we should recognise the rules, codes and conventions through which the real is constructed in media, the basic analytic paradigm continues to distinguish between the representations of reality constructed by media and the external reality in which we live. The representational paradigm can focus upon either the rules of media construction by which reality is mediated, or upon the subsequent effects or outcomes of media representations in the social world. The representational paradigm applied to new media objects and practices would, therefore, account for particular meanings, effects and outcomes within the established rules of representation, as they are practised and articulated at various levels in the cycle of culture (Hall 1997). The continuation of the representational paradigm in new media, while recognising the cultural and technical problematic of representation, still insists that representation is valuable and possible. New media practice, which embraces representational languages, would therefore wish to extend and build upon the codes of narrative and documentation, rather than reject them.

B New media, the avant-garde and breaking rules

If new media in mainstream media has been understood by us primarily as extending and building upon the rules and codes of established representational forms, new media in the contemporary arts is, as we go on to describe, typically characterised as a defining set of practices that break with the realist representational paradigm. In Part I (new media as a subject) we surveyed the institutional and cultural contexts in which the contemporary fine arts have engaged with new media as both a technology used by artists, in which it is considered as no more than a new set of tools for a continuous set of artistic purposes, and as a radical medium of expression in its own right, a 'truly' new cultural form that breaks with previous practices of art and requires new definitions. The difference between these two views revolves very precisely around whether 'tool' is understood as either a neutral carrier of the content crafted by the producer, or as having a charged content built into it, whether recognised by the producer or not. The conceptualisation of digital technologies as part of a continuous set of cultural forms and purposes, tends not to see digital tools as carriers of new content, or shaping new purposes. Artists working with digital technologies as 'neutral' tools are considered to be working within existing arts forms and practices, artists using digital photography for example, rather than fundamentally challenging the paradigm of art practice. Where digital technologies are thought to constitute a new medium of symbolic expression, then the idea of the digital tool is invested with a content particular to itself and extended to the point where the tool is defined as a new medium through which new perceptions, thoughts and experiences can be grasped. It is this later definition of digital technology as a new (artistic) medium where the radical potential of the form is seen to require a break with the continuous purposes and language of art.

Initially, we can be clear about the fact that a wide range of artists are using the WWW as a means of information and dissemination about their work, which, as we discussed in mainstream media, is continuous with existing purposes. Here, the WWW is a conventional marketing and publicity form for individual artists, art institutions and organisations. Artist websites on the WWW are little different from any website in that they are typically used as a means for users to access information contained on a database, which mirrors modes of print information, such as catalogues. Virtual galleries and museums with virtual tours have been built upon databases of digital photographic reproductions of collections produced in other forms. Images and text show and describe the documented work of performance, painting and installation. Museums and galleries also use the WWW to publicise their programmes and collections, and very clearly function as a marketing, information and educational service, directed primarily at maintaining and increasing visitor attendance. The content of individual artists' websites will vary between the design styles of personal websites and those of institutional and organisation sites. The navigation and links contained on artist websites will relate to how much material they carry and whether they function to disseminate information about the artist and their work, or whether the site itself is constituted by the artist as an artwork. There is, as is to be expected, a very large variation in the status and quality of artist websites because the WWW is essentially a self-publishing form. Museums and galleries function as gatekeepers as well as legitimators of the status of art and the question of whether the WWW has widened access for a greater number of artists to existing or new audiences, buyers or collectors, would require substantial empirical research. In our view and experience it is more likely that cyberspace reproduces reputations that are made through existing institutional arrangements. In its most inclusive grasp, art in cyberspace, or less prosaically, art on the web, has to be understood as both relatively uncharted and reflecting the existing social organisation of art practices and economies.

However, the WWW is also used by a range of younger artists and organisations dedicated to the production and development of new media art projects. It is also the case that some national and international art institutions, the Tate and the ICA in London and the Whitney and Dia-Centre in New York, for example, have developed links to specific 'digital art' projects. We should also note here, as we have earlier, that there are a small number of European-based international organisations for the advancement of electronic arts that have been in existence for well over a decade, the standing conference on Electronic Arts, ISEA (International Society for Electronic Arts) and Ars Electronica as well as the Institute at Karlsruhe and the journals *Leonardo* and *Wired*. It is in this arena, jostling alongside everything and everyone else in cyberspace, that the more serious claim for new media as a radically transforming art is to be found.

Screens and time

New media is still predominantly screen based in it reception, however much the rhetoric of telepresence and immersive and virtual environments suggests otherwise. This screen, the computer screen, is a televisual screen in origin and the flat plasma screens of today have merged the screen of the television and computer. Most of the published accounts of new media's emergence within contemporary art point out the historical importance of video as a medium and video as an art form in extending our notion of space and time within the work of art. The arrival of the video screen, whether as monitors or projections, extended the idea of representation beyond the picture frame, which some have argued is a limited and hierarchical form of representation that is ultimately illusional (Ascott 1993). In contrast to the fixed, framed image of the photograph or painting, television cameras and screens allowed for real-time communication in local space or remotely, which brings the view closer to the contingency of the real, without the mediation of representational illusion. The counter argument is, of course, that television cameras and transmission still mediate what passes before them both technically and culturally. However, real-time video does create the dynamic of telepresence. The argument about screen media being in a dynamic rather than static relationship to the external object, or referent, 'the real', is extended with the arrival of the digital because now the screen's image can be adapted in real time and thus reflect changes in the referent.

Interactivity and the virtual in new media art

A clear expression of the argument that new media art marks an end to modernist art and aesthetics is to be found in Rush (1999). For Rush the new digital aesthetic is founded upon the principal characteristics of interactivity and virtuality. He points out that 'interactivity is a new form of visual experience. In fact, it is a new form of experiencing art that extends beyond the visual to the tactile', and that 'current immersive environments let alone whatever lies beyond such virtual realities is dictating a new discourse' (Rush 1999: 216). Rush's argument here is, reasonably, speculative and comes as the conclusion to his general argument that new media is the culmination and possible closure of an avant-garde art movement that started with Marcel Duchamp. Rush sees Duchamp, along with the Dadaists, as replacing the received canon of artistic practice based upon an aesthetic of beauty, with an aesthetic of the everyday (object) derived from the machine age. With the new features of interactivity, Rush sees the final end of the artist as arbiter of the art object and the end of invested meaning. With the realisation of the virtual Rush sees the end of the object itself and its replacement by simulation.

The argument that interactivity puts the viewer in a new position of choice and active participation in the face of a digital work of art, rests upon the assumption that previous forms of art experience involved a form of looking and seeing that was passive and non-participatory. As we have said previously this is a flawed argument and makes a false dichotomy between viewer (passive) and user (active). We can say, with Raymond Williams, that for any work of art to succeed even partially, it must have an active sender and active receiver. The receiver, as much as the sender of the message, has to actively decode meaning through their cultural and experiential knowledge. It follows, therefore, that communicative interactivity existed long before computer pro- grams allowed for programmed choice. Looking and listening inevitably involve choice and selection. Bolter and Grusin (2000) cited the medieval cathedral as a hypermedia environment, because it contained several layers of simultaneous attention in the archi- tecture, paintings, stained glass windows, music, sermons and incense. The passivity of the contemporary viewer of Leonardo da Vinci's painting of *Mona Lisa*, hung behind bullet proof glass in the Louvre, is an example of the way in which the museum has produced a hierarchy of space and our access to it. We have come to see how art is pre-packaged, almost commodified, in the contemporary art experience in ways that limit the viewer's own creative agency. Rush's criticism of the passivity of packaged museum experience is the flip side of the claim that cyberspace represents a non-hierarchical space where human agency is given back to the user through the necessity to practi- cally interact with the computer. We would say that human agency is always given limits by the circumstances in which we interact, whether in front of a computer screen or the *Mona Lisa*. What we are meeting in this comparison between the painting and the computer screen is a new juxtaposition between the conventional art object and the virtual, networked communication, which Rush (1999: 216) identifies as spaceless, timeless, imageless experiences.

A pluralistic approach to new media

The assertion that new media represents another 'death of art' is less evident in Paul (2003), who takes a more pluralistic view in which digital technologies are seen as the latest in a long line of historical interest in, and relationship between, art and technology. She does make the categorical distinction, which we have discussed above, between digital technologies as either 'tools for artistic use' or digital technologies as 'a new medium'. Like Rush, Paul identifies the aesthetic of new media as arising from the char- acteristics of digital computer use, its capacity for being interactive, participatory, dynamic and customisable. In discussing these attributes of new media Paul takes the approach, also adopted by Lovejoy (2004), of classifying new media arts projects around a number of themes. Some of the themes, such as telepresence, telematics and tele- robotics, databases, data visualisation and mapping, indicate the preoccupation of new media practitioners with the technical possibilities of the medium, for remote interaction in real time, for example, or with cultural forms of accessing, traversing or realising abstract digital data. Other themes, such as text and narrative and interactive gaming, suggest the ways in which new media is remediating older cultural forms. The theme of the body and identity and tactical media activism more obviously register the cultural politics of new media and the ways in which the computer and networked online communication have created new ways of thinking, presenting and communicating about ourselves. The concerns of new media with the themes that Lovejoy identifies echo a wider set of social concerns. These can be defined as (i) the greater dimension of surveillance in everyday life, (ii) the potential fragmentation of any unified notion of the self in disembodied online forms of communication, and (iii) the undemocratic powers of corporations to dominate and control the organisation and access of the Internet. We should also note, as indeed Paul and Lovejoy do, that these concerns are not new to new media and that politics has been a strong current throughout the modernist movements of the twentieth century. In this sense the themes of digital art identified by Paul can be seen as continuous with the modernist focus upon the autonomous individual, social identity and the democratisation of art. What is different in the debates about digital art is that there is a new (post-modernist) intellectual discourse that is redefining the central relationships between art, reality, society and the individual.

These recent accounts of new media and digital art have an uneasy relationship to wider theories of technology. Primarily new media in art practice is accounted for by established modernist art history and theory. The argument here is the familiar avant-garde notion of the artist as a person who rejects established ideas and boundaries, who breaks the rules, in order to bring us new experience. But, at the same time, these accounts also argued that new media brings forth the need for a completely new language and way of thinking. 'Interactivity, though still primitive and dependent on photo-based media, might generate art for which no vocabulary yet exists' (Rush 1999: 217), or 'Current immersive environments let alone whatever lies beyond such virtual realities is dictating a new discourse' (p. 217), or 'In all likelihood, digital technologies will become more and more pervasive and will not constitute a category in themselves but become an integral part of life and art in general' (Paul 2003: 212). How far technology is moving the goal posts of what distinguishes art from other forms of technologically mediated communication remains ambivalent in the above accounts. Lovejoy (2004: 278–80) argues that artists working with new technologies embrace technology both as a medium and a tool, and that they can occupy a space that 'reconfigures the negotiation of cultural meaning'. This, she argues, can take a number of forms, from critically examining contemporary media-dominated cultural conditions, to reflexively examining the process of representation itself. This is a useful, pluralistic account which describes new media art as exploring not only the technology itself as a medium, but also recent political cultural themes such as exposing dominant narratives of mass media (control and surveillance, for example) and redefining the geography of culture by challenging received notions of identity and place.

Breaking the rules

New media art practices are united here by a common set of strategies for challenging, breaking, inverting or subverting the rules and responses of existing art and media forms and languages. But why, we might ask, should we limit the idea of new media practice as breaking the rules to an avant-garde notion of art practice? It can be argued, in the same terms as Benjamin (1939), that the new medium not only represents a new way of seeing and representing reality, but also changes irrevocably the existing function and meaning of art. Isn't the digital medium an extension of Benjamin's argument that photography, and later film, ushered in an art made for reproduction as well as reproducing by mechanical means all previous art? The digital is reconfiguring and hybridising existing media forms and isn't it, therefore, changing the function of art as well? This point is not lost on the accounts of new media art we have been considering. Lovejoy, Rush and Paul acknowledge that Benjamin's argument is highly relevant to any attempt to grasp how new media is changing the ways in which art is made and understood. What all of them point to is the less than stable boundary between art and all other digital media. While most accounts of digital art and new media recognise that the new medium changes the relationship of the artist and audience in ways that give the user more agency and control there is less recognition that new media repositions the producer.

Poster (2002) also explicitly acknowledges the importance of Benjamin's argument to the present moment of the work of art in the age of digital reproduction. Poster notes that with new media:

> The work of art is a collective creation combining information machines with engineers, artists and participants in a manner that reconfigures the role of each . . . [such that] Art is then not a delimited object but an underdetermined space in which subject and object, human and machine, body and mind, space and time all receive new cultural forms.

Poster also notes, with Rush (1999) that, from the position of new media, modern art can now only reproduce itself as an object and a commodity, which reinforces the older mode of representation and distinction between subject and object, whereas 'the art of networked computing invites the participant to change the real'.

Walter Benjamin's historical schema of artistic development

Tribal cultures of hunters and gatherers	Art as magic
Agrarian cultures of unified religion	Art as ritual
Secular cultures and the rise of capitalism	Art as beauty
Industrial cultures of capitalism	Art as art
Post-industrial and post-modern culture	Art as information [our addition]

C New media thought of as provoking a crisis in culture in which the rules of representation are abandoned in favour of the logic of the system

The argument that new media is a radically different paradigm of communication and (non)representation, taken to its logical extreme, provokes a crisis in prevailing conceptions of culture. One way in which this crisis has been popularly imagined is in the genre of literary and filmic science fiction, in which the machine, through further scientific and technological discovery, is invested with autonomous power that ultimately escapes human control. There are, of course, many versions of this central theme, from the present in which science and technology are seen as largely beneficial to human life, to the near future which has been imagined as humans living in harmony with their machine extensions, or a world gone wrong in which humans become locked in mortal combat for control of the planet against the robots and cyborgs they have created, or, indeed, that humans are reduced to the source of energy for a simulated reality controlled by a database. Such are the plots of Ridley Scott's influential film *Bladerunner* (1982), or *The Matrix* (2001) or the novels of William Gibson. As Lister *et al.* (2003)

point out, there is a history to the ways in which science and technology have been configured in the popular imagination. Within such histories the idea of human replacement by machines in the form of automatons and the merging of human and machines in the form of cyborgs has been articulated with varying degrees of seriousness. In much less totalising and apocalyptic ways we have already rehearsed the arguments, from Benjamin, McLuhan and Williams, that human perception and representation are constantly changing in relationship to technological and social developments. It is in the writings of Jean Baudrillard and Paul Virillio that the idea of technology reaching a stage where it has provoked a crisis of representation and reality has been strongly formulated.

The real as simulation – Jean Baudrillard

Baudrillard (1985) argued that digital code has changed our sense of reality from one in which there was a clear separation between object and subject, between the real and its represented, to a new state of reality as simulation. Baudrillard's earlier work (1968) was dedicated to proving that the notion of human activities governed by irreducible primary needs was a myth. Baudrillard was interested in developing an account of human activity in which the symbolic function of objects served the needs of unconscious structures of social relations. In 'The Ecstasy of Communication' Baudrillard goes beyond his account of reality, defined by the symbolic exchange of objects, to claim that we have entered a new era of simulation or hyperreality in which the scene and the mirror are replaced by the screen and a network. To understand what he means by this radical replacement we first need to understand what he means by the 'scene' and the 'mirror'. For Baudrillard, mirror and scene are both symbolic qualities of 'the object'. The object is what is external to or produced by the subject, the self, which corresponds to our intimate universe, our imaginary and symbolic world. In this equation we are 'the subject'. In a pre-digital culture the opposition between object and subject and the private and public defined our relationship in and to reality. Hence, we expressed our mental or psychological reality through making objects that opened up the imaginary depths, the deeper scene of our life. In the pre-digital world, art and communication comprised the realm of symbolic expression of our inner life and offered the possibility of reflexive transcendence, or enlightenment.

Baudrillard opposes this reality of depth with one of surface and excess. Today's reality of the screen offers a non-reflecting surface, an immanent smooth operational surface of communication. For Baudrillard it is technology, above everything else, that has brought about the situation in which simulation is dominant. He identifies three scientific and technological tendencies, which he sees as irreversibly driving social change: (i) the functionalisation and abstraction of all operations in homogeneous processes; (ii) the displacement of bodily movements and efforts into electronic commands; and (iii) the miniaturisation in time and space of knowledge and memory. Baudrillard notes that the outcome of these changes has been a dramatic 'emptying out' of the meaning of our active lives, rendering everything that used to fill the symbolic scenes of our life useless. In particular, he observes this vacuum effect upon our bodies, the landscape and public and private space. Baudrillard argues, therefore, that in place of a world of active signs and signifieds in which objects deliver messages, we are left only, as McLuhan (1968) argued before him, with the medium. In the collapse of private and public space everything becomes visible, or, as Baudrillard puts it:

> Today there is a whole pornography of information and communication, that is to say, of circuits and networks, a pornography of all function and objects in their

readability, their fluidity, their availability, their regulation, in their forced significa-
tion, in their performativity, in their branching, in their polyvalence, in their free
expression.

(1985: 131)

Baudrillard poses many important questions in his polemical argument which wants
to insist that we must now understand reality as simulation. Perhaps the most important
part of his argument for new media is whether he is right to say that signs no longer
bear any relationship to reality because in simulation there are no equivalents for the
real; simulation does not reproduce the real but reduplicates and generates it. In 'The
Ecstasy of Communication', Baudrillard was deeply pessimistic about post-modern
capitalist society. Webster (1999: 186–188) insists that Baudrillard's view of the era of
hyperreality constitutes a rejection of any credible intellectual reality principle. Other
academics and intellectuals have criticised Baudrillard as an eclectic and contradictory
thinker who is, himself, more a reflection of post-modern confusion than an analyst of
the phenomena (Kellner 1995). Other contemporary academics continue to find his work
important in exploring the effects of globalisation and the experience of cyberspace
(Morley and Robins 1995).

We now acknowledge, as a matter of historical fact, that television was a significant
element in reshaping the experience of the family from the 1950s onwards and now the
computer and the Internet are an equally important feature of the domestic environment.
As much as television is an entertainment commodity to be bought and sold, it is also
a medium of significant regulation and control. Its presence in the home, as Baudrillard
says, positions the viewer at the centre of a control screen. Although TV is dominant
and pervasive, it is also not total. People can, and do, switch television off and do other
things. Of course, Baudrillard would go on to argue that the world of 'other things' is
now defined in relationship to the TV and computer screen image. The rapid growth of
the convergence of media in domestic online services gives substance to Baudrillard's
argument of the increasing tendency towards the dominance of code and the abstract
organisation of all operations. You can work, shop and play in the 'virtual' world of
cyberspace without leaving the computer station. In the workplace, in scientific laboratories, more and more functions are organised and controlled by the operational systems
of computers. However, life is still lived in the real world which, as Turkle (1995) points
out, is still far more interesting than life on the screen. The Internet also opens up many
more possibilities of users becoming producers of their own communication as well as
consumers of information. One of the early arguments for the non-regulation of the
Internet was that it was essentially a democratic medium, which would foster new forms
of community and association. Against this claim for new forms of cyber-democracy
is the recognition that large sections of the world's population have no access to the
Internet and that most of those that do have access are already being given a fixed and
limited form of access (Castells 1996). Baudrillard would have little sympathy with
those who argue for the productive democracy of the Internet, instead insisting that those
with access only enter the world of simulation faster to become transfixed in the face
of excessive and total information.

Aesthetic of the surface

Following Baudrillard's description of the flat, non-reflective screen of total and excessive information, Darley (2000), who, as we saw earlier, compares the new moment of
new media to early cinema, identifies digital arts with that of the tradition of decorative

arts. Although Baudrillard announces the death of the spectacle with the arrival of simulation, Darley nevertheless applies Debord's (1977) critique of the society of the spectacle when considering the digital aesthetic. He draws our attention to the ways in which the entry of the digital into film, animation and television emphasise and play-up form, style, surface, artifice, spectacle and sensation. He points to players surfing the image in video and computer games through immersive graphics. Darley sees such decorative effects as a dilution of meaning and as encouraging intellectual quiescence. Digital media's surface without depth leads Darley to say that current fascinations lie in the ephemeral, superfluity of the image, rather than with the image's representation of anything. The aesthetic of the digital is then to be considered as an extension of the aesthetics of decoration and ornamentation, focused upon delight and sensation of the surface and spectacle. In emphasising the superfluidity of the digital image we are brought back, via another route, to the characteristic of excess within the post-modern experience.

The condition of post-modernity

Jameson, Harvey, Castells and Baudrillard have, in their different ways and at different times, all made a causal link between the rapid expansion, development and application of digital technologies in communication media and marked changes in the character of individual social and cultural experience, which can be broadly characterised again as the condition of post-modernity. Jameson (1984) articulates what he calls 'a cultural logic of late capitalism' in which aesthetic populism dominates, history has been replaced with nostalgia, and pastiche eclipses parody. Harvey (1989) identifies time and space compression as a feature of globalisation that brings with it an accentuation of the volatility and ephemerality of everything, the establishment of the values of instantaneity, disposability, novelty and obsolescence and the loss of a sense of future continuity. Castells (1991) places informational processing at the centre of social and economic production and suggests that the 'space of flows' of information is superseding that of the 'space of places'. Baudrillard, as we have discussed above, replaces reality with simulation. All of these accounts point out that the post-modern condition is, in part, a consequence of the application of information technologies, and that one of its key characteristics is the experience of excessive information, or information overload.

Webster (1999) takes issue with Baudrillard and the more general stance of the post-modernists who reject the idea that we can explain the post-modern as an extension of a modernist past founded upon historical progress and rational thought. For post-modernism the 'grand narratives' of scientific truth, technological progress, civilisation, capitalism and communism, which lay claim to the truth about progress and development, are no more than prescriptive and relative versions of the truth. Post-modernism points to the limits of the modernist paradigm of rational, scientific thought on the grounds of the failure of historical progress in the twentieth century. Science and politics has so far failed to stop global warming, the destruction of the world's natural habitats, Chernobyl and Aids. Rational political thought was also responsible for the rise of fascism and the failure of communism. Technology continues to produce super-sophisticated military technologies and weapons of mass destruction. The cultural and intellectual strategies of post-modernism replaced the modernist search for absolute truth with relativism or 'versions of the truth'. Post-modernists replace singular prevailing discourses in science and philosophy with a plurality of discourses, especially those that celebrate differences of analysis, explanation and interpretation. The cultural strategies of post-modernism embraced the inauthentic, superficial, ephemeral and artificial, arguing that without any means of attaining authenticity we are left with the inauthentic construction of the authentic.

Webster as well as Jameson and Harvey acknowledge these failures as contingent factors and can agree with the list of failures, but they also insist that they can be explained by rational and scientific analysis rather than requiring a break with such methods.

The digital aesthetic and the logic of the system

The globalised world, the networked society and the informational mode of development are all concepts based upon the centrality of the computer in production, exchange and consumption. The processing of data treats all knowledge as information. Attempts to define the primary aesthetic of the digital have focused upon the nature and essential characteristics, in theoretical terms the ontology, of the digital computer.

The aesthetics of analogue media, film for example, are seen to arise from its materiality, the way in which the film frame is an optically focused, light-exposed image, and that movement and duration are achieved through running twenty-four film frames per second through a camera and projector. But the aesthetic of film is not reducible to its ontology, its material technology, because film form also includes narrative language derived from literature and story-telling. As we have noted, whereas analogue media continuously inscribes without breaking down the signal or source into discrete units, digital media convert the original source through capture and sampling. This difference has led to defining code as the essence of digital media and most descriptions of a digital aesthetic start from the essential characteristic of numerical representation and procedural operations such as automation and modularity. It is the mutability of information in digital form that has been seized upon as a defining quality of a digital aesthetic. Digital code is continually open to change through endless recombination. Digital code is unsteady and immaterial and is collected, stored and transmitted through dispersed and random modes. These technical qualities have, as we have seen, led to the descriptions of digital media as non-hierarchical and non-linear. But, as we noted with film, a full account of the aesthetics of film has to include its developed languages and the same is true for a digital aesthetic, which cannot be fully discovered in its procedural functions, or reduced to its essential electronic binary form. The language of new media, as we have gone to great lengths to demonstrate, still crucially depends upon the culturally developed sign systems of image, music, orality, script and text, which the digital is technically simulating. However, this dependency is not absolute because while digital code technically simulates it also culturally repurposes. The hypermediated computer screen and online communication adds to and changes the quality of screen representations as well as the relay of the message. It is the (photo)graphic spatial representations rendered by numerical algorithms and their animation through computational scripting together with the programmed ability to intervene, that have given new media its immersive and interactive qualities.

Aesthetic of systems

In the cultural practices of new media, including their theoretical and educational discourses, we can detect arguments in which there is a strong insistence that a 'true' digital aesthetic will emerge from work focused upon code, the database and the mutability of data rather than work based upon the digital simulation of representational forms in immersive and hypermediated screen media. The argument against digital representational forms is that they reproduce all the previous analogue moments and the attendant cultural problems that post-structuralism and post-modernism identified with those representational forms. Realism, narrative and the authorial voice were exposed in theoretical analysis as closed systems that could not guarantee reality or truth. Systems of representation are, it is argued, based upon the myth of the unitary and coherent subject/self and its binary relationship to the external object and reality. If the representational forms of analogue media only give us a relative and oblique view of what is contingent and real then it follows that a new paradigm or guarantor of the real must be found. The new symbolic form of the networked database, founded upon code and the mutability of information, is perceived as a means to liberate knowledge, experience and sensation from the fixed and closed analogue forms and their hierarchical institutional regimes. However, in order to find this new means of communication and self recognition, further cultural and theoretical articulation of the ontology of the computer will have to be done. As Weibel (2001) put it: 'A digital aesthetic must therefore first and foremost be founded in a structural understanding of what goes on between the ontology of work and viewing.'

The counter to the argument that the representational paradigm should be rejected because it reproduces an outmoded subject/object discourse is, at one level, very simple. As yet, no meaningful replacement to the developed systems of representation exists and therefore they continue to operate, for good and ill, as the dominant and shared mode through which the self and external realities are communicated. Saying this does not deny either the recognition of the problems of representation, or the desire and need to find more meaningful forms which are closer to and engage with post-modern experience. The analysis of language(s) as a system of signs in which meaning is assigned to the subject and object within the signifying system and hence finally does not guarantee externality, demonstrated categorically the constructed nature of all representation. In revealing the nature of signifying systems, structuralism and post-structuralism both signalled a new crisis in representation and created the analytical means through which the constructed nature of given representational discourses was deconstructed. Deconstruction reveals the operational and mediating discourses at work within representational systems for critical producers and readers. Deconstruction of a signifying system thus constitutes a revision to, rather than a transformation of, the system itself. What is evident in both the argument for the overthrow of the notion of representability and the argument for continued revision is that the digital represents a new set of possibilities, which engage with the acknowledged need and desire to go beyond the current limits of representation.

Modernism	*Post-modernism*
Purpose	Play
Design	Chance
Hierarchy	Anarchy
Distance	Participation
Presence	Absence
Centring	Dispersal
Selection	Combination
Root	Rhizome
Depth	Surface
Origin	Difference
Cause	Trace
Determinacy	Indeterminacy
Transcendence	Immanence
Analogue	*Digital*

The central problem for developing a new media language and post-representational system based upon the networked database is that computer code is an abstract mathematical formula and data are written in a computational procedural programming language. The network of networked computers is understandable in its technological structures as are the procedures of online communication, but we don't 'read' lines of code, neither do we communicate directly through programming language. These organising levels of relay and command remain invisible. While the human–computer interface relies upon the procedures of code and programming to create meaningful communication, it actually takes place through software tools, which convert code to knowable language, i.e. text, image, sound, graphic, spreadsheet.

Non-representational strategies

In attempting to move beyond the problematic of the representational paradigm, with its subject/object dichotomy, objectifying gaze and fixed order of time and space, some new media practitioners and theorists have sought alternative models and strategies. Such strategies are present to some degree in all new media work that make technological mediation present. In such work the technology is not simply assumed as a carrier of some message or content, but is actively worked upon so that the user or participant becomes aware of the underlying orders and logic of the networked system and its code.

New media practice that sets itself the task of critically engaging with, and moving beyond, the forms of discursive power represented by online networked communication has been most recently influenced by post-structuralist and post-modernist theoretical perspectives developed from the 1980s, which cluster around a set of interests in non-hierarchical, participant, interactive and relativist modes of thought and action. But it is also the case that this agenda for change has much longer roots in two opposed intellectual traditions. The renewed focus upon the processes of computing and the social construction of networked communication can be found in the 'actor-network' theory of Bruno Latour and the 'tactical practices' suggested in Michel de Certeau's *The Practice of Everyday Life* (1988). The emphasis upon processual knowledge and practice as a means of theorising the human–computer relationship brings with it a politics of intervention consistent with the materialist tradition. On the other hand, the human–computer relationship is theorised in terms of phenomenological affects, those direct mind/body responses that come before or even escape rationality and language which have their origins in Idealist philosophy. The complex set of ideas related to 'rhizomatic systems in the work of Gilles Deleuze and Felix Guattari (1987) are an example here.

The practices of everyday life

De Certeau built upon the work of Pierre Bourdieu (1930–2001) to define culture not as a collection of texts, artefacts and fixed structures, but as a set of practices. Culture as practice emphasised the process and operations that each of us perform on text-like structures. De Certeau shifted our attention from representations in their own right to ways in which representations are used and consumed. Representation here is taken to mean anything from a newspaper to the street layout of the city. How we negotiate our encounter with representational space, media and institutional representations, all thought of in the structuralist and semiological sense as texts to be read, constitutes the practices of everyday life. The practices of everyday life are, according to de Certeau, not simply our conditioned responses to a given order of things, but acts of creative rebellion. Consumption is not a passive act, but a two-way process of resistance, through which the consumer can gain a temporary reversal of the flow of power. The idea that each one of us, in our everyday life, in work, in leisure, in consumption, practices a set of complex tactics through which we assert power, can be applied to the new practices of online communication and the strategic power of representational space can be tactically disrupted by the user/consumer. The group Tactical Media make direct use of de Certeau's work in defining the tactical (new media) practitioner who, they argue, can 'take us beyond the rigid dichotomies that have restricted thinking in this area for so long, dichotomies such as amateur vs. professional, alternative vs. mainstream, and even private vs. public' (Garcia and Lovink 2006).

Actor Network Theory

Actor Network Theory (ANT) has also been co-opted as a procedural way of understanding the relationship between humans, systems and machines in computer networked communications. ANT originated in the social sciences in studies of scientific and technological practices and networks and is most associated with the work of Bruno Latour (1988). Latour argues that the notion of a fixed objectivity in social science is no longer tenable because it is part of the very thing, 'technoscience', that it seeks to study. Instead, he develops a relativist sociology in which the viewpoints of all the participants, including the scientist/observer, at best form a metalanguage through which a viewpoint can be expressed. The impact of Latour's work upon new media lies not only in its rejection of an 'objectivistic' science paradigm, but also in the methodology he proposed to replace it. Latour defines both human and non-human elements and structures in the environment as actors who can make other elements dependent upon themselves. Actors have interests that can come into alignment with other actors' interests to form an actor-network. Both humans and non-humans may be 'actants' in a network made up of social groups, entities and artefacts who then become enlisted to reinforce a position within a network. ANT thus reverses our normal thinking about science and technology and nature and society; ANT argues that nature and society are consequences, not causes, of human scientific and technical work. The interactions of people and machines should be understood as a continuous chain of 'translations' or 'recruitments' into their own languages and values and that in a successful chain technology becomes transparent and is taken for granted. The more a technological project progresses, the more the role of technology decreases, in relative terms.

The rhizome and smooth space

A rhizome is an organic plant (the potato is an example), whose growth depends upon a rooting structure, that has no single stem and central root, but instead a branching system of roots that connect nodal points, from which other roots and nodes develop. Gilles Deleuze and Felix Guattari (1987) use the concept of the rhizome as an analytic metaphor for an alternative way of thinking about intellectual, social and spatial structures, orders and power relations. Like other post-structuralist and post-modernist thinkers we have touched upon, Deleuze and Guattari are seeking a theory of knowledge, an epistemology, which accounts for the persistence of hierarchical forms of human thought and action as well as a means by which humans can be liberated from hierarchical and binary dependencies. Deleuze and Guattari enumerate a number of principles of the rhizome, the foremost of which are connection, heterogeneity and multiplicity. These are the characteristics of a rhizome, which they define as essentially a non-hierarchically distributed, branching system in which all of the nodes, or points, are connected to each other. Deleuze and Guattari contrast the self-consistent heterogeneous aggregate of elements that are connected together in a rhizome with that of stratified organisations, which are composed of layers of homogeneous elements. The importance of this contrast between two forms of organisation and thought is that the rhizome can be considered as fluid and plane-oriented, whereas stratification is linear and point-oriented. As a metaphor for spatial or social relationships, striated space closes off a surface, defines intervals and subordinates the trajectory to the point, whereas in the rhizome, or, as they put it, in 'smooth space', the self-consistent aggregate points are subordinated to the trajectory, which can be considered as open and distributed.

It is not difficult to see the relevance of the rhizomatic system to an account of cyberspace and the network of networked computers. The Internet is a non-hierarchical and dispersed structure and traversing cyberspace can be likened to journeys or trajectories without beginning or end. Such metaphorically open travels in cyberspace can also be contrasted to closed and fixed boundaries of identities and positions in the economically and socially contingent space of the 'real' world. Deleuze and Guattari's work, theoretically difficult as it is, has been taken up because it offers the new media practitioner and user a new model of connected human agency, and a radical theoretical means of potentially realising the free autonomous subject whose desires and impulses can be cognitively mapped into networked space. One of the problems with the phenomenological account for new media practitioners is its very abstractedness in a theoretical language from which practical knowledge and action have to be metaphorically inferred rather than being able to be grasped in any programmatic way.

Computers, mind and consciousness

One of the common elements of thought to arise from the post-structuralist and postmodernist strands of thinking we have sketched above is that, with the application of computers to more and more human functions, the strict separation of human and machine can no longer be maintained. In the technoscientific domain, ANT argues that 'actants' can be both human and non-human. In Baudrillard's era of simulation the human is faced with a new ecstasy of communication, likened to the position of the schizophrenic who can no longer separate him/herself from the totality of electronic impulse. In cybernetic theory human behaviour is analysed as a functioning machine system. In Deleuze and Guattari's operation of the distributed self the human is conceived as a 'desiring machine'. In all of these accounts nature and reality are no longer opposed to human history and activity but, rather, are seen as extensions, or products, of human activity. It follows therefore that if humans produce nature then humans produce themselves and hence any absolute division between what is and is not human can no longer be maintained. Technology from this perspective is not to be considered in antithesis to nature, or the body, but as their extensions. Conversely, we can no longer define what is human in opposition to the machines and technologies that humans have built and adapted themselves to. Computer architecture is concerned with building structures for the organisation, access and navigation of electronic databases (defined as stored knowledge of whatever kind). The human mind can, by analogy, also be seen as a database consisting of all that an individual has learnt and experienced. Neurology and psychology have long been preoccupied with how human memory and thought is structured, how the mind accesses its own database.

Interactivity and its relationship to human thought is part of the larger technological cognitive mapping project in which, over a long history, machines have been conceived and built that either mimic or aid human thought. This can be reformulated as an intellectual and practical project that has a sustained interest in machines that 'think' independently of human thought, and machines that aid our thinking. Independent thinking machines are the province of the discipline of artificial intelligence (AI), while the broader application of machines to think with is the application of computational power to specific tasks previously carried out by mental processes. These two strands have a common route in the conceptualisation and writing of computational code. The computational power of the PC expands exponentially with an increase in the functions and operations of 'intelligent' software.

The anthropomorphism of the computer is not so much a reflection of the inexorable development of the computer towards independent consciousness, but more a reflection, like that of the car, of its familiar functions in everyday life. However, computer networks are also thought of as neural networks and the world network of computers is, metaphorically, likened to the human brain, just as the brain has been described as functioning like a computer. Outside of the AI computer science laboratory, the promise of an autonomous thinking machine is much more located in a cultural discussion, as the long-established genre of science fiction writing demonstrates. This is also what we earlier referred to as the technological imaginary. New media artists continue to explore the idea of machine intelligence or consciousness, but in general the main drive of computational power, whether for military or civil application, has been to assist and extend human operations in thought and action. Computers are centrally entailed in a greater and greater range of both routine and extraordinary operational systems and until relatively recently this fact, when recognised, was somehow shocking. The fear of computers taking over the world stands in marked contrast to the fact that it is getting harder to think of human activities that aren't assisted by computers.

Post-human

Whether at a metaphorical or actual level the post-human is conceived as the merging of human and machine. In hard science, in AI, in neural-networks and nanotechnology, the machine is being conceptualised as organic, self-modifying and intelligent. In medical science we are already incorporating technology into the body in routine ways such as pacemakers, artificial joints and contact lenses. More radically, biotechnology is drawing upon the discoveries of human DNA, the Human Genome Project and stem cell research to provide bioengineering, including cloning of the human body. The convergence of nanotechnology, bioengineering, information sciences and cognitive research does centre on projects that extend or merge the human and machine in real ways and for particular purposes. But it is still a large leap to the science fiction of robots, cyborgs or replicants. Fukuyama (2002) sees biotechnology creating a future in which the issue will not be about how changes in our external environment may harm us, but about changes to what being human is. Pepperell (1995) sees the challenge posed by biotechnology and the recombinant DNA possibilities of the Human Genome Project as an alteration on the level of the human soul, and that complex machines are an emergent life form.

The idea of the post-human is also employed to account for the reconfiguration of human subjectivities in cyberspace. Here, the post-human is being employed, not to envisage individual humans as technologically reconfigured bodies, but to account for how notions of identity are changed through our interactions with machines. Harraway (1990), Plant (2000) and Hayles (2002) extend the discussion of the post-human to include our cultural and psychological response to a world in which information and its systems dominate, arguing that we have the anxiety of becoming post-human, or not knowing if we are human, because of a paradigm shift in which a networked cybernetic system is installed as the medium of communication and knowledge.

Conclusion

How are we to leave these theoretical trends, cultural interventions and intellectual arguments and how do they relate to new media practices and the practitioner? Of course there can be no final conclusions, only a continual dialogue. The pace of change in new media is such that, on the surface, there is a shifting set of preoccupations. What we can say, and have said throughout this book, is that precisely because of the instability of technologies in a period of rapid change, we all need some kind of map, however incomplete, as a guide. But, rather like the Deleuzian notion of smooth space, our journeys are not to be plotted between two fixed points but, rather, thought of as trajectories, which cross and re-cross each other. But we are not saying that the map is a rhizomatic network; we are still committed to the idea that it is possible to gain an overview and that the map attempts some kind of comprehensiveness of the field that is new media. Theory has its own practice and at many points the practice of theory is only remotely connected to the contingencies of other practices. Practice proceeds through practice and its rules are different from those of theory. But theory is also an abstraction of concrete practices, an attempt to grasp the complexity of practice in another form of knowledge. What the practitioner needs, what all of us need, is really useful knowledge, which can illuminate our efforts and struggles to both make sense of a complex world and to make communicable sense within it.

Much that is really useful in new media arises within its own practice, but other things do not and theory, from a number of the sources we have identified, can shed light upon and inform practice. New media practices are fundamentally communicative practices, which take place in definable social and cultural circumstance and between groups and individuals. The most exciting and creative cultural dimension of new media is that it represents a challenge to established ways of thinking about the communicative process. It challenges the notion of the artefact and instead reminds us of the importance of process. New media confronts any settled notion of sender and receiver, artist and audiences, producer and consumer and, instead, invites us to articulate the space and method of interaction. New media invites us to explore what the medium itself is and how our thinking and ways of seeing are potentially changed and extended by it. Finally, new media challenges some of our most cherished institutional categories of human activity and encourages us to revisit settled histories.

There is a tension between the highly commercial and profit-driven practices of e-commerce, programming and research and the radical openness presented by new media. The established institutions of education, media broadcasting, the press and the cultural institutions continue to reproduce themselves along familiar lines of power and purpose, co-opting new technologies and the new medium to familiar, often uncritical, purposes. However, the convergent tendency of all new media threatens to break across established boundaries and suggest new purposes, productions and points of entry to practitioners. New media practices actively seek new contexts, new audiences and collaborations from an existing stock of historical cultural politics. Museums, galleries, universities, schools, community centres, theatres, concert halls, dance venues, clubs, even regular workplaces, are being challenged by the new communication media, whether that is recognised or not. They have been changed for the worst if technology has been introduced in ways that are not critically reflected upon, because they will, as Lyotard (1979) pointed out, be processing knowledge as units of information exchange, rather than as something really useful. They will be changing for the better wherever new media is engaged in the process of making meaning, which is critically and (inter)actively worked upon and (inter)actively received.

Life in the real world is, as Turkle (1995) pointed out, still better than life on the screen. However, she goes on to say that we do not have to choose between them, we can and do have both and one is not a negation of the other. Communication through online networked media does represent a huge challenge in developing meaningful languages capable of producing complex, deep and sustained communicative forms. The scale and scope of online communication is already great and it has already presented us with many problems to solve. The greatest challenge in the short term is to develop human–computer interfaces that reveal, rather than conceal, their own selective operating principles and which extend the openness that has carried the medium to its present point. The second major challenge is for computer users to be able to maximise its advantages while minimising its risks. There is a dialectic of opposites, which is part of the shaping of the future of new media for all of us. On the one hand, the networked computer has given us immediate access to a great diversity of material that is only a couple of clicks of a mouse away. It has given us machines that can perform a wide variety of functions at incredible computational speeds. It has given the world a new means of communication that connects the one to the many and the many to the many. All of these aspects are positive and being extended as we write. On the other hand, the new medium has presented us with a new set of problems of control over exploitative material and the exploitation of users. We are currently struggling to find better tools and forms for navigating databases and being able to make discerning judgements about the quality and worth of what we find, and there are few channels of evaluation and critical reflection within navigable modes. The third and final challenge of new media is to ensure that it develops as an open and democratic medium and, for that to happen, great efforts will have to be made by governments of the world to put limits on some of the most aggressive and monopolistic commercial instincts in order to ensure that we continue to expand its great educational and creative potential.

Glossary

....

We do not aim to provide a comprehensive glossary of unfamiliar technical or theoretical terms used across the new media field. Instead, we focus on a small number of key terms that reflect the discussion of this book and which we consider to be core terms in new media practice. As we have discussed, technological as well as cultural discourses have their own languages, which are full of short-hand terms that label and code conceptual definitions and practical processes. Traditionally, print encyclopaedias, dictionaries, as well as manuals, provided indexed word definitions, however, today online communication supplements and augments printed sources in electronic form. One would expect, therefore, to find a book on new media pointing the reader in the direction of useful websites, hyperlinks and search engines.

Google (www.google.co.uk)

Google is now the Internet's biggest search engine and currently receives over 200 million queries each day, through its various services, with over eight billion connected webpages. Google has recently been valued at eight billion dollars on the American stock market which makes it the world's biggest media company by stock market value. The popularity of Google as an accessible and simple search engine is reflected in its grand mission statement to 'organize the world's information and make it universally accessible and useful' (source: http://en.wikipedia.org/wiki/Google. Accessed 09/06/05).

Wikipedia (www.wikipedia.org)

We suggest that you build upon our deliberately limited keyword glossary by using the web to search for a wider range of technical definitions and theoretical definitions, to build up your knowledge and understanding of the new media field. It is important to bear in mind in this process something we have insisted upon throughout this book, which is that linguistic definitions are dynamic and relative to their context and use. This is particularly true in the field of new media.

Key technical terms you might need to research in more depth

Technical acronyms and terms

AI	Artificial Intelligence
AL	Artificial Life
APPS	Software applications
Avatar	On-screen presence of the user in graphical form
Bandwidth	The amount of information, measured in kilobits per second, that can be transmitted through the telephone system
Bit	A single unit of binary code, used to denote transmission rates per second
BLOBs	Binary Large Objects
Bluetooth	A short-range wireless connection between computers and peripherals
Broadband	High bandwidth modems which increase the speed of information transfer/downloading
Byte	A unit of eight bits, equal to storing 265 characters, or shades of an image, denoting data storage size; hence megabyte to denote one million bytes
CACHE	An area of computer memory used to hold recently acquired data
CAD	Computer Aided Design
CD	Compact Disc (recordable)
CD-ROM	Compact Disc (Read Only Memory)
CGI	Computer-Generated Imagery
CMC	Computer-Mediated Communication
Cookie	An information reference saved on a web user's hard disc drive by a website
Domain	The location of a website or group of websites
DVD	Digital Video Disc
Flame	An abusive email
Flash	Vector-based graphics and animation format with small file sizes
GIF	A graphic file compression
GPRS	Global Positioning Response System
GUI	Graphical User Interface
HTML	Hypertext Mark-Up Language
HTTP	Hypertext Transfer Protocol
ICT	Information Communication Technology
ISP	Internet Service Provider
Java	Programming language
JPEG	A compressed graphic file used for photographic images
LAN	Local Area Network
Modem	A device that enables a computer to interface with a telephone line
MOOS	Multi-User Domain, Object orientated
MUDs	Multi-User Domains
OS	Operating System
PC	Personal Computer
PDA	Personal Digital Assistant
Pixels	Individual units of value in a raster grid which determine by their size and number the resolution of an image
Server	Network of computers which control shared resources for workstations

Streaming	Transmission and downloading of compressed data of video, animation of graphic files (MPEGs), at frame rates which operate at the persistence of vision
TCP	Transmission Control Protocol
URL	Universal Resource Locator
WiFi	Wireless Frequency connection to Internet

New media-related websites

The following websites serve as a reference to organisations and sites involved in new media arts and creative practice. There are many sites with comprehensive listing of arts projects and discussions. These sites have been selected since they are primarily larger institutions, organisations or research centres which have long established track records or working in this area and keep up to date links. They also reflect the history of new media practice as well as more recent work. Projects and debates which have been referenced in the case studies and chapters of this book can also be accessed through the links that will be found within these sites.

URLs are subject to change and, if unavailable at the given address, readers should use a search engine for an updated location.

Ars Electronica Centre: a media centre hosting an annual festival for art, technology and society and awrding the Prix Ars Electronica awards for outstanding cyberarts innovations.
http://www.aec.at

Art Museum: Internet-based art museum experience specializing in new media works
http://www.artmuseum.net/

Australian Network for Arts and Technology (ANAT)
http://www.anat.org.au/

The Center for Art and Media (ZKM) Germany: a centre production and research, exhibitions and events, coordination and documentation of new media in theory and practice
http://www.zkm.de/

CRUMB, Curatorial Resource for Upstart Media Bliss: discussion site investigating how new media art is presented, commissioned, collected and critiqued.
http://www.crumbweb.org

The Daniel Langlois Foundation: documents history, artworks and practices associated with electronic and digital media arts
http://www.fondation-langlois.org/

Dia Centre: New York arts organisation hosting artists web art projects since 1995
http://www.diacenter.org/

The International Academy of Digital Arts and Sciences
http://www.iadas.net/

Inter-Society for the Electronic Arts (ISEA): an international organization fostering interdisciplinary academic discourse and exchange among culturally diverse organizations and individuals working with art, science and emerging technologies.
http://www.isea-web.org/

Leonardo: international journal investigating the application of contemporary science and technology to the arts.
http://leoalmanac.org/

The NTT InterCommunication Center (ICC), Japan: presents media art works which employ electronic technologies.
http://www.ntticc.or.jp/index_e.html

Resfest: a showcase of digital shorts, music promos and animation
http://www.resfest.com/

Rhizome: an online platform for the global new media art community. It includes the Rhizome ArtBase, an online archive of new media art containing over a thousand art works that employ materials including software, code, websites, moving image, games and browsers to aesthetic and critical end
http://rhizome.org/

De Waag, the Society for old and new media, the Netherlands
http://www.waag.org/

V2_Institute for the Unstable Media, the Netherlands: an interdisciplinary center for art and media technology,
http://www.v2.nl/

The Walker Art Center, USA, online exhibition space, Gallery 9
http://gallery9.walkerart.org/

Webby awards: international award for excellence in web design, creativity, usability and functionality.
http://www.webbyawards.com/

New media courses

The following categories of courses can be found on the UCAS website (www.ucas.ac. uk.). UCAS is the University Central Admissions Service, which organises applications to all undergraduate programmes in the United Kingdom. What this list demonstrates is that new media comes in many titles. In fact, only three categories actually use the term 'new media', while most others define their approach to new media either by the term 'digital' or by'multimedia'. The list also makes it clear that digital or multimedia is a feature of some other disciplines or practices – design or technology, for example. Most new media courses will have emerged from one of four previous discipline areas: broadcast and print media; film and photography; graphic design and fine art; or engineering and computing science. It is important to enquire thoroughly into the discipline basis of any new media course to ascertain its orientation and interests. New media as a distinct discipline is still emerging, while there are many hybrid practices of existing media which now include the use of digital technologies.

Creative Digital Design
Creative Digital Imaging
Creative Digital Technology
Creative Multimedia
Digital Animation

Digital Art
Digital Broadcasting
Digital Business
Digital Communications
Digital Communications Technology
Digital Design
Digital Electronics
Digital Entertainment
Digital Imaging
Digital Imaging Science
Digital Media
Digital Media Art
Digital Media Communications
Digital Media Production
Digital Media Publishing
Digital Media Technology
Digital Microelectronics
Digital Music
Digital Photography
Digital Sign Process
Digital Systems
Digital Systems Design
Digital Systems Engineering
Digital Three Dimensional Design
Digital Visual Effects
Fine Art Digital Techniques
Interactive Digital Media
Interactive Multimedia
Interactive Multimedia Communications
Interactive Multimedia Design
Multimedia Art
Multimedia Business Studies
Multimedia Communications
Multimedia Computing
Multimedia Design
Multimedia Electronics
Multimedia Graphics
Multimedia Information Technology
Multimedia Journalism
Multimedia Marketing
Multimedia Production
Multimedia Studies
Multimedia Systems
Multimedia Systems Design
Multimedia Systems Development
Multimedia Technology
Multimedia Web Production
New Media Design
New Media Technology
New Technology

Key terms

Analogue

An important term in understanding the significance of digital code. Prior to digital media all media were analogue in that they employed some form of continuous material signal such as light or sound, which was physically inscribed onto a recording medium, for example magnetic tape or chemical negative. The resulting representation of image or sound or both was analogous to the original source. In contrast, digital code is a transcription of one source of signal into another form such that the source is segmented into a discrete code. The continuous nature of analogue encoding makes the resulting media – photography, film, sound recording – less open to manipulation and change.

Code

Has a technical as well as a cultural meaning. Technically, code is a component of a message system in numerical, linguistic or auditory form, which relays a set of instructions, information or meanings. Morse code is a clear example of the relay of a linguistic system into an electronic auditory system. Semaphore used a system of flag positions to send messages where the sender and receiver were in visual sight of each other. Digital code is the base system of binary numbers, zeros and ones, which create computer data. Programming languages, such as Java or HTML, use code to create instruction patterns for computer operations. Code has a wider cultural meaning related to communication media. Film lighting formats can be said to be codes, narrative story lines and characters have familiar and repeated patterns of action and resolution which can be said to be codes. There are behavioural and dress codes which vary from culture to culture.

Convergence

Refers technically to the drawing together of previously discrete analogue technologies in digital form such that functions and tasks previously carried out by different media technologies are now functions of one machine. This is true of both the production of media, in digital image compositing and editing for example, and the distribution of media, where online services can deliver radio, television and print media. Convergence also refers to the bringing together and overlapping of media practices, where knowledge, skills and understanding of different analogue media practice are brought together in digital hypermedia and multimedia.

Cyberspace

A literary term for the Internet and online communication. A term originally coined by science-fiction writer William Gibson to describe a fictional computer-generated virtual reality. A conceptual space where computer networking, hardware and users converge. The term has become generalised to describe any kind of digitally generated three-dimensional sense of space.

Digital

A form of information that is encoded, stored and transmitted as a sequence of discrete electrical units. The units are based upon a mathematical binary code, zeros and ones, which are used by the computer to form a code or strings of information. Digital media is amenable to mathematical manipulation of its code and is hence thought to be more mutable or open than its analogue counterpart. It is the single fact of the discrete, segmented character of digital code upon which many of the claims for new media are made.

Discourse

A way of thinking about language and ideas as they are used and employed in specific historical periods and institutional settings, such that what is taken to be an objective body of knowledge is understood as the elaborated sum of arguments, theories, ideas and descriptions that surround, and are embedded in, a particular social organisation. The term 'discourse' allows us to connect the abstract power of language to define meaning with institutional forms of power so that we can see that discourse and its specific language is capable of constructing it own objects of attention and importance. New media is still emerging as a set of practices, but already, as we have shown in this book, there are a number of discourses at work seeking to define the object of new media.

Interactive

Used in two importantly different and often conflated senses, interactivity refers to both the ability of the computer user to technically interrupt a programmed sequence in real time, and the process of psychological investment and engagement as a viewer, reader, audience or spectator with a media and communication form. In the first case, technical interaction refers to the forms of making programmed choices in navigating databases: the ability of the user to interrupt a sequence and make further, branching choices within the program. In the second case, interaction refers to the complex processes of human sense perception and cognitive forms of interpretation of sensory information.

Interface

In general usage a form, physical, mental or social, which is interposed between two separate states or substances. Applied to new media an interface has a number of specific meanings: (i) The physical interface between the computer and the human user is constituted by the peripheral devices of the keyboard, mouse and screen, but a voice activated piece of software could also be the interface for command and control. (ii) The graphical user interface (GUI) consists of a software program, Windows operating system for example, which enables the user to navigate files and programs stored or accessed by the computer. (iii) Graphical user interfaces use cultural metaphors, such as the idea of a desktop and office filing formats, to make command, control and navigation of digital data intelligible, and are therefore cultural interfaces.

Navigation

Applied to new media, navigation is a spatial metaphor derived from the physical plotting or steering of a course over land, sea or air, which has been applied to the actions of programmed choices in using a database or the WWW. Since progression through a database is non-linear, and made of a branching structure, the process of moving through data is considered to be an act of navigation.

Paradigm

Paradigm is used as an alternative to the term 'discourse' and describes the governing ideas of a particular time, culture or subject. Scientific paradigms define the limits of meaningful questions and formulations about knowledge at any one time. Thomas Kuhn (1962), in his thesis on *The Structure of Scientific Revolutions*, identified a paradigm shift as occurring when the problems posed within an existing scientific knowledge frame outweigh the solutions and so provoke a crisis in the governing ideas, the paradigm. In new media the establishment of digital networked systems has been said to constitute a new paradigm of thinking and representation.

Remediation

Remediation is an important concept in new media, first developed by Marshall McLuhan (1964) to describe how a new medium in its early stages relies upon, i.e. adapts, co-opts or incorporates elements of, previous media. For McLuhan this was summed up in his idea that the content of any medium is always another medium. So, for example, early film staged narratives using theatrical conventions of scenes and acts, while television used theatrical conventions of the interlude and presenters. Bolter and Grusin (2000) developed the idea with respect to digital media by pointing out that digital media used the content and form of all previous media. In explaining this they identified two moments of the remediation process. Hypermediacy describes the multiple applications that can be active on the desktop, creating a rich media environment in which the user places a high value on the mediating functions of different applications which allow multiple forms of attention. In contrast, immediacy is a feature of media where there is little or no sense of mediating presence, only a direct sense of the content of media. Immediacy is a feature of screen media that operate like a transparent window on the world, creating the sense of immediate and direct contact with the content. Whereas immediacy is associated with new media that attempts to create immersive environments, hypermediacy is associated with extractive database searching. According to Bolter and Grusin, immediacy and hypermediacy are constantly vying with each other in the process of remediation.

Notes

....

2   New media as a subject

1   Everett, A. and Caldwell, J.T. (2003) provide a good example of how North American academics are adjusting media studies to new media studies.
2   Williams, R. (1975 and 1976). *Culture and Society* and *The Long Revolution* became the cornerstones of British Cultural Studies, further developed by The Centre for Contemporary Cultural Studies under the directorship of Stuart Hall, and later carried on by the Open University's programme of study on Popular Culture.

4   The language of new media

1   Mitchell, W. (1998) develops an analysis of the digital image on the basis of its difference from the photographic image. Manovich (2001) likewise distinguishes a language of new media on the basis of its origins in film.
2   Robins (1996) discusses the confusions surrounding the differences between analogue and digital photography. Lister (2003) concludes that the digital photograph should be conceptually understood as a hybrid of computer graphics.

10   Who are the new media practitioners?

1   Source: http://www.etforecasts.com/pr/pr1202.htm.
2   Sectors: Advertising, Auto Industry, Business Use, Customer Service, Ecommerce, Entertainment, Financial Services, Health/Medical, Internet Trading, IT/Computer Ind., Knowledge Man., Marketing/Brands, Portals/ISPs, Publishing/Media, Recruitment, Retail/Apparel, Telecom, Travel.
3   The URL for ths site is http://movielink.com and a recent review of download times and associated issues can be found at http://news.com/2100-2023-965194.html
4   Nicholas Negroponte (1996) discusses the concept of the 'digital butler' in 'Less is more: interface Agents as Digital Butlers'.
5   'The Pulse', *Newsweek*, 2 April 2001, p. 65.
6   http://en.wikipedia.org/wiki/Microsoft_PowerPoint
7   Cliff Atkinson. 'PowerPoint usability: Q&A with Don Norman'. http://www.sociablemedia.com/articles_norman.htm.

19   Human–computer interface

1   A fuller discussion of remediation is given in Part II.
2   See the MIT website, www.media.mit.edu/publications/19992000-02.htm

Selective bibliography

Althusser, L. (1971) 'Ideology and Ideological State Apparatuses', in *Lenin and Philosophy and other Essays*. London: New Left Books.

Ascott, R. (1966) 'Behaviourist Art and the Cybernetic Vision', in *Cybernetica Journal of the International Association for Cybernetics* (Namur) 9: 247–64.

Ascott, R. (1989) 'Is there Love in the Telematic Embrace?', in *Art Journal* 49, (3): 24–27. http://telematic.walkerart.org/overview/overview_ascott.html.

Ascott, R. (1993) 'Telenoia: art in the age of artificial life', in *Leonardo* 26 (3): 176–7.

Ascott, R. (1999) *Reframing Consciousness: art, mind and technology*. Bristol: Intellect.

Bachelard, G. (1994) *The Poetics of Space* (La Poétique de l'espace, 1958), Boston, MA: Beacon Press.

Barthes, R. (1957 [1973]) *Mythologies*. London: Paladdin.

Barthes, R. (1975) *S/Z*, trans. R. Miller. London: Cape.

Batchen, G. (1999) *Burning with Desire: the conception of photography*. Cambridge, MA: MIT Press.

Baudrillard, J. (1983) *Simulations*, trans. P. Foss. New York: Semiotext(e).

Baudrillard, J. (1985) 'The Ecstasy of Communication', trans. J. Johnston, in Hal Foster (ed.) *Postmodern Culture*. London: Pluto.

Baudrillard, J. (1988) *The Ecstasy of Communication*. New York: Semiotext(e).

Baudrillard, J. (1993) 'Hyperreal America', in *Economy and Society* 22, (2): 243–52.

Baudrillard, J. (1968 [1996]) *The System of Objects*, trans. J. Benedict, London: Verso.

Bell, D. (1974) *The Coming of the Post Industrial Society: a venture in social forecasting*. London: Heinemann.

Bell, D. and Kennedy, B. (2000) *The Cybercultures Reader*. London: Routledge.

Bender, G. and Druckery, T. (eds) (1994) *Culture on the Brink: ideologies of technology*. Seattle: Bay Press.

Benjamin, W. (1939) 'The Work of Art in the Age of Mechanical Reproduction', in *Illuminations* (1969). New York: Schocken.

Benjamin, W. (1939) 'The Work of Art in the Age of Mechanical Reproduction', in J. Evans and S. Hall (eds) (1999) *Visual Culture: The reader*. London: Open University/Sage.

Berger, J. (1972) *Ways of Seeing*. London: BBC and Penguin Books.

Berners-Lee, T. (1999) *Weaving the Web: the past, present and future of the World Wide Web by its inventor*. London: Orion Business Books.

Blackman, L. (1998) 'Culture, Technology and Subjectivlty', in J. Wood (ed.) *The Virtual Embodied Presence/Practice/Technology*. London: Routledge.

Blake, E.C. (2003) 'Zograscopes, Virtual Reality, and the Mapping of Polite Society', in L. Gitelman and G. Pingree (eds) *New Media 1740–1915*. Cambridge, MA: MIT Press.

Bolter, J.D. (1991) *Writing space: the computer, hypertext, and the history of writing*. Hillsdale, NJ: Lawrence Erlbaum Associates, pp. 21–5.

Bolter, D.J. and Grusin, R. (2000) *Remediation*. Cambridge, MA: MIT Press.

Boyd, F. and Dewdney, A. (1996) 'Technology and Cultural Form', in M. Lister (ed.) *The Photographic Image in Digital Culture*. London: Routledge.

Buck-Morss, S. (1995) *The Dialectics of Seeing: Walter Benjamin and the Arcades Project*. Cambridge, MA: MIT.

Bush, V. (1945) 'As We May Think', in W. Wardrip-Fruin and N. Montfort (eds) (2003) *The New Media Reader*. Cambridge, MA: MIT Press, pp. 37–48.

Castells, M. (1991) *The Information City: economic restructing and urban development*. London: Blackwells.

Castells, M. (1996) *The Rise of the Network Society*. Oxford: Blackwell.

Castells, M. (1999) 'The Social Implications of Information and Communication Technologies', World Science Report, Paris: UNESCO.

Castells, M. (2001) *The Internet Galaxy: reflections on the Internet, business and society*. Oxford: Oxford University Press.

Crary, J. (1990) *Techniques of the Observer: on vision and modernity in the nineteenth century*. Cambridge, MA: MIT Press.

Critical Art Ensemble (1994) *The Electronic Disturbance*. Brooklyn, NY: Autonomedia.

Cubitt, S. (1998) *Digital Aesthetics*. London: Sage.

Darley, A. (2000) *Visual Digital Culture*. London: Routledge.

Debord, G. (1977) *Society of the Spectacle*, trans. F. Perlman and J. Supak. Detroit: Black & Red.

de Certeau, M. (1988) *The Practice of Everyday Life*. Berkeley, CA: University of California.

De Landa, M. (1991) *War in the Age of Intelligent Machines*. New York: Zone Books.

De Landa, M. (1993) 'Virtual Environments and the Rise of Synthetic Reason', in M. Dery (ed.) *Flame Wars*. Durham, NC: Duke University Press.

Deleuze, G. and Guattari, F. (1987) *A Thousand Plateaus: capitalism and schizophrenia*. Minneapolis, MN: University of Minnesota Press.

Dovey, J. (ed.) (1996) *Fractal Dreams: new media in social context*. London: Lawrence & Wishart.

Druckery, T. (1991) *Digital Dialogues: photography in the age of Cyberspace,* Ten-8 Photo Paperback, vol 2, no 2. pp. 16–27.

Druckery, T. (ed.) (1996) *Electronic Culture: technology and visual representation*. New York: Aperture.

Du Gay, P. *et al.* (1997) *Doing Cultural Studies: the story of the Sony Walkman*. London: Open University/Sage.

Evans, J. and Hall, S. (1999) *Visual Culture: the reader*. London: Sage.

Everett, A. and Caldwell, J.T. (eds) (2003) *New Media: theories and practices of digitextuality*. London: Routledge.

Foster, H. (ed.) (1985) *Postmodern Culture*. London: Pluto Press.

Foster, H. (2001) *The Return of the Real*. Cambridge, MA: MIT Press.

Foucault, M. (1994) *The Order of Things: an archaeology of the human sciences*. New York: Vintage Press.

Foucault, M. (1995) *Discipline and Punish: the birth of the prison*, trans. Alan Sheridan (2nd edn). New York: Vintage Books.

Freedman, L. (2004) *Deferrence*. Malden, MA: Polity Press.

Fukuyama, F. (2002) *Our Posthuman Future: Consequences of the Biotechnology Revolution*. New York; Farrar, Straus, and Giroux.

Garcia, D. and Lovink, G. (2006) *Tactical Media*, http:www.waag.org/tmb/abc.html.

Garvey, E.G. (2003) 'Scissoring and Scrapbooks: nineteenth century reading, remaking and recirculation', in L. Gitelman and G. Pingree (eds) *New Media 1970–1915*. Cambridge, MA: MIT Press.

Gere, C. (2004) 'When New Media was New' in L. Kimbell and H. Cadwallader (eds) *New Media Art: practice and context 1994–2004*. Manchester: Cornerhouse.

Gibson, W. (1986) *Neuromancer*. New York: Ace Books.

Gitelman, L. and Pingree, G.B. (2003) *New Media 1740–1915*. Cambridge, MA: MIT Press.

Goldberg, K. (2003) 'Tele-embodiment and Shattered Presence: reconstructing the body for online interaction', in *The Robot in the Garden*. Cambridge, MA: MIT Press.

Hall, S. (1997) *Representation: cultural representation and signifying practices*. London: OU/Sage.

Haraway, D.J. (1991) *Simians, Cyborgs and Women: the reinvention of nature*. London: Free Association Press.

Haraway, D.J. (1990) 'A Cyborg Manifesto: science, technology, and socialist-feminism in the late twentieth century', in *Simians, Cyborgs and Women: the reinvention of nature*. New York: Routledge (1991), pp. 149–81.

Harries, D. (ed.) (2002) *The New Media Book*. London: BFI.

Harvey, D. (1989) *The Condition of Post Modernity*. Oxford: Blackwell.

Hayles, K. (1999) *How We Became Posthuman: virtual bodies in cybernetics, literature, and informatics*. Chicago, IL: University of Chicago Press.

Hayles, K. (2002) *Writing Machines*. Cambridge, MA: MIT Press.

Hayles, N. Katherine (1993) 'The Life Cycle of Cyborgs: writing the posthuman', in M. Benjamin (ed.) *A Question of Identity*. New Brunswick, NJ: Rutgers University Press.

Jackson, P. (2002) Director, *Lord of the Rings*, Miramax.

Jameson, F. (1991) *Postmodernism, or The Cultural Logic of Late Capitalism*. London: Verso.

Jencks, C. (1999) *The Postmodern Reader*. London: Academic Editions.

Jenkins, H. (2001) 'Digital Renaissance: Convergence? I Diverge', in *Technology Review*, (June), www.techreview.com/magazine/jun01/jenkins.asp (accessed 24 April 2005).

Jones, S. (ed.) (1994) *Cybersociety*. London: Sage.

Kellner, D. (1995) *Media and Culture*. London: Routledge.

Kuhn, T. (1962/1970) (1970, 2nd edition with postscript) *The Structure of Scientific Revolutions*. Chicago, IL: University of Chicago Press.

Landow, G. (1992) *Hypertext: the convergence of contemporary critical theory and technology*. Baltimore, MD: Johns Hopkins University Press.

Lash, S. (2002) *Critique of Information*. London: Sage.

Latour, B. (1988) *Science in Action: how to follow scientists and engineers through society*. Cambridge, MA: Harvard University Press.

Latour, B. (1992) 'Where Are the Missing Masses? The sociology of a few mundane artifacts', in W.E. Bijker and J. Law (eds) *Shaping Technology/Building Society: studies in sociotechnical change*. Cambridge, MA: MIT Press.

Latour, B. (1993) *We Have Never Been Modern*, trans. Catherine Porter. Cambridge, MA: Harvard University Press.

Lévi-Strauss, C. (1958 [1968]) *Structural Anthropology*. London: Allen Lane/Penguin Press.

Lister, M. (ed.) (1995) *The Photographic Image in Digital Culture*. London: Routledge.

Lister, M., Dovey, J., Giddings, S., Grant, I. and Kelly, K. (2003) *New Media: a critical introduction*. London: Routledge.

Lovejoy, M. (1992) *Postmodern Currents*. Englewood Cliffs, NJ: Prentice Hall.

Lovejoy, M. (2004) *Digital Currents: art in the electronic age*. New York: Routledge.

Lunenfeld, P. (ed.) (1988) *The Digital Dialectic*. Cambridge, MA: MIT Press.

Lunenfeld, P. (2000) *Snap to Grid: a user's guide to digital arts, media, and cultures*. Cambridge, MA: MIT Press.

Lyotard, Jean-François (1979) *The Postmodern Condition: a report on knowledge*, trans. Bennington and Massumi. Minneapolis, MN: University of Minnesota Press.

Mackay, H. and O'Sullivan, T. (eds) (1999) *The Media Reader*. London: Sage.

McLuhan, M. (1964) *Understanding Media: the extensions of man*. New York: McGraw-Hill.

McLuhan, M. (1968) *Understanding Media*. London: Sphere.

Malina, R.F. (1990) 'Digital Image Cinema: the work of art in the age of post-mechanical reproduction', in *LEONARDO* (Digital Image – Digital Cinema supplemental issue).

Manovich, L. (1996) 'What Is Digital Cinema?', http://www.manovich.net/text/digital-cinema.html.

Manovich, L. (2001) *The Language of New Media*. Cambridge, MA: MIT Press.

Markoff, J. (2002) 'Technology's Toxic Trash is Sent to Poor Nations', *New York Times*, 25 February.

Merleau-Ponty, M. (1962) *The Phenomenology of Perception*. London: Routledge & Kegan Paul.

Minksy, M. (1986) *A Society of Minds*, New York: Simon & Schuster.

Minksy, M. (1996) *The Society of Mind* (CDROM, Mac version). New York: Learn Technologies Interactive.

Mirzoeff, N. (1999) *An Introduction to Visual Culture*. London: Routledge.

Mitchell, W. (1995) *City of Bits: space, place and the infobahn*. Cambridge, MA: MIT Press.

Mitchell, W. (1998) *The Reconfigured Eye*. Cambridge, MA: MIT Press.

Morely, D. and Robins, Kevin (1995) *Spaces of Identity: global media, electronic landscape and cultural boundaries*. London: Routledge.

Mulvey, L. (1973) 'Visual Pleasure and Narrative Cinema', in S. Hall (ed.) (1999) *Visual Culture: the reader*. London: Open University/Sage.

Murray, J.H. (1997) *Hamlet on the Holodeck: the future of narrative in cyberspace*. New York: The Free Press.

Negroponte, N. (1972) *Soft Architecture Machines*. Cambridge, MA: MIT Press.

Negroponte, N. (1995) *Being Digital*. New York: Vintage Books.

Nelson, T. (1966) 'A File Structure for the Complex, the changing and Indeterminate', in W. Wardrip-Fruin and N. Montfort (eds) (2003) *The New Media Reader*. Cambridge, MA: MIT Press, pp. 37–48.

Nelson, T. (1974) 'Computer Liberation/Dream Machine', in N. Wardrip-Fruin and N. Montfort (eds) (2003) *The New Media Reader*. Cambridge, MA: MIT Press.

Paul, C. (2003) *Digital Art*. London: Thames & Hudson.

Pepperell, R. (1995) *The Post Human Condition*. Bristol: Intellect.

Plant, S. (1997) *Zeros + ones: women, cyberspace + the new technoculture*. London: Fourth Estate.

Poster, M. (1990) *The Mode of Information*. Oxford: Polity Press.

Poster, M. (1995) *The Second Media Age*. Oxford: Polity Press.

Poster, M. (2002) 'The Aesthetics of Distracting Media', http://culturemachine.tees.ac.uk/Cmack/Backissues/j004/Articles/poster.htm.

Postman, Neil (1993) *Technopoly: the surrender of culture to technology*. New York: Vintage Books.

Raskin, J. (2000) *The Humane Interface: new directions for designing interactive systems*. Reading, MA: Addisen-Wesley.

Rheingold, H. (1991) *Virtual Reality*. New York: Simon & Schuster.

Rheingold, H. (1993) *The Virtual Community: homesteading on the electronic frontier*. New York, CA: Harper Perennial.

Richin, F. (1991) *In Our Own Image: the coming revolution in photography*. San Francisco, CA: Aperture.

Robins, K. (1996) *Into The Image*. London: Routledge.

Rush, M. (1999) *New Media in Late 20th Century Art*. London: Thames & Hudson.

Sains, A. (2000) 'Sweden's Digital Debate', in *Europe* 402, (December).

Schmidt, H.W. and Zimmermann, W. (1994) 'A Complexity Calculus for Object-oriented Systems', in *Journal of Object-oriented Systems* 1 (2): 117–47.

Scott, R. (dir.) (2000) *Gladiator*. Dreamworks Pictures.

Schneiderman, B. (1997) *Designing the User Interface: Strategies for Effective Human–Computer Interaction*. Boston, MA: Addison-Wesley Longman.

Slater, D. (1999) 'Marketing Mass Photography', in J. Evans and S. Hall (eds) *Visual Culture: the reader*. London: Sage, pp. 289–306.

Slevin, J. (2000) *The Internet Society*. Cambridge: Polity Press.

Song, E.H.J. and Anderson, J.E. (2001) 'How Violent Video Games may Violate Children's Health', *Commercial Alert*, May.

Springer, C. (1998) 'Virtual Repression', in John Beckman (ed.) *Virtual Dimension*. New York: Princeton Architectural Press.

Springer, C. (1999) 'The Pleasure of the Interface', in J. Wolmark (ed.) (1999) *Cybersexualities*. Edinburgh: Edinburgh University Press, pp. 34–54.

Stam, R. (2000) *Film Theory: an introduction*. New York: Blackwell.

Stelarc, www.stelarc.va.com.au.

Stone, R. (1995) *The War Between Desire and Technology at the Close of the Mechanical Age*. Washington, DC: MIT Press.

Tagg, J. (1987) *The Burden of Representation: evidence, truth, and order*. Cambridge: Cambridge University Press.

Thompson, J. (1999) 'The Media and Modernity', in H. Mackay and T. O'sullivan (eds) *The Media Reader*. London: Open University Press/Sage.

Toffler, A. (1980) *The Third Wave*. New York: Bantam.

Toffler, A. (1990) *Powershift: knowledge, wealth, and violence at the edge of the 21st century?*. New York: Bantam.

Tufte, E. (2003) 'PowerPoint is Evil: Power Corrupts. PowerPoint Corrupts Absolutely', in *Wired* (11 September).

Turkle, S. (1995) *Life on the Screen: identity in the age of the Internet*. New York: Simon & Schuster.

Virilio, P. (1995) *The Art of the Motor* (*Art du moteur*), English edn, trans. Julie Rose. Minneapolis, MN: University of Minnesota Press.

Virilio, P. (2000) *The Information Bomb*. New York: Verso.

Waldby, Catherine (2000) *The Visible Human Project: informatic bodies and posthuman medicine*. London: Routledge.

Wardrip-Fruin, N. and Montfort, N. (2003) *The New Media Reader*. Cambridge, MA: MIT Press.

Webster, F. (1999) *Theories of the Information Society*. London: Routledge.

Weibel, P. (ed.) (2001) *Net Condition: art and global media (electronic culture)*. Cambridge, MA: MIT Press.

Weinmann, E. and Lourekas, P. (2003) *Photoshop. Quick Start Guide*. Berkeley, CA: Peachpit Press.

Wiener, Norbert (1954) *The Human Uses of Human Beings: cybernetics and society*, revised edn. Boston, MA: Houghton-Mifflin.

Williams, R. (1961) *The Long Revolution*. Harmondsworth: Penguin, p. 32.

Williams, R. (1974) *Television, Technology and Cultural Form*. London: Fontana.

Williams, R. (1975) *Culture and Society*. London: Penguin.

Williams, R. and Edge, D. (1996) 'The Social Shaping of Technology Research Policy', in *Research Policy*, 25: 865–99.

Winston, B. (1998) *Media, Technology and Society: a history from the telegraph to the Internet*. London: Routledge.

Wombell, P. (ed.) (1987) *PhotoVideo*. London: River Oram Press.

Wood, J. (1998) *The Virtual Embodied*. London: Routledge.

Woolley, B. (1992) *Virtual Worlds*. Oxford: Blackwell.

Index

....

Pages containing illustrations are indicated in *italic* type.

Related titles from Routledge

The Cyberspace Handbook

Jason Whittaker

The Cyberspace Handbook is a comprehensive guide to all aspects of new media, information technologies and the internet. It gives an overview of the economic, political, social and cultural contexts of cyberspace, and provides practical advice on using new technologies for research, communication and publication.

The Cyberspace Handbook includes:

- a glossary of over eighty key terms;
- a list of over ninety web resources for news and entertainment, new media and web development, education and reference, and internet and web information;
- specialist chapters on web design and journalism and writing on the web;
- Over thirty illustrations of internet material and software applications.

The Cyberspace Handbook explores how cyberspace has been constructed, how it is used and extends into areas as different as providing us immediate news or immersive games and virtual technologies for areas such as copyright and cybercrime, as well as key skills in employing the internet for research or writing and designing for the Web.

ISBN10: 0–415–16835–x (hbk)
ISBN10: 0–415–16836–8 (pbk)

ISBN13: 978–0–415–16835–9 (hbk)
ISBN13: 978–0–415–16836–6 (pbk)

Available at all good bookshops
For ordering and further information please visit:
www.routledge.com

Related titles from Routledge

Media and Power

James Curran

Media and Power addresses three key questions about the relationship between media and society.

▓ How much power do the media have?
▓ Who really controls the media?
▓ What is the relationship between media and power in society?

In this major new book, James Curran reviews the different answers which have been given, before advancing original interpretations in a series of ground-breaking essays.

Media and Power also provides a guided tour of the major debates in media studies. What part did the media play in the making of modern society? How did 'new media' change society in the past? Will radical media research recover from its mid-life crisis? What are the limitations of the US-based model of 'communications' research? Is globalization disempowering national electorates or bringing into being a new, progressive global politics? Is public service television the dying product of the nation in an age of globalization? What can be learned from the 'third way' tradition of European media policy?

Curran's response to these questions provides both a clear introduction to media research and an innovative analysis of media power, written by one of the field's leading scholars.

ISBN10: 0–415–07739–7 (hbk)
ISBN10: 0–415–07740–0 (pbk)

ISBN13: 978–0–415–07739–2 (hbk)
ISBN13: 978–0–415–07740–8 (pbk)

Available at all good bookshops
For ordering and further information please visit:
www.routledge.com

Related titles from Routledge

Media, Technology and Society
Brian Winston

Media Technology and Society offers a comprehensive account of the history of communications technologies, from the printing press to the internet.

Winston argues that the development of new media forms, from the telegraph and the telephone to computers, satellite and virtual reality is the product of a constant play-off between social necessity and suppression: the unwritten law by which new technologies are introduced into society only insofar as their disruptive potential is limited.

Winston's fascinating account examines the role played by individuals such as Alexander Graham Bell, Guglielmo Marconi, and John Logie Baird and Boris Rozing, in the development of the telephone, radio and television, and Charles Babbage, whose design for a 'universal analytic engine' was a forerunner of the modern computer. He examines why some prototypes are abandoned, and why many 'inventions' are created simultaneously by innovators unaware of each other's existence, and shows how new industries develop around these inventions, providing media products to a mass audience.

Challenging the popular myth of a present-day 'information revolution' *Media Technology and Society* is essential reading for anyone interested in the social impact of technological change.

ISBN10: 0–415–14229–6 (hbk)
ISBN10: 0–415–14230–x (pbk)

ISBN13: 978–0–415–14229–8 (hbk)
ISBN13: 978–0–415–14230–4 (pbk)

Available at all good bookshops
For ordering and further information please visit:
www.routledge.com

Related titles from Routledge

The Newspapers Handbook
Fourth edition
Richard Keeble

Fully revised and updated, *The Newspapers Handbook*, Fourth Edition remains the essential guide to working as a newspaper journalist. It examines the ever-changing, everyday skills of newspaper reporting and explores the theoretical, ethical and political dimensions of a journalist's job.

Using a range of new examples from tabloid, compact and broadsheet newspapers, non-mainstream and local publications, Richard Keeble examines key journalistic skills such as the art of interviewing, news reporting, reviewing, feature writing, using the Internet and freelancing.

New chapters from John Turner, Nick Nuttall and Mark Hanna explore the specialisms of local and national government reporting, investigative journalism and covering the courts.

The Newspapers Handbook includes:

- interviews with journalists about their working practices;
- examples of writing from a range of recent publications;
- a guide to training and career opportunities;
- the importance of new technologies for the newspaper industry;
- an updated glossary of key terms and a revised bibliography.

The Newspapers Handbook encourages a critical approach to newspaper practice, and maintains its standing as a must-have student and professional resource.

ISBN10: 0–415–33113–7 (hbk)
ISBN10: 0–415–33114–5 (pbk)

ISBN13: 978–0–415–33113–5 (hbk)
ISBN13: 978–0–415–33114–2 (pbk)

Available at all good bookshops
For ordering and further information please visit:
www.routledge.com

Related titles from Routledge

The Photography Handbook
Second edition
Terence Wright

The Photography Handbook provides an introduction to the principles of photographic practice and theory and offers guidelines for the systematic study of photographic media. It explores the history of lens-based picture- making and examines the mediums' characteristics, scope and limitations.

The Photography Handbook equips the reader with the vocabulary for photographic phenomena and helps to develop visual awareness and visual literacy. It will enable students to familiarise themselves with current theoretical viewpoints and to evolve critical frameworks for their own photographic practice.

The Photography Handbook introduces practical photography as a series of processes from pre-production through to post-production editing. Terence Wright discusses such topics as choice of camera format, camera angle, aperture, development, captions and editing contact sheets. He analyses photographic theory so that the photographer is able to make an informed and efficient use of the medium to deliver the desired image, while reflecting on the social and cultural environment.

The Photography Handbook includes:

- a new chapter on the ethics of photojournalism;
- coverage of digital photography;
- a new section on research in photography;
- new case studies including a study of war photographer James Nachtwey, photographic representations of Marilyn Monroe and Adolf Hitler, and the 'Bert is Evil'.

ISBN10: 0–415–25803–0 (hbk)
ISBN10: 0–415–25804–9 (pbk)

ISBN13: 978–0–415–25803–6 (hbk)
ISBN13: 978–0–415–25804–3 (pbk)

Available at all good bookshops
For ordering and further information please visit:
www.routledge.com

Related titles from Routledge

The Public Relations Handbook
Second edition
Alison Theaker

The Public Relations Handbook is a comprehensive and detailed
introduction to the theories and practices of the public relations
industry. It traces the history and development of public relations,
explores ethical issues which affect the industry, examines its
relationship with politics, lobbying organisations and journalism,
assess its professionalism and regulation and advises on training
and entry into the profession.

The Public Relations Handbook combines theoretical and
organisational frameworks for studying public relations with
examples of how the industry works in practice. It draws on a
range of promotional strategies and campaigns from businesses,
consumer groups and cause related marketing including Railtrack,
Voice of the Listener and Viewer, Marks and Spencer, the
Metropolitan Police, the Prince's Trust, Shell and Centrica.

The Public Relations Handbook includes:

- interviews with press officers and PR agents about their
  working practices;
- case studies, examples, press releases and illustrations from a
  range of campaigns from multinational corporations, local
  government and charities;
- specialist chapters on financial public relations, business ethics,
  on-line promotion and the challenges of new technology;
- over twenty illustrations from recent PR campaigns;
- a new chapter on the effects of culture on communication.

ISBN10: 0–415–31792–4 (hbk)
ISBN10: 0–415–31793–2 (pbk)

ISBN13: 978–0–415–31792–4 (hbk)
ISBN13: 978–0–415–31793–1 (pbk)

Available at all good bookshops
For ordering and further information please visit:
www.routledge.com

Related titles from Routledge

The Radio Handbook
Second edition
Carole Fleming

The Radio Handbook is a comprehensive guide to radio broadcasting
in Britain. Completely rewritten and updated for the second edition,
using new examples, case studies and illustrations, it examines the
various components that make radio, from music selection to news
presentation, and from phone-ins to sports programmes. Fleming
explores the extraordinary growth of commercial radio, analyzes
the birth of digital audio broadcasting and internet radio and
evaluates their effects on the industry.

The Radio Handbook shows how communication theory informs
everyday broadcasts and encourages a critical approach to radio
listening and to radio practice. Addressing issues of regulation,
accountability and representation, it offers advice on working in
radio and outlines the skills needed for a career in the industry.

The Radio Handbook includes:

- interviews with people working at all levels in the industry,
  including programme controllers, news presenters and DJs;
- examples of programming including nationwide and local BBC,
  commercial radio, community and student stations;
- chapters on radio style, the role of news, getting started in
  radio and the tools of broadcasting;
- a glossary of key terms and technical concepts.

ISBN10: 0–415–22615–5 (hbk)
ISBN10: 0–415–15828–1 (pbk)

ISBN13: 9–78–0–415–22615–8 (hbk)
ISBN13: 9–78–0–415–15828–2 (pbk)

Available at all good bookshops
For ordering and further information please visit:
www.routledge.com

Related titles from Routledge

The Television Handbook
Third edition
Jonathan Bignell and Jeremy Orlebar

The Television Handbook is a critical introduction to the practice and theory of television. Jonathan Bignell and Jeremy Orlebar discuss the state of television today, explain how television is made, and how production is organised, and discuss how critical thinking about programmes and genres can illuminate their meanings. This book also explores how developments in technology and the changing structure of the television industry will lead the medium in new directions.

The Television Handbook gives practical advice on many aspects of programme making, from an initial programme idea through to shooting and the post-production process. The book includes profiles giving insight into how personnel in the television industry from recent graduates to television executives think about their work.

The Television Handbook bridges the gap between theory and practice. There are chapters on the vigorous debates about what is meant by 'quality' television, how news and factual programmes are changing as new technologies and formats such as Reality TV have risen in prominence, and how drama, sport and music television can be understood.

The Television Handbook includes:

- interviews with directors, editors, producers and trainees;
- a revised glossary of specialist terms;
- career case studies.

ISBN10: 0–415–34251–1 (hbk)
ISBN10: 0–415–34252–x (pbk)

ISBN13: 978–0–415–34251–3 (hbk)
ISBN13: 978–0–415–34252–0 (pbk)

Available at all good bookshops
For ordering and further information please visit:
www.routledge.com